CONCRETOPIA

A journey around the rebuilding of postwar Britain

JOHN GRINDROD

First published in Great Britain in 2013 by Old Street Publishing Ltd
Trebinshun House, Brecon LD3 7PX
www.oldstreetpublishing.co.uk

This paperback edition first published in 2014.

ISBN 978-1-908699-89-3

10 9 8 7 6 5 4

A CIP catalogue record for this title is available from the British Library.

Printed and bound by CPI Group (UK) Ltd, Croydon, CR0 4YY

For Adam Nightingale

'So we can build a new home for ourselves: a new Britain.
No difficulties, except of our own making, stand in the way.
Knowledge, enthusiasm and unbounded skill
Wait for the opportunity. We alone
The people of this nation are its deciders, it creators, its builders.
A new world we *must* make: with what success we make it
Rests in ourselves.
The choice is our own.

The future begins to-day.'

from *Building Britain: 1941*, a film script by Thomas Sharp, in
The Town Planning Review, October 1952, p204

CONTENTS

Introduction

INTRODUCTION

It is difficult to understand the place you come from. You grow up so much a part of it, and yet your home, street and town remain mysterious, full of questions no one seems able to answer. Why is one of our bedrooms so small? Why can't we play ball games on that grass? Could we live in a tall block of flats like those kids do? For the most part you put up with these unanswered questions, distracted by the overwhelming banality of real life. We have to keep putting 50ps in the meter under the stairs. Other people own their houses. The buses don't come down this end of the estate. Why? Who knows. These things just *are*.

I grew up in New Addington. The place has always felt odd, like an inner-city housing estate abandoned in the country outside Croydon. I remember my O-level geography teacher arriving at a lesson in 1985, armed with an AV trolley and the ominous words, 'I think you'll find this very interesting.' When she pressed play on the Betamax recorder, a scrawny man in seventies clothing popped up on the screen, describing a town planning experiment that had gone horribly wrong. Then a caption: 'New Addington'. There was no reaction from us – mainly because at my school to express interest, surprise or engagement of any sort was a fatal sign of weakness – but that programme did something to me that a decade of geography lessons had entirely failed to do. It made me think. As the presenter made his way around the estate over the next half an hour, I felt increasingly as though I were listening to a surgeon explaining my symptoms to a group of medical students while I lay there with my gown open. What did he *mean*? Sure, New Addington was far from perfect, but what was so wrong with it? There it was, acres of it, getting on with inertly just being there – and we, the class of 1985, were all its children. If this was *bad planning*, did that make us *bad people* from a *bad estate*?

In all likelihood you have not heard of New Addington. It has few claims to fame. The most enduring export of this south London estate of 22,000 people is the Croydon Facelift, the no-mercy

A bad estate?
Tower blocks mingle with low rise flats in New Addington.

ponytail worn by strung-out working-class mums from the estate. 'Racist Tram Woman' Emma West – source of Twitter outrage in 2011 – briefly became its most famous citizen, after a video of her racially abusing a fellow passenger was viewed 11 million times on YouTube. Kirsty MacColl wrote a song about the place: *The Addington Shuffle*. It seems fitting that it was a B-side. And in the summer of 2012, while the Olympics were briefly transforming the rest of London into a zone of peace, harmony and love, a truly dreadful news story kept the residents of New Addington transfixed. Twelve-year-old Tia Sharp was first reported missing from her grandmother's house in The Lindens, and a week later her body was found wrapped in a blanket in the attic. Images of the fruitless searches, the wasted vigils, the shrine to the young girl were shown for days on the news, alongside Olympic champions proudly displaying their hard-won medals a few miles away in Stratford. A case like that does a lot to change a town. Owen Jones, author of *Chavs*, wrote on Twitter that he felt it said as much about life in poor communities as Harold Shipman did about GPs. New Addington has the lowest voter turnout of anywhere in the south of England, what politics it does have shifting over the years from staunch Labour to a recent flirtation with the far right.

This vast estate was built seven miles outside Croydon town centre, on top of a hill so chilly, windswept and isolated it has earned the nickname Little Siberia. In 1935, just as 'green belt' legislation

Flats on the Fieldway estate.
The tree gives some idea of the high winds experienced in 'Little Siberia'.

was being introduced to protect the area around London from urban sprawl, the land was bought by developer Charles Boot, whose company had been responsible for building more interwar houses than any other. Not everyone was thrilled at the prospect of a new estate being built on this wooded hill. 'We know people have got to live somewhere, but there are so many other spaces more suitable for building,' opined the vicar of Addington Village, which sat at the foot of the hill.[1] Relations between the two settlements, ancient village and new estate, have not improved over time.

1,000 red-brick semis were built by Charles Boot in the late thirties.
© *Croydon Local Studies Library and Archives Service*

Yet 1,000 red-brick semis and maisonettes were built before the war and a further 1,000 prefabricated council houses and flats joined them in the fifties and sixties. In 1970, the year I was born, my parents moved from Nine Elms, a working-class district of Battersea, into one of the prewar maisonettes.

There was green space everywhere on this prewar section of the estate, most of it ruthlessly mown: grass verges, patches of grass between blocks of flats, broad avenues of grass separating rows of houses, enormous grass roundabouts, the contours of the hillside shorn like a lumpy scalp. By the time I was growing up, most of these areas had acquired 'no ball games' signs.

A pair of New Addington's prewar maisonettes.

Small blocks of flats surrounded by acres of mown grass at North Downs.

The postwar estate was more tightly packed, all alleyways, walkways and clusters of garages: the folk living here had to walk to the outskirts to see anything more than pinched slivers of green. Despite the farmers' fields and woodland that still ring New Addington today, to me the place always felt more inner-city than suburban. It slotted neatly into my teenager's view of British life in the eighties – a mental map composed of the riot-ravaged suburbs of Brixton and Liverpool, the desolate urban landscapes evoked by bands such as The Specials or The Smiths, and the concrete, post-apocalyptic settings of television sci-fi and *Threads*. Looking back, I see that New Addington wasn't really like any of those places. It isn't easy to pin the place down. This curious hotchpotch of a housing estate, plonked on the hill and surrounded by woodland, was unlike anywhere else I'd ever visited – until, that is, I started to research this book.

The mothership is Croydon, a place lazy comics reflexively reach for as a synonym for shit. It's shorthand for a rather dated English idea of ugliness, boredom and embarrassment, alongside Olive from *On the Buses*, woodchip wallpaper and school dinners. As a teenager I began to stray into the centre of Croydon, eventually getting a job there, but I understood it no better than I did New Addington. There were the office blocks, of course: 'Manhattan built in Poland' as one wag had it. And there was a lot of antipathy to the place, I knew. 'It was my nemesis, I hated Croydon with a real vengeance … it represented everything I didn't want in my life, everything I wanted to get away from,' was David Bowie's verdict, and many of my friends agreed.[i]

Croydon is one of the biggest towns in Europe: a third of a million people live there. If it were a city it would be the twelfth largest in Britain. From 1977 onwards, it has repeatedly been identified by the Home Office as a prime candidate for city status, only to be overlooked – most recently in 2002, in favour of smaller towns like Newport, Stirling and Preston. The perennial experience of rejection has made the ambitious council chippy.

Croydon's origins are as a medieval market town, blossoming under the patronage of various Archbishops of Canterbury. It grew into a prosperous Victorian town that, by the turn of the twentieth century, was eager to rival England's big cities. Then an airstrip built during the Great War to help the Royal Flying Corps tackle the zeppelin raids on Britain changed everything. When the war ended, the airstrip became glamorous, art deco Croydon Aerodrome, and suddenly, in the heart of suburban Surrey, was London's airport,

i Oddly enough, many pop stars have lived, worked or studied in Croydon, from Art College punks to more recent BRIT School alumni such as Amy Winehouse and Adele, but it's rarely mentioned alongside pop powerhouses like Sheffield, Liverpool or Manchester. Even Bob Stanley, architecturally savvy member of Croydon pop champions Saint Etienne is faintly disparaging. 'South London's not really London, is it?' he told the *Guardian*. 'It's just an endless suburb.' Fans of dubstep, the quintessentially urban music genre born in the borough, might disagree. .

home to Imperial Airways. Britain's richest citizens passed through Croydon on their way to jolly jaunts around Europe, or on the first leg of grand tours to His Majesty's Dominions. It was what the Empire was to Liverpool and Bristol, or the Industrial Revolution was to Manchester and Leeds. For two decades, the airport put Croydon at the cutting edge of technology, design and innovation.

The Second World War bloodied the borough, with doodlebugs damaging some 54,000 houses (and giving a boost to town planning), but it was the advance of technology that eventually made the airport redundant. The Second World War brought with it a need for ever-bigger planes to carry ever-heavier weapons ever-longer distances, and by the end of the war, Croydon Airport was too small to house the new generation of airliners. Instead, the town looked to London's office boom to supply a fresh *raison d'être* and fund its expansion.

In the sixties, thanks to some wily dealing by local council leader James Marshall, the infamous office blocks – like scaled-up *Mad Men*-era G-Plan wardrobes and filing cabinets – loomed onto Croydon's skyline. The resulting cityscape made sense during the week, when the ground-level car parks were crowded and the surrounding streets were bustling with suits and briefcases. But if you wandered in the empty space among their girlishly turned ankles on a Sunday,

Amid the skyscrapers in central Croydon.

you couldn't escape the impression that they had turned up in the wrong place, like giant social misfits. They seemed all the more awkward when you considered that they were standing where once there had been homes and gardens, whose owners had been encouraged to sell up for a few bucks.

The Post Office depot, one of many towers being built at East Croydon in the late sixties. © *Ian Steel*

Architecturally there was all sorts going on: here, the kind of blue mirrors you'd see on children's sunglasses; there, Tetris in concrete; beyond them, what looked to be a space freighter from a seventies sci-fi series, all glass curtain walls and concrete gables. By the early seventies this landscape of 'total work' would be familiar throughout the country.

Not all of Croydon's development was vertical: let's not forget the urban motorway splitting the centre into East and West, or the shopping precincts sprawling across the centre of the town like so many fallen Titans. One such, the Whitgift Centre, was deemed the 'showpiece,' and has become the ninth busiest shopping centre in Britain. It was heavily featured in the opening credits of the original 1979 series of *Terry and June*, where Purley's foremost couple were shown getting lost all over the centre of town as they attempted to find each other in the landscape of exposed concrete beams, squared-off steel railings and frosted wire glass panels. By the time I was working in a bookshop there eight years later, that style had fallen so out of favour that the entire structure was being clad in creamy, fibreglass Neo-Victoriana. Frumpy, functional Rosa Klebb had been given a makeover and was emerging as flouncy, fairytale Princess Di. It was fascinating to watch the whole edifice regenerate around me, the future being tarted up as the past.

The Whitgift Centre in 1971. © Ian Steel

By 1993 the Berlin Wall had tumbled, and Croydon's office centre in the east was looking decidedly frail too. Thatcherism's great architectural legacy had been the Docklands, a vast new London business district of giant silver skyscrapers. It was built for the age of PCs, privatisation and the space shuttle, as East Croydon had been built for the Trimphone, devaluation and the Austin Maxi.

Understandably worried that Docklands would woo all the major investors and financial service corporations away from the town, Croydon Council invited the Architectural Foundation to pimp for entries for a competition they called 'Croydon: The Future', designed to showcase the town as a major corporate investment opportunity. Among them were a boomerang-shaped bridge across Wellesley Road, a giant propeller, an underground art gallery to replace the underpass, and travelators in the sky. My personal favourite were the inflatable Tokyo-style 'dromes' (or inverted bouncy castles) to be set on top of the multi-storey car parks in the centre of town, creating instant arenas for concerts, skiing, horse jumping and basketball. But the most outrageous solution was by the James Bond-style villain who intended to demolish Lunar House, bury its offices underground and replace it with a boating lake.

Needless to say, none of these projects were ever realised, but in bigger cities all over the country private investment was flexing its muscles where government planners had once held sway. In the last 15 years, massive regeneration schemes in Newcastle, Liverpool, Birmingham, Leeds and Manchester have transformed these cities, and brand new shops, apartment blocks and offices now stand where postwar concrete buildings once towered. Ambitious Croydon is rattled.

The history of Croydon in the last 200 years has been the story of a town evolving and adapting in an effort to keep pace with the times: from Chaucerian market town through nineteenth-century industrialisation to the housing and commercial projects of the twentieth century. Today, while Croydon looks warily on, the concrete, prefabricated and high-rise buildings of the postwar era are being eradicated, and structures made with new, high-tech materials are taking their place. Where once nostalgic figures such as John Betjeman sprang into action to defend our Victorian heritage, now a small band of architectural historians and mid-century modernists are arguing for the preservation of our most important postwar monuments before they are all developed beyond recognition.

This is no easy task. There is an accepted narrative to the way we think about our postwar architectural legacy. That narrative is somewhat akin to the plot of a superhero blockbuster: a team of supervillains – planners, architects, academics – have had their corrupt, megalomaniac way with the country for 30 years. Then, at long last, a band of unlikely heroes – a ragbag of poets, environmentalists and good, honest citizens – rose up against this architectural Goliath and toppled it in the name of Prince Charles. In this story, prewar modernism equals good, postwar modernism equals bad. One only has to look at an episode of Channel 4's *Grand Designs* to see that people are still keen to build glass-fronted white boxes of the kind popularised in the twenties by Le Corbusier.

Hence, while early modernism is still much imitated, the default word for what we ended up with after the Second World War is *monstrosities*. The towers, the blocks, the redeveloped city centres, the new towns: *concrete monstrosities*, mostly – even if they're not concrete, or, for that matter, monstrosities. Postwar buildings are *concrete monstrosities* in the same way that political correctness is always *going mad*. It's a potent and irresistible cliché, worming its way into your psyche, even if you don't agree with the sentiment. A litany of planning decisions, from the demolition of the Euston Arch to the remodelling of cities from Glasgow to Portsmouth, all appear to tell the story of a bloodthirsty elite out to smash the decent British way of doing things, to crush the life out of it beneath *concrete monstrosities*.

And yet, was that what actually happened? Were these architects and planners the philistine barbarians of popular myth? Are the places they planned and built as awful as *Crap Towns* might make us believe? And is their legacy one of catastrophic failure? After all, they inherited a nation where millions lived in overcrowded conditions in cities, where factories belched toxic fumes onto the slums next door and the most basic sanitation was a dream for millions. It isn't all that hard to understand the demand for change and the excitement of new ideas. A mere half-century had brought the motorcar and aeroplanes, antibiotics and nuclear physics. The possibilities for human progress seemed endless, and after the catastrophic upheaval of two wars, people around the world were

'We went forward':
The town centre is a vision of the future from the past.

open to new ways of living. Croydon's postwar Borough Engineer Allan Holt's view was, 'I think that Croydon had either got to deteriorate or go forward. We went forward.' And so did thousands of other projects, from homes to offices, power stations to pylons, airports to motorways, and in some cases, entire new towns.

On 8 August 2011, while I was researching this book, riots erupted in Croydon. I was in Sheffield at the time, watching events unfold on television, a strange reversal of the situation in 1981, where Sheffield had been one of the places I'd seen rioting break out in on the news. One thing that was apparent from the media coverage afterwards was that no one seemed to know anything about Croydon. It had long passed under the radar of crime correspondents and journalists, and the reportage consequently had an empty feel. Pundits seemed at a loss to explain what Croydon was, let alone how the riots had started there.

When I was a kid I wanted to be a robot. A big, clunking, Marvin-type android. Today, as I look out at Croydon, it seems obvious why. These supersized, solid-state monoliths have stood patiently by for decades, just waiting for their robot friends to turn up and give them meaning. Croydon makes sense as a town to be approached by jetpack, where paranoid androids hum early Human League songs in the underpasses and flying saucers land on top of shopping centres, transforming Terry and June into George and Jane Jetson at the zap of a ray gun. Like those aliens and androids, I feel quite at home wandering among the office towers of East Croydon, caught forever on the cusp of decimalisation, silicon chips and the death of our sci-fi vision of the future. Surely there are millions of people like me in Britain, who don't recognise the village green, country cottage or Georgian square as the epitome of our nation, but whose identities have instead been moulded by *concrete monstrosities* or *bad planning* – or rather, the postwar optimism that sought to build a better future.

This book is my attempt to get to the root of this obsession, and to plug the gaps in my own knowledge of the world I grew up in. How did estates like New Addington come to be built, and what were the ideas behind them? Why did towns like Croydon completely rebuild their town centres? What principles, if any, lay behind these decisions, and whose principles were they? How did they meet the challenges of city centre Blitz damage, vast Victorian slum clearance and endless suburban sprawl?

Over the years the fortunes of these grand modernising projects have ebbed and flowed, from admiration and the kudos of listing to demonisation and demolition. Often the original feelings of pride have been lost over time. 'It cannot really be claimed that any of the rebuilt cities of Britain are works of art,' wrote historian Gavin Stamp,[2] while geographer Alice Coleman's view is that 'the modern movement's brand of utopia is a virtually universal disaster.'[3] Yet in recent years the era has found its champions too, not least in the Twentieth Century Society.

In July 2011, I set off round the country to explore some of these extraordinary places, and meet some people who helped create the world that was built after the war, to find out what that time was really like. They shared their experiences of everything from designing the Barbican Centre to growing up in a Gorbals high-rise, from building the Elephant and Castle to planning new towns in Wales and Scotland, from helping in the reconstruction of Coventry Cathedral to visiting the Festival of Britain. I've also delved into a lot of books, journals and newspapers from the era. It's fascinating to me that my copy of the book on Hook – the Hampshire new town that never was – came from the University of Wisconsin Library; and Dame Evelyn Sharp's dry-as-dust tome on the Ministry of Housing had to be prised out of the possession of Ohio University. They demonstrate that these experiments in Britain had worldwide fame.

I didn't know what to expect when I set out, but what I found was a story of design triumphs and planning disasters, of heroic struggles and thwarted schemes, widespread corruption and utopian ideals. This is the story I have tried to tell in the pages that follow.

Part 1
SO DIFFERENT, SO APPEALING

1. 'A Holiday Camp All Year Round'
THE TEMPORARY BUILDING PROGRAMME AND PREFABS (1944–1951)

I was excited about my grand odyssey around Britain, so it was almost disappointing when it turned out that my first journey would be a mere three-mile stroll from my flat in Forest Hill. On a rainy spring morning I set off on foot for Catford, south-east London, home to the largest estate of wartime prefabs still standing in Britain. Even with the help of the GPS on my phone they weren't easy to find. A damp, half-hour walk through streets of small, terraced Victorian houses revealed little. So there was a mild rush of relief when I rounded yet another red-brick corner and came face to face with a sleeping army, barely peeping above privet hedges, wooden fences and parked cars, and dwarfed even by the two-storey houses. Here were the 187 forties prefabs that formed the Excalibur Estate.

I was surprised by how immediately my heart went out to them. It may have been their size, so modest and low-lying in this vertical urban landscape. Or the signs of ageing which many made little effort to hide, with their paint peeling off external walls. Or perhaps it was the knowledge that soon there will only be six left, Lewisham Council planning to demolish the estate and replace the prefabs with twice as many new homes. Here was the evidence, soon to disappear, of a heroic tale from the end of the Second World War: not the usual story of destruction and catastrophe, but one of ingenuity and humanity. A story of how enterprising engineers turned factories from building aeroplanes to making homes for the bombed-out, the displaced, the exhausted generation.

The immediate aftermath of the war was a hard time. Rationing was at its height: bread joined the long list of basic controlled items in 1946, and potatoes in 1947. The population had been either dispersed – to fight, to work the land – or flung together, forced to share overcrowded homes. The country was bankrupt, and day-to-day life for millions was increasingly colourless and threadbare – a fact all too clearly brought home by the sleek, well-fed US troops who'd been based all over Britain. By 1951, eight million homes had been declared unfit for habitation, of which seven million had no hot water and six million no inside toilet. In 1949, a fifth of London homes were officially classed as slums. For bombed-out families crushed into sharing homes with relatives or strangers, the relief of peace was soon overshadowed by pressing problems. New homes were needed – not so much fast, as instantly.

The war had shown people what modern materials and production techniques could achieve in munitions factories up and down the land. 'Why not switch these factories over to the production of houses, using the light, efficient and beautiful materials, like steel duralumin, and light alloys, which are stretched to such efficiency and economy in aircraft,' asked Donald Gibson, the progressive young city architect for Blitz-damaged Coventry, in 1940.[1] Prefabrication was not a new idea – over the past few decades thousands of huts, shacks and billets had been created using the technology, from the curved corrugated roofs of Nissen huts to the slatted timber of houses imported from Sweden – but it was about to be embraced on the home front with the fervour of a 'Dig for Victory' or 'Make Do and Mend' campaign.

Late in 1942, with housing shortages worsening at an alarming rate and predictions that four million new houses would be needed within 10 years, the government began to take action. Sir George Burt, who ran the construction company Mowlem, was tasked with finding new ways of building homes, given the dearth of materials and labour. In no time the committee was flooded with hundreds of proposals for building prefabricated houses, and a painstaking process of sorting the wheat from the chaff commenced. In October 1944, the Housing (Temporary Accommodation) Act was passed, authorising the government to spend up to £150 million on the provision of temporary housing: the Burt Committee began to roll up its sleeves and start work in earnest. Hopes were high. '[T]he government hope to manufacture up to half a million of these prefabricated houses,' reported *The Times*, while Churchill declaimed, with typical panache: 'The erection of these emergency houses will be carried out by exceptional methods, on the lines of a military operation ... The success of this undertaking is not to be impeded by reliance at any point on traditional methods.'[2]

The first fruits of the government's research into temporary houses were made public that autumn, when four experimental prefabs were exhibited at the Tate Gallery in London. The first was a design by the Ministry of Works, known as the Portal House, named after the Minister himself. This all-steel bungalow, lined with plywood for insulation, had been constructed by two car manufacturers, Briggs Motor Bodies and the Pressed Steel Company. It was never put into production due to a wartime steel shortage. Next there was the Selection Engineering Company's Uni-Seco prefab, which was timber framed and clad with asbestos cement panels. In due course 30,000 of these flat-roofed little bungalows were manufactured, and these were what greeted me in Catford at the Excalibur Estate. The head of the company, Bernard Brunton, wasn't impressed with the strength of the government's commitment to the Temporary Housing Programme, and wrote to *The Times* in February 1945 complaining of 'a deplorable lack of coordination as between various Ministries concerned'.[3] As if to prove his point, three months later 3,000 Uni-Secos originally destined for the capital had to be relocated around the country instead because the London County Council couldn't clear space fast enough to site them. Also on display at the Tate was a prefab made by the Hull company Tarran, built from reinforced concrete panels around a lightweight timber frame: 19,000 of these were built. The final exhibit was the Arcon house, whose pitched roof gave it the familiar look of a scout hut. Manufactured by construction firm Taylor Woodrow, the corrugated asbestos walls and roof were attached to a steel frame. Nearly 40,000 of these were put into production.

It was, however, the design that replaced the rejected steel Portal that would go on to become the most numerous of all the temporary houses. This aluminium prefab issued not from the construction industry, but from the military industrial complex. The Aircraft Industries Research Organisation on Housing, or AIROH, manufactured a total of 55,000 of these metal bungalows, on production lines that, until very recently, had been churning out heavy bombers. They were built from aluminium from melted-down aircraft. The AIROH prototype wouldn't be exhibited until the following year, 1945, when one was erected behind Selfridges department store in London.

The Times was a little sniffy about the original four they had seen at the Tate. 'The present exterior is dull and unpleasing,' wrote their reporter, opining that 'repetition of these units would, in fact, be wearisome.' Inside, he found there were 'all sorts of awkward connexions; that from bed rooms to bath room and w.c. being through the kitchen'. Yet, in summary, the article refrained from condemnation: 'To say that the emergency house cannot be properly judged until it has been lived in is to state the obvious ... All will agree that a very significant first step has been taken in the direction of building by mass-production.'⁴

Before I could reach the Uni-Seco houses at Excalibur I had to negotiate the estate's strange and wonderful tin tabernacle. The church, St Mark's, has the curved, corrugated roof of a Nissen hut. Its neighbour, the community centre, is like a temporary mess for Battle of Britain pilots. It was as if these two militaristic sentries were guarding their little estate against the bigger brick buildings all around. They were embodiments of the effort that was made to create a discrete, bona fide *neighbourhood*.

All of the roads and pathways on Excalibur were Arthurian-themed: Mordred Road, Ector Road, Pelinore Road ... These

The Excalibur Estate's 'tin tabernacle' St Mark's Church, a former Nissen hut.

heroic names – like calling a hamster Samson – contrasted with the modesty of the prefabs, whose height, or lack of it, was the most striking feature of the estate. There really wasn't a lot going on above head height, other than the odd tree or telephone pole. Though factory-produced, there was something strangely organic about these houses. Whereas the surrounding Victorian brick buildings had the look of giant fossils – long dead beasts that had become immovable features of the landscape – the prefabs had none of that sense of rock-solid permanence. Instead, they were

Some of the estate's prefabs were falling into disuse or disrepair.

slowly sagging, stricken by rickety joints and crumbling skeletons, worn out by the constant, losing battle to halt the decay evident in their mottled skin.

Yet back in the early postwar years, these huts were at the cutting edge of British construction technology. 'It is the scheme which is temporary, not the houses,' ran a Uni-Seco advert in 1945.[5] In 1952, four years after the last temporary house had been delivered as part of the government's programme, the company was still vigorously marketing its products: 'Building programmes can be maintained in spite of the steel shortage by using Seco,' ran one opportunistic advert.[6] Another led with the mildly alarming claim that anything 'from a light factory to a labour camp' could be 'delivered immediately from stock'.[7]

A huge amount of public resistance to rehousing people in prefabs had been expected, and the government-sponsored media campaign launched to promote them went far beyond a few show houses at the Tate. A public information film was made, the first of many I'd see in the course of my research, covering every new development from the forties to the seventies. This one was directed by Lewis Gilbert, who went on to mastermind three James Bond films as well as *Alfie* and *Shirley Valentine*.

The Ten Year Plan followed a dogged young journalist on his journey to discover just what these new temporary houses were all about, and what people thought of them. Who played this womanising, chain-smoking young journalist? That's right: Charles Hawtrey. In big round glasses, he's a hoot, whether fearlessly interviewing mouthy mums or listening to earnest briefings on prefabrication by a panel of military types, like a scene from *Reach for the Sky* (which, funnily enough, Gilbert later directed).

In the event, the prefabs were received more favourably than anyone had expected. 'It was beautiful,' recalled Islington prefab-dweller Betty Vodden, who moved into hers in 1947. 'There was a fridge, which was something I'd never had before, an electric cooker, electric kettle.'[8] 'Mother went to the housing office every Wednesday,' remembered Mary Sprakes, 'and my father went every Saturday to see where they were on the list. Such was the demand that the housing officer had a nervous breakdown. In the end my mother found a councillor that she vaguely knew, contacted him and they got a prefab.'[9] Former Labour leader Neil Kinnock grew up in one too. 'It seemed like living in a spaceship,' he said of the modern amenities like fridges and plumbed-in baths that few at the time had.[10]

One of the residents of Excalibur, Eddie O'Mahoney, had lived there from the time it was built and was still there when this book was being written. 'I'd been demobbed from the army and my wife was living in some bomb-damaged property with the two children,' he told the *Guardian* in 2012. 'When the council offered it, I immediately said, "I don't want a prefab – I want a house." I'd had enough of living in tents and Nissen huts. They told me to go and look before I decided. We opened the door and my wife said, "What a lovely big hall! We can get the pram in here." There was a toilet and a bathroom. I'd been used to a toilet in the garden. The kitchen had an Electrolux refrigerator, a New World gas stove, plenty of cupboards. There was a nice garden. It was like coming into a fortune. My wife said, "Start measuring for the lino."'[11]

One of my interviewees also had fond memories of them. Retired builder Peter Barry had grown up in a prefab straight after the war. A large, avuncular, excitable figure, he told me how his family had moved to one of Oxford's temporary houses on the Barton Estate in the forties when he was a kid. Not much hit by bombing in the war, the Barton Estate was an example of how cities like Oxford were still able to get involved in the scheme, using them to relieve overcrowding rather than bomb damage.

'They were *so* well equipped!' he told me as we chatted in his modernist house in Milton Keynes.

'I think it was 1946 when we moved into there. When you think of 1946–47, what basic equipment there was in the house!

We moved into this little prefab bungalow and all the kitchen was steel. It had a refrigerator. It had an immersion heater. It had a gas boiler to do your washing in. And everything was built-in. It was like going into a futuristic environment you see on television programmes! It was all built-in units, which are quite common now, but not *then*. The boiler was, I suppose, a forerunner to the washing machine. You lit it and it boiled the water and then you did all your washing in it. It was all part of the fitted kitchen, it was an amazing bit of kit.'

He made it sound more like a much-loved sports car than a kitchen. Like many of the new prefab occupants, Peter's family had moved out of an overcrowded and awkward situation, squashed into his grandmother's house. 'My parents were thrilled to have their own place,' he remembered, 'albeit council. They had their own house and they could do what they wanted. My grandmother: if you're living in *her* house, you're living under *her* rules, which are not *your* rules. They're not what you want to do as a married couple.' In his case, religious tensions had aggravated the relationship between Catholic father and Protestant mother-in-law. 'I don't think she went to my mother's wedding. She wouldn't have anything to do with it. And dad had to come home from Egypt to live in that sort of atmosphere. There was tension.' It was a huge relief to be able to live as they liked. 'My father was a great gardener, he grew all his own veg. My mother kept chickens. It was a good lifestyle, really. I remember what it was like being able to have a hot bath every night, which was unheard of at that time. And fields to play in. I was off playing cowboys and Indians or whatever. In the prefab from where we lived you could see open country out of the garden. You could roam.'

The prefabs at Excalibur sit along a network of narrow paths that stretch between a simple grid of roads. The layout serves no fancier purpose than to fit in as many buildings as possible in the space, allowing for small gardens around each home.

A row of well-maintained Uni-Secos on the Excalibur Estate, 2011.

I'm sure the Selection Engineering Company would be proud – and perhaps also shocked – to know that a whole estate of them is still standing, nearly 70 years after their construction. Despite their initial popularity, it soon became apparent that these miracle boxes, and many others like them, weren't perfect: there were leaky roofs; their thin walls and single glazing let the warmth out and the cold in; and the concrete, or sometimes wooden, bases allowed the damp to rise. For otherwise homeless families they must have been a godsend in the winter of 1946-7 – the harshest on record – but no doubt their flimsiness was frequently cursed. These days a damp cardboardy smell permeates many of the remaining buildings. And while their frailty and small scale makes it easy to feel a connection with them, the same qualities can also prompt resentment – even without the many tragic cases of asbestosis and bronchitis that have been attributed to them.

Naturally enough, moving to a more permanent residence was the dream for many a prefab-dweller. But that didn't happen quickly. By 1948, around 157,000 temporary houses had been produced – significantly less than the half-million Churchill had promised. They'd been far more expensive to make than had been anticipated. 'This was partly because the basic materials used were expensive (particularly aluminium and steel),' was the view from 1966 of the government's advisor on construction, Cleeve Barr. The assumption was that prefabs were a much cheaper solution than building traditional bricks and mortar homes, but Cleeve Barr was at pains to point out that this was not the case. He wasn't much taken by their homely charms, either. 'Two hundred standardised houses on a flat site can look like a shop floor full of shoe-boxes.'[12]

By 1964, 15 years after they should have been emptied and dismantled, 71 percent of these shoe-boxes were still standing. In Manchester, of the 3,004 prefabs built in the city, just one had been removed by 1960, and that was only because it had burned down. This was understandable given the scale of the city's housing problem: in 1955 alone, 68,000 houses in the city had been condemned, 13,000 people had been forced to live in lodgings and 800 old homes had simply fallen down of their own accord. Despite the expiration of the original licenses that had allowed the prefabs to occupy what had been parks and open spaces – often where makeshift airfields and military camps had been built during the war – the council had no option but to allow them to remain.

Not that all prefab dwellers wanted to move out, even when they did get the chance. 'Council officials came round this morning and offered some families the choice of three new houses to move into,' a Mrs Barnes, resident of Heaton Park's improvised prefab town, told the *Guardian* in 1961. 'But we don't want to go. The vast majority of us are satisfied with where we are now. We're settled in, have got the prefabs nicely decorated and find them very comfortable. We'll even pay more rent if they let us stay.'[13] Not so in Birkenhead, where in 1961 the tenants of 41 prefabs handed a petition in to the town hall demanding to be rehoused.

'They were built with a stated life span which was by far exceeded,' recalled Peter Barry, 'because they were there long after we were rehoused. And I think in the end they were sold by Oxford City Council to anyone who wanted them. And a lot of them ended up on the coast. Because all you needed was a concrete base with the services and you could plonk it down and plumb it in and they made wonderful holiday chalets! You still see them around in places in Somerset, Devon and Cornwall.' Excalibur resident Ian Goold told the *Guardian*, 'To me it's like a holiday camp all year round.'[14]

Many of the houses in the Excalibur Estate are painted white or magnolia, but a number are in striking pastel colours, and some have painted the Uni-Seco's structural frame a mock-Tudor black. There's a flush of Georgian front doors, and the odd leaded window, but many still have the original single-glazed metal frames, identical to those on the prewar council house I grew up in, with nets hanging in most of them. Mid-century modern-style kitsch is nowhere in evidence. Sure, there's the odd neglected one gradually mulching where it stands, but for the rest it's an even split between the very well kept and the considerably more lived in: portacabins versus cottages. There's an amazing variety considering that they all started off the same. And unlike the surrounding Victorian terraces, they are all detached, with their own gardens.

The friendly, nostalgia-inducing cosiness of these prefabs belies a dark side to their history. Many were built by prisoners of war: Germans from Rommel's Tank Corps, as well as some Italians. Britain was slow to repatriate PoWs, even to countries that had been far more devastated by the war and were desperately in need of labour to begin the work of rebuilding. In 1946, over 400,000 Germans were still in British camps, and were used as forced labour, not just in construction but also in agriculture, as a form of reparation.

'When we had the keys to move in there were no pavements laid, no entrance down to the house,' recalled Ruth Haynes, of her AIROH prefab in Plymouth. 'Every day, German PoWs came by lorry to work on the estate. Seeing our predicament, they very kindly laid a few blocks as stepping stones for us to get to the door "mud free". Seeing we weren't really allowed to fraternise, when I was baking there would always be some small warm cakes, left on the doorstep, for them as a thank you.'[15]

By no means were all of the prefabs built as part of the temporary housing programme. Some became prototypes for the most enduring housing types of the postwar period. The BISF – British Iron and Steel Federation – house was typical of these permanent structures. This was a two-storey semi, designed by engineer Dominic Lee and architect Frederick Gibberd (who would go on to be the master planner of Harlow). A steel frame was erected first, then steel panels were used for the roofs and upper storeys, with more conventional building materials used for the lower floor. The BISF house was one of the prefabs on show at the *Daily Herald* Modern Homes Exhibition in Dorland Hall, Lower Regent Street, in spring 1946. Opinion pollsters Mass Observation were on hand to record the thoughts of the public: they described the crowd as containing 'a very high representation of the artisan class', with more than half of the men and almost half of the younger people they interviewed having no home of their own or expressing dissatisfaction with it.[16] The kitchens, fitted with the latest gadgets, and the sturdy new utility furniture were the most popular exhibits, but people were less taken with the one-room flat that was on display, which was considered impractical due to its size.

The Dorland Hall exhibition featured several examples of prefabs other then the BISF. There was the Orlit, a two-storey house made from reinforced concrete, designed by Czech architect Erwin Katona, and produced in Scotland and the Airey house, from Leeds, made from concrete panels and reinforced with tubing made from decommissioned military vehicles, and available in flat or pitched roofed variants. To the visitors the Orlit 'looked more permanent …

had a personality', while the BISF houses seemed 'a bit barracky... Imagine rows and rows of them.'[17] Many of the visitors gave them a hard time. 'You know we were offered the choice of a prefab?' one told the Mass Observation interviewer. 'Well, I wouldn't have it. They're nice inside, but they look dreadful from the road.' Another was rather more blunt. 'Those prefabs are awful – when you see a lot together they look like pigsties or hen-houses I always think.'[18] We had some BISF houses in New Addington; their steel panels were always painted bright colours and were fascinating to me as I was growing up, with so much of the estate being red-brick and uniform. They seemed somehow to speak of adventure, with their improvised-looking metal walls and the moss growing on their corrugated steel roofs. I didn't know then that the estate had once been home to hundreds of temporary prefab bungalows, before the red-brick houses were built in the fifties. This whole prefab story was closer to home than I'd realised.

The experience of living in a prefab, like the experience of rationing, is disappearing from popular memory. For the 44 percent

Prefabs in New Addington in the early 1950s: Arcons in the foreground, AIROHs top left, and BISF houses along the top of the hill.
© *Croydon Local Studies Library and Archives Service*

of residents at Excalibur who voted to keep the prefabs rather than redevelop, their slow and painful dispersal is causing much heartfelt opposition: photocopied A4 notices in windows read *I'm not moving I'm takeing the council to court so is the rest of us who loves owe prefabs.* [sic] These notices and the whole estate have a dignified air of doom that stays with me as I walk away. I feel unexpectedly moved: perhaps by faint childhood memories of prefab holiday homes by the sea, or school buildings past, or the story of my parents' life in Battersea after the war.

'To move out of here … quite frankly, I'd rather be finished,' said Eddie O'Mahoney, fiercely loyal to his prefab and the little estate when he was interviewed in 2012. 'If they want to evict a 92-year-old war veteran, good luck to them. I've been happy here, all my memories are here. Be honest: what will they offer someone like me? What I bought, I want to keep. I took a pride in this place. I loved it.'[19]

GARDEN CITIES AND THE FIRST NEW TOWNS (1946–51)

The big manor house stood surrounded by horse chestnut trees in the heart of the Hertfordshire countryside. A group of highly skilled technicians had taken Terlings over in the forties with the government's blessing, erecting two rows of prefabricated huts in the garden to form their offices. Their urgent, detailed work was overseen by ex-military commanders, senior civil servants, doctors, even Bertrand Russell's pipe-smoking wife, Peta. 'Everyone worked terribly hard and played hard during their lunch break,' wrote Ena Elliot, one of the many secretaries busy at work there in the late forties and fifties. 'I remember tennis and swimming, and then the annual garden parties, cricket matches and cross-country runs ... I remember the great enthusiasm and interest of the staff – many of them would take work home each night.'[1]

I met one of those members of staff, Janet Search, in her ranch-style house in the Hertfordshire village of Sawbridgeworth. 'It was all right unless it poured with rain and there was flooding,' was Janet's rather less romantic memory of working at Terlings. 'You all cycled on these high pavements to get into the building. But it was a beautiful building. And all of the drawing offices were these prefabricated wooden places.' It's easy to see Terlings, with its huts teeming with intellectuals, experts and their committed support staff, as another Bletchley Park. But the place wasn't full of secret code-breakers. It was home to a dynamic team of planners, architects, draughtsmen and women, and administrators – all working frantically to create something vast and new in the English countryside with a minimum of time and resources. A *new town* –

one of the first four designated by the postwar Labour government. The team at Terlings were inventing Harlow.

'I worked at Terlings when I first left school,' said Janet, who'd arrived in Harlow as a teenager in 1952, as the first phase of the town was in progress. 'And that was quite interesting really because it was all planning.' What was her job? 'Tracer. Plotting lampposts!' She laughed. Sounds like a thankless task, I said. 'It was.' Yet the plotting of lampposts perfectly encapsulates how all-encompassing the work at Terlings was, from the grandest vision to the most basic detail. The *Harlow Journal* reminded its readers two years later that 'during the autumn and winter of 1951 there was just one lamp standard in the new town. There were no shops, no cinema, no new school, no Moot House and no pub. There was, however, mud, more mud, and still more mud.'[2]

John Reed, whose family had also moved to Harlow in 1952, pointed out the concrete lampposts as we walked together around Mark Hall North, the first area of Harlow new town to be built. 'I'm told these lamp standards, the concrete part was built before the war for a big job in Germany' – he gave a hearty laugh at the absurdity of the situation – 'and after the war someone found them lying about so we've got lamp standards. One of the things my dad told me once, I dunno where he got the information from.'

Both Janet and John had fathers who were builders, which explains their early arrival in a town that had been announced to the public only five years previously and, by 1952, had barely begun to be built. As Janet plotted lampposts and John's father pondered their provenance, much bigger decisions were being made by the senior planners. 'When I worked at Terlings, Frederick Gibberd used to come in quite regularly,' said Janet. 'He always had a buttonhole. He was ever such a nice chap. He'd always acknowledge you and come round.' Gibberd, he of the government-sponsored temporary steel house, had been chosen as the master planner for the town in September 1946, well before the designation of the town had been made public, in an effort to ensure they had some attractive plans to reveal when the announcement was made. 'Apart from having an attitude to design acceptable to the new generation of architects, I was one of the few among them with planning qualifications,' said Gibberd, explaining his appointment for such a plum job.[3]

To understand the genesis of new towns like Harlow, and the ways many existing cities set about solving the problem of overcrowding, we must look to the work of an extraordinary man with no planning training: Quaker, Hansard clerk and fluent Esperanto speaker Ebenezer Howard. In 1898 he had written a groundbreaking book, *To-morrow: A Peaceful Path to Real Reform*, more famously reprinted in 1902 as *Garden Cities of To-morrow*. It was these garden cities, whose construction was overseen by Howard from 1903 until his death in 1928, that became the direct inspiration for the postwar new towns programme. Like many engaged citizens of the late Victorian era, Howard was repulsed by the quality of life in the industrialised cities, particularly for the poor. Pollution and overcrowded slum housing had ensured the spread of diseases such as cholera, tuberculosis and rickets. Between 1848 and 1872 the child mortality rate for boys in Britain was a staggering 36,000 per million of the population, and children had only a 50 percent chance of surviving their first year. In response, a number of philanthropic employers, such as William Lever in Liverpool and George Cadbury in Birmingham, created healthy 'model' villages for their workers to live in at Port Sunlight and Bournville, along the lines of New Lanark, built on the banks of the Clyde for millworkers in the late eighteenth century. Ebenezer Howard envisaged a world where the menace of overcrowding would be relieved by decanting a significant portion of the population to new settlements beyond the boundaries of the city: healthy, spacious, self-contained towns that were part rural, part urban. 'There are in reality not only, as it is so constantly assumed, two alternatives – town life and country life,' wrote Howard, 'but a third alternative, in which all the advantages of the most energetic and active town life, with all the beauty and delight of the country, may be secured in perfect combination.'[4] He named this ideal hybrid settlement a garden city, and such a phenomenon was his book that by 1902 he'd set about securing funding to actually build one of these towns in Hertfordshire: Letchworth.

Howard conceived the garden cities as functional towns, each housing 32,000 people, and, crucially, self-supporting, rather than mere commuter hubs for the nearest big city, as so many suburbs were. Partly to ensure this, they would be separated from the city by a 'green belt' of land, and the plans allocated generous space for light and air within the garden cities themselves. Howard went so far as to envisage a ring of six of these towns, connected by road and rail to form one huge, leafy garden city of nearly 200,000 inhabitants. Being a practical man, over half of *Garden Cities of To-morrow* was concerned with the funding and management of such a project – more a how-to guide than an abstract treatise. Although raising the money to build Letchworth was almost as hard as actually building the place, Howard managed it and the resulting town became something of a sensation among town planners and architects around the world.

Miniature versions of garden cities sprang up all over the country as garden suburbs and garden villages in the early years of the twentieth century. One such was Rhiwbina, begun just before the outbreak of the First World War and finished shortly after the cessation of hostilities. Rhiwbina was built to the north of Cardiff, largely because the local train company, Cardiff Railway, had been encouraged to create a stop there in 1911. The houses were white-rendered Arts and Crafts detached, semi-detached and terraced cottages with steep pitched roofs and totemic chimneys, set back from the road behind broad grass verges.

Once derided for its cultish devotion to the garden city ethos, this suburb has now become one of the most desirable places to live in Cardiff. I spoke to two residents, Jim and Jo Griffiths, who have lived there since the seventies. 'I still feel slightly like a newcomer here,' said Jo. 'These houses were rented through the maternal line.

If your mother rented one you could put your name down to rent one in the garden village. But then in '68 or whatever, they got sold off to sitting tenants.' This was how they had managed to move there in the first place, from the new town of Cwmbran. 'It was different coming here because it was very established and you had to be very careful that you didn't contravene any of the unwritten rules and regulations.'

'About parking and keep your hedges trimmed, for example,' said Jim. He pointed out the street layout, the generous green spaces, the gently curving roads, the large gardens front and back – typical both of early garden city design and the more established anti-industrial Arts and Crafts movement, championed by William Morris. Rhiwbina was designed by Arts and Crafts architect Richard Parker and Ebenezer Howard acolyte Raymond Unwin, whose careers neatly track the rapid evolution of planning ideas: the pair had previously built a Victorian-style 'model village' for Joseph Rowntree's workers near York, planned Hampstead Garden Village in London, and worked on Letchworth.

Such was the success of Letchworth that, immediately after the First World War, Ebenezer Howard bought further land in Hertfordshire to build another: Welwyn Garden City. I spent a day driving round it with comedy writer Mark O'Sullivan, a former resident, offering a darkly subversive running commentary of all we saw. The original western part of the town was beautifully maintained in all its interwar glory: big brown brick cottages with steeply sloping roofs and elaborate chimneys, exhaustively planted gardens pining for rosettes and highly commendeds, tree-lined roads bordered by immaculate grass verges. The centre was low-wattage triumphal: grand vistas at right-angles formed by broad, straight ribbons of neatly mown and planted park and a Versailles-style fountain splitting the two sides of the high street 200 feet apart. The low-lying brick neo-Georgian shop units peeped modestly over the hedges at each other. As Mark pointed out as we strolled down the high street, there were very

Welwyn's grand, yet also remarkably low energy, vista.

few young people about. In fact, most were over 70. The longer we were there, the more I was struck that there was something uncanny about the immaculate nature of it all, the careful ordering of nature, the broad, quiet pavements, the folk clipping hedges. They all gave Mark a friendly wave between clips (it turned out he was somewhat of a local celebrity). It was a little spooky, like the perfect families waving to camera in the opening moments of David Lynch's *Blue Velvet*.

'It always felt quite quiet as a child,' was Mark's recollection as we stood by the fountain on the central reservation looking back to the town centre.

'It's so spacious it's almost soporific,' I remarked.

Mark laughed. '*We will not have people over-stimulated in our town!* I imagine a lot of that comes from that Quaker ideology of not overloading the senses, of giving people space.'

We talk for a while about the population-calming effects of all this order and room. Mark felt it had created a very definite risk-averse mindset among the population here.

'What's that Woody Allen quote? "In the event of a war, I'm a hostage." I think you could say that for most of the people in Welwyn Garden.'

This is the Britain of bucolic railway posters, those mythmaking images where the latest locomotives were seamlessly blended into the rolling landscape, as if they had always been there. Yet those posters also represented something the garden city visionaries, and later the postwar town planners, were keen to put a stop to – the sprawl of metroland. During the interwar period a lack of planning controls and a housing shortage had led private developers and building contractors to create vast new settlements along the railway and road network. A line of suburban semis chased the arterial roads out of every major city, and the town planners' horror at the Victorian slums was quickly matched by their disgust at the cavalier way that developers were eating up the countryside with what was later termed 'subtopia' by critic Ian Nairn. Ebenezer Howard had forseen the consequences of the endless city, and had suggested enforcing a green belt around cities as the solution: an idea eagerly adopted by the postwar planners.

It struck me that this older part of Welwyn could be viewed as the prewar estate at New Addington on a big budget. The brick was the same, but we didn't have any of the pretty Arts and Crafts finishes these cottages had been given, from huge ornate chimneys to curving roofs and porches. I recognised the green spaces too, but these ones had lush planting and fountains, not just mown grass and broken saplings. We pulled up at one of the smaller parades of shops,

Garden City cottages, deluxe cousins to the plain red-brick houses in New Addington.

and it seemed strangely familiar. Could it even have been the actual model for New Addington's Central Parade? The difference was, this row of shops was meant to serve just one small neighbourhood in Welwyn's population of 43,000; in New Addington it was all there was for all 22,000 of us. I suddenly saw Charles Boot's activities in Croydon in a new light: he had been trying to create a private garden village of his own, on a hill, surrounded by trees. But it was a garden city on a squeezed budget, with none of the comforts or attention to detail that Howard had put into Welwyn. For the first time, I saw where I'd grown up in some kind of larger context. We were the bargain-basement model of a garden city, lacking even the basic facilities Howard had seen fit to provide for his citizens.

By the twenties, apart from his two cities, and the limited application of his ideas in garden suburbs like Rhiwbina and cheap housing estates along the lines of New Addington, Howard's crusade was coming to an end. Funding was a large part of the problem, and Howard bankrupted himself in the attempt to secure the future of Welwyn Garden City. He died in 1928, the town unfinished. He hadn't won the green belt argument, nor had he stemmed the rapid development of metroland, with its endless, unplanned ribbons of semi-detached houses eating up the countryside. And the slums in the big cities remained.

Yet the Second World War was to change things dramatically on the planning front. By its outbreak, the government was beginning to publish reports on the neglected area of town planning. As Welwyn Garden City staggered to a halt, Howard's agenda seemed for the first time to be seriously on the government's mind. By 1943 a Ministry of Town and Country Planning had been set up, and Patrick Abercrombie, a professor of town planning, had been asked to produce plans for the postwar rebuilding of London and Plymouth. There was optimism even amidst all the rubble. 'City dwellers saw new vistas,' wrote Howard's planner Frederic Osborn. 'They were astonished at the amount of sky that existed … the "urban blinkers" were dislodged from many eyes. What would replace the former crowded buildings if and when we won the war? Might we not have much better homes and workplaces and retain this new sense of light and openness?'[5]

One of the biggest conversions was undergone by Lewis Silkin, who'd been deeply sceptical of garden city principles when he'd been leader of the London County Council's planning committee back in the twenties. Like many city planners in positions of authority in the first half of the twentieth century, he'd been in favour of high-density cities that, as far as possible, maintained the existing social structures (and, importantly for a successful politician, the electorate they contained). Yet the prewar planning reports were paving the way for a policy that spread people and industry more evenly across the country, and the creation of satellite towns was a key recommendation of Patrick Abercrombie and John Henry Forshaw's *County of London Plan*. A committee was formed to look into it, chaired by the newly ennobled Lord Reith, autocratic founder of the BBC. Reith was the great public service 'doer' of the age – and its irritant in equal measure, which was partly why by the end of the war this former Minister for Information had been left twiddling his thumbs. Reith's whirlwind stewardship saw the genesis of the New Towns Act 1946, and Silkin, now Minister for the newly created Ministry of Town and Country Planning found that instead of the four towns he'd been expecting to approve, 20 were ready to go from the off. He referred to the resulting Act as 'a leap into the unknown', and the first four new towns to be approved were all around London: Stevenage, Crawley, Hemel Hempstead and Harlow. Once behind the project, Silkin quickly became evangelical. Looking back in the late sixties he proudly described the challenge: 'They set out to show that we in Britain could do something better than soulless suburbia, ribbon development, single-industry towns, and one-class housing estates of the thirties.'[6] Yet the only recent examples of building entirely self-contained new towns, as opposed to the many vast, under-supported estates, remained the two garden cities of Letchworth and Welwyn.

One of the most striking interviews held in the Museum of Harlow's oral history archive is that with former local Labour councillor Jim Desormeaux, who described life in London as a demobbed soldier before he and his wife moved out to Harlow.

'I found myself one of a family of six living in one room, The house was a four-room house plus a scullery. Each room was occupied by a separate family. There was one cold water tap for the whole of the four families, and one outside toilet. Conditions such as those were quite common to many thousands of people.'

The task of rescuing millions from the city slums had become critical. Even 20 years later, though the overcrowding had eased, city life was still tough for parents raising young children. Jo Griffiths, who I'd interviewed in Rhiwbina alongside her husband Jim, recalled life in Islington in the late sixties:

'One of the reasons that convinced us to move, I remember, was one day taking Lucy in the pushchair up Chapel Market, and getting home her face was covered in little black specks of carbon monoxide or whatever it was. I remember thinking, if it's like that there, what are her lungs like? And also I was brought up where you could play on the street and you could go down the road and see your mates, and I thought it was really a natural thing for kids to be able to do, to play out in the street. It wasn't going to happen in Islington, was it? It's nice to think we could go somewhere where you could open the door and the garden gate and the kids could play out in the street. All that traffic noise and all that angst of crossing every road ...'

'When Parliament passed the New Towns Act,' reported the *Harlow Citizen* in its first edition in May 1953, 'it decided that the new towns, like children, should be given a decent start in life, and not left, as so many places were left in the past, to make their own way in the world.'[7] Reith drew on his experience of setting up the BBC, so that the building of each new town was managed by a corporation. Funded by the treasury through loans repayable over 60 years, and run by a part-time board appointed by the Ministry of Town and Country Planning – or the Scottish Office in Scotland – it was these development corporations, rather than central government, who were responsible for buying the land to build the towns. Harlow's general manager described the corporation as a developer with a conscience. The idealistic desire to 'do right' by the people who would live there, would be one of the driving forces behind these towns, but it was a daunting challenge. 'Despite the pioneering work of Ebenezer Howard and his colleagues, we had no real knowledge of the organisation and finance required, nor could we readily see the social problems that might emerge' wrote Silkin.[8] Yet despite all of these worries, and with the confident, can-do attitude left over from the war, on 25 March 1947 he designated Harlow a new town for 60,000 people.

In fact, Stevenage was the first new town to be designated. Mass Observation carried out surveys on the streets of the village of Old Stevenage in April 1946, a place that 36 years before had been the setting for E. M. Forster's celebrated novel *Howards End*. The area earmarked for the new town was already home to over 6,000 people, whose opinions of the scheme were largely optimistic (57 percent of the sample thought that the new town would be good for Stevenage). 'It's time this town was woken up,' said a 45-year-old signwriter. 'It's far too sleepy. We need a little life in the place … They still do things here because their grandfathers did them … I've recently come out of the Forces and I notice it.' Practical considerations were frequently voiced: 'Perhaps my husband will be able to get a job here then, instead of having to go out of the district to work,' said a 25-year-old woman. Not everyone was so keen: 'I don't like to see the beauty spots being violated,' said a 60-year-old car park attendant. 'I shouldn't like to see the beauty taken away.' The unhappiest response recorded by Mass Observation was that of Mrs M. H. Tetley, owner of The Priory. 'We've been advised that the government will very probably compel us to sell this house and land,' she lamented. 'It's certain that we shall be hemmed-in by new houses and buildings of one sort and another – which is exactly what we moved here to avoid.'

When the designation was announced there was immediate uproar, which Silkin's visit to the village to sell the project did little to quell. Through a barrage of cries of 'Dictator!' and 'Gestapo!' he attempted to paint a picture of how important this project would be. Stevenage, he declared to a hostile public audience, 'will in a short time become world famous [*laughter*]. People from all over the world will come to see how we here in this country are building for a new way of life.'[9] For his pains, his car received a dose of sand in its petrol tank and its tyres were let down. In a photo-op worthy of UK Uncut, the protest group even renamed the station Silkingrad and called on E. M. Forster to become involved, who obliged with the observation that the new town would 'fall out of a blue sky like a meteorite upon the ancient and delicate scenery of Hertfordshire'.[10] A local enquiry followed, which found the designation to be quite lawful. This decision was then challenged in the courts, moving on to the Court of Appeal, and finally to the House of Lords, where the protesters had to finally admit they were beaten.

Protests greeted the designation of most new towns, but such was the energy and belief in them that the first tranche, from 1946–51, were all waved through. There were Harlow, Stevenage, Hemel Hempstead, Crawley, Basildon, Bracknell, Hatfield and even the unfinished Welwyn Garden City: all intended to ease the overcrowding in London. In the Midlands, Corby was built to house steelworkers, and two small mining towns were conceived in County Durham: Peterlee and Newton Aycliffe. Wales was granted just the one, Cwmbran, between Cardiff and Newport. Scotland had two: East Kilbride, to deal with overspill from Glasgow, and Glenrothes, a mining town in Fife. Some, like Stevenage, Welwyn, Corby and Hatfield, were already home to many thousands of people, while Cwmbran and the two Durham towns were largely unpopulated.

Harlow was to be 6,400 acres in size, and in 1946 consisted of four villages, containing a total of 4,000 people. A large house, Mark Hall Manor, stood in the northeast corner of the designated area, and the development corporation had an eye on its land. Godfrey Arkwright, the landowner, wrote to Eric Adams, a member of the corporation, about vacating the area where his family had lived for 130 years for the sake of the new town. 'It is a very, very sad moment for me … I've got criticisms about the new town, but I admit the necessity for these satellites.' Despite his attachment to the house and the area where he'd grown up, Arkwright was loath to stand in the way of progress. 'I hope that we can remain friends,' he wrote.[11]

'It's the neighbourhood that best represents the Gibberd plan,' enthused Museum of Harlow curator David Devine of the first area to be built, Mark Hall North, on the site of Godfrey Arkwright's former land. 'It was built with everything as he wanted it, the right size plots, the right sized gardens, the roads. Afterwards, as the town was being built, pressures were on the corporation from the government for the density and to build faster.' In many ways, Mark Hall North is an undiluted glimpse of the vision the planners and architects had been nurturing all through the war. Large houses were set well back off the road behind vast verges, overlooking beautiful 'green wedges' where municipal lawns were interrupted by huge old trees growing in copses and playgrounds. Then there are the smaller, sparsely detailed red-and-yellow brick terraces that sit behind neat lawns on narrow, quiet roads. Even the smallest of these side roads feature grand old trees and expanses of grass. 'The idea of the landscape wedges breaking up the housing wedges? Integral,' explained David. Of all the new town planners, Frederick Gibberd was particularly fascinated by landscape architecture, and hired the mother of the modern form, Sylvia Crowe, to make the most of rural features such as wooded valleys within his design. Her influence was most expansively demonstrated by the Town Park that drifts in an unstructured way from the centre, a perfected wilderness as vast as any by Capability Brown. This all served to embody Gibberd's theory about the best relationship between the buildings and the green spaces: 'Housing, instead of being spread all over the town as a mixture of buildings and open space, was concentrated together in a more urban form. The land thus saved was added to the broad belts of landscape which separate one built up area from another.'[12] The roads too were screened from the built up areas by dense banks of trees and shrubs. Green wedges would become one of the defining features of the early new towns. 'To see children riding, playing with kites or chasing butterflies on those wedges in spring or summer is to see Gibberd's vision bearing fruit, and a moving sight it is,' wrote a journalist visiting for *The Times*.[13] Although later areas in Harlow would be more densely packed, in Mark Hall North the green wedges were victorious.

When I visited the south Wales new town of Cwmbran the green wedges were much in evidence there too. Retired planner Jim Griffiths led me through the neighbourhood of Coed Eva, where he and his wife Jo had lived in the early seventies. Although one of the later estates in Cwmbran, it bore many similarities to Mark Hall North, most obviously in the landscaping.

'That area we walked through is pretty generous with greenery outside of gardens compared to any other residential estate I've ever been on,' Jim commented later, when we were sitting in his kitchen.

'It did mean you could have quite a small garden because of your vista,' added Jo. 'It did very much feel countrified.'

It was at this point that Jim's background as a planner began to show:

'Everywhere there are builders building regular housing estates, which have a few trees in them,' he said. 'Compare that with a housing estate round here or Milton Keynes – there's a difference. And it's in the trimming. Even at the same densities, the regular house builders will not afford a great wide strip of trees or an avenue. They might put a tree in your front garden or a green corner. He's paid a lot of money for this land and he's going to get as many houses as he can on there. It's a battle with the town planners. Whereas *this* is a designated area. All of it's green and it's all for the corporation and it was all bought at agricultural value. And they had room to breathe and room to manoeuvre. They had plenty of space to make things happen, to make the park big enough for 24 football pitches or whatever. Not squidged in the corner with a little play area. It's a mind thing: do you start with a blank sheet or do you start with a great big bill you've just paid for a small field?'

The first-generation new towns, of which Cwmbran is one, had a lot in common in terms of design. They took much from Ebenezer Howard's disciples in the United States, where his ideas were being actively promulgated, in their desire to marry the best of the countryside with the best of the town. For instance, they adopted the idea of 'neighbourhood units', areas for anything up to 7,000 residents – a number derived from the population that could be supported by a single primary school. The unit would have its own small centre – a parade of shops, a pub and a community centre – and the neighbourhood itself would be made up from various smaller clusters of housing. In Harlow, these neighbourhood centres were called 'Hatches', an old Saxon word. Howard's vision for the garden cities had been that industrial, residential and central areas could be separated, rather than muddled together as they were in the overcrowded centres of the big towns and cities. Neighbourhood units, the theory went, would encourage neighbourliness: those green spaces and community centres would be buzzing with activity as residents pursued healthy activities. As Harlow planner Frederick Gibberd characterised it, channelling the idealism of *Garden Cities of To-morrow*, '[the new town resident] prefers segregation of home and work, has an innate love of nature, enjoys open air exercise – and, while demanding privacy for the individual family, likes some measure of community life.'[14]

Gibberd had been a rising star before the war, and brought in fellow big name architects to design the housing in these early areas: married modernists Maxwell Fry and Jane Drew, who later worked with Swiss master Le Corbusier; F. R. S. Yorke, fresh from an architectural partnership with Bauhaus refugee Marcel Breuer; and Powell and Moya, a dynamic pair of 20-somethings who'd designed the Skylon for the Festival of Britain. Yet Gibberd's most remarkable feat was to design many of the buildings himself while also master-planning the entire town.

'How he managed to do all of this,' said Harlow museum curator David Devine, 'is *amazing*.' Yet his powers were not without limit. 'He moved into a house on Marsh Lane on the edge of the town in 1956 and applied to have an extension. He applied to his own corporation, and guess what? *No!* The man who built the whole town can't even get his own extension!' The acclaimed architects weren't the only ones behind the building of the new towns: almost all of the development corporations were run by retired colonels and the like – in the case of Harlow, it was Churchill's pal General Ridley Pakenham-Walsh – and the workforce was made up of men and women who had been so recently fighting in Europe.

Cwmbran's Jim Griffiths had a theory:

'They'd built new towns in the desert, they'd built new towns in Italy, they'd built new towns on the Ardennes: why wouldn't they build one here? And they had the same get up and go about it. *We just get engineers over here and we put it there* – there was no finesse about the new towns. That came a bit later as they got a bit more sophisticated. But the first wave were just: *map it out, give us a diagram and here we go!* It was a product of the thinking of the Second World War. An awful lot of people had nothing to do in 1945. They could turn out a sewage works, they could make a road nice and straight.'

John Reed, who'd moved to Harlow's Mark Hall North as a boy in 1952, vividly recalls the situation his parents' generation found themselves in after the war:

'The bloke next door had been in the army with Slim in Burma. My Dad had been in the desert. Gone there via, I might add, Cape Town. He'd been to see the pyramids, Cairo, places like that. These were places people had never seen! Another bloke had been a submariner. My teacher had been a navigator in a Lancaster. Well, of course, people had seen these things, they'd come home, and they thought, *so we'll go back to living in an upstairs flat in Holloway or something?*'

John and I went on a slow walk around his neighbourhood. He pointed out landmarks as we strolled along, and waited patiently while I took bad photos of design detailing with my phone.

'My father was a builder. It was obviously a happy hunting ground for bricklayers and the like. I used to be sent out with his lunch. I used to go round asking if anyone knew where he was working today 'cos if he found someone else was paying another tuppence an hour down the road then off he'd gone. He was certainly involved in those houses up the top of the road there, that's one of the places I found him.'

We were looking at some austere two-storey brick terraces with flat-roofed porches. 'Of course, when it started to slow down round here, he trotted off to Basildon and Stevenage.' We rounded a corner and ahead of us was a sloping green wedge, with a small row of corner shops at the bottom – a 'Hatch'. 'It consisted originally of a chip shop, a greengrocers, a grocers, a newsagent-tobacconists and a pub,' he explained. 'The pub's the White Admiral.' All of Harlow's pubs were named after butterflies. John vividly remembered the workmen from when they first arrived there. 'The chip shop queue used to go round the block! A lot of the men were still stag, they were living in wherever they could find anywhere, waiting for their houses to be issued, so of course they made a lot of use of the chip shops and such like.'

Everyone expected the new towns to be garden cities with Arts and Crafts cottages for everyone, but the planners had other ideas. Gibberd and his peers were keen to create something that felt urban: they built flats. For the most part these were small blocks of four or five storeys, but in Harlow Gibberd pushed it further, and introduced a new form to British housing: the high-rise 'point block' from Sweden. Point blocks were residential towers where the flats were situated off a central lift shaft or stairwell. Several had been built in the Stockholm district of Danviksklippan in the early forties, and they became one of prime lures for visiting architects. They were a symbol of how Swedish architecture had been in the ascendant as an international force since the 1930 Stockholm Exhibition. 'While other nations have been talking about building landscapes of towers,' wrote Gordon Logie admiringly in his book *The Urban Scene* in 1954, 'the Swedes have quietly gone ahead and done it.'[15] Pages of beautifully shot photos of point blocks followed.

Point blocks had several advantages over their lower-lying cousins: by piling flats on top of each other they freed up space on the ground for parks; town planners loved them because they provided a vertical feature akin to a church spire; and they

The Lawns, Britain's first 'point block', designed by Frederick Gibberd, nearing completion in 1951.
© *Harlow Museum and Science Alive*

were perfect for the elderly or single people who didn't have the time or energy for a garden of their own. Gibberd saw the chance in Mark Hall North to build something shockingly modern: 'A tower block of bed-sitting and one-room flats for single people.'[16] John Reed and I wandered up to The Lawns. The 'block' is really a rather pretty fan shape, and each small flat has its own balcony. The paintwork looks fresh and it seems generally in good nick for a festival-era building – it even has a plaque to commemorate its history and listing. The most obvious point is that it really does work as a landmark. It's the only tall building in the district, and this prototype for the tower block must have felt huge when it first appeared, with nothing comparable anywhere else in the country and when so little of the town had been built. Still surrounded by large trees and rows of low-rise flats, houses and garages, the block may no longer look unique, but it remains a dignified country gent mellowing with age.

Gibberd admitted later that there was

'a selfish reason for the block in that, as joint author, along with F. R. S. Yorke, of *The Modern Flat,* this would be an opportunity to try out some of its theories. There was the special appeal that a point block would orientate the new town towards Le Corbusier's vertical city – the "ville radieuse" – and away from the garden city movement.'[17]

Le Corbusier's powerful vision of a city of parkland punctuated by mighty tower blocks as a solution to urban living had inspired and incensed architects and planners in equal measure. In Harlow even a modest nod to this idea, in the form of a ten-storey, Swedish-style, concrete-and-red-brick point block, was almost derailed by government opposition to the cost of constructing such an experimental building. 'One of the test samples of the reinforced concrete failed,' recalled Gibberd in 1980. 'As a result the columns had to be stripped down to the reinforcement. The situation was a gift to journalists but thanks to Adams' [the General Manager] control over every situation it did not leak out.'[18] The opening ceremony was performed in May 1951 as an official event of the Festival of Britain.

Like many of the people I interviewed about Harlow, Janet Search expressed a fondness for the block. 'They were nice flats in there. I have a friend who lived in one.' She'd been very keen to get a look inside. 'We were only being nosey really. We were dying to find someone who lived

The Lawns in 2011, still well maintained and surrounded by mature trees.

there.' Did her friend like it? 'Oh yes. The view, and the fact it was *something*, it was something different. They've built two or three since but somehow that one seems special.' Two months after it was opened, Walter Gropius, the founder of the Bauhaus, made his thoughts known on the state of town planning in the UK: 'He is a keen advocate of blocks of flats in the country,' reported the *Observer*, 'such as that just finished at Harlow, pointing out their advantages for the newly married or the old couple.'[19]

With all this revolutionary building work going on, relations between the newcomers and the residents from village of Old Harlow were not without friction. Janet Search was 14 when her family moved from the village of Langford in Essex to the new town in 1952, where her father was to be a Clerk of Works on the new industrial estate.

'We did all our shopping in Old Harlow. A lot of people, well, they didn't like the new town coming, and I can understand it – all this beautiful rural ground and all this concrete arriving. As children we weren't really liked in Old Harlow. The people were all, *Keep your children away from us!*'

Yet this was a boom time in Old Harlow for the shopkeepers, before any of the new town's own shopping centres opened. She remembered how the pioneers banded together to overcome the inconveniences of living without the most basic infrastructure:

'There was no soul or character to it to start with. You all had to put your own mark on things. When the gardens were all cordoned off it was amazing how people put all different paths down. My dad put brick down. You had to do that yourself. All you got was a concrete standing outside your back door. And it had to be open plan at the front. There were no gates or hedges.'

In fact, Gibberd was determined that residents should not cordon off the front of their houses at all, and fences and hedges were banned. Walking round with John Reed it was remarkable to see how widely this rule was still being adhered to.

'The rate of growth was *phenomenal*,' he told me. 'By the time I went to secondary school in '57 there were 40,000 people in the town. And when I came here in '52, just five years earlier, there were literally hundreds. I don't suppose there were 200 houses.' I also spoke to a boundlessly energetic Michael Caswell, whose family had lived next to a paint factory in Canning Town, been bombed out three times, and moved to Harlow in 1953 alongside a vast cohort of his extended family.

'I was four and I *loved* it. The door numbers weren't on the door. I remember holding my mother's hand. The men were still laying the paving slabs, the roads were just being built. I remember my mother saying, "where's number 77?" and the workman going [he mimes counting the doors of their street]. We were making camps in the ditches, it was great, all of us kids had grown up in slums. It was *fantastic*. My parents were amazed they had a bathroom, and a garden instead of a yard. I think what we found when we came to Harlow was that the community spirit was still very much the London spirit.'

Michael's experience wasn't shared by John Reed, who felt the dislocation endured by many after their move to a town of strangers.

'In those days there were no extended families. A few people had cars, no one had phones, so when they came out here they were very isolated. Some of the women particularly found it very difficult I think, 'cos women didn't work.'

Not all Harlow residents had been city dwellers. Janet Search's family had arrived from a small village, and found it hard to adjust. 'My mother never settled, she hated it,' said Janet. As a teenager, Janet had been similarly unenthusiastic at first, although they'd all loved the house itself. 'I just thought it was fantastic to go to an inside toilet and *bathroom*. Never had a bathroom before. Three bedrooms, oh yes, it was marvellous.'

'The building of a new town is not merely a great task of physical construction, it is also a great adventure in social construction,' wrote Lewis Silkin in his introduction to the New Towns Act 1946, 'for the new towns must be lively communities with their own civic consciousness and civic pride.'[20] But constructing communities amid the mud, drudge and chaos of a building site wasn't easy. The theme tune for all of the early postwar new towns could have been 'Getting to Know You', from *The King and I*. It was certainly the tone adopted by the local paper and the development corporation: the first edition of the *Harlow Citizen* in 1953 included notices on the formation of a new scout troop, the laying of a foundation stone for a new Methodist church, the debut of a young wives club, an old-time dancing society and the town's inaugural pigeon race. Yet the adverts sold a different, more inward-looking dream, featuring television repairmen warning those lucky enough to own a set to make sure it was ready for the coronation.

'There was a great friendship because everybody moved in with the same boat,' said Janet Search. 'On the Queen's coronation one person had a telly and we all took sandwiches or whatever into this Mrs Sullivan's and we all watched the coronation there together. You all helped each other. There was outings arranged in factories and if there was any spare seats you sort of got offered those.' Community groups were keen to explain the rules of new town life to new arrivals from the off.

'When we first moved to Harlow all the kids were given a booklet on how to behave in the countryside,' explained former city kid Michael Caswell. 'They told us that you mustn't kill birds, leave birds eggs alone, don't break trees, respect. Very nice, it's what the countryside's all about, because we'd come from towns.'

Almost two decades later, in the brand new Cwmbran neighbourhood unit of Coed Eva, Jim and Jo Griffiths also had to deal with the dislocation of moving from London to a town where they knew no one.

'You're all migrants,' said Jim, recalling what it was like for them to be the first generation of people moving into a new estate. 'There was a Scotsman, there was someone from Yorkshire we knew, there was another guy from Barnsley, and so on, and that immediately pushed you together. And the Welsh dimension was, I suppose, 50/50.'

'We happened to have family who were quite near – my parents were in Newport,' explained Jo. 'Most people didn't have the backup of a family, and I think that makes people much more friendly if you know your family aren't going to turn up every Sunday for lunch.

Babysitting had to be done amongst friends and babysitting circles and things like that.'

'One of the things that happened with a new town,' recalled Jim, 'there isn't that structure – religious structure or community structure – that already exists in every suburb. It made people more inventive.'

'It all seemed to be made up of cardboard boxes and things,' agreed Jo. 'The fun was generated without it costing a lot of money, so everyone had a fair crack of the whip. Because the amenities weren't there. The most expensive thing you could do was go to the pictures or go swimming.'

'It was out in the field playing kickabout,' said Jim wistfully.

Local shopping centres were springing up everywhere, creating some very fifties PR opportunities.

'Pram town': Woolworths, Dolcis and H. Samuel beseiged by young mothers with children in the late fifties. © Harlow Museum and Science Alive

'Different shops had different celebrities to open them,' remembered Janet Search. 'Sabrina was one in Bush Fair. Hermione Gingold opened W. H. Smith in The Stow. She got given a teddy bear for doing that.' Yet shopping and old-time dancing were not the only pastimes in Harlow in the early days. By 1956 it had the highest birth-

rate in the country, and cheeky *Daily Mirror* journalists coined a phrase
that would haunt Harlow for decades: 'pram town'. In the Museum
there were amazing photos of high streets completely rammed with
coach-sized baby carriages. 'If you went into Sainsbury's or Boots or
Woolworths you just parked your pram outside – *with the baby in it!*'
said Janet, shaking her head in disbelief at the memory. The photos
highlighted the unbalanced nature of the town's population, which
was heavily weighted towards young professionals. Indeed, Ben
Hyde Harvey, General Manager of the corporation, predicted in 1957
that 'virtually no one will die in Harlow for 30 years.'[21] This youthful,
middle class workforce had been attracted by the concentration of
high-tech industry: something all the new towns had in common,
bar the handful that had been built around coal or steel.

'If you were a businessman with a start-up business like my
own father,' said museum curator David Devine, 'they said, *well
you're going to bring enterprise to the town, you're going to bring
employment, you can come to Harlow.*' His family moved there
from Croydon, his father setting up a factory specialising in the
impossibly futuristic business of encasing electrical components in
plastic. They were by no means the only high-tech firm. 'We had
Cossor's, which is basically radar; we had STC, Standard Telephone
and Cable, which is valves and everything like that; then you had
STL, Standard Telephone Laboratories, the research arm of STC,
which later became ITT and then became Nortel; we also had Pitney
Bowes, who do all your franking machines.'

By October 1952 the number of industrial workers
outnumbered the builders for the first time, and the town's
amenities were growing. In an attempt to embrace modern art as
well as architecture, Barbara Hepworth's 'Contrapuntal Forms' had
been re-sited from its original home in the Festival of Britain, soon
joined by her archrival Henry Moore's 'Family Group'.[i] There were

---

i A decade later when the Gulbenkian Foundation bestowed a £3,000 grant for the
town to commission a sculpture, *The Times* remarked on the modernist tone of the
existing examples that 'so far there is no one on horseback'. (*The Times*, 6/2/62, p14)

53 social groups, and 25 shops had opened. One of the standard factory units in the industrial estate had been converted into a temporary cinema. The Essex Skipper became the first pub. There was one primary but no secondary school. A mere five years later, 15 million square feet of factory space, 300 social groups, six pubs, 150 shops and 11 schools had sprung up. As befitted any self-respecting high-tech postwar town, a heliport opened in 1955, and the first passenger was the new head of the development corporation, the building magnate Sir Richard Costain, choppering in from Battersea.

An ever-more skilled workforce was needed to oil the wheels of commerce in this state-of-the-art town, and a gulf began to appear between the new town's founding principles and their reality. Unless they were builders, the working-class former residents of big city slums – the very people the new towns were built for – were left out in the cold. The experience of Londoner Jim Cattle, interviewed in 1986 for the LWT programme *The Making of Modern London*, was shared by many trying to jump through the requisite hoops to get a home away from the city.

> 'When they started to build the new towns like Stevenage they said, *Well, would you like to go?* I said, *Yeh, cor, I'd love to go.* They said, *What do you do for a living?* Well, when I turned around and said to them I worked at Smithfield Market they looked at me and said, *Well, you'd better go back there.* We weren't qualified for anything like that. With me not being skilled we had no chance.'[22]

Not all the residential areas in Harlow were like Mark Hall North with its great wedges of green. Their styles were varied, as was the quality of their housing and design. The Potter Street area, for example, was built as part of Macmillan's housing drive and 1,000 houses were built more swiftly and cheaply than the development corporation would have liked. Other districts near the centre, such as The Dashes or The Hides, were tightly packed. Here blank-faced red-brick terraces and part-rendered semis were often built around a complex arrangement of pathways, where the house numbers were bafflingly hard for an outsider to follow. Gibberd acknowledged that the problems his development corporation faced were compounded by a brain drain. 'With the advent of the later new towns with new concepts, like Redditch and Milton Keynes, the *Mark I* new towns found it harder to attract the same calibre of staff, and their work on the whole became less imaginative.'[23]

The appeal of the new towns was international. Ben Hyde Harvey reported back from a town planning conference in West Germany, where his experience appeared to confirm Lewis Silkin's prediction that the new towns would become world famous. 'The main topic of conversation was Harlow new town,' he claimed, 'which many of them had visited.'[24] Yet by then, the West Germans were building 540,000 homes a year, almost double the figure in England and Wales. By the seventies Harlow was receiving visitors from the Soviet Union, who had built large garden cities of their own, such as the steel town of Magnitogorsk in the Urals. 'We are very interested in both the architecture and the sociology of the new towns,' Mr V. S. Vysotski, the chief design architect at the Russian Institute of Town Designing was quoted as saying in *The Times*. He was one of a delegation of three experts from Russia who, in a peculiar footnote to Cold War détente, visited Harlow, Stevenage, Runcorn, Cumbernauld, Thamesmead, Glasgow and the Barbican in 1971. It was reported as a triumph of the British new town movement, though the visitors were not enamoured with everything they found: 'They were surprised ... at the many low houses and maisonettes compared with their own mainly tall blocks of flats. The extensive road network around Harlow has also come as a shock to them.'[25]

The sheer quantity of tarmac may have seemed shocking to delegates from a Soviet bloc mired in stagnation, but in fact the road network would turn out to be a universal failing across the first wave of new towns. Gibberd was the first to admit that they'd massively miscalculated the growth in car ownership. In 1940 the Ministry of Health, then responsible for housing, was recommending that Britain would need just one garage for every 10 homes. Two decades later Welwyn Garden City's development corporation reported that they were still building only 106 garages a year – despite a waiting list of 3,955. 'It is becoming apparent,' they wrote with a modicum of understatement, 'that whatever the national proportion of car owners may be, the statistics have little relation to the problem in the new towns.'[26] Facilities for cars still leave something to be desired today. John Reed pointed out to me that his next-door neighbours alone had five cars to one house.

'Even now the roads are quite narrow,' said Janet Search. 'A lot of them are cul-de-sacs and you weren't ever supposed to park in the hammerheads because that was for turning.'

And roads were to cause another huge headache for the master-planner, as curator David Devine explained to me. 'The motorways were going to be on this side of the town,' he said, indicating the northeast corner where we were stood, 'and that's why the industrial areas are on this side of the town. But then the government in 1972, or thereabouts, decided to put the motorway here' – he pointed to the south of Harlow on the map – 'and that's because they wanted to have a Norwich-Cambridge-London link.' David was getting quite worked up at this point. I was beginning to recognise this proprietorial note in all of the people I interviewed in Harlow. 'It's buggered up the plan. People drive in on Southern Way, which is a minor road. Freddie Gibberd at the time went absolutely mad. He actually said – and this is the polite version – that it was like planning a seaside town and then they moved the sea.'

'It was nice when the town centre was first built,' Janet Search recalled of Gibberd's showpiece, which for the early residents had been a long time coming. Her mild praise was echoed by the

Manchester Guardian, who in 1957 found it a rather meek affair, with 'an engaging air of restrained gaiety, of tastefully tentative fun'.[27] He'd left the centre (known as 'The High' due to its position on a hill) blank on the plans, but by the end of the fifties, at the insistence of Macmillan's Conservative government, this space was being sold off to private developers rather than carefully planned out by the corporation. One of the successful bidders to build 'superblocks' along a new Broad Walk was Ravenseft, a slick operation specialising in building shopping centres in bombed cities such as Plymouth, Exeter and Hull. The first 'superblock' on Broad Walk opened in 1957, part of the first wave of pedestrianised precincts outside America, and just behind Stevenage and Coventry. The *Harlow Citizen* carried a special sponsored supplement extolling the joys of the 52 new shops, which included H. Samuel, MacFisheries, Timothy Whites and Dolcis.

Gibberd recalled that the process of choosing between Ravenseft's sketches of proposed developments was 'like choosing a hat'. He was distinctly unimpressed with the plans, which fell well below the standard of design he'd been keen to uphold in the town. After much wrangling, however, he claimed that the developers had come to accept 'that the appearance of the building mattered as much to the company as it did to the corporation.'[28] Ravenseft, on the other hand, were quoted as saying that 'on aesthetics we didn't really care, provided we didn't feel the building to be offensive'.[29] Their plain red-brick superblock ended up facing the colourful marble 'crazy paved' gables and gently swooshed asymmetric awnings of Seymour Harris and Partners' parade, across Broad Walk. The zigzag-patterned precinct floor led pedestrians into the earlier Market Square, commanded by a large modernist clock, not unlike the sort once used to count down schools' programmes on the telly, affixed to the wall above a shop unit. The design of the shopping centre may have been tentative, but The High was soon home to a huddle of more impressive civic buildings: St Paul's Church with its beautiful John Piper mural; a modernist water garden designed by Gibberd;

The Market Square taken shortly after completion.
© *Harlow Museum and Science Alive*

and the Town Hall, a stout tower block with a lighthouse-like viewing gallery perched on top. There was also Britain's first purpose-built postwar cinema – operated by J. Arthur Rank – in 1960.

The High came in for a great deal of criticism when it was finally built. Roger Berthold in *The Times* wrote in 1977 that it was 'like a morgue at night, the dance hall is expensive, the only cinema often only shows X films … a coffee bar has only recently opened in the centre, and many young people cannot stand youth clubs.'[30] This was a dig at the new town fetish for social organisations such as sports, arts and social clubs as the centre of community life, which showed no signs of abating by the late seventies. Harlow's showpiece Town Hall and water gardens have since been demolished.

Jim Griffiths showed me around Cwmbran's central area, built a few years after Harlow's in the early sixties. They shared a design principle: the centres look inwards, presenting a blank brick-and-concrete face to the rest of the town. In Cwmbran a ring road circles the centre beneath pylon-topped hills. From the roof of the car park Jim pointed out the earliest areas, houses and maisonettes of a mildly Scandinavian modernist bent, built from local brick, their roofs barely pitched. Then there was a slender 20-storey concrete point block, which had a huge industrial-looking duct snaking up the side. This was the chimney for the town centre's district heating plant, suggesting that the entire point for this block of flats was less to provide a landmark, as in Harlow, than to disguise the flue as far as possible. To its left we could see the industrial zone, with its small factory units, and beyond that a ribbon of thirties semis that followed the existing road – exactly the kind of unplanned sprawl the new towns were developed to counter.

The shopping centre itself was a pretty mellow place: elderly people sat outside coffee shops; kids played by the old corporation office block, with its concrete and mosaic frescoes of kings and dragons; and a few drunks hung out by a sunken water garden. A theatre and a bus station were built into the edifice, and the car park offered free parking. I took a few snaps, and before we knew it we were surrounded by fluoro-jacketed security guards. *Excuse me, have you got permission to take photographs?* one of them asked. I admitted that I didn't. Jim was outraged as we were ushered up to the centre's management offices. We waited around for a while as the staff dealt with a young mum who'd stubbed her toe on a paving stone and needed a plaster. Eventually we were seen, and Jim explained I was researching a book. *Did I*, the administrator asked, *have a certificate for that?* After an exasperating half hour spent trying to explain that authors don't come with certificates, we were released, a promise having been extracted that I would not take any further photographs. It was a reminder that the centre was no longer public space, as it had been when built: like all new towns, the development corporation had been wound up, and the centre sold off.

The backlash against Harlow and the other early new towns struck early and viciously, before many of the first wave even had populations in the thousands. In the July 1953 edition of *Architectural Review*, editor J. M. Richards and art editor Gordon Cullen decided to put the boot in. The hitherto celebrated green wedges were suddenly accused of dislocating these fledgling communities, the vast green areas of sucking the energy and vitality out of the place by separating everyone to an unnecessary extent. 'Prairie planning' was Cullen's dismissive description of the concept, and one that stuck in architectural rags as quickly as 'pram town' had in the tabloids. He took a number of swings at the 'un-use' of land by the planners, which created 'a feeling of hopelessness in the face of a terrifying eternity of wideness, punctuated at intervals by seas of concrete'.[31] He illustrated his piece with drab photos of the 'sulky monotony' of Hemel Hempstead's wide streets and long, low municipal lawns. Richards insisted that a town should be 'a sociable place, for people who want to live close together ... The new towns, by and large, have none of these attributes ... Their inhabitants, instead of feeling themselves secure within an environment devoted to their conven-ience and pleasure, find themselves marooned in a desert of grass verges and concrete roadways'.[32]

Cullen, generally better known for his beguilingly colourful architect's drawings than for vitriol, had a field day with these 'prairies'. 'In spite of all the administrative energy, publicity, and cash expended on them,' he wrote, 'what should have been a great adventure has come to nothing and less than nothing. And so far with hardly a word spoken in protest'.[33] Their portraits of 'footsore housewives and cycle-weary workers' were a startling and unexpected blow to Frederick Gibberd and his fellow new town planners, who believed they'd successfully moved beyond the soporific garden city to create something exciting and new that really worked. Richards even went so far as to suggest that there was little to differentiate these towns from the sprawling ribbons of privately built suburban semis of the interwar years, claiming Gibberd and his peers had built houses 'in the wrong place, of the wrong size and laid out in the wrong way'.[34] A new wave of younger architects was equally contemptuous. Peter and Alison Smithson, a recently qualified and increasingly influential pair of architects, described them as 'English towns as off the mark as any English scene by Hollywood'.[35] And they didn't stop there.

'Drive or walk into any example of the garden city idea and you will lose your sense of direction in the wide streets that lead nowhere. Wide tarmac rivers wave off in every direction, any of them may be the way out.'[36] Even Lewis Mumford, American planner and friend of garden city champion Frederic Osborn, wasn't convinced by these early postwar experiments: 'Because the new planners were mainly in revolt against congestion and squalor, rather than in love with urban order and cooperation, the new towns do not yet adequately reveal what the modern city should be.'[37] The new town planners were bewildered by the vehemence of these reactions to their masterworks. 'We, the architects, found it all rather discouraging,' said Gibberd, with characteristic understatement, 'and we were only reassured when we talked to householders.'[38]

'I think most people would agree that the new town concept has worked by and large,' said David Devine when I interviewed him. 'I think it's been absolutely brilliant.' In 1977, in an attempt to assess the quality of life in Harlow, *The Times* analysed statistics covering crime rates, population density and so on. 'On balance,' they concluded, 'its inhabitants have pleasanter surroundings, better living conditions, social services and recreational facilities ... than in most towns of comparable population in most parts of London and in the deprived inner areas of our major cities.'[39] Despite this, there's little love for the new towns beyond their boundaries.

'I went to Letchworth about a month ago,' said David as we wandered among the exhibits in the Museum. 'They were putting a big show on to celebrate the garden city, and they invited other towns – pre-new town places – to visit and put an exhibition on. So they had one from Port Sunlight, Saltaire, Hampstead Garden Suburb, one or two others. And we were there representing the new town. And people were coming into the tent, looking at the wonderful panels that the civics had put up and saying, *Oh, Harlow, well, we're not going to bother with that, that's really boring. Oh! Wretched!* And it's just this idea that people have in their heads.' Yet for Frederick Gibberd and many other new town planners, builders and residents, they were missing something much bigger. 'The spirit of those years was elevating,' Gibberd wrote in 1980. 'There was a determination to make Britain a better place to live in.'[40] In an era when so much more seemed possible, it was easy for the critics of the day to overlook the achievements around them, pushing on as they were for ever more radical solutions. But the early new towns were undoubtedly an incredible achievement of organisation, planning and sheer bloody mindedness. They sit alongside the creation of the welfare state, the NHS and the postwar revolution in education as monuments to a nation's desire to move on, not just from the destruction of the war years, but from the inequalities and squalour inherited from the Industrial Revolution. For the political rulers of a bankrupted nation to push ahead with such schemes in an age of rationing and shortages must have taken guts. To this day, in an era of faux austerity where political will is such that widening inequality is seen as inevitable, and grand schemes unimaginable, the spirit of these pioneering souls and their projects should still strike even the most curmudgeonly of us as visionary and inspirational.

3. 'A Real Effort to be Jolly'
THE FESTIVAL OF BRITAIN ON LONDON'S SOUTH BANK (1951)

Just before I set off round the country, a friend presented me with a gift: a copy of the *Festival of Britain Guide for the South Bank Exhibition*. Grubby, tatty, with mould creeping across the cover, the booklet, with the bunting-clad festival logo across the cover, turned out to be an absolute joy to read. And that was before I'd even got as far as the exhibition blurb and map. It was full of glorious painterly colour adverts for the Standard Vanguard car, Coalite smokeless coal, Craven A cigarettes and British Electricity's new power stations. As I leafed through it, two loose photographs fell from within its pages. My friend had bought the booklet on eBay, and the original owner had stowed inside a couple of small souvenirs of days out. The first wasn't recognisable – a vista flanked by bandstands and ornamental ponds, leading to a large fountain marked with the letters E.R., suggesting it was taken some years later, after the Queen's Coronation in 1952. But the next looked like a blurry still from *The Day the Earth Stood Still*, depicting queues snaking for hundreds of yards to the entrance of a great flying saucer. It was unmistakably the Festival of Britain, and that alien visitor the Dome of Discovery. Both photos showed crowds of early-fifties revellers: men in drab overcoats or tweedy suits, boys in long shorts and sensible shirts, women in the fitted waists and full skirts of Christian Dior's 'New Look'. In many ways these clean-cut, formal and buttoned-up citizens looked as alien as the Dome to me.

Sixty years later, as the Festival Hall celebrated its birthday, I happened to meet John Gyford, a retired planner from the London

Queues for the Dome of Discovery,
in a snap that fell from my programme for the Festival.

County Council, at a talk. An eminent panel were explaining the background to the festival, and during the Q&A a man next to me stood up and offered first a terrifically vivid recollection of visiting it as a child, and then an account of the indomitable attitude within the LCC's planning department when he'd joined it a decade later. We chatted afterwards, and met up a few months later. John had visited the Festival of Britain twice, once in May when it had just opened, and once in late August when it was soon to close. With school-boy-like enthusiasm, he explained to me how he'd felt:

'There was a book that was published some time early in the sixties called *The Age of Austerity*. And one of the chapters, I think it was by Michael Frayn, said that the best thing about the Festival of Britain was simply *being there*. And in some ways that quite well summed up what I felt at the time – just what a marvellous place this exhibition was. It just contained so many *things*.'

Today, the Festival of Britain is the sort of thing we are primed to be cynical about. It's easy to imagine snarky Twitter comments on the do-gooding exhibits or damning Instagrams of the wilfully quirky designs. And as it happens, it was easy to be cynical then, too. 'We know we're caught but must support this patriotic prank/ and though we'd rather have shot ourselves we've got ourselves to thank,' was Noël Coward's acerbic verdict in his satirical song 'Don't Make Fun of the Fair'. 'The size is petty,' reported a *Daily Express* not over-burdened with good will just before the festival opened. The paper criticised everything from the cost to the socialist vulgarity of it all. 'The theatre can't house either the show or the audience', it complained, dubbing the architecture 'a muddle of styles'.[1]

Of course cynicism can be a useful corrective, but it can also be a great inhibitor of new ideas. And after the destruction, pain and misery of the Second World War, Britain was in dire need of a shot of optimism. Surely the key to the national recovery would be to turn the mighty organisational capacities of the armed forces to more positive peacetime purposes.

Several top military figures were appointed to head up the new town development corporations, but one of the most exciting positions was taken by Winston Churchill's chief military assistant, General Lord Hastings Lionel Ismay (known to his friends as 'Pug'). In 1948, this formidable public figure was appointed chairman of a whimsical-sounding civilian affair called the Festival of Britain. 'By continuing to press on,' he told the *Daily Mirror*, 'we proclaim to ourselves and to the world that we are determined to take up our lives, and move forward again after the hideous waste of the war years.' The paper greeted the news with a screaming front-page headline: 'Britain to Go Gay For Year'.[2]

The idea for a festival to mark the centenary of the Great Exhibition that would also reward the British people for their fortitude during the war, and point the way to a brighter, happier, more modern way of life, had been knocking around since 1943. The cause was taken up by two dynamic figures: Herbert Morrison, who'd been deputy prime minister since the Labour party's victory in 1945; and Gerald Barry, former editor of the *News Chronicle*. In the century since the pioneering Great Exhibition at Hyde Park, international fairs and 'expos' had become big business. The daringly modernist Stockholm Exhibition of 1930 had made a huge impact in the world of architecture; Chicago's World's Fair of 1933 showcased the latest in new technology; and the highly charged 1937 Paris Expo became a political face-off between the Nazi German swastika-topped tower and the Soviet Union's gigantic steel sculpture: workers wielding a hammer and sickle.

A more modest industrial showcase, 'Britain Can Make It', had been the inaugural exhibition when the Victoria and Albert Museum re-opened in 1948. Aimed not at Britons but at boosting exports of British-made goods (and thus universally known as 'Britain Can't Have It') it had been designed by a dandyish young Edinburgh architect, Basil Spence. It hadn't set the order books alight. Morrison's triumph was to overcome the grave reluctance of his fellow MPs, stoked by the failure of 'Britain Can Make It'. Yet financial constraints soon began to loom large, with a politically disastrous devaluation of the pound in 1948, and the festival had to shrink from an international extravaganza in the Great Exhibition mould to a smaller, more domestic affair. There were other harsh realities to be faced – not least the punishingly short schedule. Even its location was a tough call. Celebrations would be held across the country, but the focus was to be an exhibition in London. A shortlist of sites was drawn up: Hyde Park, home of the Great Exhibition, was deemed too nice – it hadn't been dug up for war, and digging it up for peace was reckoned intolerable vandalism; the south bank of the Thames was too squalid, with its industrial relics and notorious slums; but the grounds of the Earl of Jersey's stately home in Osterley Park, west London, was just right – until ruinous infrastructure costs came through. The committee was stumped.

Meanwhile, playing no part at all in frivolous festival planning, the London County Council was setting about the serious task of reconstruction. The *County of London Plan* of 1943 had been commissioned by Lord Reith, wartime Minister of Works and Buildings, and written by eminent planner Patrick Abercrombie and the LCC's own Chief Architect John Henry Forshaw. They hoped to remedy four major defects of London: traffic congestion, depressed housing, inadequacy of open spaces, and the untidy mixing of industrial buildings and houses all over the city. The plan focused heavily on the West End, East End and the south bank of the Thames, which Abercrombie described as having 'a depressing, semi-derelict appearance, lacking any sense of that dignity and order of appearance to its location at the centre of London'. Furthermore, 'this gloomy aspect is intensified to-day by war damage.'[3]

The *Plan* addressed these shortcomings with an ambitious redrawing of the map of south London, beginning with 'a riverside embankment, a series of buildings of various character, starting, perhaps, with a great cultural centre, followed by theatres, concert halls and assembly halls; with offices at the new Waterloo Bridge head, terminating at the eastern extremity in commercial and other buildings'.[4] One of the most notable casualties of the London Blitz had been the city's greatest concert auditorium, the Queen's Hall in Langham Place, near Regent Street. Abercrombie and Forshaw suggested that a replacement might be built on this largely derelict, unfashionable and post-industrial site. The Ministry of Works was also keen that the area should accommodate civil service sprawl as Whitehall expanded across the river. Charles Holden, the architect most famous for his London Underground station designs, was initially engaged by the LCC to flesh out this plan. He envisaged a waterfront rebuilt in monumentally formal fashion, as in the plans for Plymouth and his own thirties Senate House building for the University of London[i]. But before he could even file his report,

---

i The following year Holden's colossal 19-storey university building would form the inspiration for the Ministry of Truth in George Orwell's *Nineteen Eighty-Four*.

Holden's plan was challenged from within the LCC by a dashing young star of the modern movement.

Robert Matthew was a former Edinburgh College of Art classmate of 'Britain Can Make It' designer Basil Spence, and very much the outsider for the post of LCC Chief Architect and Planner. John Henry Forshaw had quit in 1946 following a bout of spectacular Machiavellian internal politics. Matthew, keen to make his mark, moved in to ensure it was his department, not freelancer Holden, that would be responsible for this major chunk of South Bank reconstruction. A new auditorium on the South Bank was exactly the opportunity he needed to rebuild the esteem of a demoralised team, although he noted that even within the depressed staff he inherited, 'the aura of Abercrombie was strong down the corridors, and enthusiasm for postwar planning was tremendous'.[5]

However, it was clear that a project of this scale would allow him to bring in some fresh blood, and transform it from a shadow of its thirties heyday to a beacon of modern design and planning ideas. The replacement for the Queen's Hall was to be built on the site of the derelict Lion Brewery, between Sir John Hawkshaw's wrought-iron Hungerford Bridge of 1864 and a brick tower, built in 1826, which had been used in the manufacture of lead shot. It was the perfect opportunity for Matthew to create London's first strikingly modernist postwar public building.

It was at this point that the two great plans for London's postwar civic revival crashed headlong into each other. On 21 July 1948 the festival council also settled on the 27 acres of the South Bank site as the ideal location for their exhibition, under the government proviso that the LCC invested in building a proper embankment. The government put further pressure on the county council when Herbert Morrison insisted that they get the proposed new concert hall ready in time for the festival. There was little choice in the matter, and so they pushed ahead as fast as they were able, draining the famously marshy land on the South Bank and erecting a new river wall. Conditions on this wetland were tough, with workmen mired in claustrophobic holes 20 feet down, while water from the Thames constantly flooded in.

The sudden influx of energy played brilliantly to Robert Matthew's plan to build up his department. He had made the most significant of his early appointments within days of the Festival of Britain being announced: that of talented, easily bored and highly-strung architect Leslie Martin as his new deputy. Martin is generally credited with the design for the Royal Festival Hall, but Matthew had sketched out the initial plans before the appointment was made, working flat out – literally, as a bad back forced him to work lying down – with his drawing board suspended above him on a Heath Robinson-style contraption, and all the while, according to his brother, 'pumped full of morphia'.[6]

Building a concert hall next to a busy railway bridge was hardly ideal, and the problem of keeping the rumble of the trains out and the concertos in was a difficult one, solved with an ingenious 'egg in a box' design, with the auditorium suspended inside the building to protect its delicate content. 'Whilst this conception undoubtedly met the scientific requirements,' Leslie Martin later said, 'I cannot say that it was achieved by logic. It came, like all ideas, out of the blue, as an arrangement which suddenly seem to fit and to bring into order all the requirements.'[7]

In the summer of 2011 the Southbank Centre ran a festival of its own, commemorating the 1951 exhibition in a flurry of bunting, beach huts and idiosyncratic events. Abram Games' famous festival logo – Britannia's profile topping a star surrounded by bunting – was adapted to make way for branding from MasterCard, as if to hammer home just how far we've strayed from the era of the welfare state and nationalisation.

The South Bank and the Festival Hall have long been my idea of the apex of civilisation. As a timid teenager from Croydon I'd travel to watch plays at the National Theatre, rummage for second hand books in the stalls under Waterloo Bridge or hang out in the quiet cafés and drink hot chocolate (coffee being one step too far

Abram Games' Festival of Britain logo from the cover of the souvenir brochure, and a spread from Design in the Festival, *another official publication.*

towards sophistication). Abercrombie and Forshaw's 'great cultural centre' was the place I'd been looking for all my life. And the Festival Hall, beaten up, tired and quiet as it was back then at the end of the eighties, was still one of the most beautiful buildings I had ever seen. There were fossils in the polished marble, contrasting with the warm parquet and the threadbare net-and-ball design carpet that smothered the sound of my footsteps. The glass walls looked out on the Thames, so much of which was shielded from the public by the miles of private developments along the river. There was wood everywhere: ribbed wall panels, cantilevered staircases and chunky curved rails that felt silky smooth to the touch.

To anyone brought up in postwar Britain, aspects of the design feel familiar from schools, civic buildings and provincial theatres. The brass-tipped cigar shape, so familiar from fifties furniture legs and standard-lamp stems, crops up everywhere, from the shape of the bar to the detail on the balconies. The Festival Hall popularized many styles that were later much imitated elsewhere, but it was built with the best materials around, and as a result retains a sheen of luxury.

Etched glass on the doors of the Festival Hall, just part of the fine detail in this luxurious building.

An extensive refurbishment in the noughties has left us with a brighter, more logical, busier building, bustling from morning to evening with what seem to be locals rather than tourists. Yet even though it's heaving these days, I still think of it as my secret.

Back in the late forties, over in the Festival of Britain office, another young designer, Hugh Casson, was appointed as the festival Architect. Given a list of exhibits he was expected to deliver in celebration of the British spirit, he set about appointing his own team of architects to create a diverse array of buildings on the small, awkward site split in half by Hungerford Bridge.

To many of the festival's visitors, it was not only the buildings or exhibits that would have such a startling effect, but the way the entire festival had been laid out. In the Festival Hall café, John Gyford and I took tea amid the melee of the sixtieth birthday celebrations. An unassuming-looking man, balding and casually dressed, he spoke with the ease, charm and confidence of someone used to commanding a room. He recalled how marvellous he had found the exhibition. And it wasn't necessarily what was inside the different buildings that had attracted him – it was the whole experience.

'I didn't talk that sort of language at the time,' he explained, 'but I now realise that what I was talking about was design, and the arrangement of buildings and spaces, all that sort of stuff. I just had not dreamt that such things could be. It was a complete revelation.'

We'd both visited the Museum of 1951, an exhibition commemorating the sixtieth anniversary of the festival, featuring a nostalgic and engrossing mixture of gentle modernist design, faded relics from the exhibition and oral history. 'One of the films they've got on downstairs about the Festival of Britain,' said John, 'was mainly narrated by one of the architects who was involved. I was totally too young to appreciate this at the time, but whereas most great exhibitions, like the World's Fairs, had been laid out on axial principles' – John was chopping the air into great right angles at this point – 'these great *axes*, this one was laid out on the principle of small spaces leading into and off one another. I could see as he said that how absolutely true that was as an organising principle. I'd never come across something like that before, and so without knowing it was a design principle I was just overwhelmed by it all.' I thought back to prewar Welwyn Garden City, with its axial layout, and compared it to Harlow, with its wedges, winding roads and deliberate lack of formality: the festival provided another early example of that new approach to laying out buildings. 'When I was studying planning as a postgraduate student, one of the key books I read was by an American called Kevin Lynch.' John was referring to an influential 1960 work on planning theory called *The Image of the City*, which explored the way in which people navigated through urban areas. 'It was about what was then beginning to be called "townscape". And he proposed a vocabulary for how to talk about the arrangement of urban spaces and the linkages of openness and closure and the importance of being able to see long distances – or *not* being able to see long distances. It provided me with the kind of vocabulary that had not been available at the time of the festival.'

Like many postwar planners experimenting with new ideas in 'townscape', Hugh Casson decided early on that the layout of the Festival of Britain was as much about what you couldn't see as what you could. Hungerford rail bridge cut right through the centre of the festival site, so the team decided to use this to help organise the exhibits into two groups. The upstream section by County Hall was to be The Land of Britain; the downstream section by Waterloo Bridge would showcase The People of Britain. Hugh Casson saw the first section as 'the Origins of the Land, Agriculture, Mining, Industry all grouped around the shining cranium – as we saw it – of

The Festival Hall, Dome of Discovery, Skylon and all the other Festival of Britain buildings on the South Bank. © Lambeth Archives Department

invention (hence the Dome of Discovery)'.[8] Ralph Tubbs, who had shown his mettle by withstanding the pressure of working in the architecture practice of fearsome Hungarian émigré Ernő Goldfinger, gained the most extravagant commission of the festival for this 'cranium'. This great umbrella was to house exhibits on the living world, polar exploration, physics, and most dramatically, outer space. His eminent former boss, by contrast, was allocated a rather less impressive structure to design for the festival – a souvenir kiosk on the embankment. George Grenfell-Baines, who'd designed wartime factories, was the perfect person to design the macho Power and Production pavilion, while Basil Spence produced the glass-walled Sea and Ships pavilion, on the site now occupied by the London Eye. 'The object of an exhibition is to excite and even shock, above all to tell some story quickly and fully,'[9] declared Spence, whose building, featuring massive bisected ships held aloft, wowed the crowds. Yet he felt that his nautical-themed design was treading water: 'By the time I designed the Sea and Ships pavilion,' he confessed, 'I was bored with the stretched glass skin over a frame.'[10]

A counterpoint to all this masculine endeavour was the downstream section, the People of Britain, built around the LCC's concert hall site. In Casson's words this was 'the Origins of the People through and under the bridge of Education, the English at Home, their character and recreations, the Arts and the Seaside … all grouped around the Festival Hall, still to be built'.[11] Here Tubbs' former colleague H. T. Cadbury-Brown was responsible for the People of Britain pavilion and fountains. 'It was joyous to work on the first big anything, after years of small exhibitions, alterations and a little housing work,' he recalled. 'It was an event for a new dawn, for enjoying life on modern terms, with modern technology.'[12] Wells Coates, the Canadian architect of many of Britain's most celebrated thirties modernist houses, including the pristine white Isokon flats in Lawn Road, Hampstead, created the 400-seat Telekinema, the first cinema in the world designed to show both film and television. The Regency Shot Tower was transformed into a memorial to the 1851 Great Exhibition, but also housed a radio telescope linked to the Dome of Discovery, where visitors could use it to beam signals at the moon.

A pair of inventive industrial designers, Robert Goodden (fresh from 'Britain Can Make It') and Dick Russell (who'd styled cabinets for Murphy radios) put together the most famously eccentric exhibit of the festival: the Lion and Unicorn Pavilion, derided by some as sentimental and silly, but loved by many thousands of visitors for precisely the same reason. This barn-like structure featured eye-shaped windows and contained a riot of exhibits on everything from law and religion to the 'national character', all extravagantly captioned by a young Laurie Lee of the GPO Film Unit, who'd been appointed to the gloriously titled position of Curator of Eccentricities and Caption-Writer-in-Chief. 'Don't tease the locomotives – penalty forty shillings' ran one caption, while another read 'Storks nesting over the Birdcage Restaurant'.[13] Even the restaurants – storks or no – were of exciting modernist design: one was drawn up by early Harlow pioneer architects, the husband and wife team Maxwell Fry and Jane Drew (who also designed the schools exhibit), and another by Leonard Manasseh, one of the innovative souls behind Hertfordshire's ground-breaking scheme to build prefabricated schools. Casson and his team of over 100 architecture and design staff worked round the clock, desperate to meet the near-impossible deadline for the opening of the festival.

Over at the LCC's concert hall site a young architecture student, Jean Symons, had volunteered for what could have turned out to be the work placement from hell. And not just because of the site's swampy conditions. 'The whistling and catcalls subsided once they got used to having me around,' she recalled in the remarkable diary she kept of her time working on site. 'In fact, catcalls became one of my patent methods of finding out where a new gang had started work.'[14] The foundation stone was laid in September 1949 and Symons found the process of watching a building rise from plan to completion utterly fascinating. Her diary is full of delicious details of those frantic months. She noticed, for example, that the architects tended to 'come to the edge of the sheet just where they encounter a tricky detail – a sort of "continued in our next" attitude and "let's hope that by then someone else will have worked it out".[15] Similarly, engineers casually allowed additional half-inches to creep in here and there, only for them later to cause mayhem for the builders and window-fitters, forced to re-cut Portland stone or concrete to fit the windows. 'It was often hard to believe they were all working for the same firm on the same contract,' she observed.[16]

Such had been the lapse in civilian construction during the war years that many of the people working on the project had no experience of building anything of such scale. Frank Lloyd Wright, the grand pioneer of American modernism, visited the LCC while they were working on the Festival Hall. Upon meeting Robert Matthew and Leslie Martin the eminent architect exclaimed, 'Why you're just a coupla boys!'[17] Yet, at 45, Matthew was an elder by the standards of the concert hall or Festival of Britain teams.

The turbulent political situation was a further complication. There had been a general election in February of 1950 and Clement Attlee's majority was cut from 146 to a precarious 5. Britain was then dragged into what would be the opening conflict of the Cold War: the Korean War that would last four years. At home, meat rations were cut and coal was in short supply. Yet despite the turmoil, by July 1950 the roof was going on the Festival Hall, and the workers celebrated with an impromptu concert. 'The first music emitted by the piano,' noted Jean Symons in her diary, 'is "Put another Nickel in", and the first concert, after the meal, consists of traditional Cockney and Irish songs. There is a race up to the roof, to crack a bottle of beer over it and hoist the flags.'[18]

Back in 1949 Casson had realised that something was missing from his already well-advanced festival plan. One of the original concerns with locating it in a notoriously seedy area was how a crowd might be attracted. 'As the South Bank is a part of London that people don't ordinarily go to very much,' Casson remarked, 'we must try to somehow link the South Bank to the north bank and make it very easy to go from one to the other.'[19] A temporary bailey bridge (a lightweight prefabricated design invented during the war) would be constructed next to the Hungerford rail bridge to help lure visitors, but what was needed, Casson now reckoned, was an eye-catching vertical feature to attract attention from the north bank.

It was decided to launch a competition. A total of 157 entries were received, and in January 1950 it was revealed that the dynamic partnership of Powell & Moya had won with a structure that became known as the Skylon: a 250-foot, 12-sided hollow metal erection, to be made from steel and aluminium. Philip Powell and Jacko Moya were both still in their twenties, but when it came to audacious competition victories they were already veterans. In 1946 they'd triumphed in a rather different Thames-side project – to turn the bomb-damaged wasteland of Pimlico into a vast housing estate of 1,600 flats. Not completed until 1962, Churchill Gardens became one of London's most significant and influential modern housing estates, still held in high regard by residents and architects alike.

'Jacko and I did separate entries,' recalled Powell of their Festival of Britain design. 'I did a pyramid, a slightly tapering thing, with a zigzag bracing and a coloured pattern, but Jacko's first sketch felt so right that there was no point going further and we collaborated after that.'[20] Moya's design would then undergo a transformation at the hands of Felix Samuely, their former lecturer at the Architecture Association whom they had also requested as engineer on the project. In Moya's words he turned the Skylon into 'something so simple and clean looking that it seemed quite remarkable that it could remain standing'.[21] Samuely's engineering expertise meant that the heavy cables the team had envisaged to hold up the floating cigar design were either drastically reduced or dispensed with altogether. Moya may have had the inspiration, but it was Felix Samuely's talent that ensured that the 'vertical feature' was given the one quality for which it is so fondly remembered: that of seeming to be lighter than air. A final stroke of genius ensured that this late addition to the festival plan by its most youthful team would become the most memorable. A further competition was held to find a name for this extraordinary structure, won by writer Margaret Sheppard Fidler (wife of the chief architect of one of the new town development corporations, at Crawley). 'We toyed with words like Skyhook and Pylon,' she said. 'Suddenly it seemed that "Skylon" would be a good name for this beautiful and exciting adornment to the London sky.'[22]

The other colossus of the festival was Ralph Tubbs' vast umbrella, the Dome of Discovery. With a diameter of 365 feet, this was the largest aluminium structure in the world. While workers on the Skylon dangled at dangerous heights with a minimum of safety equipment, those in the Dome faced a whole other world of problems. 'Work inside the Dome was uncomfortable and very dark,' the artist Barry Evans recalled. Not ideal conditions in which to paint a vast mural representing Captain Scott's ship, 'Discovery'. 'The atmosphere was damp and cold, the lighting was minimal, one electric lamp of 100 watts for a 20 foot or so wall … We were dressed in winter clothes and wearing mittens.'[23]

Meanwhile, from her vantage point on the roof of the Festival Hall, Jean Symons looked out at Ralph's Tub and the Thames beyond: 'St Paul's seemed to be rearing its head, looking across at Big Ben and saying, "Even if this interloper is going to be the biggest dome in the world, it is only temporary and it is very flat".'[24]

As the festival launch date neared it became clear that the LCC team would have neither the time nor the money to complete the concert hall to plan, so elements were dropped to ensure that there would be something serviceable open in time for the festival. Plans for a small hall, art gallery and backstage space were postponed, and instead a temporary back wall was erected from asbestos cement panels.

The acoustics of the concert hall were deemed to be of paramount importance. The 'egg in the box' scheme cancelled out the rumble of the trains, and acoustician Hope Bagnall was employed to ensure that the hall's sound quality would compete with the best in the world. While the outside of the building was being finished with Portland stone, and lobbies were being stuccoed, the auditorium had been lined with high-quality materials rare in any buildings of the austerity generation, such as Derbyshire marble. Fabrics were hung around the auditorium, and doors were insulated with leather. The celebrated designer Robin Day, who along with his wife Lucienne would go on to revolutionise the domestic taste of a generation, was employed as furniture consultant, designing the seats in the hall with the aim of minimising reverb and echo. When all the leather, fabric and wood were in place in the hall, it emerged that Bagnall's team had done the job of minimising unwanted reverberation rather too well – instead of a recommended concert hall reverb time of 2.2 seconds, they had ended up with a deadening 1.5 seconds. It would be decades before this could be put right.

At one point a dispute about carpentry overtime threatened to derail the construction of the auditorium, but when a ballot of workers was taken, only 12 out of 800 voted in favour of industrial action. Even so, the planners were haunted by fear of worker action. 'One day, when crossing the foyer, I see about 20 men with their arms raised and assume some form of vote is being taken,' wrote Jean Symons in her diary. 'A couple of steps later, a light-reflection reveals the sheet of glass they are carrying.'[25] In the event, even a fire in the roof of the Festival Hall didn't stop work being completed a month ahead of schedule in December 1950. It was a near miracle, but both the LCC and Festival of Britain teams hit their deadlines.

The start of 1951 saw a steady stream of high-profile visitors to the South Bank as the LCC, and Gerald Barry's festival committee attempted to hype their wares to the world at large. The King dropped by in a torrential rain shower. A string of modern architecture's luminaries followed Frank Lloyd Wright to visit Robert Matthew's young team, including former Bauhaus masters Marcel Breuer and Walter Gropius, and the holy father of modern

*The much-tweaked Festival Hall in 2013,
a building finished just in time for the Festival in 1951.*

architecture himself, Le Corbusier, who declared that 'the whole world will admire your concert hall'[26] before fixating on the most startling detail of the entire building, the boxes in the auditorium, extruding from the wall like a succession of filing cabinet drawers. 'These boxes are a joke, of course,' he declared. 'But a good joke.'[27]

Many of the auditorium's designers at the LCC thought the design of the festival around their hall was a joke too far, one of the team remarking that 'we despised the Casson approach which was the Festival of Britain; we all thought it was crap, actually.'[28] They were not alone: Beaverbrook's media empire, led by the *Daily Express,* was energetically stoking anti-festival feeling in a way reminiscent of recent press coverage of the London Olympics. Cheerleaders such as the left-leaning *Picture Post* leapt to the defence of the exhibition. 'In its two years a-building the South Bank has, after all, plugged along against the inevitable pressure of sour ill-will from the professional knockers,' a fiery editorial proclaimed, pointing out that 'those who most loudly attacked Socialist austerity equally deplored Socialist festivity'.[29] Instead, the magazine predicted that 'Londoners, always last to observe the miracles in their midst, will become abruptly aware of a transformation that will last them long after the Skylon has disintegrated into its million separate nuts.'

For many architects and designers of the British modern movement, painfully aware that they lagged behind their continental cousins, the success of the Festival of Britain and the Festival Hall was of critical importance: either it would make them, or consign their utopian impulses to the dustbin of history. On the night of 3 May 1951, hours before the Royal gala concert and opening ceremony for the Festival Hall, Robert Matthew, who had done so much to modernise his LCC architects' department, sat down to dinner with a few friends. 'Robert displayed not the slightest anxiety about the crucial test to which his great work was about to be submitted,' recalled one of the guests, the architect Clough Williams-Ellis, 'but continued to play the role of the entirely relaxed and genial host without a care in the world.'[30] Now it was down to the public to decide what they thought of this vision of a modern Britain.

The festival was a nation-wide event, taking place in church halls and village greens around the country as well as on the South Bank, but its centre was in London, where another lesser-known site was built for the occasion. 'The whole area had an atmosphere of foreboding, gloom and despondency,' was Jack Godfrey-Gilbert's initial impression of the district he'd been allocated in Poplar, east London, in which to create a Live Architecture Exhibition. It was on an 'open derelict landscape, formerly occupied by terraced houses which had been completely devastated by the bombing and cleared away'.[31] Poplar had been one of the areas worst hit by the Blitz of 1940-41, and the East End, with its slums and squalor, had been targeted by Patrick Abercrombie and John Henry Forshaw in their *County of London Plan*. They saw 'large areas of dreary and monotonous streets' there, made bearable only by 'the invincible cheerfulness and neighbourliness of the Londoner'.[32] They criticised the haphazard mixing-up of housing and industry, and were convinced that only through lowering the population of the area could decent living conditions be achieved. Instead of the tightly packed back-to-back slum housing, they recommended a radical European solution: 'a proportion of lofty blocks of flats, placed well enough apart for groups of trees, with terraced houses disposed in regular but not monotonous form, the whole interspersed with open space.'[33]

In 1947, this district became the Stepney-Poplar comprehensive development area. The CDAs were a new government initiative to speed up the planning and rebuilding of large areas of urban decay. A bright young team were brought in to inject radical new ideas: Arthur Ling, senior LCC planning officer and fervent communist split the vast East End district into eleven neighbourhoods, along the lines of the new town ideal; Harlow mastermind Frederick Gibberd joined him in June 1949 to develop what would become the centre of the first neighbourhood, Chrisp Street Market, in the newly named Lansbury Estate; and sociologist Margaret Willis was hired to canvass the existing residents.

Gibberd developed Willis' results into a new plan for the area, which became the Festival of Britain's Live Architecture Exhibition. It consisted of a mixture of permanent and temporary buildings, since the redevelopment of the whole neighbourhood would not be complete until 1954. The temporary structures included a huge temporary café, the Rosie Lee, and a Town Planning Pavilion, and the Building Research Pavilion, home to a spoof mock-Tudor house called 'Gremlin Grange', meant to represent all of the basic flaws of the suburban semi, from bad lighting and rising damp to cracks in the walls, leaking water tanks and a smoking fireplace. The permanent buildings included a shopping centre and market square, a couple of pubs – the Festive Briton and the Festival Tavern – and three schools. Walking around Chrisp Street Market today, it remains a recognisably festival-style development, with its slim pillars, flat roofs, atom-diagram railings and classic postwar clock

Chrisp Street Market 2011, one of the few remaining relics of the Festival of Britain.

tower, with the hands and hour marks affixed directly to the brick, as in Harlow's Market Square. 'I suggested we should not stop at a clock but also make it an "outlook tower" from which to survey the surrounding panorama of dockland,' said Frederick Gibberd, describing it as 'a practical folly that gave pleasure'.[34] Sadly for the exhibition, the tower was not ready until the following year, and was closed soon after for reasons of health and safety.

The market was intended as the focus of local life, or as Robert Matthew put it, to make 'the community look inward towards itself – to be really neighbourly, in fact'.[35] Despite its location in the heart of the East End there's nothing particularly 'urban' about the Lansbury Estate, perhaps because it was designed more to exemplify what was being built in the new towns rather than the 'lofty blocks' of the inner cities. Some found it 'a modern oasis set in a vast area of overcrowded streets',[36] but for Gibberd himself, the overall design was 'conventional and a bit tame'.[37]

All over Britain, towns and cities enjoyed historic pageants of their own. The major Scottish exhibit was held in the impressive neoclassical Kelvin Hall in Glasgow: The Exhibition of Industrial Power. Here was a serious counterpart to the English whimsy on show in London, designed by none other than that busy exhibition expert Basil Spence. 'Since the end of the war the only real work I could get was the design of exhibitions,'[38] he recalled in the early sixties.

In Glasgow his vast scheme included an artificial waterfall to demonstrate hydroelectricity, a Tesla machine that flashed sparks up into a high black dome, a working pit cage, a blacksmith's forge, and, to celebrate the completion of the National Grid in 1945, two full-sized crofters cottages, one without electricity and one with all mod cons.

While the main London and Glasgow events may have been wholesome and educational, there was another side to the festival. A few miles upsteam from the South Bank, in London's Battersea Park, sat the ultimate in gaudy Americanised amusement: a gigantic funfair. Worthy it was not, but this riot of carousels, big wheels and candyfloss served up a less demandingly festive atmosphere.

On 3 May 1951 at 11am, exactly 100 years after Victoria's opening of the Great Exhibition in Hyde Park, King George VI declared the Festival of Britain open, and all the good intentions and the years of work were suddenly put to the test. John Gyford visited the festival twice as a child – three times if you counted the funfair at Battersea. His childlike delight was still palpable some 60 years later. 'It was the sheer sense of novelty and revelation and amazement, even down to the level of things like these chairs' – he indicated the metal-framed chairs we sat on in the Festival Hall café – 'and obviously these aren't the original ones. But even the idea of spindle-legged furniture was a complete revelation. Lightness and airiness and all that. In the film one of the designers says they quite deliberately went for light colours because at that date, before the clean air act, the buildings of London were black. And that was a complete amazement to me, that you could have buildings that weren't either soot-stained

Portland stone or battered red-brick. Some of it was quite dramatic, like the Skylon, and the size of the Dome of Discovery. But over and above that it was all the other details – it was the furniture and the colours, both on the stupendous scale and on the novelty scale.' And novelties there were in spades, from hot air balloon flights to pearly kings and queens who would whisk you away on a boat trip to the Battersea pleasure gardens. Impresario Eric Morley, who in 1949 had dreamt up the format for *Come Dancing*, one of television's first hits,[ii] created a media sensation with his festival bikini contest. When the press dubbed the contest 'Miss World' Morley's second mega-brand was born. Geraldo and his orchestra played each afternoon and people danced on the fairway. Rare butterflies were bred on the site as part of an exhibit on British nature. There was even a high-wire crossing of the Thames. As people flocked from all over the country to the South Bank, Mary Brown in the *Daily Mirror* felt bound to remind her readers not to take advantage of their relatives' hospitality when visiting the festival: 'Unless your London relative lives in a mansion – remember that she too is a sixteen-hour day housewife.'[39]

Reactions to the extraordinary exhibits varied widely: some detected a preachy tone ('Why carve up all over the place hollow pomposities like "Land is the blanket of man's birth, his launching ground to the stars?"' complained the *Daily Express*[40]) while others disliked the contemporary aesthetic. 'Awful steel chairs, all modern, no grace and no beauty and no elegance,' was how one visitor, Vere Hodgson, saw the schools exhibit. Yet when it was dark and the lights came on she found herself charmed: 'Now it is all lovely. The Skylon looks fine inside the exhibition.'[41] Rapidly becoming the star of the festival, the Skylon found itself the recipient of the sincerest form of flattery when Mr E. Gilbourne, Mr J. W. Wildey and Mr H. R. Towlson took six weeks to build a 32-foot high replica

---

ii Morley went on to monetise his *Come Dancing* format through a lucrative deal with Mecca dancehalls, ironically spearheading their demise as halls of dance, and conversion into temples of bingo.

from scrap metal to decorate their street for a carnival in Ilkeston, Derbyshire. *Picture Post* took great delight in describing the *Daily Express'* outrage that the festival looked likely to be a success, noting gleefully that the paper was now 'complaining crossly that the Skylon is held up by wires, and not by magnetism'.[42] For its part, *Picture Post* reckoned that the Dome of Discovery 'might be thought the most exciting piece of functional architecture of contemporary times'.[43] Although what exactly that function might have been was unclear.

Much like the summer of 2011, when the Festival Hall held its sixtieth anniversary celebrations, 1951 was the wettest for some years, but that didn't stop 8.5 million visitors turning up to experience the modernist curio on the South Bank, and the same number again tucking into wet toffee apples in the Battersea funfair. 'What everyone I know, and have observed, seems to like most in it,' wrote Dylan Thomas, with characteristic passion, 'is the gay, absurd, irrelevant, delighting imagination that flies and booms and spurts and trickles out of the whole bright boiling.'[44] Even the hard-to-impress *Architectural Review* declared it 'the greatest architectural event of the postwar years'.[45] The final day of the festival was Sunday 30 September, a gala headlined by Gracie Fields having taken place the previous evening as a last huzzah. 'The thing that left its longest memory with me in some sense,' John Gyford said, with a certain sense of melancholy,

> 'had nothing to do with the quality of the exhibition. As we got towards the end of our second visit here we were sitting over, down on the corner, almost opposite one of the entrances to County Hall where one of the exits was, and we were more or less getting ready to go. And I suddenly realised that we'd never come back – 'cos this was it, and none of this would ever be here again. And that was the first moment I think that I can recall suddenly understanding that not everything lasts. It wasn't an intimation of mortality, but it was that sort of realisation that nothing is forever, which – I was 12 at the

time – was quite an eye-opener. I mean, I didn't break down and go into a nervous collapse, but I can remember quite clearly suddenly realising that, and I've never forgotten that, it was one of the key moments of my growing up.'

Eight weeks after the festival closed its doors Clement Attlee, stuck with his wafer-thin majority, set the date for the second general election in 18 months. In one of those quirks of the British electoral system, a not-exactly-resurgent Conservative party claimed victory with half a million fewer votes than Labour. Winston Churchill's 'government of national nostalgia' was not predisposed to embrace the socialist, modernist spirit of the Festival of Britain.

Yet even before the government had a chance to intervene, the temporary exhibits were set for rapid dismantling and demolition. 'The Telekinema, the Lion and the Unicorn, the Dome of Discovery and the Skylon are likely to be preserved, though homes have not yet been found for all of them,' reported the *Manchester Guardian* in early October, well before the election. 'There have been several bids for [the Skylon] for seaside resorts,' they noted, before urging that 'if they use a fraction of the imagination that the festival authorities had, the Ministry and the council between them should be able to find some way of using the site to the advantage of London.'[46]

But the saga dragged on without resolution. 'A landing ground for hover planes is being considered,' reported the *Daily Express* in December. 'And the government hopes the LCC will move the Dome of Discovery to the Crystal Palace.'[47] In the end no homes were found for any of the glorious temporary structures, and demolitions were well on their way by May 1952. The dismantling of the Skylon took six weeks, the same time it had taken the intrepid Ilkeston trio to build their replica. The structure was sold to London scrap merchants along with the aluminium Dome of Discovery and the remains of several of the other metal-framed buildings. Art from the festival was scattered around the country: Henry Moore's beautiful, specially commissioned bronze sculpture 'Reclining Figure' ended

up in the National Gallery of Scotland. The few relics left on the
site included the Telekinema, which was renamed the National Film
Theatre, and was only demolished in 1957, its replacement built
beneath Waterloo Bridge. The lion, rescued from the top of the old
pre-festival brewery, still stands beside Westminster Bridge.

The Festival Hall, the reclaimed South Bank, its embankment
and railings, and the Lansbury Estate remain the three major
architectural legacies of the summer of 1951. The Festival Hall has
endured a number of structural changes over the years. It took over a
decade to replace the temporary back of the building, whose rugged
grey asbestos cement tiles had been the feature most admired by the
'hard' – and perhaps rather contrarian – faction within the LCC,
who despaired at what they saw as the 'effeminate' Scandinavian
modernism that characterised both the hall and the festival.[iii]

Every 10 years, it seems the lost festival buildings are mourned and
the Festival Hall is celebrated in exhibitions and the media. The
sixtieth anniversary celebrations were the most extensive yet, with
their recreation of the beach and beach huts on the embankment,
a kinetic sculpture erected in honour of the Lion and Unicorn
Pavilion and a multimedia exhibition in the basement. A year
after the festival closed, Marghanita Laski wrote a gloomy epitaph,
commenting that 'far from marking a rung on the ladder of progress,
this might be the furthest pinnacle we could reach.'[48] Two decades
later, *The Times* published the recollections of Paul Overy, who had
been just 11 at the time of the exhibition. He remembered 'those
people walking past bright, light, glass-and-metal pavilions in their
long, shapeless dark coats and hats, waltzing in the evening drizzle
to the music of Geraldo.'[49] For these people, as for John Gyford and
for many thousands more, the festival was a hugely significant event
– a putting-away of warlike things and an affirmation of a bright
new future – and the swift demolition of its buildings a cause for
mourning. 'Why, oh, why did they have to pull that down, the silver

iii See Chapter 5

dream bubble of my childhood?' demanded Paul Overy of the scrapping of the Dome of Discovery. Marghanita Laski was even more emotional. 'It was the nicest thing that happened in England in the whole of my life.'

Even the warring parties who had worked to design and build the Festival of Britain and the Festival Hall agreed on one thing. 'Harmless jollification',[50] was Gerald Barry's description of these life-changing events on the South Bank; and even the usually earnest Leslie Martin recalled that 'we did make a real effort to be jolly.'[51] The pair might be surprised by the growing regard in which their jolly, hastily conceived schemes are held – symbols of a moment where, even in the midst of austerity, efforts to bring the country together to celebrate the best of the past and look ahead with excited eyes were not brought low by the cynicism of markets or media.

REBUILDING BLITZED PLYMOUTH AND COVENTRY (1940-62)

'I was only a couple of hundred yards away from here the night the Blitz started.' Bob Chaney, a garrulous 92-year-old dressed in an airforce-blue blazer, his tie emblazoned with the Red Arrows and Concorde, met me in the Chapel of Unity at Coventry Cathedral. Alongside him, beaming beatifically at me, sat 89-year-old Irene, his wife. They made a great double act, Bob hamming up a pomposity he didn't really have, Irene deflating it at every turn. Within minutes of sitting down he was recounting, in his rich, gravelly voice, the story of the night of 14 November 1940. 'I was posting a letter to my brother, who was waiting to go on board ship out to the Middle East with the Army Service Corps. Sirens went, you see, and within five minutes I was encircled in flame all round the roofs of the centre of Broadgate.' He was alone in the street apart from a few fire-watchers posted on the buildings of the city centre. 'I thought the best was to high-tail it out of it!' He turned to Irene. 'I got up to where you were eventually.'

'He was coming up to take me to a dance,' said Irene.

'But we never got there.'

'Sat under our table instead,' she said. 'There were too many of us to get under our stairs.' They relay all this in a light, matter-of-fact tone ('You can't live your life being afraid. You've just got to get on with it,' Irene had told me) but Bob's escape from the city centre was little short of miraculous. In fact, so unprecedented were the events of that night that they spawned a new word: to Coventrate, from the German *Koventrieren*, described the effects of a firestorm caused by aerial bombing. The Luftwaffe raid, codename 'Moonlight Sonata', killed 568 and injured over 1,000, leaving the industrial powerhouse, as one eyewitness described, 'a city of the dead, utterly devastated'.

Amazingly, the bombed-out local paper was able to get an edition printed within days, reporting what was to become one of the great emblematic acts of the Blitz:

> 'The provost of Coventry (the very Rev. R. T. Howard) who, with a volunteer squad of three besides himself put out incendiary after incendiary at the Cathedral until sand and water were exhausted, said to a *Coventry Standard* reporter: "The Cathedral will rise again. It will be rebuilt and will be as great a pride to the generations of the future as to the generations of the past."'[1]

St Michael's Cathedral, Coventry, in ruins after the Blitz of 14 November 1940.
© *Coventry Heritage & Arts Trust*

Bob and Irene felt the loss keenly – they'd both been regulars in the congregation since before the war. But the cathedral was just a small part of a much bigger story that unfolded that night, one that affected the entire population. I craned to hear Irene's delicate whisper as she recounted her experiences:

'There was a girl I worked with, Eva, and Bob knew the boyfriend. They went to the cinema in Primrose Hill Street, not far from here, and the sirens went in the middle of the film. And you had to make your mind up whether you were going to stay there or whether you were going to a shelter. If they'd have stayed in the theatre they'd have been safe. They came out and got killed, just like that. You'd go to work the next day and there'd be people missing, it was awful.'

Bob, it transpired, still works part time for the Blitz Museum, situated in the crypt of the ruined cathedral next door: he is so involved that they both refer to it as 'the Bob Chaney experience'. 'When I talk about it to people who come to the museum,' he tells me, 'I say, unless you've actually lived through air raids you can never have any conception as to what it's like.' But he has a good go at conveying it.

'A shredded bus here' – aftermath of the Coventry Blitz, 1940.
© *Coventry Heritage & Arts Trust*

The aftermath too was terrible to endure. The following day Coventry City Council's young deputy architect Percy Johnson-

Marshall was at the spot Bob Chaney had been standing when the Blitz began. 'In the morning, I walked up over piles of smouldering rubble to Broadgate.' He saw 'a shredded bus here, a car balanced crazily on the roof of a ruined building there, and the cathedral, the library and nearly everything one could see was still burning and smouldering in great masses of devastation.'[2] This wasteland was all that remained of the medieval streets that had been at the heart of the city: 60,000 buildings were either razed or damaged by the raid; 4,000 homes were utterly destroyed.

'The centre of the city that night was wiped out,' Irene told me, the awe still there in her voice. 'The big stores and the whole of the market were flattened.'

The reason for the raid was clear. 'Taking the cathedral as a centre, within about a mile radius all round you had about 20 factories,' said Bob. 'So you see, Coventry was an obvious target.'

The historic naval port of Plymouth held a similar attraction for the Luftwaffe. The first bombs fell on the Devon city on 6 July 1940 and the bombardment continued on and off until the end of April 1944. On 2 May 1941, after a series of heavy raids, Winston Churchill visited the city, newsreels capturing the naval-capped prime minister waving from an open-top car with a look of shock upon his face. His secretary Jock Colville recorded in his diary that 'scarcely a house seems to be habitable.' Over 4,000 houses were destroyed in the Plymouth Blitz, with a further 18,000 damaged. Churchill's party were greeted by scenes similar to those seen by Percy Johnson-Marshall in Coventry: 'I saw a bus which had been carried bodily by the force of the explosion, onto the roof of a building some 150 yards away from where it had been standing.' As for the military efficacy of the bombing, Colville noted that 'the whole city is wrecked except, characteristically, the important part of the naval establishment.'[3]

Plymouth would end up the most intensely bombed British city in relation to its size: over 1,000 residents were killed in the Blitz and its population almost halved over the course of the war, as the raids

made life intolerable. 'The fabric of the city was shattered,' recorded
the official planning report. 'Plymouth, bragged the Germans, had
been wrecked beyond repair.'⁴ Thousands fled from the city in fear,
never to return, but the legend of the plucky Brit in wartime was
cemented by stories such as the one printed in *Picture Post* some
years later, which reported that 'after the raids people gathered on
the Hoe, looked back on the tracery of blackened roofs, struck up
the military band – and danced.'⁵ The wartime press, too, had played
up this 'bulldog spirit' and passed silently over the terror and despair
felt by many.

Many British towns and cities were devastated by bombing. The
London Blitz lasted 76 consecutive nights. Industrial cities such as
Manchester, Glasgow, Belfast and Birmingham suffered raids, as
did the ports of Cardiff, Hull, Liverpool and Bristol. The clear-up
operation would be immense and severely limited until the war was
over, but that didn't stop plans being drawn up to inspire thoughts
of a peaceful and brightly modern future. In fact, many of these
cities had already had great plans for rebuilding well before the war
started, and none were more advanced than those for Coventry.

Donald Gibson wasn't yet 30 when he was appointed city
architect in 1938. He was part of a young generation who were keen
to stress the link between town planning and architecture, and his
background, working for the experimental, government-funded
Building Research Station, put him at the forefront of the latest
thinking in the field. Gibson appointed a dynamic new team, and
Percy Johnson-Marshall became his assistant the same year: 'A few
of us went to help start the new office, and we went bursting with
ideas; ideas about prefabrication in building, about new kinds of
housing layout, about carrying good design into every detail of the
townscape, and about making the whole city a collective work of art.'⁶

Such cutting-edge attitudes might have seemed extraordinary
for a council running a city with a historic medieval fabric, but that
fabric had seriously frayed. At the start of the twentieth century,

Coventry's population was under 70,000. By 1941 it was approaching 200,000, an increase of 279 percent in just 40 years, more than any other town in the country over the same period. The main reason was the invention of the motorcar. Coventry had become Britain's Detroit, the centre for the car manufacturing industry.

Bob and Irene, who have observed the city change around them over the last nine decades, recalled how the war effort triggered a further population explosion. 'It was at that time that Coventry completely changed,' said Bob.

> 'Up until then we had all the motorcar factories, well, anything that could be made was made in Coventry. Towards the end of '38 and '39 we had a terrific influx into the city. We had all the car workers on to assembling parts for aircraft and tanks and whatnot. Alvis wanted to do their tanks, and all the same with the Daimler. All round they were swapping over to aircraft. And so there was a terrific influx into Coventry. Coventry changed at that point, because we had different people coming in. Where we lived we hadn't got a road, we'd got a cart track, and we were more or less at the edge of Coventry. Now Coventry goes way beyond.'

Gibson and team were charged with rescuing the medieval streets from strangulation by traffic; in Percy Johnson-Marshall's words, the prewar city had 'some very fine buildings which very few people care about,' and 'streets designed for a fraction of the traffic which now clogs them'.[7] In the immediate aftermath of the Blitz, Gibson spoke to the *Midlands Daily Telegraph* about his already advanced plans for the city. 'Over a year and a half ago I prepared a civic centre scheme which, grouped round the two noble medieval churches, embodied all the public buildings in one ordered conception, at the same time suggesting a central park space, which is so badly needed.'[8] Gibson's plan was the radical architectural embodiment of the social changes that had hit the city in the last few decades.

In place of the medieval streets, Gibson planned a new rationalised network of roads that would leave a few historic buildings isolated within a landscaped park or 'pedestrian gardenway'.[9]

The scheme brought together a variety of influences: most notably the gentle form of Scandinavian modernism that had so captivated the new town planners, and the beaux arts tradition, whose formality had influenced the grid layouts in cities as diverse as Paris and Welwyn Garden. In June 1940, five months before the Blitz, Gibson and Johnson-Marshall had staged an exhibition of their plan. It featured new buildings such as a daring pedestrianised shopping centre, and civic amenities including a library, art gallery, swimming baths, police station and town hall. It also factored new green spaces into the densely built-up centre, and surrounded it all with a ring road to ease the motor city's congestion.

'There is a great opportunity here for the rebuilding of Britain to begin,' the *Manchester Guardian* declared, resurrecting Gibson's plan a mere week after the Blitz. The exhibition model of Gibson's new civic centre was described as 'a plan for a hundred years instead of tomorrow,' with the architect quoted as remarking that the opportunity the Blitz afforded was 'an architect's dream'.[10] A couple of weeks later Gibson gave a talk, reprinted in the *Midlands Daily Telegraph*, where he expanded on this theme. 'In one night the entire site is cleared ready for this regeneration, and it rests with the fortunes of war and the desires of a great people to see it accomplished.'[11]

In 1941 John Reith was still in his post as First Commissioner of Works for the government, and he encouraged Coventry's city reconstruction committee to 'plan boldly and comprehensively'.[12] The Labour council were smitten with Gibson's bold vision. Yet there was an alternative. City engineer Ernest Ford prepared a far less drastic plan that left many more of the buildings and roads intact. Businesses, notably the shopkeepers, were keen. The prospect of a pedestrianised shopping precinct seemed alien and threatening, and they were reassured by Ford's more conventional plan. 'Shopkeepers, generally, have fought the introduction of precinct planning in Great

Britain,' wrote Coventry's planning officer, Wilfred Burns, some years later, 'but this has been largely due to the inevitable reluctance to accept change.'[13]

Just months after V. E. Day, in October 1945, Gibson held another public exhibition of his plans, called 'Coventry of the Future'. It was estimated that one in four Coventrians saw the exhibition; one recalled that 'whatever they proposed to do in the rebuilding you just went along with it in a zombie-like fashion'.[14] The new Labour government in Westminster were less enamoured of Gibson's plans, due to spending restrictions and a national shortage of materials. They demanded cuts, and in 1949 finally approved a much scaled-down plan – but one nevertheless that saw the creation of three comprehensive development areas, like those in the East End where the Festival of Britain's Live Architecture Exhibition was held: there was the central area; the district of Spon End, to be cleared for the inner ring road and homes for a projected 1,790 residents; and Hillfields, another residential estate.

If the business community had been wary of Gibson's huge plan, they were won over by his scheme to double the square footage of shops in the centre. Owen Owen, the Co-op, Woolworths, Marks & Spencer and British Home Stores were among the first slated to move in, just as soon as the new structures could get off the ground.

'The city should be the focal point for the diffused rays of the many separate beams of life; it should be the centre of culture and learning, of entertainment and the market,' was how Patrick Abercrombie, arguably the most influential and respected town planner in Britain during the twentieth century, saw it. Along with many of his generation, he felt the Industrial Revolution had turned the city 'into something more like a labour pool for the large industrial works – soulless and meaningless'.[15] It was his job to change that. Documentary maker Jill Craigie's 1946 film *The Way We Live*, followed him as he worked out his plan for Plymouth. She showed a tall, slim, immaculately dressed and inscrutable man stiffly stalking through the Victorian remains and rubble-strewn wreckage with the cool detachment of a spy scouring a war zone, his spotty bow tie the one incongruous detail. He looked like William Burroughs with a monocle. A professor, first in Liverpool, then at London University, he was invited by cities as diverse as London, Bath, Glasgow, Hull, Edinburgh and Bournemouth to produce plans for their reconstruction. Abercrombie drew his inspiration from the beaux arts movement, which had influenced the monumental grids not just of Paris, but American cities such as Chicago. These newly laid-out cities, along with New York and its skyscrapers, had left the old world of Europe behind. 'We in America are more used to new building and radical planning,' wrote the U. S. Ambassador John G. Winant in the introduction to Abercrombie's *A Plan for Plymouth*. 'Our greater spaces, our shorter traditions make it less painful and less difficult to construct and reconstruct.'[16] A recurring theme of *The Way We Live* was the envy felt by some locals towards the New World and its greater possibilities for innovation.

I went on a tour round the city led by Jeremy Gould, an energetic architecture professor and leading light of the Twentieth Century Society, an organisation which, according to their website, 'exists to safeguard the heritage of architecture and design in Britain from 1914 onwards'. Plymouth was the second of Abercrombie's great plans, and Jeremy was in no doubt that it was the most comprehensive of all his schemes. In Plymouth, Abercrombie had the opportunity to design the city he'd been teaching about for decades. First published in 1943, *A Plan for Plymouth*, was co-written by James Paton Watson, the city architect, and it was he who would be responsible for putting its ideas into practice.

In *The Way We Live*, Paton Watson was a striking contrast to the dapper, crisp Abercrombie. His smooth Dundee accent and more down-home manner acted as a bridge between the highfalutin tones of the Professor and the pre-scripted vernacular of the Plymouth townsfolk. The plan was certainly ambitious: the 114 Blitzed acres in the city centre provided a space in which, they declared, 'man must show what he is capable of in the way of artificial design for purpose and delight.'[17] The pair were keen to rise to the challenge. 'This magnificent opportunity,' they wrote, echoing the optimism of Donald Gibson in Coventry, 'should result in the creation of a virile Regional Capital.'[18] As with the Midlands city, the plan set out to solve the problems not just of war damage, but various other ills of the modern age – most notably slums, overcrowding and road traffic – 'to build better not only what has been destroyed, but also parts which, although left intact, are no longer worthy of her glorious past and her present heroism'. Their job was no less than 'to obtain a maximum of health, safety, convenience, prosperity and enjoyment of everyone'.[19]

There were major problems to overcome. 'Most of the houses in Plymouth were antiquated without the quality of antiquity,'[20] was their sniffy view of the mainly Victorian residential areas. Then there was the central junction at St Andrew's Cross, judged to have the worst congestion of anywhere in the south outside of London. In Craigie's film, Abercombie dryly refers to this bottleneck as 'the ideal street for getting knocked over'.[21] He and Paton Watson aimed to unknot the tangle by separating the city into different 'functions', along the same lines as the new towns.

Yet they saw their role as going far beyond mere problem-solving: they were also determined to create the kind of huge statement that only someone re-planning a city centre from scratch could make. To this end they envisaged a grand symmetrical metropolis, based around a single main road which led from the railway station right down to the Hoe, that historic ground where Sir Francis Drake had been casually playing bowls as the Spanish Armada gathered. The drama of this grand vista would be accentuated by placing the two sides of the street a full 200 yards apart, with gardens planted down the centre for the entire length of the shopping section. Abercrobie and Paton Watson saw the vista as a grand memorial for those who lost their lives in the Blitz. It would be rebuilt in cheerful bright white limestone and concrete, materials that would shine in the seaside sunlight. *The Way We Live* flashed up their drawings and models in the way Hollywood films dramatically cut to newspaper headlines or animated maps to illustrate the epic scale of their story. The stripped classical style would create an impressive pattern of smooth white surfaces, and the grid pattern had the captivating formality of a topiary maze within a landscaped garden. Even the inner ring road formed a dignified part of the symmetrical whole.

The Way We Live also showed the town's reconstruction committee. Perhaps the most telling detail was not what was said, but who said it: elderly bald men slugged it out with older, balder men, like withered bull seals fighting for territory. I spotted one woman in a room of 40 or so councillors. She didn't speak. The film shows a motion to water down the plan being overwhelmingly rejected by the committee, who were keen to begin work as soon as possible. In July 1946, *The Times* reported that 'Plymouth City Council has taken what is believed to be the first step of its kind by any blitzed city towards acquiring a large area of the land needed for reconstruction,' at an estimated cost of £20 million: 178 acres in the centre of the city were to be bought in what the newspaper called 'the first executive operation prescribed in the mechanism of compulsory purchase.'[22]

James Paton Watson was less excited by the rate of progress, and Jill Craigie's film records the still-existing acres of rubble, rickety and overcrowded houses, as well as that classic emotive forties trope of mop-capped toddlers plonked out to play in bleak cobbled streets. The town planner decided to stir things up a bit, and succeeded in creating a very public spat: 'After four years we in Plymouth are still looking at ruins,' he wrote in the *Observer*. 'We expected great things not only in our city centre but on our new estates, but so far they have not materialised.' He complained that 'we were advised to plan boldly' but later 'to narrow our streets, to whittle down our cross-sections, to amend our designs and forget our foresight because the Treasury again controls all things and says that open spaces are of no use unless they can be trodden on.'[23] The minister Lewis Silkin hit back, describing local authorities like Plymouth and Coventry as 'very backward in making up their minds' despite his having 'spent months trying to hurry them up'. Litigation in Plymouth appeared to have been one of the biggest problems, with 370 objections from local property owners to be dealt with. As regards the changes he'd proposed to Abercrombie and Paton Watson's original designs, Silkin remarked acidly that he knew 'only two people who would say that the plan was perfect and must not be changed'.[24]

Progress may have seemed frustratingly slow, but Plymouth was the first of the Blitzed cities to complete its public enquiry into its rebuilding plans. On its release Jill Craigie's film broke all box office records in the city. The period she spent making it would also change her life, for it was then that she met her future husband, the young firebrand MP Michael Foot.

One symbol of reconstruction soared above the rest in the national consciousness. The provost of Coventry Cathedral's defiant cry that it would rise again was almost instantaneously followed by the engagement of the nation's most celebrated living architect, Sir Giles Gilbert Scott. He was a scion of a Victorian architectural dynasty: his grandfather Sir George Gilbert Scott had created such masterpieces as St Pancras Station and the Albert Memorial. Giles himself was the versatile designer not only of Liverpool's colossal Anglican Cathedral but also Battersea and Bankside power stations, and the ubiquitous K2 red telephone box.

Yet the problem of what to do with the site at Coventry, particularly with the skeletal remains of the bombed out medieval cathedral with its pencil-thin spire, was not an easy one to solve. Gilbert Scott was keen to place the altar at the centre of a cross-shaped cathedral. 'It should be centrally placed on the main axis of the new plan so that it stands in the centre of the main approach,' he wrote in *The Times* in February 1944, before moving on to discuss the difficulties of achieving this: 'The present limitations of the site prevent this, and the plans are put forward with the hope that it may be possible to adjust the boundaries of the site.'[25] His doubts were confirmed when the Royal Fine Art Commission expressed its dissatisfaction with the scheme two years later, whereupon Scott bowed out, claiming he was too old to supervise such a large project. In fact, he died some fourteen years later, midway through his work on a small Roman Catholic church in the centre of Plymouth.

In 1947 a competition was launched to design the new cathedral. On the face of it, the brief was wide open: 'No restrictions are placed upon Competitors as to style or materials to be used in any of the building,'[26] went the blurb on the entry booklet. Yet the awkward site and the problem of what to do with the old cathedral had already been enough to see off the most prominent architect of the day.

Nevertheless, 219 architects and practices were inspired to enter. One flamboyant young man was particularly obsessed with cathedral architecture, and went to visit the site for inspiration in 1950. 'This first visit to the ruined cathedral was one of the most deeply stirring and moving days I have ever spent,'[27] wrote Basil Spence of his fact-finding trip. Spence's instinct was that the old cathedral should not be destroyed to make way for the new; rather, the two would have to co-exist, a vast architectural representation of the death and resurrection of Christ. As he looked out from the north end of the ruin to the ground reserved for the new cathedral, Spence 'got one of those pictures that architects sometimes get. This one, however, was unusually clear – a great nave and an altar that was an invitation to Communion, and a huge picture behind it. ... I could not see the altar clearly but through the bodies of the Saints. In those few moments the idea of the design was planted. In essence it never changed.'[28]

The competition came at a busy time for Spence. During the winter of 1950 he was hard at work troubleshooting his design piece for the Festival of Britain, the Sea and Ships Pavilion. The cathedral was relegated to an evening project. The stress gave him an abscess, but the drugs he was prescribed induced a dream that further embellished his vision – or at the very least, the myth. 'I was walking through the cathedral and it looked marvellous,' he wrote. 'I could not see windows until I went right in and turned half back – the walls were zigzagged.'[30] And zigzagged the walls of his eventual design certainly were. At the last moment Spence had second thoughts about entering his design, but Joan, his wife, gave this idea short shrift. 'You have sweated all these months,' she said. 'You hand in and don't be such an ass.'[31]

All 219 entries were displayed at King Henry VIII School, Coventry in August 1951. One entry was from hardline modernist Arthur Korn, a German émigré and associate of Bauhaus founder Walter Gropius. Korn had spent much of the war imprisoned as an enemy alien, but when the British authorities released him he became a prominent member of the Modern Architecture Research Group (MARS), working on their plan for London. This extraordinary project reimagined the city as a series of 'herringbones' radiating out to the north and south of the Thames 'spine'. Each herringbone consisted of the sort of buildings advocated by Le Corbusier – namely, high blocks – and between each one was a large strip of parkland. As this plan would have necessitated the demolition of most of London it was a bit of a non-starter, and Korn focused instead on his new and influential job as lecturer at the Architectural Association.

Perhaps the most ambitious entry of all was from the couple set to become the *enfants terribles* of British architecture, the newly-married Alison and Peter Smithson. They were keen to prove that modernism could be every bit as spiritual as more traditional forms, and visualised something that was both as high tech as jet planes and as starkly monolithic as Stonehenge: a vast kite-like shelter that soared above a platform containing the open box of the chapel.

On 15 August 1951, two days after his forty-fourth birthday and while the Festival of Britain was in full swing, Spence was at Associated Electrical Industries drumming up trade when he received a phone call telling him he'd won. The electrical company's reaction was immediate: drinks all round. 'I could have done with some strong whisky,' remarked Spence, 'but perhaps George Walker was thinking "Cathedral", for all I got was dry sherry.'[32] He was overwhelmed to have won such a major commission , and was soon the recipient of both hearty congratulations and fruity insults from all corners of the press and public.

'We were sold on it because Provost Howard was so keen,' Irene Chaney, who'd initially been taken aback by the drawings, told me. 'And when he talked to us, our little nucleus of congregation – he'd got a talk he did with the drawings – we were all sold on it really.'

'We thought it'd be good,' nodded Bob.

'We weren't condemning it out of hand,' explained Irene, 'because you don't know what you're talking about.' Not all of the people who saw the drawings felt the same. Spence was completely unprepared for the volume of hate mail he received. 'Some did not even have stamps,' he wrote, 'which shocked me as a Scot.'[33]

'You could imagine that building to be an abattoir, a cinema, anything, but not a church,' said Bob of the initial reactions.

'Oh, the things that were said …' Irene shook her head, smiling at the memory of the more colourful insults.

'Everybody took a great dislike to it. Even doing tours of the cathedral as I've done in the past 10 years there's still quite a number of people who couldn't accept Coventry Cathedral.'

'Because it's so different,' said Irene.

'The old was beautiful,' said Bob, 'it really was. To see this one, no. Mind you, I did have an accolade one day, when a lady came round at the end of a tour and she says, well, she says, "I'll be quite honest. I hate modern art. But since I've been round with you I can now understand it. Thank you very much."' He paused for a moment. 'I know I've got a big head … But everyone we've talked to really appreciated what the cathedral means.'

From the moment of victory on, Basil Spence and his design were public property. The dandyish architect took both fame and notoriety in his stride. He put a model, revised through consultation with the cathedral provost, on display at the 1952 Royal Academy Summer Exhibition, a show that featured other major postwar architectural developments: there was a model of Frederick Gibberd's Festival of Britain Chrisp Street Market in east London, and Alwyn Sheppard-Fidler's 'gaily coloured' drawing of the shopping centre for the new town at Crawley. No sooner had this model been displayed than Spence produced a further major revision. 'Mr Spence, in announcing the amendments, said that they resulted from impressions he gained while visiting Italy recently,' wrote *The Times*. In fact they came at the suggestion of engineer Ove Arup.[34] Meanwhile Provost Howard and his flock, including Bob and Irene, made do, using the two crypt chapels in the ruins until the new cathedral was ready.

The individual, often anonymous objections Basil and Joan Spence received through the post were one thing, but a more tangible and formidable opponent soon began to make its feelings felt. The council were dead set against the scheme from the start, claiming it would take away much-needed money, manpower and resources from the urgent rebuilding of the fabric of the city. 'Houses must have priority after the war,' had been the Bishop of Coventry's entirely reasonable call in 1944.[35] The council jumped on this and opposed the cathedral plan all the way, even taking their argument to the House of Commons.

In the event Coventry Council never had to put a penny towards the cost of the new cathedral. They were wholly immersed in their own mighty challenge: to reconstruct the entire city centre and rehouse its population. One of their first acts was to commission a statue of Coventry's most famous daughter, Lady Godiva, by Sir William Reid Dick to occupy the devastated Broadgate site. In front of it a new shopping centre began to grow up, on an avenue that lined up beautifully with the cathedral spire in the symmetrical beaux arts manner. By 1953 a dual-level shopping precinct along American lines had been completed. Where cars had once driven on Coventry's narrow medieval streets, trees were planted on this pedestrianised precinct. The separation of pedestrians and vehicles was meant to cut the shockingly high number of road traffic accidents. In Jill Craigie's film, Abercrombie points out that the number of wartime casualties on the roads exceeded those of civilian bombing. Coventry's traffic-free precinct was at the cutting edge: it even preceded those in the new towns of Stevenage and Harlow. Here gentle Scandinavian-influenced red-brick modernism was perked up with the odd playful Festival of Britain-style flourish: a mural here, a sculptural clock there, and concrete planters everywhere.

The materials shortage that held back construction at Coventry had been, to some extent, avoided in Plymouth, where the rebuilding schemes were more quickly off the mark. A snapshot taken in January 1951 shows how busy the city had been with reconstruction: new branches of Woolworths, Dolcis, Norwich Union and three schemes for the Co-op were all nearly complete. Building contractors Bovis were confidently predicting that a new M&S would be open by Christmas.

James Paton Watson had employed Thomas Tait, the eminent Scottish architect of Selfridges and Sydney Harbour Bridge, to set the style for the town centre, ensuring that all new development followed some basic rules – such as setting the size of blocks and the height of cornice lines – so that his vision of beaux arts symmetry would be realised.

Thomas Tait set the rules for the rebuilding of Plymouth's town centre on Armada Way.

Steel was often the deciding factor in whether these grand schemes were built or remained forever on the drawing board. In 1951 a spokesman from one of Britain's leading steel producers was quoted as saying that the steel position was 'growing exceedingly complex' and that it was 'difficult to forecast from one month to another what priorities would be allocated by the government.'[36] In this increasingly complex and bureaucratic world, Plymouth council were anxiously pushing on, aware that the brakes could be slammed on at any moment.

The housing situation was the most pressing. 'The housing figures for the country were short of what was promised in 1945,' thundered Sir Clifford Tozer, leader of the Conservative party in Plymouth City Council, who appeared in Jill Craigie's 1946 documentary sporting an Anthony Eden moustache along with more than a little pomposity. 'Instead of 500,000 or 600,000 houses a year, something like 200,000 houses were built last year. The Conservatives had promised 300,000 if they returned to power. In western Germany 350,000 had been built in less than a year.'[37] This magic number of 300,000 was the vote-winning brainchild of the Tories' ambitious new housing spokesman, Harold Macmillan. But with materials and skilled workers both short on the ground, it sounded like a fantasy figure rather than one that was actually achievable.

Even so, the building contractors were hard at work. Laing were creating new housing estates using an unconventional method they'd devised called Easiform, where concrete was poured into frames on site to create the walls, to be given a pebble-dashed coating later. By January 1951 they'd used it to complete their thousandth house in Plymouth. Easiform was created in response to George Wimpey's hugely popular (with councils, at least) 'No-Fines' construction technique, where coarse concrete was set in house-shaped moulds. It would become the most ubiquitous modern form of house building in Britain.

In September 1951, Plymouth's town centre received its biggest boost yet. The first postwar department store, Dingles, designed by

Thomas Tait, opened on a prominent corner of Armada Way. Forty thousand shoppers descended on the store on its opening day, 1 September. 'Plymouth people this week have been mutely testifying to years of frustration by standing six deep to stare at a Dingles' window full of unremarkable tinned goods,'[38] the *Observer* reported cattily. The article also touched on the Conservative council's frustrations at having its wings clipped by the Labour government's building controls. 'The city points out that it is not now asking for more public money to spend, but simply that private builders should

When Dingles, the first of the rebuilt shops in Plymouth, opened in 1951, 40,000 shoppers descended on the store on its first day.

be allowed to spend money of their own.'[39] When the Tories won the general election two months later, many expected these controls to be swiftly removed, but when Macmillan, now the minister responsible for housing, inspected Plymouth in 1952 he found a city still chomping at the bit for more freedom. 'We visited housing sites all the morning; visited the "Blitzed" areas all the afternoon,' he wrote in his diary. 'I could give out no news about reconstruction ... This "Capital Investment Programme" is really intolerable.'[40] The

Treasury-inspired programme was the cap on local government spending for reconstruction, a limit that threatened to undermine Macmillan's precious 300,000 houses a year.

Yet despite the frustration felt by many of its citizens, Plymouth was doing relatively well. When in 1954 *Architecture Journal* published a review of comparative progress in the bombed cities, Plymouth's quick start put them ahead of the field by a country mile. They'd succeeded in attracting a great deal of skilled builders to the city, with one man in 12 employed in the construction industry (in laggardly Coventry, the figure was less than one man in 50). The city had restored 40 percent of business premises and constructed 46 new dwellings per 1,000 inhabitants.[41] This was also the year the ten thousandth council house was completed. In 1954, Plymouth was on a roll.

On 7 March 1955, a group of workmen in Coventry made their way through the unseasonably late driving snow to finally make a start on construction of the cathedral.

'We watched every stone being laid,' said Bob.

By this point my imagination was beginning to invest the Chaneys with some form of divine power: a pair of *It's A Wonderful Life*-style angels watching over the cathedral's reconstruction.

'When Princess Elizabeth laid the foundation stone we were in the congregation,' said Irene. 'The only thing we didn't attend was the unveiling of the St Michael and the Devil, but that was very quiet and that was Lady Epstein. Hadn't he just died?' she asked Bob of the sculptor Sir Joseph Epstein. No response. 'I can't remember. He never saw it installed. But everything else, yes.'

The contractors, John Laing, were wholly committed to the project: the company had secretly decided to put all of its profit from the job back into a donation for St Michael's. The eminent engineer Ove Arup had been appointed to turn Basil Spence's design into something that could be built. His skill transformed aspects of the original plan into something even more exciting. 'The problem is not just to design an efficient and economical roof spanning 80 feet,' he wrote in *The Times*. 'It is to create a visual impact, to create abstract sculpture, if you like.'[42] He spoke of the building's 'structural honesty': a modernist preoccupation with not disguising the inner structure of an edifice, preferring, for example, to expose the steel frame supporting a building to concealing it with brick or stone.

Even so, the cathedral contains many tricks of structural 'dishonesty', used to great effect: most notably, perhaps, the concrete pillars that terminate a few inches above the floor to reveal a narrow steel strut inside, connecting earth to pillar like the spark zapping between God and man on Michelangelo's Sistine Chapel ceiling. The struts are there simply for effect, but the effect is beautiful, more than compensating for any 'dishonesty'.

Spence commissioned a wide range of artworks for the cathedral, from windows to sculpture, engravings to ironwork. One of the most remarkable was the Great West Screen, designed and etched by the New Zealand artist John Hutton; on it, a host of angels appear to hang between the old and new cathedrals. This vast window, encompassing the whole of the west wall of the cathedral, was constructed by Crittall, an Essex company better known for producing modern, steel home and office window frames. Its proud advert ran that it had been 'eight years in the planning and making, the technical design and construction carried out in its entirety by Crittall'.[43] Then there was John Piper's celebrated Baptistry Window design, depicting a burst of sunlight radiating outwards: it was as colourful and exuberant as John Hutton's creation was ghostly and pale.

Spence's zigzagged walls each contained a series of slender floor-to-ceiling stained glass windows completed by a number of artists. Three sections had been finished by the month construction started, March 1955. The following year the windows went on display at the V&A, prompting a visiting Bermondsey housewife to exclaim, 'they're different, all right – but they're beautiful.'[44] For a time these windows were housed in the basement, or undercroft – the first section of the new cathedral to be completed. There they created a temporary Chapel of the Cross for the loyal congregation, which naturally included Bob and Irene.

'As soon as the cathedral had got up to floor level we consecrated the offices underneath,' said Bob, 'and we had that as our Chapel of the Cross. We were attending services in here before it had a roof on. It was an absolute building site. They had all the scaffolding up. Once you get the zigzags going up you realise what you can't see on a drawing: what the windows are going to be like and the effect of the windows. And the effect of the windows is really absolutely wonderful. I mean, now I've got nothing but praise for the whole lot. I feel it was a privilege being associated with it while it was being built.'

The undercroft was consecrated at lunchtime on New Year's Eve, 1958. 'Workmen's voices were raised in unison at lunchtime today to sing the first hymn – "All People that on Earth do Dwell" – ever heard in Coventry's new cathedral,'[45] reported the *Coventry Evening Telegraph*. Later that night a televised service was broadcast by the BBC to a curious nation.

The unrivalled *coup de grâce* of theatrical flourishes came four years later, when Basil Spence engaged the RAF to lift the flèche, the aerial-like bronze spire, to the top of the finished cathedral. 'Helicopter experts of No. 38 Group Transport Command believe that it can be done by one of the latest Westland Belvedere Mark 1 twin-engined helicopters,'[46] reported *The Times* amidst a flurry of media excitement about payloads, wind-speed and turbulence. In April 1962, Squadron Leader J. R. Dowling, the pilot, failed at his first attempt, because it was too windy, but managed it on his second. Coventry had finally regained its cathedral.

Donald Gibson left Coventry in 1955. He was replaced by ex-London County Council planner Arthur Ling, who'd been Arthur Korn's chief helper on his fantastical MARS Plan for London. By 1961 Coventry had twice as many cars per head as the national average, and the inner ring road had become a busy urban motorway. Its effect on the centre is most apparent if you walk from Coventry train station to the shopping precinct.

You set out from the beautiful white-tiled, wood-detailed and marble-floored 1962 train station – a tribute to the modernist white villas of the thirties, with flat roofs generously overhanging an expansive glass frontage – and soon you're crossing under a long, low section of motorway, the civic gardens ahead framed in a letterbox format by the underpass. Suspended above, the busy local and through roads wind and swing, while you climb stairs and descend ramps in a vast non-place created by the tangled motorway loops. It's a relief to reach the precinct, with its monumental concrete murals and colourful mosaics, its slate and brick-clad squares – and its thorough lack of cars.

The vast, tangled moats of traffic restlessly circling the precinct were perhaps an unavoidable consequence of separating pedestrian and vehicle so thoroughly in the motor city. Many citizens appreciated the tranquillity of the centre. 'It was always pleasant to go in the precinct and do your shopping,' recalled one Coventry resident interviewed some years after it was built. 'You know, there was places where you could sit, there was the trees, there was the flowers, there was the shops, and like I say, there was no traffic. It was great. And it was very modern.'[47]

Ling added two residential tower blocks to Gibson's resolutely low-rise city centre, deliberately messing with the beaux arts symmetry in order to create a less formal vista. His freer style wasn't everyone's cup of tea. 'I still think that Gibson's idea would still have been the best here,' says Bob. 'Because what he envisaged was to have an open vista right from St James's Church right up to the cathedral. But now they've got all the blocks in between.'

Coventry's shopping centre was trail-blazing in more ways than one: not only was it pedestrianised but it was built on two levels. This latter development turned out to be rather too ahead of its time. Not enough thought had been given to how shoppers were to be encouraged to visit the upper levels. With no lifts, escalators or ramps, those with prams, heavy shopping or mobility problems were effectively barred from the upper level, and many of the shops there closed until facilities improved.

In Plymouth, the reconstructed city centre had created a consumer boom. By 1954 Dingles reported takings of three times what they needed to break even. The big chains which moved into the shiny new units were a runaway success, but small businesses suffered. 'Every new shop in Plymouth is taking business from someone else,' commented Mr Knight, an out-of-pocket jeweller, to *Picture Post*, as he looked over the impressive Portland stone façades of Armada Way. 'Maybe I'll have to move to a small market town.'[48] It was an early indication of the whirlwind that would transform the high street over the following 50 years.

Other problems began to surface. Unemployment in the town was running at twice the national average because of the lack of industry catered for in the reconstruction. Only three postwar factories had been built – for Bush radio, Berketex clothing and toolmakers Tecalemit. Yet for those lucky enough to find employment, the rebuilt centre offered the post-austerity consumer a wide array of treats. And James Paton Watson had certainly seen off the overcrowding of the old Victorian centre. 'Even on Saturday afternoons there's plenty of room on the pavements,' commented one happy local. 'Even in the rush hours the traffic never jams.'[49]

It's remarkable how evident the postwar plan still is in today's Plymouth. The plastic signs and corporate logos of the shops are still framed by Thomas Tait's strict rules for cornice lines and block size. The vast boulevard of Armada Way has been pedestriansed, and retains a vestige of a garden running down the centre. The original garden, Jeremy Gould explained on our tour, had been exactly the same width as the central reservations in Welwyn Garden City; this suddenly made sense, because the rebuilding of Plymouth belonged more to the interwar mania for beaux arts planning and stripped classicism than the postwar hankering for informality and asymmetry.

The shopping area feels too big for the city; too spread out. As in Welwyn, a surfeit of space saps energy: twice the population are needed to make it work. The abundance of white stone and classical grandeur give the lethargic and empty centre a vaguely Olympian – or post-Olympian – feel. Even the spaces behind buildings, such as the loading bays for shops, are vast. The town that Abercrombie and

A two-flagpole McDonalds.

Paton Watson built was handsome and clean, but also fatally low-energy, with no bustle. By the late forties a new generation of architects and planners was already emerging to challenge this becalmed and formal way of building towns. "'Before the war it was a picturesque town,'" one resident told *Picture Post*. "'Now it's a draughty barracks … We call that place," (nodding to Armada Way) "'Pneumonia Corner'. On a winter's day it's as cold as charity.'"[50]

Yet I can see what enthuses Jeremy Gould about the city. These grand vistas and handsome classical buildings are a unique monument to a very important moment in recent history. The symmetry is, in its way, beguiling, and the detail and pride taken with the rebuilding is a delight, albeit a faded one. I have never seen so many flagpoles. Every building seems to have at least one. McDonalds has two. Then there are the numerous pretty nautical reliefs carved into the pale stone. The most controversial building of the reconstruction was the last to appear: the multi-storey Civic Centre. This tall 1962 office block, complete with water garden and rooftop restaurant, is a handsome knock-off of the United Nations headquarters. It was designed by Hector Stirling, then city architect. The current council hate it so much that they've covered great chunks of it with apparently purposeless scaffolding in some form of futile self-harm. They seem to be hoping for the centre to be razed again, so they can rebuild in the mode of the day once more.

By 1961 preparations for the opening of the cathedral of St Michael at Coventry were well advanced. The midlands regional television station ABC threw a ball at which they announced a £5,000 gift, while Sacha Distel and Ted Heath and his orchestra performed. The BBC donated some television lights and set up a temporary radio studio in the building, soon replaced by a permanent broadcasting studio in the undercroft. A festival of the arts was organised, and the new works commissioned included a new cantata by the master of the Queen's Music and two new operas. There were productions from the Royal Opera House, the Royal Ballet, Sadler's Wells, the Berlin Philharmonic and the Royal Shakespeare Company. The Coventry mystery plays were performed. Over 2,000 people squeezed in for the consecration ceremony on 25 May 1962, including the Queen, Lord Snowdon, Princess Margaret, representatives of Lutheran and Reform churches from Germany, and government ministers including Duncan Sandys and John Profumo. Bob took the collection.

'On consecration day,' said Bob, 'someone looked at me, I've been told, and they said, "He has come! He is here!"'

'And then they found out their mistake when he went round with the plate,' interjected Irene.

'You see, the Chaney experience...' Bob shook his head. It must have been an amazing and memorable occasion, I suggested.

'You couldn't see anything,' said Irene. 'We were on the end of a row with all the bishops. We were on about row four or five. We did see Richard Dimbleby coming round and looking before he went off. And when the Queen came up all the bishops went' – to demonstrate, she stood up and leant forward, craning her neck. 'We didn't stand a chance! We had a vague feeling of what colour she was wearing.' Dr Ramsey, Archbishop of Canterbury, declared the new cathedral 'a house in which all the arts and the craftsmanship of their time had united; stone, wood, glass, metal, tapestry; the designer, the builder, the painter, the sculptor, a generation had made its offering of beauty in the service of God'.[51] By 11 June, 300,000 visitors had flocked to the cathedral, with up to 20,000 in a single evening. Irene was still overwhelmed by the response from the public. The cathedral was mobbed.

Basil Spence's Coventry Cathedral, in 2011.

'Five deep right up to Broadgate,' she said. 'Five deep! And *nobody* asked for money and *everybody* gave. And they paid off the bill for the cathedral just like that.'

Contemporary reactions remained mixed, though rather more enthusiastic than when the plans had been unveiled. 'Although the cathedral may look like a jam factory outside,' wrote Susanne Hughes from Loughborough, 'there is much to commend inside.'[52] P. D. Patel, a worker at GEC in Coventry, found it 'a very nice building ... I have seen temples in Delhi, and I would compare it with them.'[53] 'I think this cathedral is wonderful,' said retired commercial traveller, Mr J. Williams, reflecting the go-ahead spirit of the age with the provocative thought that 'the old cathedrals are outdated, in my opinion.'[54]

For some, however, Basil Spence hadn't been radical enough. 'The trouble with Coventry Cathedral is not that it is modern,' wrote Nevill Francis from Ipswich. 'The trouble is that it is extremely old fashioned.'[55] Many architectural critics, and a new wave of architects, led by competition losers Alison and Peter Smithson, agreed. There were many elements of the gothic here, mingled with a more modern sensibility. Basil Spence was well aware of this. In fact, it had been one of the central tenets behind his design: 'I felt,' he wrote, 'there must be continuity and unity with the old.'

This blend of the old and the new was one of the things that most attracted me to the cathedral. Back in the nineties, on the way home from boring business trips for meetings with the head office of Barclays Bank, I used to nip in for a quick fix of art, beauty and mortality – before getting the train back to Croydon. My favourite part of the cathedral is the Chapel of Unity. It's the plainest by far of the chapels, and the vertical slit windows are ordinary clear glass, looking out onto the more recent university buildings. But after all the drama, excitement and beauty of the cathedral, gazing through the windows onto the rather bathetic scene is a powerful reminder that the everyday world outside, so recently destroyed, is what all the great art inside – the Elizabeth Frinks, Graham Sutherlands, John

Pipers and Jacob Epsteins – is about. For a soul as unspiritual as mine, that's as close to an epiphany as I'm likely to come in any church.

Still, as I sat chatting with Bob and Irene in the cathedral, it was hard not to be moved by their attachment to the place. Our interview nearing the end, we were preparing to leave when Irene took a moment to reflect on the enormity of it all.

'It's been an experience all our lives, really,' she said, with great understatement.

It began to sink in how extraordinary it was that they both used to attend the old cathedral, that they survived the Blitz, that they worshipped here while it was still being built – and that they were still here now, chatting to nosy strangers.

'Nothing stands still, does it?' said Irene. As if to prove her point, their bus drew up at the stop.

HERTS, MINDS AND BRUTALISM (1949–54)

At first glance, *John Betjeman Goes By Train*, the extraordinary British Transport Films feature following the future Poet Laureate's journey from Kings Lynn to Hunstanton looks like it was made before the war. The train is a lumbering steam giant, the film is faded black and white, and Betjeman's demeanour is pure Wodehouse. This was the anachronistic world of Britain in 1962: Richard Beeching's drastic slashing of Britain's railway network was just around the corner, and the country was on the brink of the tumultuous changes a left-out Philip Larkin would glumly describe in *Annus Mirabilis* as taking place 'Between the end of the "Chatterley" ban/And the Beatles' first LP'. Aside from Betjeman's dismissive wave at a 'concrete lamp standard' that spoiled his view of the village green, the film gives no hint that back in the late forties the sleepy Norfolk seaside town of Hunstanton had been the cradle of Britain's most shocking architectural craze – new brutalism.

The Kings Lynn–Hunstanton branch line has long since closed, so I took a coach through the flatlands of Norfolk with a bunch of folk from the Twentieth Century Society. Our destination was the world's very first new brutalist building, Hunstanton Secondary Modern School, designed by two of the most controversial figures in modern British architecture, Peter and Alison Smithson. As I would soon discover, the story of the postwar education building boom was defined by the fierce rivalry between the era's two dominant schools of thought, embodied by two extraordinary married couples: the Smithsons, out to stamp their intense conceptual vision on the world; and David and Mary Medd, a pair of resourceful problem-solvers. It was a battle between theoretical rigour and practical nous.

Secondary moderns, like the one at Hunstanton, were the result of another of those radical wartime government reports: this time the 1944 Butler Act. While Percy Johnson-Marshall worked on the rebuilding of Coventry, his younger brother Stirrat dedicated himself to the cause of education architecture. 'All children should have an equal educational opportunity,' was his take on Rab Butler's reforms. 'Secondary education was to be free for all.'[1] Equally significantly, the school leaving age was raised to 15 and three types of high school were created: grammar, technical and secondary modern. They were conceived as equals, although by the late forties, Labour's education minister George Tomlinson had imposed a more traditional hierarchy on the system, with grammar schools seen as the most prestigious of the three, while the technical school programme languished.[2]

School building was a mammoth task, and about to be made a whole lot tougher by an unforeseen national baby boom: 325,000 new primary and secondary school places were soon required across England and Wales. This swarm of babies afflicted some counties more than others. In Hertfordshire, local authority architect Charles Herbert Aslin faced a veritable population explosion, fuelled by the construction of several huge London County Council estates to help relieve inner-city overcrowding, as well as its four official new towns. Herbert wrote that 'apart from questions of brief and design, the first problem after the war was the physical one of building anything.'[3]

He began to put together a team who would get things done. The first architect to make her mark was Mary Crowley, who'd had a classic Quaker garden city upbringing in both Letchworth and Welwyn. She'd spent the war experimenting with nursery prefabrication, becoming Hertfordshire's pioneering local authority architect. She produced their first prefabricated school, Burleigh Infants, Cheshunt, in 1946. Then Stirrat Johnson-Marshall was appointed Aslin's deputy. A later colleague described his approach as 'highly analytical', and 'mechanistic': 'Stirrat wrote, or designed, virtually nothing. He'd always say, "I draw through other people's pencils – I speak through other people!'"[4] In postwar Hertfordshire, Stirrat saw at once 'that there was not enough site labour to build the many new schools needed by conventional means'.[5]

The unconventional means would be prefabrication. As he cast around for a solution to a seemingly intractable situation, Aslin experienced the truth of the adage – necessity did indeed prove the mother of invention: 'A search for new materials, or new ways of using old ones was commenced in 1945 and resulted in frames either of light steel or pre-stressed concrete, and a variety of methods of walling and roofing.'[6] Hills, a company that had manufactured prefabricated steel-framed huts during the war, were contracted to produce and build these hurriedly conceived and ingeniously planned schools.

By this time Mary had teamed up with the 'puckish and terrier-like' David Medd, who had been brought in to adapt the Hills system.[7] While Mary had been devising huts for school dinners in Hertfordshire during the war, David Medd had worked with Stirrat at the extraordinary Camouflage Development and Training Centre in Surrey, manufacturing the inflatable tanks with which the army was to perpetrate many a cunning wartime deception.

Rather than high-handedly imposing the design of schools on their teachers and pupils, Mary Medd worked with the education officers to observe the behaviour of the kids for whom they were building. The whole team, Stirratt wrote, were clear that this new Butler-inspired spirit in education 'would require buildings quite different in shape and spirit from even the most advanced prewar designs'.[8] Out went the familiar Dickensian classrooms with their rows of desks facing a blackboard, to be replaced by experimental new layouts, including moving teachers away from the front of the room and placing them at the centre.

These pioneering schools quickly drew national, then international attention. An admiring article in the *Observer* in 1950, by which time Hertfordshire had already constructed 31 of these new schools, noted that 'no two schools are alike. Mr Aslin's young team spend happy hours fitting the parts into an infinite variety of shapes.' Remarking that the tarmac playgrounds were sensibly placed away from the largely glass-walled buildings, the reporter Cyril Dunn spotted a wall built in the midst of the open playground. 'An isolated playground naturally has no wall for bouncing a ball. So the council built one for this and no other reason.' Interviews with the staff were equally surprising. One female teacher ('she was not one of those self-conscious progressives,' he observed, 'but an ordinary painstaking and devoted schoolmarm') gave her passionate verdict: 'This,' she said, 'is the school I have always dreamed about.'[9] By January 1955 the Minster for Education, David Eccles, was opening the hundredth postwar school in Hertfordshire, now having to cope with a pupil population that in less than a decade had expanded from 56,000 in 1946 to a 'pram town'-busting 95,000.

A month after this milestone, another *Observer* journalist surveyed the educational architecture scene, noting that 'the broad fabric of the welfare state – with all its blemishes – does, even in architectural terms, slowly emerge.'[10] He was perhaps being generous towards the welfare state as a whole. Virtually no new hospitals were built between 1939 and 1955, the year in which the Ministry of Health unveiled their new plans for a building programme. In fact, the Vale of Leven Hospital, built to serve Dunbartonshire and Argyll in Scotand, was the only postwar general hospital completed by the time Hertfordshire had built its hundredth prefabricated school.

Hertfordshire's friendly use of colourful tiles and textiles, and lightweight modern furniture was rapidly imitated across the country. As far away as Sheffield, secondary moderns were being built using the southern county's cunningly flexible modular kit. 'Children, architecture and, presumably, education were all "modern", wrote the *Observer*, 'and it seemed not a bad world, if much maligned.'[11] So who were the naysayers and what was their problem with the progress education authorities like Hertfordshire had made? The education debate at the 1954 Conservative party conference in Blackpool gave some clues. Attendants from Hertfordshire were scathing about the schools programme. The *Manchester Guardian* reported that Lieutenant P. W. T. Kine 'condemned the wasteful and extravagant new school buildings', and Miss A. Mackie 'also condemned the "totally unnecessary extravagance" of local education authorities in commissioning works of art to decorate schools'.[12] Minister of Education, Florence Horsbrugh, reminded them that these schools 'were planned and built by the Socialists', but then did little to allay their fears about the amount of money being pumped into school building, declaring 'we want to build more schools. We want as many as we can get.' An announcement that the Tories were spending £392 million on education, more than Labour, was greeted by gasps from the crowd.

No doubt Peter and Alison Smithson would have been just as scathing as the Conservative faithful about David and Mary Medd's colourful Meccano Hertfordshire schools, though on aesthetic rather than financial grounds. The fuss surrounding the Herts programme was as nothing to the enduring controversy that has dogged Hunstanton Secondary Modern School in Norfolk and its pair of iconoclastic architects. As the Twentieth Century Society coach took its final turn in the dainty suburban streets of Hunstanton, the school suddenly revealed itself: a long, low, black monolith sprawling along the edge of an enormous playing field. It was a stretch limo of a building, the most serious-looking school I had ever seen, more CIA silo than Secondary Modern.

Two storeys high, the walls were a combination of glazing and stealthy black panelling. Even the exposed steel frame was painted black. The only colour was from the doors, painted a shocking cardinal red, and the walls at either end, the buff yellow of the local gault bricks. At the front, a number of small single-storey brick buildings sat in perfect symmetry to the front door: workshops to the left, boiler rooms to the right. The only features from the original building to break the regularity of the pattern were the gym, which sat off to the right, the boiler's brick chimney and the school water

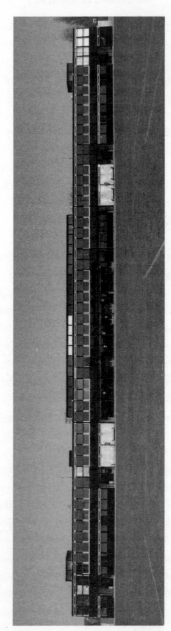

Hunstanton Secondary Modern: more CIA silo than school.

tank, built on tall struts like a grain silo from *Paris Texas*. In stark contrast to the friendly, open Hertfordshire schools, Hunstanton glinted in the spring sunshine like a particularly dangerous-looking beetle. It looked amazing.

Inside, the rigorous brutalist integrity of the exterior gave way to the visual rag-bag of a busy secondary school, and we were forcibly reminded that we were not walking around a museum. The first thing we saw was an incongruous wall of roughly hewn rock: this was for a school production of *The Wizard of Oz*. Later on our tour, the swooning visage of Robert Pattinson stared down from classroom walls, and I spotted a number of Stonewall posters declaring that *Some People Are Gay. Get Over It.*

Hunstanton is now a very modern, fully functioning school, but the Smithsons' style was as removed from the Medds' pragmatic approach in Hertfordshire as could be imagined. Far from spending hours carefully observing children and consulting with teachers, Peter and Alison didn't even visit the site before they designed the school. When it was completed, they insisted that it was photographed without a shred of evidence of children or furniture to clutter their masterpiece.

The Wizard of Oz set was being assembled in the main hall: a flexible central space that sits between two symmetrical wings of classrooms, an area also used as the school's lobby, dining room and assembly hall. Elain Harwood, one of our lecturers for the day, told us that the jaunty Mondrian-inspired décor was a recent addition designed to help kids and staff make the connection between modern art and architecture.

In the course of my research I discovered that Daniel Weir, a friend I'd made via Twitter, had been a pupil at Hunstanton in the early eighties. We chatted over email about his recollections of this most peculiar school. 'I remember one afternoon a teacher mentioning that some architects had visited at the weekend,' he wrote. 'Seemed odd at the time. He also mentioned something about brutalism which seemed even odder, especially as it went largely unexplained. At no point in all my time at the school was the building celebrated or even talked about.' As a kid, Daniel wasn't particularly impressed: 'I think when I was there I was largely indifferent to it, although to be honest, given I was largely indifferent to schooling generally that's perhaps not a surprise. However, over time, my increased knowledge of the building and the opportunity to pass by it on a regular basis means I've grown to be enormously proud of it.' These days Daniel is a modern architecture buff, and I wondered if that interest had been fostered by attending such an extraordinarily designed school. 'I'd never thought about this until you asked but I think there may very well be a link. To be honest, this part of Norfolk is bereft of buildings of significance built in the twentieth century. I can't really think of another. So for me to have gone to school at Smithdon [the school's modern name] must have registered somewhere along the line.'

If the informal, modular approach of the Hertfordshire schools system was a triumph of Britain's austerity years, the Smithsons had intended that Hunstanton Secondary Modern would be a homage to the new steel and glass structures of the USA. Alison Smithson

The Smithsons based their school design on a Mies van der Rohe building for IIT.

had experienced – and rejected – the Hertfordshire system while working on schools for the LCC; at Hunstanton she and Peter sought to design something with much greater purity. More than the neat little prefabricated schools of the home counties, it deliberately resembles the starkly modern 1943 Minerals and Metals Research Building at the Illinois Institute of Technology. This was the first American project to be designed by former Bauhaus boss Mies van der Rohe, and as part of our tour of Hunstanton, Twentieth Century Society Chair Alan Powers showed us the impressive black-and-white photos of the IIT building that Alison had torn from the pages of *Architect's Journal* to send to Peter.

The Smithsons weren't just architects; they were pop artists. They were formative members of the Independent Group, a cross-disciplinary artistic collective whose most famous product was the 1956 exhibition *This is Tomorrow* at the Whitechapel Art Gallery in London. The Independent Group had formed over coffee at the Primrose Hill flat of artist Mary Banham and her husband, the critic Peter Reyner Banham. Architects, artists and art historians would drop by on a Sunday morning for intense debates on the latest ideas. The biographer Mark Girouard paints a vivid picture of this quintessential fifties London bohemian scene, where one morning the artist Eduardo Paolozzi entered with a grand announcement: 'Right! Make way for THE architects!'[13] In walked Peter and Alison, who'd shaken up the conservative British architecture scene with Hunstanton and their peerlessly innovative entries for the Coventry Cathedral and Golden Lane housing estate competitions.

Like the Medds, Peter and Alison had married in 1949 – the year they'd triumphed in the Hunstanton competition. By 1950 they had left their day jobs at the London County Council and set up their own practice. They were a deeply serious couple, but Peter's intensity was occasionally leavened with a streak of dry wit. Alison was an altogether more eccentric proposition. Even from afar she made an impact, thanks to her extraordinary dress sense. 'She was a Mary Quant before Mary Quant even thought she was Mary Quant,' was artist Magda Cordell's view.[14] Mary Banham recalled a typically lurid homemade affair: 'she knitted herself a kind of green gnome suit, like a baby grow, with a hood, and she looked absolutely extraordinary in it.'[15] Behind the carefully maintained image was a razor-sharp mind. 'She had a touch of genius, there's no doubt about it,' recalled Mary. 'I was terribly fond of her ... And yet she was terribly difficult to get on with.'[16]

This fizzing, creative band of bohos set to work on their exhibition, *This is Tomorrow*: their plan was to force collaborations between young artists and architects. Up-and-coming figures in the art world such as Victor Pasmore, Theo Crosby and Eduardo Paolozzi worked with architects like James Stirling, Colin St. John Wilson and Ernő Goldfinger. The star exhibit was undoubtedly Richard Hamilton's glorious proto-pop art collage *Just What Is It About Today's Homes That Makes Them So Different, So Appealing?*, in which he wittily juxtaposed near-naked beefcake and cheesecake models with televisions, hoovers and tinned ham. That spring the Smithsons had contributed the House of the Future to the *Daily Mail* Ideal Home Show; the moulded plastic sci-fi structure boasted a dizzying plethora of fantastical innovations, such as remote controls and self-cleaning baths. Their exhibit for *This is Tomorrow* was as dystopian as their House of the Future had been utopian: a shack equipped with everything one might need to survive a nuclear attack. This provocative statement had a profound effect on the young J. G. Ballard. 'I thought: here is a fiction for the present day,' the novelist later recalled of his reaction to the exhibition. 'I was interested in the evolving world, the world of hidden persuaders ... of the vast conformist suburbs dominated by television – that was a form of science fiction, and it was already here.'[17]

The Smithsons' buildings demanded a level of technical expertise that was hard to come by in the enfeebled postwar British building sector, and sometimes the architects themselves made mistakes. 'We are using the steel in the same way as medieval builders used wood,' they claimed.[18] Yet one unforeseen consequence of revealing the steelwork rather than burying it within the construction as was more typical, was that the metal frame buckled in the heat. Window frames would spontaneously shatter as the sun baked the exposed metal. At Hunstanton, thick wooden battens have been added around the edge of each steel framed panel to prevent warping. This was not the only effect temperature would have on the school. I managed to grab a few words with the caretaker as he puffed past, and asked him what it was like to work there. Without stopping he replied, 'freezing in winter, boiling in summer,' and then was gone. Daniel Weir agreed: 'The extremes of temperature did make some of the winter and summer months a challenge,' he told me in an email. 'I did enjoy the glass though – meant I could stare into the distance in almost every lesson ...'

The Smithsons' school was an experimental playground for the architects, engineers and builders. Windows shattered when steel expanded and contracted in the heat.

Yet if early fifties technology had lagged behind the Smithsons' inventiveness, the finished building still managed to cause a stir. 'What has caused Hunstanton to lodge in the public's gullet,' posited the *Architectural Review*, 'is that it is almost unique among modern buildings in being made of what it appears to be made of ... Most modern buildings appear to be made of whitewash or patent glazing even when they are made of concrete and steel. ... One can see what Hunstanton is made of, and how it works.'[19] No doubt most pleasing for Peter and Alison was the reaction of Philip Johnson, Mies van der Rohe's chief collaborator in the U. S., who was full of praise for the school in *Architectural Review*. 'All the more credit to them for mastering and using the language so well,' he wrote of their interpretation of the IIT, 'in my opinion as well as anyone ever has on either side of the ocean, not excluding the Midwesteners who have worked directly with Mies.'[20]

The Smithsons would term the architectural style they had striven for at Hunstanton the new brutalism. It's a name and a philosophy with seemingly endless interpretations. One thing was clear: it was a direct reaction against the new empiricism, the dreary -ism coined by the architecture journals to describe the dominant Scandinavian style of the day, seen most clearly in the Festival of Britain and the new towns. New brutalism was certainly a more memorable brand, 'adopted as somewhere between a slogan and a brick-bat flung in the public's face', even if no one seemed able to decide quite what it stood for.[21] For the Smithsons it was about a 'reverence for materials',[22] a celebration, in Alan Powers' words, of the 'thingness of things' – be it concrete, steel, wood or brick – without dressing them up as anything else.

Nikolaus Pevsner, the foremost architectural critic of the day, was dismissive of the term. 'Brutalism has been used to mean much,' he said in a BBC Third Programme broadcast, 'too much, for the Hunstanton School with which Peter and Alison Smithson made their name and which served to launch the term is entirely unbrutal.'[23] For him the most puzzling thing was that up until that point, brutalism in architecture, if it could be attributed to anyone, would have been the specialism of concrete-obsessed Le Corbusier, and not Mies van der Rohe, whose steel and glass work Hunstanton so clearly imitated.

Why Le Corbusier? Because in the immediate postwar period, he'd become fixated with the primitive allure of rough concrete – *béton brut* in French. But for the Smithsons it was Le Corbusier's desire to show 'the thingness of things' in his buildings that was brutalist, not his love affair with rough concrete, even if, confusingly, the name suggested it was. Theo Crosby, the new editor of *Architectural Design* magazine in 1955 immediately saw new brutalism, ill-defined as it was, as a call to arms. He championed the cause of the Smithsons, which by this stage had gone far beyond a protest against the Medds and their super-flexible Hertfordshire schools, and was now a rallying cry against the prevailing Scandinavian style so beloved in the new towns. 'For many years since the war we have continued in our habit of debasing the coinage of M. Le Corbusier,' he wrote, attempting to reclaim the radical spirit of the modern movement, 'and had created a style – "Contemporary" – easily recognisable by its misuse of traditional materials and its veneer of "modern" details'.[24] Hunstanton and new brutalism was the hero of the hour, vanquishing pastiche, whimsy and uncontrolled prefabrication.

Commentators often described brutalism approvingly as a reaction against 'effeminacy' – a label which, at a time when homophobia was rife, was calculated to cause maximum damage. The new empiricism of the new towns and the Festival of Britain was cast as the effete teddy bear-clutching Brideshead toff to new brutalism's plain-speaking, authentic and earthily heterosexual working-class hero. Yet if the Festival of Britain's Lansbury Estate could be characterised as effeminate and cosy, was the brutalism of much postwar architecture not simply a kind of butch drag? After all, its much-vaunted authenticity was itself a species of artifice, with schools, offices or houses 'dressed up' as factories, power stations or machines. Of course, the results were sometimes glorious and inspiring, but were they necessarily *better* than those of their opponents? There were fierce battles in the profession, and its press, between the two schools of thought, though sadly no one at the time thought to say, '*Some buildings are gay – get over it.*'

The winds of change did not blow only for the new brutalists. Charles Herbert Aslin's team at Hertfordshire were proving hugely influential. It was inevitable, given the outstanding success of their programme, that its key figures would move on to a bigger stage. In 1949 the Medds moved from Herts to join the Ministry of Education: a considerable boost to the department's skill set. The couple were on a mission to spread the message of prefabrication to other education authorities. In 1957, a pilot scheme was set up in Nottinghamshire to test a new prefabricated system of flexibly jointed steel-framed buildings, spring-loaded to cope with the county's notoriously tricky problem of mining subsidence. With the Medds providing central support, a number of local authorities banded together to develop and fund the system, in order to make the manufacture of standard parts on a large scale cost-effective. The result was the Consortium of Local Authorities Special Programme, or CLASP. By 1964, 17 authorities had joined the scheme, with 103 projects in train that year alone. With frames designed to be clad with timber, tiles or concrete panels, the results were varied and extremely flexible. 'The light, airy, colourful and attractive character of these schools is a product of their economy and function; it is not a stylistic gloss,' wrote the eminent planner Sir William Holford in *The Times*. In particular he praised 'the impetus they have given to the formation of development groups in other types of building such as hospitals, laboratories, barracks, university hostels, transport buildings and even prisons'.[25]

This dynamic new system was championed by Stirrat Johnson-Marshall, who in 1956 formed a slightly awkward partnership with the LCC's ex-chief architect, Robert Matthew. Thanks to Stirrat's contacts, their practice, RMJM, won a major contract at York University campus. 'To speed up the construction,' reported the *Guardian*, 'the university is taking part in CLASP.'[26] The company was split between those who shared Stirrat's love of system building and the more traditional architects who loathed it: 'Robert thought CLASP was a complete load of rubbish,'[27] recalled Ken Feakes, who worked for RMJM at the time.

CLASP was only one of many systems being developed by local authorities or private companies to build schools cheaply and effectively. One of the most successful was Intergrid, whose first building was a secondary technical school in Worthing in 1955. The joint patentees of this precast concrete system were private contractors Gilbert Ash and the Prestressed Concrete Company Ltd. By 1966 a whopping 22 percent of all schools in England and Wales were system-built, including many of the new comprehensives, the first of which had opened its doors to children in Kidbrooke, south-east London, in 1954. Hertfordshire rather than Hunstanton had certainly won out as the prevailing philosophy in education: cheap, modular, flexible and designed in consultation with teachers, the school buildings of the sixties were inspired by the ideas of the Medds and the other pioneers of prefabrication. In the words of Lionel Brett, former new town planner, these developments amounted to 'more than a technology, they were an ideology'.[28]

Back in at Hunstanton Secondary Modern, life had overtaken brutalism. The Smithsons had placed the classrooms at either end of the building, around two courtyards designed as little more than light wells, and inaccessible to students. These have been colonised by mallard ducks. The ducks waddled after us as we wandered around the perimeter of the building; they were quite unafraid of all the people, offering the occasional friendly quack and generally looking hilarious in that duck way. In the hall, while we tried to focus on admiring the formal

Hunstanton's ducks enjoy their new habitat.

simplicity of the layout, the Wicked Witch of the West flew up and down on a wire in rehearsal for the school play. Even the society members were overtaken by a certain juvenile *joie de vivre*: through a window I spied a small splinter group giving each other piggy backs on the playing field. Inside, we played hide and seek around corners, as we attempted to create a pure Smithson moment and photograph the building without any sign of human life.

By the mid-fifties, the first phase of postwar British history was drawing to a close. Partly with Marshall Plan money from the US, the Labour government had established the welfare state, built the new towns and put on a spectacular Festival of Britain. Rationing ended in 1954, and as if in celebration the first Wimpy bar opened its doors. Yet much of Britain remained bomb-damaged and slum-ridden – and now it was the Conservatives' turn to work out how to transform it. They saw private enterprise rather than public planning as the answer.

The next decade would see another deeply divided group of planners, architects, builders and politicians set about transforming the island of Great Britain in diverse ways and at an extraordinary rate. Yet, as this boom took hold, none of them saw that the greatest threat to reconstruction would come not from the economy, shortages or conservative attitudes to change, but from within the warring factions themselves.

1. 'A Flying Saucer Taking You to Mars'
GLASGOW AND COMPREHENSIVE REDEVELOPMENT (1957–65)

'I grew up in the Gorbals. Actually, the posh end of the Gorbals: Hutchesontown. It was always classed as the posh end.' I met Danny Gill, an energetic and chatty retired builder, at his cosy flat in south London. We'd been looking at a photograph of the tenement where he'd grown up, taken in the late fifties, and now I was failing to pick him out of the crowd in his school photo. 'I came home from school one day, and 'cos our building had been up – as they all were – about 120 years at that time, the back of our building completely collapsed.' He was quite matter of fact about it. 'Nobody was killed, thank God, like. About six of the families were shifted out to one of the new housing estates on the outskirts of Glasgow.'

In 1961 the Queen came to the Gorbals to lay the foundation stone for her namesake buildings in Queen Elizabeth Square, which would soon rise over the old tenements. While she was there she paid a visit to the old streets, where she was reportedly shocked by the overcrowding and lack of basic amenities. 'The Queen saw both sides yesterday,' reported the *Herald*. 'She visited six families in a blackened Victorian tenement … But even as she stood on the pavement, smiling at the milling crowd who struggled to see her, she also saw at the corner the tall towers of the first Hutchesontown-Gorbals redevelopment area, the gigantic 20-storey flats that are now nearing completion.'[1]

The story of Glasgow's attempts to tackle its housing crisis is one of the more extreme episodes in the history of postwar rebuilding, and marks the start of a radical new wave of redevelopment. In the fifties, tenement life for people like Danny hadn't changed much since the Industrial Revolution first gripped the Clyde valley: whole families still lived in single gas-lit rooms, side by side with a disturbing complement of bugs and rodents, with no hot running water (and often no cold water indoors), and a single outside toilet shared by several households.

Eddie McGonnell, another former Gorbals resident I met, is regularly invited by local schools to describe the reality of tenement life to the children. He clearly revels in the shocked reaction he gets.

> 'It was an outside toilet; your mum was bathing you in the sink,' he recalled. 'It was like *Steptoe and Son*! You made sure the curtains were shut, the street was just outside – literally. And don't get me wrong, I wouldn't criticise the old Gorbals because that was what people were used to. When you see programmes about Newcastle or whatever, these were the kinds of tenement dwellings people went into, you didn't know any better. You look back now at the state of the backs where the bins were ...'

Eddie made a face, shuddering at the memory. By the mid-twentieth century, the Gorbals had become the most overcrowded and impoverished area in western Europe. A succession of planners and politicians were clear about one thing: the patient was in need of radical surgery if it were to survive. Two opposing plans, both produced in 1946, were drawn up to tackle the problem. Robert Bruce, the City Engineer, proposed that the city's entire population should be rehoused within its own boundaries, in modern high-rise flats. Meanwhile, two outsiders brought with them the fashionable garden city vogue for green belts, neighbourhood units and decentralisation. Naturally, Sir Patrick Abercrombie, the establishment's favourite planner, was one of them, assisted this time by a young Robert Matthew, in the days before his triumphs at the LCC and the

Festival Hall. In their *Clyde Valley Regional Plan*, the pair advocated 'a general policy of housing decentralisation'[2], noting that the area had 'reached saturation point as regards population.'[3] A substantial chunk of the city's population should be (in the fashionably posh planning lingo of the day) 'decanted' to three new towns, at Cumbernauld, East Kilbride and Bishopton. The historian Miles Horsey claimed that 'to cleanse the region of its Industrial Revolution legacy, it would be necessary not just to demolish the slums but also to reduce Glasgow's population and political dominance.'[4] This was to be engineering in the widest sense: not just of new buildings and towns, but of social and political reality.

Robert Bruce's more modernist plan was sidelined, and Sir Patrick prevailed once again. The *Clyde Valley Regional Plan* estimated that some 250,000 Glaswegians would need rehousing beyond the borders of the city. It was not a popular recommendation among the local political classes. 'The Glasgow view was that it would be unnecessary to lose any population or industry at all,' recalled one of the proponents of the scheme many years later.[5] Even so, the new town of East Kilbride was given the green light in 1947 – although not before facing the full fury of Glasgow City Council at the public enquiry. It was now that the planners' most exciting new toy – the comprehensive development area, used so effectively in Blitzed cities such as Plymouth and London – came into play. In Glasgow, the mania for creating these radical CDAs reached a peak that was unmatched anywhere in Britain: an astonishing 29 were declared, as a prelude to the razing of thousands of acres of decrepit cityscape for the construction of a better future. As far as the planners were concerned, very little in Glasgow was worth preserving. Factories, for example, were a dangerous menace, dotted about as they were in the most densely populated areas. In 1961 a fire destroyed 50 tramcars and a sawmill. 'When the fire was at its height, showers of sparks landed on tenements in London Road and Mauldslie Street and families were ordered to leave,' the *Herald* reported. The provost of Stranraer, Mr R. E. Caughie, expressed his opinion that the perils of mingling heavy industry with housing were clear: 'Again last night it was demonstrated that there could not be a fire in an industrial building in Glasgow without half of the population having to be evacuated.'[6] John Maclay, Secretary of State for Scotland, backed Sir Patrick's strategy to the hilt, seeing the benefits not just for the population but for business too: 'I feel sure that Glasgow industry will follow the inevitable trend in London and other great cities and move out, with those workers, to the new sites with better surroundings.'[7]

The most comprehensive of the development areas was the Gorbals, a working-class Catholic and Jewish immigrant district that ran along the south bank of the Clyde near the city centre. It had a colourful and fearsome reputation, stoked by the 1935 novel *No Mean City* which had luridly mythologised its notorious 'razor gang' battles. The architectural guidebook *The Buildings of Scotland* noted that 'the great development schemes of the 1950s and 1960s were aimed as much at rehabilitating the Gorbals' reputation as at physically improving it.'[8] So extensive was the Gorbals, and so large the problem, that six of Glasgow's 29 CDAs were declared on this 2,000-acre area alone: Hutchesontown-Gorbals (split coolly into areas A, B, C and D), Hutchesontown-Polmadie (E) and Laurieston-Gorbals. This massive, ambitious project was to become one of the defining architectural stories of the era.

Hutchestontown-Gorbals A, the smallest area, would be tackled first by an in-house team of city planners and architects. Robert Matthew's new firm, RMJM, was selected to tackle riverside area B, while area C, was given over to a rather more flamboyant character: Basil Spence. Attitudes to these proposals were mixed. The *Herald* reported that of the 26,000 or more people affected by the proposals, '56 percent would prefer to be rehoused there after the redevelopment of the area has been completed,'[9] noting grimly that in fact only 38 percent would be. Rowland Nicholas, the city surveyor of Manchester, had prophesied back in 1946 that 'many families, particularly where they had no young children, would prefer to accept flat accommodation in the area in which they had spent their lives.'[10] But for the 16,000 Gorbals residents who were to be displaced, estates were being proposed further out, on the suburban fringes of the city.

By the late fifties, area A was complete. A low-rise estate largely consisting of pitched-roofed Scandinavian-influenced three-storey flats, it wouldn't have looked out of place in any of the early new towns. But the need for high density in the city forced the planners to look for more innovative solutions than this form of polite modernism. As early as 1946 ideas of a more radical high-rise Glasgow had been in general circulation. The letters pages of the *Herald* were full of people vigorously arguing the pros and cons, few as vehemently as one garden city enthusiast who signed his or herself 'Town and Country Planning':

'Fifteen storeys! Let us be practical. How many wirelesses, how many shouting youngsters? ... After all, it is human beings who are expected to live in the multi-storey flats. ... Human beings are not bees or ants. Why in the middle of the twentieth century should they be denied their simple wish for a little home of their own on God's earth? Letchworth and Welwyn have shown what can be done.'[11]

Yet the editorial line of the paper mirrored the authority's enthusiasm for high density living, enthusiastically endorsing high flats for all but those families with young children. 'There are, in fact, many classes of tenant to whom a flat is not merely tolerable, but desirable,' went one leader, offering the startling apologia that 'planners have to reconcile so many claims, technical, economic, topographical, and aesthetic, in designing our new communities that they can hardly be blamed if there is a risk that the convenience, or even the comfort, of the ultimate householder may be lost sight of.'[12]

Both Robert Matthew and Basil Spence saw high-rise as an essential part of the schemes they were building in the Gorbals. For

the residents, watching Matthews' and Spence's titans grow up in
their midst was a memorable, if divisive sight. Danny Gill, a trainee
builder at the time, remembered the construction work: 'When I
was growing up, doing my apprenticeship, I could see all these tower
blocks going up and I didn't like it. I thought to myself, those poor
people stuck up there, you know. It broke up generations of families
that lived there. They all knew each other.' The author Colin
MacFarlane recalled his neighbour Mrs Carey pointing to the newly
built blocks and saying 'Look at them – how dae they expect people
tae live there? They're no real hooses, they're boxes.'[3] Yet others had
a more hopeful view: 'We watched the multis grow and each of us
dreamed of occupying one some day.'[14]

Robert Matthew's blocks under construction in Hutchesontown-Gorbals area B,
1961. © Glasgow City Archives

'I've got an old photograph and it's me leaning against a car,'
recalled former Gorbals kid Eddie McGonnell, 'and I'm only about
four or five years of age, and in the background you can see the
construction of the flats. So my street was running right down onto
where the new flats were built.' He was one of the lucky 38 percent
to be rehoused within the district. The scale of the changes was
breathtaking. The *Herald*'s 22 September 1960 issue alone featured

a list of compulsory purchase orders for Hutchesontown-Gorbals that ran to four broadsheet pages of closely-set notices, listing the imminent demolition of over 60 tenement buildings and hundreds of individual properties.

One sunny summer afternoon I took a walk east along the south bank of the Clyde to see what remained of Robert Matthew's Hutchesontown-Gorbals B estate, now quaintly renamed Gorbals Riverside. A lot of work has gone into cleaning up the dirty old river in the last decade, and there is little evidence of its industrial heritage. On my way I passed the mosque and City of Glasgow College, and as the path narrowed the riverbanks became thick with an immigrant weed, pink-flowering Himalayan Balsam, and the drooping branches of old trees. The rough concrete parapet was blotched with moss and lichen, like an old gravestone. I passed a heavy iron weir and ducked under a strange over-grown metal gangway, with the formal parkland of Glasgow Green on the opposite bank. With not a soul to be seen and the river as still as glass, it felt less like the setting of *No Mean City* than a sequel to *Don't Look Now*. Then the path abruptly opened out and there it was: area B of the Gorbals comprehensive re-development, crowned by four sturdy 18-storey slab blocks turned at an angle to the path like flowers seeking the sun.

Recently refurbished, Robert Matthew's blocks have been rebranded 'Gorbals Riverside'.

Robert Matthew, like Frederick Gibberd, was of the generation who'd been to Sweden and had seen first-hand those exciting 'point blocks'. His take on the idea is one of the last bastions of this once new Gorbals. Renovated by Glasgow Housing Association in the late noughties, as part of a scheme that also included a glorious seaplane service from the Clyde to Oban and Tobermory, the once rough concrete and brick gables with their asymmetric windows have been re-clad in silver fibreglass – with surprisingly handsome results. All over the curiously irregular frontage, glossy glass screens have replaced wired glass balustrades, their complex pattern due to the mixed nature of the flats within. *The Buildings of Scotland* accurately describes the estate as 'an undemonstrative, friendly-looking mixed development'.[15] Mixed because between the blocks snake a variety of buildings: terraces of three-storey maisonettes, a few random shops, and a single-storey flat-roofed pub – The Riverside Tavern. It's one of those slightly alarming pubs where everything apart from the battered doors has been bricked up. It's hard to tell if it's been armoured against the outside or from what lay within. I wasn't tempted to find out. Still, after the eerie quiet of the walk up, it was a relief to see people everywhere, of all ages and races, on phones, pushing prams, jogging, lugging shopping, taking photographs for art school projects, doing precisely those things that architects are always so keen to show on their drawings. Amid all this bustle in the car parks, plazas and pathways, I spotted a number of gaunt old men making their way to the tavern. These were the relics of the old Gorbals, moving like ghosts through this regenerated landscape to a refuge that hadn't changed for decades. The presence of two pubs on the new estate had initially been a source of controversy: some of the original residents due to be rehoused petitioned the council to ban every single one, while others were heartbroken to see the Gorbals' 48 legendary pubs replaced by a measly nine.

These were the first tower blocks in the Gorbals. Michael Noble, Secretary of State for Scotland, opened them in November 1962 with the promise that 'here the world is going to see the real "*Miracle in the Gorbals.'"* His speech was followed by 'a burst of applause from those watching, cheering when the interior lights were switched on and startled comments when a maroon-type rocket was fired with a loud report and a falling cluster of stars'.[16]

'The techniques of building, through the imagination of the architect, point the way to a new level of human environment,' wrote Robert Matthew in *The Times*. 'This age-old business is taking another exciting leap forward.'[17] Hutchesontown-Gorbals B was that leap. Among the first to move in were young married couple Joe and Mary Davie, and four decades later they were still in the same flat. Mary described her feelings when they arrived at their new home: 'I was delighted to be moving into a brand-new house. We moved here from a room and kitchen, and I was very pleased with my new inside bathroom and fitted kitchen. Back then the rent was very high but I felt it was money well spent.'[18] But the size and layout of the flat have become difficult for them to manage: 'We have two sets of internal stairs in our flat,' said Joe, 'and you have to go up both to get from the living room to the front door. Mary, who is disabled, finds it very difficult to manage the stairs and get about the flat in general.'

Joe and Mary had witnessed the arrival of tacky pitched roofs, plonked incongruously onto this most flat-roofed of estates in the eighties. They have now been dispensed with. Also gone are the original high walkways: these days Gorbals Riverside is accessed only at ground level. I'd checked out the drawings for the estate in the library a few days before, and it looked to me that many of the horse chestnuts, maples, planes, elder and whitebeam originally planted here had been lost to new car parks. Yet despite all the work, the fabric of the estate has changed little since it was designed by John L. Paterson for RMJM in 1957. The angling of the blocks for maximum sunlight, the variety of homes on offer, the green spaces, the amenities, the nursery school and playgrounds – all these spoke of a compassionate and thoughtful vision, and one that remains surprisingly intact, considering the ups and downs of the Gorbals.

Ups and downs certainly describes the fate of the Gorbals' most famous postwar development, Hutchesontown-Gorbals C – also known as Queen Elizabeth Square; or, more poetically, as the Queenies; or, in the black humour that so characterises Glaswegians, as Alcatraz, Barlinnie and Sing-Sing. Nothing now remains of these

Despite cladding and some remodelling, John L. Paterson's design for Robert Matthew in 1957 largely holds today.

extraordinary structures, once situated next to Robert Matthew's estate, and described in *The Buildings of Scotland* as 'the most complex of all the city's multi-storey blocks, powerful in silhouette ... elevation and detail but brutal as an environment, with dark and dramatic spaces between the strongly-curving concrete pylons at the level of the square'.[19] They may be long-gone, but their shadow still falls on the area – as does that of their architect, Basil Spence. The *Herald* characterised this 'sprucely bearded' architect as 'an Edinburgh man with a golden tongue, and a light, almost frivolous manner, which he uses as a sort of cloak'.[20] Perhaps the most famous anecdote about Spence recounts his eccentric pitch to the housing committee for this job: 'On Tuesdays, when all the washing's out, it'll be like a great ship in full sail!' In the words of one of the corporation architects present, this was 'a patter merchant if ever there was one!' – but his ambitious plan was waved through.[21] The minutes of the housing committee recorded the less-than-ringing endorsement from the Department of Health for Scotland, who had decided not to raise any objections to the plans only 'on the understanding that the scheme was an experimental one and would not create a precedent'.[22]

I met Eddie McGonnell, a former resident of Queen Elizabeth Square, one evening in the Waterfront Bar in Laurieston, the western end of Gorbals. The place had a vaguely Wild West atmosphere, which the barman fed by putting Johnny Cash's 'Ring of Fire' on the jukebox three times in the space of an hour. Eddie was neat in his office clothes, and at first seemed reserved. He soon turned out to have the most colourful turn of phrase of anyone I interviewed, describing the flats at various points as Buckingham Palace, a flying saucer to Mars and the Hanging Gardens of Babylon.

'People decry them, but I've been in a lot of flats – high-rise, Gorbals and Glasgow, and to me, none of them touched this,' he said, as I sipped my slightly-embarrassing-to-order-in-a-Gorbals-pub Diet Coke. 'I stayed there from when I was five till when I was 18. I stayed in A Block, 2 Queen Elizabeth Square, 7-up.' Because of the way the flats were arranged, this was actually the fourteenth floor. How had his family ended up there? 'It was like a raffle ticket – your key and which floor. I actually picked it 'cos I was a young kid. Initially there was my grandmother, my mother, my mother's two sisters and myself.' With just two bedrooms things were still pretty tight for Eddie's family, though he was quick to remind me that 'the same five people had been staying in one room, effectively. It was like going into Buckingham Palace, bearing in mind where you'd come from. For us to go into those flats was a total transformation. And another thing as well, we had under-floor heating. Not a lot of the flats that were getting built at that time had that. This was like walking on hot coals, walking on it in bare feet. It was a great experience. I loved it.'

Eddie's extended family soon made the new flat the centre of their social life. 'My grandmother was the matriarch of the family,' he recalled. 'She was like a Rose Kennedy kind of figure, and we had a big family. My grandmother had six daughters and a son and they've all got kids as well. And they all came there on a Saturday.' This included a whole group of uncles who used the flat as a waiting room before the pubs opened. 'The pubs used to shut in the afternoon, half-two and open at five, in the seventies. We'd be playing on the veranda, they'd be sitting in the kitchen playing cards, the women were in the living room, my grandmother would be making soup. It was like a Butlins!'

The veranda was one of the most startling aspects of the Queen Elizabeth flats. Rather than the poky individual balconies of Robert Matthew's blocks, four flats shared a single large outside space – the area Spence had expected to see in 'full sail' on wash day. Eddie soon claimed this space for his own. 'I learned to ride my bike on there – a racing bike! I used to take a snooker table out there, set it up. Used to take a couch out there – a settee – and have a party, have fun with the radio on. Way up, up in the sky. It more or less encompassed the whole skyline of Glasgow. We used to go out there and play football as well. And the only disappointment was when you shot, you kicked the ball over the veranda, you had to run down and get the ball. That was the killer!' He laughed. 'That's where I learned to shoot, to keep the ball low.'

Fun for the kids wasn't restricted to the verandas; the sharply angled stilts that held up the building fascinated them too. Eddie took advantage of the eddying gusts that swirled around the base of these huge blocks. 'It was great when it was a windy day, 'cos they built these stilts into a kind of wind tunnel. You'd have your jacket on and it was like a hang glider. You'd see the kids all underneath it, you know? You'd maybe see older people struggling to get through, but when you came home from school you'd get blown away, it was great! You'd lean against it, it was like a sail, like a dhow. An Arabian dhow, *that's* what it was with your parka.'

The complexity of Spence's designs slowed down the building of the Queenies, but down the road at Royston it took just eight months for Wimpey to erect three 20-storey blocks. As Miles Glendinning pointed out in his book *Tower Block*, although they were 'commenced at the same time as Spence's elaborate Hutchesontown slabs, which contained roughly the same number of flats, these were finished and let before even Spence's foundations were complete!'[23] It was like the Smithsons versus the Medds all over again. Wimpey used

Slow to build, Basil Spence's Queen Elizabeth flats became the most famous element of the rebuilding programme, due to their unconventional and monumental design.
© *Mitchell Library*

prefabricated elements to speed up the building process, but Queen Elizabeth Square was built with 'in situ' concrete, 'the medium *par excellence* of the sculptor-architect and of the sculptor-engineer'.[24] The mix was poured into giant moulds made of wooden shutters by the builders on site. The rough board-marked or 'shuttered' surfaces of the concrete that resulted were combined with an aggregate made from large pebbles, so that the estate bore either the imprint of wooden planks or was studded with thousands of smooth stones, like an abruptly upturned shingle beach.

Spence's Area C was as different from Matthew's Area B as it was possible to be. The startling design had none of that calm Scandinavian simplicity. There were no low rise blocks here to create a feeling of human scale or 'townscape'; the bold visual statement created by this cliff face of ribbed concrete walls and sculpted balconies was everything. Today we'd call this 'starchitecture'.

Spence's unconventional design, his startling 'ship in full sail' and 'hanging gardens' imagery, his triumph at Coventry Cathedral and the added glamour of the Queen's visit to the site made him a great deal more famous in the Gorbals than any of the other architects involved. The accounts of the redevelopment in the many memoirs by locals might lead you to think that Spence had planned and designed the lot, rather than just one of six schemes. Even so, he was scarcely a household name. 'When we were younger,' said Eddie, 'we thought Basil Spence was a snooker player. We had no interest in who Sir Basil Spence was.' These days, however, Eddie enjoys confronting the naysayers, people who had never lived in the Queenies but were ready to shoot their mouths off: 'The thing I say is, "Who was the architect of your flats?" They don't know. Everyone knows who did Queen Elizabeth.'

The Queen Elizabeth Square flats were eventually joined in 1969 by a shopping centre, the Cumberland Arcade, in a similar brutal concrete style. 'The thing with the shopping centre was, I'd never seen a supermarket,' said Eddie. 'The tenements was corner shops, you know, like *Coronation Street*: The Kabin. You had a bank; you had Galbraith's, that was like a supermarket; chip shops; a Chinese carry out; a Laundromat; a chemist; fruit shops; shoe shops. But when you'd come from that tenement you'd never seen that. You'd have to go up town to see that. And here it was, built in downtown Gorbals.' As with pubs, the planned reduction in shops in the district was eye-watering: from 444 down to 57, but it was hoped that bigger and more central shops like those in the Cumberland Arcade would prove popular with the residents of the rebuilt areas.

The late arrival of the shopping centre was the story of new estates across Glasgow; in fact, Queen Elizabeth Square's was a speedy affair in comparison. 'In general, shops were not built till the housing was finished so that in the larger estates hundreds of people might spend years under semi-camp conditions,' reported Pearl Jephcott's sociological study. She cited two estates, with some 700 and 500 homes respectively, that illustrated the extent of the delay: 'Though both had been occupied for over five years they still had no shops nor apparently any likelihood of them.'[25]

The Gorbals was just the tip of the iceberg when it came to high-rise blocks of flats in Glasgow. Thousands of former Gorbals residents were to be rehoused in other areas. 'Some were deeply apprehensive about being moved to the housing estate of Castlemilk,' recalls Colin MacFarlane in his memoir *The Real Gorbals Story*. "'There's no even wan pub in Castlemilk. The place is a desert wi windaes. It's worse than bein' in jail. At least in Barlinnie ye've got a bit o'atmosphere.'"[26] By the early sixties two influential figures were reacting against the ideas behind Abercrombie and Matthew's 1946 plan to disperse the population. David Gibson, Glasgow's housing convener, and local authority architect Sam Bunton were keen to rehouse as many people as possible within the city borders, rather than in the new towns of East Kilbride, Glenrothes, Livingstone, Irvine and Cumbernauld. Gibson's ugly solution was to dot high-rise flats on every available gap site in the city in order to squeeze in as many homes as possible. This was putting two fingers up to the whole concept of 'comprehensive planning': the opportunistic

plonking of blocks anywhere they would fit made it difficult to see
how the ideals of creating open space for all, relieving overcrowding
or rationalising roads could be realised. Nevertheless, Gibson got his
way. 'Over the next three years the skyline of Glasgow will become
a more attractive one to me,' he told colleagues in 1962, 'because of
the likely vision of multi-storey houses rising by the thousand …
The prospect will be thrilling, I am certain, to the many thousands
who are still yearning for a decent home.'[27]

Sam Bunton, Gibson's brother-in-arms, was the biggest advocate
of high-rise flats in the country. Glasgow had grown up as a cousin to
the industrial U. S. cities of the nineteenth century; now it was time
to bring it into the skyscraping present. Bunton and Gibson altered
the skyline of Glasgow far more radically than the 1946 plan had
anticipated, with huge high-rise estates and lone tower blocks rising
all over the city. Between 1961 and 1968 high-rise blocks of flats
accounted for three quarters of all housing completions in Glasgow.

Bunton's greatest achievement would be pushing through the
construction of the Red Road estate, which until the Barbican
in London was finally completed, boasted the tallest residential
towers in Europe. I went to visit the estate some months before the
demolition of the towers began. Standing between miles of suburban
semis on one side and waste ground on the other, these colossal,
pastel-coloured blocks were undoubtedly a striking sight, as well
as a remarkable feat of engineering. Yet there was also something
absurd about them, this huddle of slim forms straining to stand tall,
like a gang of anxious meerkats scanning a plain.

Red Road was one of the estates studied by sociologist Pearl
Jephcott in her 1971 book *Homes in High Flats*, and she found that,
as predicted by those letter writers to the *Herald* in the late forties,
nearly half the residents with a child under five were dissatisfied
with tower block life. Far from the spacious verandas to be found in
Queen Elizabeth Square, these more conventional blocks had tiny
balconies with no space for children to run, bounce a ball or pedal a
bike. A young mother with a one-year-old living on the nineteenth

floor commented that 'there are play areas for the children but they are all stone. Would be better with grass ... I feel a playpark should have been enclosed in the scheme.'[28] Perhaps most ominously, Jephcott found that 'the areas where adults expect to be responsible for their children's behaviour have not been firmly established either in the block or on the estate.'[29] Earlier warnings, such as that from Sir Alexander MacGregor, the Medical Officer of Health, who declared in 1945 'that multi-storey flats were not the proper houses in which to bring up families of young children,'[30] had been largely ignored in

The Red Road flats, designed by Sam Bunton.

Gibson's drive to install as many homes in as small a space as possible. Sam Bunton may have shared with Basil Spence an ambition to create iconic, transformative buildings, but the looming silhouette of Red Road became iconic in all the wrong ways, a symbol of all the negative stories associated with high-rise estates, from suicides to crime sprees. It stood there like a lighthouse, warning us to stay away.

There is no doubt that many were unhappy with the radical rebuilding of Glasgow. Colin MacFarlane remembers spotting some telling graffiti as the Hutchesontown estates were rising: 'Someone had even spray painted a wall with giant letters asking "Who murdered the Gorbals?"'[31] Yet for many others the slum clearances led to new and better lives. Though critical of many things, particularly Red Road, Jephcott's study recorded many other appreciative comments about the new high-rise blocks in which they had been rehoused. 'One tenant who felt just everything about the house and its situation satisfied her, quoted her husband as saying that he only started to live when they came here.'[32] There was also the old man who loved to spend a couple of hours in the evening looking out at the city lights, or the many couples who admired the peace and quiet and the modern conveniences. 'A mother pointed to her three-year-old who, accustomed to being washed in the sink, would splash about forever in this lovely shiny bath. They showed the snow-white toilet next to the bath, and some recalled the horrors they had known, maybe a murky, unlighted den off a stone passage outside the house.'[33]

And of all of the revolutionary tower blocks in Glasgow, Eddie McGonnell was in no doubt as to which was the best. 'I've stayed in three lots of flats in the Gorbals,' he explained. 'I stayed in Queen Elizabeth till I was 18, then I moved to Sandiefield Road.' This was area D of the Hutchesontown-Gorbals redevelopment, built in more conventional high-rise style by Gilbert Ash, an arm of the construction giant Wimpey who'd also built Britain's first point block in Harlow. 'And then these flats here,' he points out of the window of the Waterfront Bar at the black-and-beige rough concrete façade of 1 Norfolk Court, the last remaining of four blocks built by Scottish contractors Crudens. This was the sixth and final comprehensive development area in the Gorbals, a district called Laurieston. 'So I've stayed in three blocks, but none of them touch the Spence ones. They were just flats. I stayed in them, big deal.'

When I asked him to describe what it was about the Spence flats that made them so different, Eddie used words such as 'iconic' and 'powerful'. There was real admiration and wonder in the way he described Queen Elizabeth Square, emotions that were quite absent in the way he spoke about the rest. 'It was a mundane, stereotypical block of flats,' he said, pointing up at 1 Norfolk Court. 'Nothing going for it. You see a lot of flats over there,' he waved a hand dismissively at Robert Matthew's blocks in the distance, 'they're all bland looking – square and the same shape of windows and there's nothing different.' In contrast, Queen Elizabeth Square 'was like a flying saucer taking you to Mars. It was life on Mars, that's the way they seemed,' he said, with a characteristic flourish. 'He modelled them on a block of flats in Paris, was it?'

'Marseille,' I said, trainspotter-style. 'Le Corbusier's Unité d'Habitation.'

Eddie nodded vigorously. 'He modelled it on that one there, hanging gardens in the sky. We used to have on the veranda flower pots, and these people who were maybe green-fingered had shrubs – it *was* a hanging gardens of Babylon!'

2. 'A New Dimension Added to the Street'
SHEFFIELD AND STREETS IN THE SKY
(1957-61)

Park Hill, the immense single-block housing estate that overlooks Sheffield city centre, was almost deserted when I wandered around taking photographs on a hot summer's day in 2011. At that very moment in cities all over the country, including Croydon, riots were taking place. Park Hill's quietness was almost eerie, but there was a simple explanation: the place was in mid transformation. Three iterations of the building now stood side by side on the hill. There was the ghostly central section, now mostly derelict, with boards, painted in a street art style, hammered across the doors and windows. To the left, behind temporary barriers, was the newly renovated part of the structure, looking less like one of Britain's most daring social housing schemes than an office development in Barcelona. Its vivid wall panels, chosen by developers Urban Splash, were so bright that they all but precluded any sense of the building's shape. Finally, to the right, there were those areas of the original estate that were still occupied, and whose black windows stared blankly out at me.

Often compared to a castle or a medieval walled city, Park Hill presented an invulnerable front, but once I was inside the many pathways, spaces and enclosures began to reveal themselves. A network of paths delineated by red railings led me through the estate. There was still a community here – by all accounts one that didn't want to leave. Occasionally I glimpsed people wandering above me along one of the 'streets in the sky', or heard children playing in an adjacent courtyard. There was also the buzz of prowling helicopters, keeping a weather eye out for any sign of rioting. Yet this was no

Old and new Park Hill.

place for spectacular, high-visibility wrongdoing. Instead, the many quiet nooks of the newly depopulated estate provided the perfect environment for low-profile sketchiness. Drug-dealing, mostly. Dealers go there because it's quiet, and so handy – just a hop and a skip over the tramlines from the town centre.

I'd walked through the estate in the late morning, and returned after lunch to photograph it from the outside. A man had been shot. A forensics guy decked out in the full regalia – overalls, latex gloves, plastic bags on his feet – stood loading evidence into the back of a police van, while behind him coppers with bundles of crime-scene tape emerged from the peaceful place I'd been wandering just two hours earlier.

The redevelopment of the 800 houses and 63 prefabs at the notoriously crime-ridden slums of Park Hill had been one of the top priorities of new city architect Lewis Womersley when he moved to Sheffield in 1952. 'I climbed to the top of the roof of the library and looked down at the skyline,' he recalled of the day he went for his interview, 'and it seemed to me that it was a very, very exciting city; the topography excited me tremendously.'[1] Womersley kept his eyes out for suitable talent to bring on board. And when he saw the brilliant plans drawn up by youthful Ivor Smith and Jack Lynn for flats in Rotherhithe, he snapped the recent graduates up for his department. Jack and Ivor had been students of the wily iconoclast Peter Smithson at the Architectural Association in London. Despite their inexperience they brought with them an intellectual brio reminiscent of their teacher.

The project at Park Hill was to create nearly 1,000 flats. The site's dramatic location, looming over the city centre from atop a craggy hilltop, raised its profile, so that the project became something of an advert for the benefits of redevelopment. The planners considered it essential that the locals from old Park Hill should be rehoused in the new scheme, whatever it turned out to be, and much consideration was given as to how a suitable environment might be created for these transposed families. After all, the slums may have been unfit for purpose, but they had helped to forge communities. 'Despite its sanitary shortcomings,' wrote Jack Lynn, these old streets had 'fostered a community life' that was 'essentially healthy'.[2] He and Ivor were determined to replicate a vibrant street scene – vertically.

At the time when Park Hill was being planned in the early fifties, one building above all others fascinated architects. Designed to be a 'vertical garden city' and known locally as the madhouse, Le Corbusier's Unité d'Habitation in Marseille, built immediately after the war, instantly became the pin-up of young architects around the world. This mighty slab housed 337 apartments, along with a row of shops, a nursery, a gym and a hotel. The reinforced rough-concrete frame was likened to a 'bottlerack', with the apartments slotted in like colourful bottles; halfway up the structure, the tidy grid was disrupted by a bigger floor that housed the public areas.

Le Corbusier had based the dimensions and details of

this immense building around a set of standardised human measurements that he'd been mapping, called the Modulor. It was rational approach to design, helping to ensure that no matter the size of the project, human scale would prevail as the most important element. No matter if it were the height of door frames, the width of corridors or the depth of steps, the Modulor was there to guide the architect, engineer and builder in every aspect of the planning. Of course, it took a lot for granted, such as the size of actual people and their physical fitness – or disabilities. On every third floor the apartments were connected by internal corridors known as 'mid-air streets'. Ship design was one of Le Corbusier's obsessions, and observers were soon likening the Unité to a moored ocean liner. And there were many observers when the building opened in 1952. 'For us, a trip to the Unité d'Habitation in Marseille was almost mandatory,' wrote London County Council architect John Partridge, 'and Stan Amis and I duly made this pilgrimage (in a prewar Morris with a leaking petrol tank stopped up with chewing gum), returning in total awe of the great master.'[3] Amis and Partridge were part of a team led by Colin Lucas who, inspired by Le Corbusier, were determined to add a hard edge to the department's work. The group set themselves up in opposition to the Arts and Crafts inspired communist faction, whose work, like the new towns, was sneeringly dismissed as 'picturesque', obsessed with cosy 'people's detailing' and therefore 'soft'. Frederic Osborn, garden city guardian and softy par excellence, found his views increasingly eclipsed in architectural circles. Yet he found surprising support at a conference of the International Congress of Modern Architects. 'I was amazed, and momentarily encouraged, by support from all of the French housing people present,' he wrote, 'whose spokesman not only brilliantly exploded Le Corbusier's mad 14-storey glass house at Marseille, but expressed astonishment that England, the envied country of the family home with garden, should be increasingly piling houses on top of each other.'[4]

But the LCC's 'hard' faction quickly knocked up five fun-size

Unités at the leafy Alton West estate at Roehampton – the first of many British homages that included the Queenies, Basil Spence's blocks in the Gorbals. Down the road at Alton East an outcrop of new Scandinavian-style point blocks, planned by the 'soft' group, were suddenly old hat.

Park Hill had much in common with the Unité. Streets were raised into the air. A 'bottlerack' frame held a mixture of shops, flats and public buildings within a single structure. Yet it wasn't to be just another miniature version of Le Corbusier's 'vertical garden city'. Instead, it would be an immensely stretched, undulating structure, the largest development of its kind in western Europe, connecting the entire ridge above the city centre and dividing as it progressed into a series of crescents, protruding like ragged claws.

The 'bottlerack' frame of Park Hill holds several different types of flat, as well as shops, cafés and pubs.

The technical challenges for Ivor and Jack, the young design duo, were daunting. They relied heavily on structural engineer Ronald Jenkins of Ove Arup, who provided many a detailed critique of their designs' shortcomings, and spurred them on to better solutions. 'These were exciting days,' wrote Jack, 'when we felt we were on the threshold of what would now be called a "breakthrough".'[5] Their most famous innovation was the 'streets in the sky'. Whereas the streets in Le Corbusier's Unité d'Habitation were in reality no more than internal corridors, Park Hill incorporated great landings open

Walkways connect the streets in the sky to different limbs of the building.

to the elements, on a much bigger scale than the poky galleries on thirties blocks of flats. Another idea was to keep the roof level the same height throughout the complex, despite the steep hill on which it was built. The section built at the top of the hill was a mere four storeys high, and as the land fell away towards the bottom of the hill the estate rose to 13 storeys to maintain that constant roof line. A cunning thought from the designers further exploited this quirk of topography. Park Hill's streets in the sky actually began at ground level at the top of the hill. The further you walked along the same level, the higher you found you were in the building, as it grew beneath you on the lower slopes. Because of this, the architects figured, that residents wouldn't have to use lifts or stairs, because all streets in the sky touched the ground somewhere. But it was their third innovation that proved to be the most significant: 'Each level has been provided with a sort of street in mid-air, with front doors opening onto it,' wrote the journalist Geoffrey Moorhouse, 'where children can play and their parents are thrown together as much as they were along the old terrace streets on the ground.'[6]

Former Park Hill caretaker and latter day local celebrity Grenville Squires met me to talk about his memories of working there. His reminiscences of his time on the estate have enlivened numerous television and radio programmes, as well as the interactive exhibits at the local museum. Just a week before I met him I'd heard him on the radio, as part of a programme tracing the origins of Britain's most famous piece of pre-Banksy graffiti: *Clare Middleton I love you will u marry me*, which had been wonkily spray painted in the eighties on one of Park Hill's bridges, facing the city centre. Now retired and walking with the aid of a stick, he showed me into his front room, which was bedecked with homemade Fabergé-style eggs and an extensive collection of Betty Boop figurines. Grenville had prepared well for our chat, having dug out folders of information, including photographs from around the estate and some of his own poetry, which I'd once heard him reading on an Open University programme. He talked me through how the complex layout of Park Hill's streets in the sky actually worked.

'For each one of those landings,' he said, pointing to one of the 'streets,' 'you had three levels. A going-in level, you'd got a downstairs level and you'd got an upstairs level.' As in the Unité d'Habitation, doors off the landings led to flats on levels immediately above and below. 'And what they did, when you looked at Park Hill, you could see by different coloured brickwork: the top three was a different colour, the next three was a different colour.' It is this scheme of subtly coloured bricks that Urban Splash's acid-coloured iridescent panels have replaced.

As a caretaker, Grenville saw sides to the building that the public and residents never knew about. 'A lot of people think Park Hill is just a block of flats, but it isn't. There's an infrastructure underneath, and if it weren't for that infrastructure, Park Hill wouldn't work.' He showed me pictures of dark and dingy ducts under the building that instantly made me feel claustrophobic, and regaled me with cheery tales of flooding, blocked plumbing and power failure. Then there was the Garchey waste disposal system – which with the assistance of plungers at every sink, helped fire waste down into the bowels of Park Hill, where, ingeniously, it was recycled and converted into energy to keep the flats warm.

This mind-boggling structure was built not by a private contractor like Wimpey but by the council's own Direct Labour organisation. When Park Hill was finished in 1961, Ivor Smith and Jack Lynn's modern utopia quickly found itself an essential stop on the itinerary for other young architects and planners, much as Le Corbusier's building had been a decade before. 'Sheffield has become an object of pilgrimage for many people concerned with the social and the architectural aspects of housing,' reported *The Times*. 'Some of the architectural details and finishes are, it is true, on the grim side,' was their verdict, before concluding with unintended comedy that 'these are not unsuited to the character of a northern industrial city.'[7]

It's touching to look at the photos and footage of the early days, showing hopeful residents of all ages moving in and coming to terms with their new homes. The shock of the new still resonates from those images. Elderly working-class folk, who had grown up in the last days of Queen Victoria, shuffled incongruously about on those pale grey streets in the sky. The antiquated Austins parked against the dazzling bottlerack façade looked like ghosts, tiny and out of time. Grenville recalled one clip that stood out for him.

'In one of these films, it's a classic, there's an old lady, she's got rollers in her hair, she's got a crossover pinafore, little glasses. And she says, "Does tha know, love, we thought we'd died and gone t'heaven." She said, "We didn't have to get up in the morning and make fire tha knows. 24-hour hot water. Toilet were in there, not at t'bottom of yard." That's *classic*. They moved into Park Hill, and everything was here. You weren't cold when you were lighting fire, you just turned a dial on the wall. Everybody could wash – you didn't have a wash *day*, you had a wash *week*. And everyone could have a bath.'

The variety of shops and public spaces in the complex soon made it a vibrant social centre.

'You'd come off t'lift and you'd got Earl George pub,' recalled Grenville, walking through the shops in his head, 'then you'd got Douggie's hardware shop, Talbot's butchers, another little grocery shop, a bespoke curtain shop, another little greengrocers, then you'd got estate office, newsagents. Then right in middle you'd got wines and spirits. You'd got a wallpaper shop. You'd got frocks, Dempsey's shoe shop. And other side you'd got Co-Op, a gents' hairdressers and two ladies' hairdressers, chip shop, betting shop, post office, Indian takeaway, and a sandwich shop. Virtually everything. You could live for weeks without leaving Park Hill.'

The planners in Glasgow had often omitted such amenities from their schemes, and their residents had dreamed of them. One local who appreciated them was planner Jo Meredith, who moved to Sheffield in 1970. We met in a café by the Crucible Theatre, Sheffield's most famous postwar landmark. Over some tea and cake she proved to be both vigorously no nonsense and drily funny. 'When I lived opposite Park Hill it was still vibrant,' she said. 'The shops were used not just by the people in Park Hill flats. I remember, the whole of that area would shop there, because it was a good local shopping centre. All the sort of essentials of life in the early seventies. And I rented a lock-up garage there. They built lock-up garages there but no one wanted them.' It was a reminder how few working-class people could afford cars in the early seventies. At around the same time, *The Times* sent a journalist who came to much the same conclusion as Jo – Park Hill was a success. 'Today, eight years after the flats were opened, it is obvious that the idea has worked. It has helped create a community that is close enough to the centre to be a part of the city's life yet at the same time can support a flourishing parade of shops, a couple of public houses, a lively tenants' association and a wide range of social activities.'[8]

What of the famous streets in the sky? City architect Lewis Womersley was at pains to explain to the middle classes the ways of

'Small children like to play together in a common garden outside their houses where they are safe from traffic.'

the tenants on these decks, famously broad enough to drive a milk-float along. 'These people like to talk to one another without dressing up and making special calls. The women like to sit on their doorsteps and chat on warm summer afternoons and their small children like to play together in a common garden outside their houses where they are safe from traffic.'[9] For a time almost everyone seemed happy with this spectacular and intimate new Park Hill – which was just as well, as equally monumental sister projects Hyde Park and Kelvin were being built along the same lines too.

Park Hill stood at the cusp of an architectural changing of the guard, as an established prewar generation in thrall to Le Corbusier's ideas began to give way to a postwar cohort, whose most colourful representatives were Peter and Alison Smithson. At its fourth meeting, held in 1933 on a cruise to Athens, the International Congress of Modern Architects had boiled the whole complexity of city life down to four functional problems: the demands of home, work, recreation and transport. It was the job of all modern architects to solve these problems as neatly as possible. Yet the new generation was beginning to rebel against this formula. 'Young architects today feel a monumental dissatisfaction with the buildings they see going up around them,' wrote the Smithsons. 'They feel that the majority of architects have lost contact with reality and are building yesterday's dreams when the rest of us have woken up in today.'[10] At one CIAM meeting, to the bafflement of the older generation, they showed photos of kids playing and having fun on the streets of old Bethnal Green, the kind of area being comprehensively redeveloped. Yes, the houses were squalid and failing, but the social life these streets had fostered was to be envied – and recreated.

Peter and Alison spearheaded a group they called, with typical superhero flash, 'Team 10', whose task was 'to find new equivalents for these forms of house-groupings, streets, squares, greens, etc, as the social reality they presented no longer exists.'[11] Their manifesto set out how the vibrant spirit of traditional city life could be fostered in new ways, in 'a multi-level city with residential "streets in the air" … linked together in a multi-level continuous complex'. This sprawling, organic vision of a many-layered and complex city opposed the tidy functionalism embodied by the Unité d'Habitation. Park Hill, combining a bottle-rack frame and raised streets with the rambling informality of more familiar street patterns, was caught between two revolutions – Le Corbusier's and the Smithsons'.

The Smithsons had stressed their departure from CIAM's overly functionalist ideas by presenting their 1951 entry for the Golden Lane housing competition as a pop art collage rather than a sterile architectural drawing. As usual they didn't win, but here was an urban, modern, arty and excitingly pop vision. The idea was to replicate life on the street in all its colour and fun, but in a modern way. 'Decks would be places,' they insisted, 'not corridors or balconies.'[12] They weren't alone. In 1952, former Royal Engineer Denys Lasdun's proposal for what he called a 'cluster block' in the flattened district of Bethnal Green looked more like a space station than a block of flats: three 14-storey columns of maisonettes were splayed like solar arrays from a circular core. Lasdun was keen to emphasise the humanity behind his design. 'I used to lunch with [local people] to try and understand a bit more about what mattered to them, and they were proud people,' he said. 'It was an attempt to get some of the quality of life retained as distinct from being treated like a statistical pawn in a great prism. And they were very appreciative of this in the end, and this distinctly touched me.'[13]

Yet, as John Gold showed brilliantly in his book *The Practice of Modernism*, very little systematic community research actually took place. By 1957, Peter Willmott and Michael Young had completed their thorough sociological study of Bethnal Green, *Family and Kinship in East London*, which became one of the most influential reports on the effects of modern planning. Though acknowledging the need for slum demolition after the war, the pair concluded that planners had thrown the baby out with the bathwater: 'The sense of loyalty to each other amongst the inhabitants of a place like Bethnal Green is not due to buildings. It is due far more to ties of kinship and friendship which connect the people of one household to the people of another.'[14]

Projects like the Bethnal Green cluster blocks and Park Hill paved the way for many huge experimental 'streets in the sky' estates. Yet for all the planners' talk of community, their design was based on little evidence from the very communities they were built to house. As the decades rolled by, Park Hill lost its appeal for students of architecture. Social problems made sections of the estate no-go areas, and its reputation for drugs and mugging alienated all but the most hardy of outsiders. By 1980, *The Times* was writing that Park Hill was an estate 'now identified in official jargon as "areas of worst deprivation", whose environment is "bleak, dreary and hostile".'[15] Even Park Hill architect Ivor Smith was quoted as saying 'there were some misgivings among us that the community structure would be irrevocably upset, as indeed it was.'[16]

'It's very fashionable for people to say that the design of buildings determines the way that people behave,' said former planner Jo Meredith, 'and I'm not disputing that, because I believe that, but I think you've got to look at it with the social context and the whole demise of social housing and the lack of management on estates.' She became increasingly despondent as we talked, with bleak news of the riots underway in my home town of Croydon colouring our conversation. 'As the pool of housing declines after the sell-off, then the housing departments start using estates as dump estates. And I'm afraid everyone isn't a saint. And there are people who are anti-social. And once you start putting all those people together in one place then that's more or less the nail in the coffin, isn't it? There's the whole thing about the loss of working class culture and working class pride, and that's to do with employment and the loss of manufacturing jobs, and all the stuff about belonging to a firm, like the big steel companies, or in my father's case, a colliery, and the pride of being part of that group. I find it quite depressing, especially this week because of the riots.' She gave me a sad look. 'Apart from being very angry it makes me want to sit down and weep.'

Grenville's tone was more defensive as he recalled the impossibility of looking after the thousands of residents and the gigantic estate towards the end. 'That was the way things were with caretaking – *you took care!* When they decided they didn't want resident caretakers we had to move off. We could have stayed there, but people would still have come and knocked on your door. I were the last one to move off …'

And so sprawling, vandalised and put-upon Park Hill had to fend for itself.

After Park Hill, streets in the sky quickly became a ubiquitous feature of urban life. I revisited a place I'd lived in the noughties, the Elephant and Castle in south London, which is still full of raised walkways. Danny Gill, the Glaswegian brickie who'd talked to me about growing up in the Gorbals, later helped build many of these estates in south London, such as the Heygate. Like Grenville, he answered the door on sticks, and had prepared for my visit by

Walkways at the Heygate, planned to connect up three miles of south London estates with streets in the sky.

pulling together his collection of photocopied newspaper articles and poems he'd written about the estates. Perhaps there was something about the streets in the sky that inspired poetry.

He remembered the scale of the Greater London Council's streets in the sky plan with awe. 'The initial architects' thinking was build North Peckham, link it up with the Heygate, link it up with the Aylesbury,' he said, of three of the vast estates he'd helped build. 'All linked together on the walkways which meant you didn't have to go down to ground level. You could walk on first floor level all the way from North Peckham down to Elephant. And I think that's brilliant! That's got to be three miles without ever touching the ground.' But Danny's memories of the estates he helped build were conflicted. 'It was super-duper for about the first 10 years, and then you had a few undesirables, and then mugging came in. So ... it was something the architects tried – and they were wrong.'

Demolition of the Heygate Estate's streets in the sky began in 2014 .

After the police had left Park Hill with their forensics evidence and crime-scene tape, I wandered around the top end of the estate, the part that was mostly still occupied. There were window boxes. Two women of a certain age were leaning on the balustrade of a ground floor flat, having a classic over-the-garden-fence gossip. At this end of the estate, people had gone to great lengths to personalise their flats, with shiny new paint, satellite dishes and creepers growing up trellises. It was hard to see how this could be done in the gaudy new Urban Splash zone.

As the evening sun hit the façade, the whole of Park Hill, refurbished, derelict or inhabited, turned a warm gold. The colours on the renovated section glowed like a bank of LCD screens, and from the city centre the estate blazed bright on the hilltop, rising above the metropolis like a man-made Vesuvius. In its scale and ambition, Park Hill seems less a run-of-the-mill housing estate than an experiment with nature. Perhaps Jack Lynn had it right. 'Walking in the city,' he wrote, 'has acquired some of the quality previously found only on the fells or on cliff tops by the sea.'[17]

3. 'A Wild and Romantic Place'
SHOPPING AND DRIVING IN BIRMINGHAM AND THE ELEPHANT AND CASTLE (1959-65)

This is the tale of the Bull and the Elephant. In the midst of England's two biggest cities, these two beasts had lived stoically through centuries of tumult and change. The Bull had thrived in Birmingham for nearly a thousand years, while the Elephant arrived in mysterious circumstances in south London during the reign of George III. Over the centuries they had taken many forms, as great events overtook them. By the age of the Victorians both had gained something of a reputation for wildness and mischief. Then, during the Second World War, they found themselves engulfed in the chaos of the Blitz, and afterwards the people of the two great cities didn't quite know what to do with them. The Bull and the Elephant, creatures of national legend and local folklore, were about to be magically transformed once again ...

New shopping centres, ambitious civic schemes and bold urban road plans hit the centre of Britain's towns in the sixties. Drivers belted across new flyovers in their Minis in search of multi-storey car parks, while beneath them mini-skirted shoppers walked through mosaic-tiled underpasses on their way to huge indoor malls. The councillors of the era were ostentatiously busy, keen to be seen working for local businesses and pumping new blood into the heart of their communities.

'It was very futuristic,' said John Mulrenan, a mordantly humourous former shop steward I'd interviewed about the Elephant and Castle, where he'd grown up. 'Particularly the shopping centre. The thing about having a shopping centre *with escalators* going from one floor to another was pretty amazing ... There was such a contrast ... I hesitate to call it the shock of the new, but it *did* look futuristic ... I think that electrical substation thing' – the Faraday Memorial, the reflective metal box built on one of the Elephant and Castle's roundabouts – 'was almost like something out of the space programme. It was futuristic and it was stunning.' And of course, it *was* the space age. In the mid-fifties the Soviets had shocked the world by sending a satellite into orbit. By the end of the sixties a couple of Americans were bouncing around on the surface of the moon. Britain, meanwhile, had had a rocket put up it by its property developers. As the *Guardian* put it, 'it's said that as the Apollo astronauts swept over England, they couldn't see the north-west for builders' dust.'[1] As John reflected: 'All of these things would have influenced the way people thought about these things, whether consciously or subconsciously.'

In the Elephant and Castle and the city of Birmingham, the legacy of space-age optimism has lived on barely altered until today in many of the buildings and road schemes. The 'can do' attitude of postwar politicians, builders and planners spearheaded a massive transformation of city centres up and down the country, with an optimism more reminiscent of dynamic America than conservative Britain.

Writing in the local paper in 1959, Birmingham councillor Frank Price explained how two massive projects he was helping to push through – the city's inner ring road and a shopping centre – were connected. 'Although primarily designed to cure our central area traffic problem,' he wrote of the plan as a whole, 'it will also be instrumental in curing our shopping cramp.'[2] With a town centre grandly rebuilt by Victorian industrialists less than a century before, Birmingham was hardly cramped, but it did have fewer shops than, say, Manchester – and the council had ambitions for it to become a great world city. Of major junctions like the Elephant and Castle, Sir Patrick Abercrombie had written during the war that 'the necessities of traffic-weaving will dominate their design'.[3]

It's impossible to overestimate the importance of transport in the development of British towns and cities. After all, it was the steam engine that made the Industrial Revolution possible. But by the late fifties the railway network, still reliant on antiquated steam technology, was hopelessly out of date. Cars were king. But the automobile revolution brought with it extraordinary risks. Sir Patrick revealed that in England alone over 68,000 people had been killed on the roads in the 10 years leading up to 1943.[4] This is double the number who died in the Blitz across the whole country; and twice as many as those who lost their lives on the roads across all of Britain in the decade following 1998. And then there were a further two million road users injured too. Even taking into account wartime blackouts, which caused a spike in road traffic accidents, in the days before standardied road markings, traffic rules, signage and other safety features, Britain's roads were as lawless and deadly as the Wild West.

Safety wasn't the only conundrum the car presented town planners. There was also the traffic jam. For centuries the street layouts of Britain's towns had carried nothing more mighty than the horse and cart. Now they were being asked to cope with the onslaught of thousands of motorcars, lorries, trams and double-decker buses. Enter Metropolitan Police Assistant Commissioner Herbert Alker Tripp. The Commissioner took the traffic part of his brief very seriously, devoting much of his time to puzzling over a solution to the problem. He even wrote a book on the subject – 1942's *Town Planning and Road Traffic* – envisaging a network of fast pedestrian-free 'arterial' roads, leading to 'distributor' roads, from which you could reach a 'precinct' of local roads. Alker Tripp's book would influence a generation of transport planners, including Sir Patrick, who found Tripp's work an invaluable reference when writing his many city redevelopment plans. For London he trumped Birmingham's long-planned ring road scheme, envisaging not one but *four* of Tripp's mighty 'arterial' roads, from a squeezed inner ring out to a distant orbital expressway.

Britain's first modest stretch of motorway, the Preston bypass, was opened by Harold Macmillan in 1958. The splendid commemorative brochure produced for the occasion dubbed it, with some accuracy, 'the beginning of a new era of motoring in Britain'.[5] Decades after the German autobahns and American freeways had been constructed, here was the first link in what would soon be a countrywide motorway network. A year later the first section of the M1 opened.

Nevertheless, Britain's cities remained choked with traffic. By the mid-fifties the average journey speed in Glasgow had slowed to a dawdling 8.2 mph – below that of a horse-drawn carriage. The first section of the city's inner ring road opened in 1960, elevated on huge concrete legs and busting through street lines at tenement rooftop level. Within two decades the average traffic speed in Glasgow centre had shot up to a pulse-quickening 50 miles per hour.[6]

Not everybody was delighted with these developments. 'Parked and moving vehicles obscure the scene day and night,' wrote Professor Colin Buchanan, a traffic planning specialist, in *The Times*.[7] 'A generally hideous array of signals, beacons, signs, railings, petrol stations, sales depots and advertisements has come into being.' His report for the government, *Traffic in Towns*, became a bestseller in 1963. At a town planning conference in 1966 he described the negative effects of the car with a bleak Reggie Perrin-like howl of despair: 'confusion and congestion, delays, lack of parking space, inadequate facilities for loading and unloading goods, and the same sad story of death and injury, anxiety, noise, fumes, and the large-scale intrusion of the motor vehicle into the visual scene'.[8]

Yet if the nation's roads were a mess, there was at least one development that injected a dose of elegance, coherence and practicality into the motoring scene. Graphic artists Jock Kinneir and Margaret Calvert, fresh from working on the signage at Gatwick Airport, had been commissioned by the government in 1957 to produce standardised signage for Britain's fast-expanding road and motorway system. Their familiar symbols – red-framed speed limits, hurrying school children and motorway road 'trees' – were first

tested on the Preston bypass and by the mid-sixties had become one
of the most conspicuous symbols of modernity across the country.

Even before Buchanan had presented his report, ideas to save our
dangerous, congested streets from the car were circulating. Wilfred
Burns, planning officer for Coventry, favoured the pedestrian
precinct theory, which had been used to great effect in the Blitzed
city centre. The precinct was 'clearly the norm of the future', he
wrote: 'it satisfies the pedestrian, it provides reasonable conditions
for the motorist and for the shopkeeper, it has great architectural
possibilities.'[9] In his timely 1959 book, *British Shopping Centres,* he
went so far as to declare that the pedestrian precinct was 'the only
sensible plan on which to base designs for shopping centres in the
future, whether they be town centres or major suburban centres'.
As if to prove that he wasn't against all four-wheeled vehicles, he
pointed out that precincts were 'also ideal for pram traffic'.[10]

Other planners were thinking on another level altogether. 'If the
city is large enough, the pedestrians must be on a level above that of
traffic,' announced Percy Johnson-Marshall, brother of Stirrat and
another former Coventry planner. 'This will give the pedestrians
freedom of movement.'[11] Percy was not alone. Buchanan, in impatient
table-thumping form, defended the notion in *The Times* in 1961: 'It
is not a matter of aerial gangways or frightening catwalks, nor is it
open to the feeble criticism that "you cannot make people go up". It
is a new way of arranging buildings, with city life literally on a new
plane.'[12] However, as Wilfred Burns couldn't help pointing out, 'such
a system has the drawback, from the pedestrian point of view, of
canalising them along the walkways and making it impossible for
them to flit from one side to the other.'[13]

Taken together, the rise of both pedestrian precincts and streets
in the sky might even combine to hasten the end of the street,
that ribbon lined with overlooking buildings, as we knew it. 'The
"corridor street" – façades up to street lines – is obsolete,' wrote the
Observer's architecture critic in 1956 with great confidence.[14] With
so many new buildings placed at angles facing away from roads, or

pedestrian decks built to replace the old street pattern altogether, no longer would shops, offices or houses necessarily abut those increasingly busy traffic arteries.

Into the new world of pedestrian precincts and multi-level streets envisaged by the public planners marched armies of private developers to provide for the post-austerity boom. Specialist companies such as Ravenseft and Arndale sprang up, with all the skills necessary to plan and construct giant new shopping centres – and whose particular expertise lay in maximising the profit from any given project. Since the fifties, local authorities had been encouraged by the government to work in partnership with private developers on their large redevelopment schemes. Lionel Brett, a planner who'd worked on many such city centre projects, described the effect the government was aiming for: 'The result would normally be a brand-new inner relief-road feeding multi-storey car parks, a pedestrian shopping mall and lettable office slabs that paid for it all.'[15]

For some years after the war Ravenseft, trading on their knack for not only negotiating land deals with councils and private owners, but attracting big-name retailers into their new builds, were the undisputed masters of the shopping centre. The rise of their straight-talking Bradford-based rivals Arnold Hagenbach and Sam Chippindale – who amalgamated the first and last of their names to create Arndale – was swift and dramatic. Their first shopping centre was begun in Jarrow in 1958, and within two decades they had built 24 across Britain, from Aberdeen to Poole. 'When we started the very name of Jarrow made the multiples shudder,' recalled Chippindale of the chain store clients he came to woo so successfully. A new shopping centre could do wonders for a town – and even more for the bottom line of a company like Arndale, whose reputation was sealed by their early successes in Jarrow and Bradford. 'What was decisive was getting Woolworths to come in, and that's something the local authority couldn't have done,' ex-estate agent Chippindale bragged. 'They came in because they have learnt from experience to trust my judgment.' In Accrington he simply 'persuaded the local authority to do a deal; we promised to get in Marks & Spencer if they would let us do a shopping centre.'[16] Easy.

Shopping had been transformed since the war, partly by the arrival of American-style supermarkets. According to figures gathered by Dominic Sandbrook in his book *White Heat*, in 1947 there were estimated to be 10 self-service grocery stores in the country; 3,000 by 1956; 12,000 by 1962; and double that figure just five years later – 3,000 of which were supermarkets, the rest corner shops and the like.[17] Rationing finally came to an end in July 1954, and in the same month, the relaxation of hire purchase regulations, governing everything from televisions to fridges, vacuum cleaners to cars, helped ignite a high street boom.

With customer demand and retail practices changing so rapidly, the pressure to modernise shopping environments escalated. Arndale and Ravenseft led the way. It was in the late fifties that town councils for the first time sought to use their new powers for comprehensive redevelopment. There was the chance to remake and remodel densely crowded, derelict and neglected town centres, and Arndale and its rivals seemed to offer nervous councils the expertise that would ensure these vast projects were a success. It was capitalism at its most transformative. 'We are confident we can make a considerable contribution to the planning of a better Britain,' said Arnold Hagenbach at the company AGM in 1964, cranking up the public service rhetoric lest anyone should accuse them of money-grubbing opportunism. 'Today all political parties are pledged to promote schemes for social betterment. This must include the modernisation of town centres all over the country, where people can do their shopping and conduct their business under pleasant conditions of safety and comfort.'[18] It was a nice philanthropic spin on the £3 million of building work they had in progress, the £5 million ready to go, and the further £15 million-worth in the pipeline. They were keen, too, to dispel any fears that what they were doing was frighteningly modern in any way. 'We are not keen on "contemporary" architecture,' said Sam Chippindale to the *Architects' Journal*, unable to resist the thrill of dissing the entire architectural establishment on their home turf. 'We feel that approach is unsuitable in some of our locations, but in a completely new town the idea might appeal.'[19] His message was clear: the 'establishment' planners and architects could play with their little new towns if they liked, but entrepreneurial firms such as Arndale were getting on with the serious business of redeveloping the country's big city centres.

The first Arndale projects were simple, functional developments, such as the Headingley arcade in Leeds. Yet, as the company grew it began to go upmarket, specialising in elegant surroundings built to high standards – especially when compared to their cost-conscious out-of-town rivals, the hypermarkets, which began to spring up in the late sixties. When the *Guardian* visited Bolton they found that the Arndale, 'with its air-conditioned walkways, and wheelchair ramps, and predictably surprising fountains and budgerigars, is the hub of the trading area.'[20] Exotic wildlife came as standard, and pavements were carpeted. The centres were becoming social spaces as much as retail experience, and advances in the psychology of 'hidden persuaders' promised ever more subtle manipulation of shoppers' desires.

Initially, shopping centre designers tailored their schemes to appeal to women, on the assumption that they controlled household spending. They aimed to replicate the bustle of traditional shopping streets. 'For a housewife the natural and most insistent social centre of a modern town is the local shop, the pavement, the bus queue, or any place where she may run into a neighbour without pre-arrangement,' wrote the landscape architect Geoffrey Jellicoe in 1961.[21] Though less sanguine in tone, Wilfred Burns echoed this view, observing that 'to the hard-working housewife, shopping is not just a necessity: it is one of the few occasions she can mix with other people.'[22]

As they sought to increase footfall and spending, shopping centres attempted to attract men too, with the addition of that traditionally male-friendly space, the pub. Husbands 'can slip into the centre's pub for a quick beer when wives are in the dress shops' was the *Guardian*'s blokeish take.[23] By the late sixties Arnold and Sam had sold Arndale off to conglomerate Town and City, and returned to their earlier businesses as surveyors and property consultants. The new company swiftly overturned Chippindale's much vaunted preference for instinct over analysis. 'The company has undertaken some interesting research into shoppers' attitudes,' it was reported. 'Research has always been a Town and City strongpoint.'[24]

One of the accusations Arndale and the local authorities who had worked with them found hard to shake off was that amidst all this 'just-add-water' instant redevelopment, British high streets were losing their personality. But Robert Ogden, Bolton's planning officer, was 'not remotely disturbed by the old cry that "it's just like everywhere else", which he readily accepts it is', went a report in 1973. Instead, he stressed that the complex 'served only to complement the "real Bolton" around it'.[25]

Arndale and Ravenseft were keen on shopping centres, but they tended to avoid larger town centre redevelopment schemes, with their ring roads, bus stations and covered markets. Many councils, though, were dead set on just such integrated projects, and it was held against the developers that 'they picked up all the plums of urban renewal, leaving the local authorities to do the unremunerative chores.'[26]

In the late fifties at the Elephant and Castle – the great, tangled road junction forming the gateway to south London, and at the heart of a large working class community – just such a complex scheme was underway. The sheer scale of the development there – whether of the big roads with their roundabouts and underpasses, or of the massive multi-level flats, offices, college, cinema and shopping centre – was awe-inspiring. South London had seen nothing like it.

For several years I lived round the corner from the Elephant, and despite the promise (or threat) of numerous regeneration schemes, it remains to this day a monument to that postwar moment when the planners took control. The only visible change to most of these buildings since they were erected is owing to the ravages of pollution. I've seen many pictures of the area before the bombing, but it remains hard to reconcile the two Elephants: one a jumble of Victorian squalor and gentility, the other a towering modernist metropolis. From time immemorial a large, bawdy pub, the Elephant and Castle Hotel, had been the fulcrum, the thumb on the knot at the centre of a string of roads that fed five Thames bridges: Lambeth, Westminster, Blackfriars, London and Waterloo. The largest cinema in Europe, a great department store and many shops and drinking dens had faced onto the junction, which became known, not entirely ironically, as the Piccadilly Circus of south London. Yet by the thirties the towering hotel stood alone, isolated on a roundabout that had once been circled by horse and carriage, but as time went on was increasingly cut off from the rest of the buildings by speeding – or snarled up – motor cars.

The London County Council had failed time and again to solve the transport mess at the Elephant and Castle. The Edwardians' attempt to remove the pub from its island site had been scuppered by the Great War; a 1930 plan was thrown out for being too expensive; and a further proposal in 1937 was trounced by the Blitz, which devastated the entire area. After the war the district lay in ruins for many years. Visiting in 1949 for *Picture Post*, the writer A. L. Lloyd painted a vivid image of a place whose population had been almost halved since the bombing, from 172,000 to just 94,000. 'The backstreet bricks are sooted by the wash and drift railways smoke; and in the centre, in that inferno of trams, drays, trucks, lorries all debouch on to the doorstep of the Elephant and Castle public house … it is hard to escape the feeling of being in a metal prison.'[27] But it was the notorious slums of the area that affected him most strongly: 'Even the dead windows of the burnt-out rows are not so sad as the living windows of some streets that would be better gone.'[28]

Over a coffee, John Mulrenan and his brother Patrick, who'd grown up in an overcrowded Victorian terrace in the sixties, helped me bridge the two eras with their memories of the long period the Elephant lay in ruins. 'We used to spend most of our time as kids playing on the bombsites,' said John. 'I think we were told not to play on the bombsites, but the reality was there wasn't anywhere else. The bomb shelters were still around. The funny thing is that there was no conscious link in my mind as a kid between the words bombsite and bomb. It was just something that had a name.'

In the mid-fifties the London County Council approved a comprehensive development area covering a massive 40 acres. Their leader, Sir Isaac Hayward, made an inspiring speech when the CDA was launched: 'By imaginative and realistic planning and with goodwill and cooperation between the council and business and trading interests, the Elephant and Castle can, I am sure, become one of the main shopping and entertainment centres of south London.'[29] The scheme featured two large roundabouts to siphon off traffic into the many distributor roads. 'The committee are giving further consideration to the design of the subways around the larger roundabout,' announced an LCC press release, 'because they think it would be desirable for users to be able to pass from one section to another without ascending to a higher level.'[30] Only a decade earlier, Southwark Council had poured scorn on the notion of pedestrian underpasses for the Elephant: 'The first question is how to deal with pedestrians,' a planner had announced, 'and this council does not consider subways a satisfactory method of dealing with the problem.'[31] But subways won the day, with the planned new underpasses promised to be 'a complete departure from the drab and noisy subway atmosphere' with 'modern lamps ... and mosaic tiling on the walls and bright green granite chips on the walls of the ramps.'[32]

As the pedestrian underpasses were hollowed out beneath the ground, a dramatic silhouette of offices and shops rose into the sky. 'Not only will they make the Elephant and Castle an effective landmark in south London,' wrote another press officer in 1958 of the modern designs the LCC hoped to create, 'but with the combination of tall and horizontal elements, they are of the size and scale needed for the large areas of land created by the road improvement.'[33] Big name architects were at work to create this space-age landscape. The Hungarian emigré Ernő Goldfinger won the competition to design a new Odeon cinema and Alexander Fleming House, a suite of offices for the Ministry of Health. The

The shopping centre seen from the pedestrian underpasses at Elephant and Castle.

clash of cultures created by this mini-Whitehall was a godsend to journalists eager for a piece of topical wit in the class-obsessed era of Macmillan's toff government and the satire boom. 'More men from the Ministry with bowlers and white collars will rub shoulders with the "wide boys" of the Elephant and Castle next week,' wrote one trainee wag at the *South London Press*. 'A local layabout said, "Things ain't been the same since they started knocking the place about. Now we get all of these Civil Service geezers breathing down our necks. Still, if they come from Savile Row they must know that we ain't exactly scruffy".[34]

Yet another married team of architects, Paul Boissevain and Barbara Osmond, won the 1959 competition to design the shopping centre and office complex at the heart of the redevelopment. Like many of the pioneer modernists, Paul's background was as much product design as architecture. A Bauhaus-inspired table lamp he'd designed for his family's company, Merchant Adventurers, was exhibited at the Festival of Britain, and he had taught at the Architectural Association. Barbara had studied at the fashionable Regent Street Polytechnic, which had turned out many of the LCC's own architects. By the late fifties they'd had a run of high profile competition entries, winning some and just missing out on two – luckily for them, as it happened, for these would turn out to be poisoned chalices for the winners: the National Gallery extension and Sydney Opera House. The Elephant and Castle scheme was a chance to design something excitingly modern. 'The shopping centre is one of the few new building types created in our time,' wrote Boissevain.[35] And as they were to discover, new building types obeyed new rules.

Boissevain and Osmond's project was soon compared to such American malls as the award-winning Midtown Plaza in Rochester, New York: a huge civic project designed to breathe new life into the downtown area of the city. Boissevain had carried out research in the US and was keen to explain the merits of malls to a potentially bewildered British public. 'It is hoped that the comprehensive facilities of the shopping centre will help satisfy the varied needs of the housewife. She can shop with her children without worry, meet her friends at the cafés, purchase her daily, weekly or monthly needs all under one roof.'[36] The centre was to house supermarkets, department stores, banks, restaurants, a car park, a petrol station, two pubs and that most American of features, a 28-lane bowling alley. It was, as the promotional brochure explained, 'an entirely new approach to retailing, setting standards for the sixties that will revolutionise shopping concepts throughout Britain'.[37] Willets, the developers, were convinced that it would 'become the ideal place to break a journey and often the goal of the journey itself'. In fact, it would become – why not? – 'the most convenient and congenial place to meet one's friends in the whole of south London'.[38] The *Guardian* ran a feature in which they quoted the architects' hopes that it would 'combine Oxford Street's glamour with Petticoat Lane's versatility'.[39] Built on three floors, this mall had one ingenious trick to suit the British climate: a vast retractable glass roof. On fine days it would become an open-air shopping centre, bathed in sunlight, and in bad weather it would close itself off from the elements, allowing shoppers and shopkeepers to remain warm and dry. The local press loved the thought of this 'glass-topped sunshine roof that will slide back in summer' and the 'blend of Italian and American styling, the Italian influence providing the sweep and panache and the American the comfort'.[40]

Construction began in 1962. Danny Gill, the builder I'd met who'd worked on many of the big housing schemes in the area, reminded me of the feats of human endeavour it took to bring such projects to realisation, and what a dangerous place vast building sites such as the shopping centre had been in those pre-health-and-safety days. 'I have a couple of mates who worked on it,' he told me, 'that's how I know that three tower crane erectors died on the one day.' Nothing about building projects on this scale in the sixties was easy for the teams of labourers and skilled workers on site, forced to adjust rapidly to new ways of working, new materials and new designs.

It was also an eye-opener for the people who were watching their neighbourhood change around them. John Mulrenan was one of the locals watching the whole district redevelop on a colossal scale:

'I remember the Elephant and Castle shopping centre being
built because it was a huge, huge thing. I'm not sure there was
a lot of demolition that had to be done for the shopping centre
to be built, because it was just open bombsite land opposite
the Tabernacle. I remember us being terribly excited by the
concept of a huge shopping centre.'

'It was the biggest one in London at the time,' chipped in his brother
Patrick.

'Though it would be fair to say,' said John, putting his finger on
one of the questions that would haunt the centre throughout its life,
'we were never short of shops. Down the bottom of our road you
could get anything. There was a bakers, a grocers, a newsagent, a
pub, an egg shop, a dress shop, an electrical shop. You could get
anything you wanted.'

Every town wanted a shopping centre as a magnet to attract business
and increase their regional influence. In Birmingham, the new ring
road scheme was growing up next to the 'draughty and mucky' Bull
Ring market hall, a Victorian building hit by an air raid in 1940.[41]
As in the Elephant and Castle, a competition was launched in 1959
for designs to transform what was described as 'at times a wild and
romantic place'.[42] The council had a nightmarishly demanding wish
list: they wanted 140 shops, market stalls, a car park and office block,
a bus station, a ballroom and a link to a rebuilt New Street railway
station. This list of prerequisites was enough to scare off the likes of
shopping-centre specialists Arndale and Ravenseft, and in the event
the contract was won by construction giants Laing. 'The market will
be the most up-to-date in Britain and will be an added attraction
leading into an improved Bull Ring,' wrote Labour councillor Frank
Price proudly.[43]

The promotional brochure featured beautiful illustrations of the
centre's calm, liberating environment, alongside a myriad of stats: the
bus station would handle 18 million passengers a year; a whopping

350.000 square feet of retail space would be squeezed into a four-acre site; the largest Woolworths in Europe; 19 escalators able to cope with 128,000 people an hour. The centre was to be completely enclosed, so there would be an air conditioning system; and to encourage the pram-pushing mothers, a crèche would be provided. 'Music by Muzak is to be installed in all the public areas of the centre to create a warm, gay and welcoming atmosphere,' went the blurb. Claims for the dark magic of the cutting-edge piped music system were extravagant. 'Customers are relaxed and encouraged to linger, shopping is made a pleasure. Muzak is also designed for the benefit of staff, easing the strains brought on by fatigue and boredom, reducing errors and making service truly a pleasure.'[44] Laing described their futuristic project as 'a new concept in city centre shopping ... probably the most comprehensive multi-level trading centre in the world'.[45] Even the public service planners, like Colin Buchanan, were effusive: 'Great progress has been made with an inner ring road system and associated with it is the Bull Ring shopping centre. This last, which might be described as an in-town shopping centre (as opposed to the American pattern of out-of-town centres) provides traffic-free shopping conditions ... close to the centre of a major city, and on any count, this is a considerable achievement.'[46]

The journalist Geoffrey Moorhouse toured regional England in 1963 to research his impressionistic state-of-the-nation book *The Other England*. He described the vast changes being wrought in Birmingham in awe-struck prose, making comparisons with the work being carried out in Germany and Holland: 'Nowhere else in England is there more excitement in the air ... No other major city has yet identified its problems, tackled them and made more progress towards solving them than Birmingham.'[47] The great construction ventures, such as James Roberts' cylindrical Rotunda, the pedestrian underpasses that allowed 'women pushing prams' to cross busy roads without needlessly slowing the traffic, and the ring road were all enthusiastically endorsed. But nothing attracted more praise than the Bull Ring itself, at the centre of it all. 'The sky is cut with a great horizontal slab of concrete, embellished at one end with a fierce symbolic taurus in metal,' observed Moorhouse wonderingly. Over the past two decades the council had taken back into public ownership double the acreage of the city centre they'd owned in 1950, and by the early sixties they had embarked upon a huge number of public-private partnerships, with 59 major new building projects underway. There was even to be a collaboration between two of the most powerful British developers, Jack Cotton, and Charles Clore, and modernist superstar Walter Gropius, on a vast new scheme of shops and offices at Cannon Street. 'I'm very much impressed,' a cigar-smoking, bow-tied and grizzled Gropius told an ATV news interviewer in 1960 when asked about the plans Birmingham had in place, 'because it's an extremely rare case that a big city can collect sufficient land to do a wholesale new affair which gives a new face to the city. With the additional problem of a ring road, which is a deeply progressive idea to relieve the inner city today, it is really possible to make something really extraordinary out of Birmingham.' Sadly his own plans for the city came to nothing.

Yet given all the work that was being done, it was little wonder that Sir Frank Price, the chairman of the city's public works committee, was in no doubt that they were watching the construction of 'one of the finest city centres in Europe'.[48]

The hardened professionalism of shopping centre specialists such as Arndale contrasted with the overweening optimism of less experienced developers. Croydon, like many other towns, features the fruits of both approaches. On one side of the town centre was St George's Walk, a 2,000 square foot shopping arcade and 4,000 square foot office block scheme developed in the mid-sixties by a couple of local businessmen who bought the land from the church. Meanwhile, shopping centre experts Ravenseft bought the lease on an adjacent 12-acre plot of land, home to the Trinity School of John Whitgift. The school were happy to sell up their prestigious town-centre site and make a killing, relocating to the less expensive suburbs. The

Whitgift Centre, which opened in 1970, contained over double the square footage of shops and half as much office space again as its rival. St George's Walk buckled under the competition, becoming a desolate wind tunnel, while the vast sprawl of the Whitgift Centre kept pace with the changing fashions in retail design, becoming enclosed and reclad in the eighties to resemble a grand Victorian conservatory. On a recent trip through the semi-deserted arcade of St George's Walk, the strange echoing atmosphere of a dying mall, with its barren planters and stained hexagonal paving stones, was heightened by the grandiose pop nostalgia of Nik Kershaw as it boomed from the doorway of a pound shop. *Wouldn't it be good to be in your shoes*, he sang, *even if it was for just one day.*

The Whitgift Centre, 1971: Croydon's 'showpiece'.
© *Ian Steel*

In Portsmouth, the architect Rodney Gordon, working for Owen Luder, tore up the rulebook for shopping centre design. Following a failed entry in the Elephant and Castle competition, here he took the default luxury of Arndale and the cool efficiency of Ravenseft and re-imagined it as something altogether more spectacular. Alec Coleman Investments had bought a site away from the town centre, and Gordon designed something that more closely resembled an *avant-garde* sculpture than a building. The Tricorn Centre, initially known as the Casbah, opened in 1966. Its heavy geometric shell was cast in rough concrete. Gordon had chosen this as his medium because of the cost savings it afforded over other building materials, but soon realised that 'the shuttered concrete was not going to be up to the quality of the South Bank.' The odd geometries of his design were partly an attempt to hide the relative lack of skill and experience of the construction team. 'I learned that the more convoluted you made the shape,' he told historian John Gold, 'the less the inaccuracies of the pourer of the concrete are going to be noticed.'[49]

Unfortunately, despite the daring ingenuity of Gordon's design, a bad site chosen by an inexperienced developer failed to attract big names, and it ended up home to a rag-bag of small shops and struggled for decades to earn its keep. 'The first rule was that a new shopping project had to be built as an extension to an existing successful shopping street,' Rodney Gordon later wrote. 'Yet at Portsmouth we were given a site for a major shopping and multi-use scheme that was the shape of a huge rugby ball, bounded on one curved side by Charlotte Street, a very narrow secondary shopping alley containing market stalls, and on the other side by an impenetrable dual carriageway.' As the architect rather than planner or developer, Gordon just got down to work. 'My job was to design the scheme and not ask questions.'[50] Another project by the same team, this time in Gateshead, opened a year later. Trinity Square, made internationally famous in the ultra-violent crime film *Get Carter*, was a 15-storey giant with seven tiers of car parking. Rodney Gordon and the director Mike Hodges were friends, and Hodges always denied that the pair of effete, cynical architects featured in the film were based on Gordon and Luder, which seems fair enough given Gordon's description of Luder as 'an amiable bloke who spoke developer language in a cockney accent'.[51] Filmed a year after Trinity Square had opened, the 'architects' appeared in a memorable scene on the roof of the car park, in the empty shell of a restaurant – a unit designed by Gordon which remained unlet for the life of the building.

Just as the relaxation of hire purchase rules and the end of rationing had transformed shopping in the fifties, decimalisation, pushed through by the technocratic Heath government in 1971, saw the old, complex system of pounds, shillings and pence swept away by cool metric European efficiency. Yet the ongoing economic crises of the early seventies ushered in an age of bust rather than boom. By 1977 the *Guardian* were writing that the new Arndale in Wellingborough was 'likely to be one of the last shopping centres of its kind to be opened in Britain for a few years … Although this is lovely for the shoppers, it is increasingly difficult for developers to afford to build these days.'[52]

In March 1965 a tarpaulin printed with the legend 'Shops Now Open' in letters almost a storey in height flapped above the entrance to the Elephant and Castle Shopping Centre. In token acknowledgement of the 40-acre site's history, the Minister for Labour Ray Gunter unveiled a bronze statue of an elephant carrying a castle on its back, removed from the top of the old hotel. The smooth concrete façade of the centre, dashed with narrow 'arrow slit' windows, resembled the Festival Hall's temporary back wall that had so stirred the architects of 1951. Shoppers, drooling in consumerist anticipation, could climb a long walkway to the first floor to enter, or sneak in via the much-heralded underpasses below. Willetts had done well to attract some big retailers to the ground level – Woolworths, Burtons, Boots, Tesco and W. H. Smith were all present – but 36 of its 40 top floor shop units were empty. 'The Jeremiahs are being effectively silenced,' ran a typically bullish headline in the *South London Press*, a year after the centre had opened. In fact, a dangerously low 65 percent of the shops had been let.

After all the planning and reconstruction, the shopping centre found itself as stranded as the Elephant and Castle Hotel had been at the turn of the century. Budget restrictions imposed by the Ministry of Transport had reduced the promised spacious and elegant pedestrian subway system to a warren of poky tunnels less than nine feet wide. 'Have you, by any chance, been to the Elephant and Castle on foot?' asked *Concrete Quarterly*'s editor in 1970. 'It is not to be recommended. ... There is nothing except swirling traffic and a labyrinth of underground passages into which the poor pedestrian is forced.'[53]

Isolated by traffic: the Elephant and Castle Shopping Centre in 2013.

Sam Chippindale was fond of contrasting the dull, research-led approach of 'planners' with the instinctive knack of the real experts: 'We rely on experience. You've got to have a flair.'[54] In reality, Arndale planned meticulously and knew their market well, but plenty of less

experienced developers were rebuilding city centres and making a
hash of it. The success of the Elephant and Castle scheme had rested
on the flimsiest of premises: that the centre would draw people from
a wide catchment area, including affluent Westminster and Victoria
across the Thames. As planning nous goes, it reminds me of the
episode of *The Fall and Rise of Reginald Perrin* where our bored hero
defines two market research areas not through careful analysis, but
simply by plonking a waste paper bin and a handbag onto a map
without looking and drawing round them. So careless was he that
one of these areas turns out to be in the North Sea. The shopping
centre was built at the height of the supposed age of 'white heat',
an era that championed the scientific necessity of research. Yet it's
hard not to conclude that in establishing the need for the centre
at the Elephant and Castle, the LCC had pretty much given up
on rational decision making and pulled a Reggie. Windswept and
largely inaccessible, for all but the most determined it may as well
have been built out on the North Sea.

The Bull Ring's launch was equally shambolic. It had been postponed
by almost a year while reps from Laing desperately ran round
the head offices of various major chain stores offering them ever
cheaper leases, to the point where they were making a loss on many.
'What price a great big bubble of hot air?' asked Diana Rowntree,
reviewing the centre for the *Guardian*. While being full of praise
for the open-air market, 'the minute you enter the building on foot,'
she wrote, 'you lose all sense of direction.' And she was in no doubt
of the root of the problem. 'The emptiness – the sense of no place –
stems from a shiftiness of purpose. The architect is building shops
but he doesn't know for whom.'[55]

The eminent travel writer Jan Morris, who had spent her life
visiting the wonders of the world, from Mount Everest to ticker-
taped Manhattan, was less sniffy. 'There is the genuine brawn and
gusto of Birmingham's Bull Ring,' she wrote, praising the new
shopping centres as 'beautiful, exciting, useful'.[56] The council was

delighted to have replaced the old romantic but redundant central area with a more functional space, increasing the shopping space by 30 percent. Borough Engineer Neville Borg was convinced that if they hadn't, a silent majority would have judged the city 'on a lack of modernisation of retail shopping conditions', and taken their custom elsewhere.[57] But four years after praising the Bull Ring as a 'considerable achievement', Colin Buchanan echoed the opinions of many when he wrote that it had become 'a sordid, ugly, brutal place, where wind eddies muck and paper and cardboard into corners'.[58]

The Bull Ring Shopping Centre in the early 1970s:
'beautiful, exciting, useful'. © Co-op Historian

The sixties consumer boom was visible far from the new shopping centres. By 1963 there were 12 million vehicles on Britain's roads, 7 million of which were private cars. Buchanan, reporting for the government, announced that those figures were likely to double within a decade. By 2010, he predicted, there would be a staggering 40 million vehicles on the road, 30 million of them cars.[i] 'The problems of traffic are crowding in upon us with desperate urgency,' he wrote in his remarkably plain-spoken and somewhat frightening report.[59] The increase in traffic would have disturbing consequences for the nation unless action was taken.

In response, the government announced ever more massive increases in spending on urban roads, but some were sceptical as to what this could achieve. 'Makeshift schemes like the Elephant and Castle roundabouts and the Birmingham Ring Road continue to be pushed forward,' reported the *Observer* in 1960, 'although they are out of date before they have been built.'[60] The blunt instrument of a ring road or bypass could only ever hope to have a minor effect on the complex reality of drivers' journeys. Something more sophisticated was required – and that may not have needed roads at all.

New forms of transport such as monorail, hovercraft, helicopter, Rotodyne, and vertical take-off aircraft were being championed, with the *Observer* speculating that 'if we were bold enough, we might knock down great wedges of our sprawling industrial cities,' which it considered to be dead in parts and in need of severe pruning, and instead 'concentrate new development along fast lines of communication connecting one centre to another.'[61] This was almost a return to the ideas of suburban ribbon development from the twenties, although this time around monorail stops rather than main roads. Earnest town planning journals were full of essays such as J. W. Dark's 1963 *Why not the monorail?*, and there were rumours that a futuristic new town in Buckinghamshire, to be called Milton Keynes, might become the British standard-bearer for such a project. 'In the city centre,' wrote Leicester's planning consultant W. Konrad Smigielski, 'the priority should be given to pedestrians and full use be made of modern technology capable of

---

i RAC figures released in 2011 showed how grimly realistic they were being 50 years ago, as the 2010 number was 34 million vehicles in total, of which 28.4 million were cars.

providing more efficient means than motor cars of moving people in the concentrated areas.'[62] His recommendations were for a network of travelators, high pedestrian walkways and a monorail.

Air travel was also very much on the agenda. Indeed, most of the original plans for postwar redevelopments I looked through at some stage had a heliport mooted for a quiet corner. Even Buchanan was moved to speculate that 'perhaps some kind of individual jet-propulsion unit will eventually be developed' though, practical as ever, he was one of the first to think through the issues around jet packs: 'The problems of weather, navigation, air space and traffic control appear so formidable that it may be questioned whether such a device would ever be practical for mass use.'[63] The Smithsons, naturally, were less cautious, writing in 1970 that 'we may find that a revolutionised railway system, or the use of helicopters for local high speed passenger services, will make our proposed 120 foot wide "ring roads" ridiculous.'[64]

So what would Britain look like by the impossibly distant year 2000? Sixties planners did their best to imagine. One of the most ambitious speculative schemes was the superhuman shopping megastructure named High Market. It had been sponsored by the glass manufacturers Pilkington Brothers, and drawn up by yet another husband and wife team, Gordon and Eleanor Michell (who had advised Colin Buchanan while he was writing *Traffic in Towns*). The Michells imagined an artificial ridge stretching between two hills in the countryside near Dudley in the Midlands, creating what was effectively a dam of shops. 'It would be approached by helicopter or high-speed monorail, as well as by high-speed roads,' wrote Wilfred Burns. A glazed slab, 2,000 feet long and 400 feet wide, would join the two hills, under which would be car parks, a bus garage, and mechanised services such as parcel pick-ups, while above would stand the more 'intimate' shopping courts – all one million square feet of them. It would even come equipped with a revolving periscope, so that images from the surrounding countryside could be flashed up on a large screen inside. 'It is the kind of scheme which many will dismiss as a pipe-dream,' Wilfred concluded, not unreasonably.[65]

Reasonable or otherwise, Pilkington Brothers had funded a lot of speculative research and development for their cutting-edge Glass Age Development Committee. The landscape architect Geoffrey Jellicoe went so far as to design an entirely new template for towns for the committee, which he called Motopia. This project combined ideas from the age of John Nash ('when landscape architects were doing everything in their power to reduce by illusion all dreary matters such as drives and approach roads from their conception of the landscape') with those of Le Corbusier.[66] The resulting book resembled less a sober reflection on the state of town planning and more a megalomaniac's Pinterest page. Here was a vast city in a park: five-storey terraces built in a continuous grid, with green space in the big squares within, and roads built on the roofs of the terraces. 'The ideal town,' wrote Jellicoe, 'would seem to be one in which the traffic circulation were piped like drainage and water; out of sight and out of mind, to go as fast as it likes, to smell as it wants, and to make noises.'[67] The designs and models he produced looked like a cross between postwar Plymouth's town centre and *Tron*. What was the best thing about it? 'It can be extended indefinitely,' enthused Jellicoe.[68]

The countryside may not have become home to High Market-style megastructures, but American-style out-of-town malls and European-style hypermarkets did begin to appear. Sadly lacking space-age transport infrastructure, these malls would instead continue to rely heavily on the car. The early sixties planners would no doubt be shocked that their futuristic plans for city centres never came to pass, and by the ongoing ad hoc sprawl of car-dependent trading estates. A few years ago I visited New York and explored Rochester's huge Midtown Plaza, the inspiration for the Elephant and Castle's shopping centre. This jauntily designed trinket box of a scheme was eerily deserted. Almost all the shops had closed and it was scheduled for demolition, the optimistic early sixties vision of urban renewal overtaken by out-of-town developments and the long arm of the internet.

On 7 April 1971, the Queen opened Birmingham's completed inner ring road, an idea that had been gestating since 1917. The local dignitaries who gathered that spring day to see their ambitious project given the royal blessing, less than a decade after Buchanan's *Traffic in Towns* was published, could not have known that, apart from the odd project, the age of the grand urban road scheme was over. They would have been shocked that of the Bull Ring, the Elephant and Castle, Trinity Square and Tricorn shopping centres, all but one would be demolished within 40 years, with only a lack of money keeping the final one standing. Unlike the Bull Ring, glitzily redeveloped in 2003, south London's white elephant clings on to its sixties roots. Walkways, escalators, floor tiles and in some cases shop frontages, hark back to its opening day in 1965. Yet apart from the odd original tenant, such as Boots, the centre now is occupied by a vast array of more colourful local shops than had ever been envisaged by the LCC. There are small supermarkets dotted about the floors selling produce from around the world, appealing to Walworth's diverse population. A vibrant street market has sprung up between the underpasses and the ground floor entrance. For a long time it had the air of a large house with one elderly tenant, where the décor is dingy, most rooms have been abandoned for years and everything could do with a good scrub and a lick of paint. Yet these days it's coming back to life, in an unplanned, scruffy, organic way. Cheap rents have let in entrepreneurial businesses, and visited on a weekday the place is buzzing, full of chatty shoppers and canny traders. It may be eccentric and ramshackle but it has also become a friendly place. It certainly has character. But then, despite the efforts of planners and architects to start anew and bring on the space age, both the Elephant and the Bull Ring have never been short of that.

4. 'A Natural Evolution of Living Conditions'
NEWCASTLE-UPON-TYNE AND SYSTEM BUILDING (1959-69)

The advance party for the swinging sixties arrived in Britain in 1956. It came from America, with media reports of cinemas being ripped up by frustrated teenagers jiving their way through the film *Rock Around the Clock*, and Elvis Presley corrupting the nation's youth with his filthy gyrations to 'Heartbreak Hotel'. The frustrations of a young postwar generation were captured by John Osborne in his play *Look Back in Anger*, which premiered at the Royal Court in London; and the frustrations of an ageing postwar Empire were played out for all to see in Britain's disastrous intervention that triggered the Suez crisis.

Then the following year the Soviet Union's 'man-made moon', the Sputnik, was sent into orbit and the space age began in earnest, infiltrating everything from B-movies to newsreels. Closer to earth, the new Conservative prime minister Harold Macmillan articulated the results of a consumer boom he'd inherited with the deathless remark that 'most of our people have never had it so good.'

But while the rockers and rollers, the beatniks and angry young men, communists and consumer boomers seemed to be infusing the late fifties with colour, energy and dynamism, progressives in the fields of planning and architecture were becoming increasingly frustrated by the slow pace of material change. It wasn't just that a modernist future of the sort that had been advocated in the thirties had yet to appear, but rather that more basic considerations – the rebuilding of Blitzed cites and the clearing of bomb sites and slums – were largely still on the drawing board. More was needed

– more political will, more technical innovation and more visionary chutzpah.

It was from this stagnant world of local government prevarication that a new generation of politicians began to emerge, determined to make good their campaign-trail promises of slum clearance and a better future for all. One such was a 43-year-old painting-and-decorating contractor, who, following local council elections in 1958, was given responsibility for the housing needs of one of the great cities of the north of England. Not only would he inject exactly the kind of dynamic energy needed to reinvigorate the postwar crusade for decent homes for all, but he would go on to become a national symbol of both the triumphs and the excesses of the era. Round-faced, twinkly-eyed and always ready with an earthy quip from his famously runaway mouth, T. Dan Smith was a charismatic and outspoken politician, the Brian Clough of local government. The son of a miner, his rise through the Newcastle Labour party to the position of Chairman of the Housing Committee, and later Leader of the Council, was achieved through sheer force of personality.

Right from the off Dan Smith dismissed not only the work of the opposition but of his own party, presenting himself as an entirely new breed of politician. 'I don't feel that Newcastle City Council has much to be proud of,' he said in his maiden speech as a councillor in 1950, 'it is a hundred years since it did anything, and I mean to change that.'[1] No timid follower of the consensus, this was a man later described by a colleague as 'a politician with a vision of the sort of city he wanted'[2] – and a man who would do his utmost to realise it. This vision would turn out to be so compelling that over the next decade, Smith would pull the entire council with him in his attempts to transform Newcastle.

In *Peril in the City*, Dan Smith set out how he would rebuild a metropolis fit for the people who lived there. He had rapidly concluded that high density urban rebuilding was the only possible way they could reach their target of 2,000 new homes a year. As in Glasgow, they would have to build upwards. 'The erection of tower blocks is a natural evolution of living conditions,' he said in 1958 with characteristic boldness, simultaneously painting the proposed high-rise structures as a great leap forward in human development, and a simple certainty.[3]

The Scotswood Road, whose long, straight course runs parallel to the Tyne from the city centre out to Blaydon, would be the testing ground for Smith's vision. The *Guardian* reported in 1962 that 'the desolation of the Scotswood Road and the area behind it matches the worst that Liverpool, Birmingham, Manchester or Leeds can show in the way of slums'[4] and Dan Smith recalled visiting a house there where rats swarmed continually up from the broken drains and over the kitchen table. Clearly change was urgently needed.

I met two former residents of the area, Ken and Margaret Denholm, to learn more about the changes T. Dan Smith had brought to Newcastle. Four generations of Margaret's family have lived at Cruddas Park, one of the estates that replaced the slums on Scotswood Road ('It was Mam and Dad, and then us, then our Leslie and now his stepson'). A sprightly and talkative elderly couple, they frequently finished, repeated or contradicted each other's anecdotes. They had both dressed up for the occasion: Margaret was immaculate with her coiffed silver hair and dainty court shoes; Ken affably stylish in a light, summer jacket. As we trudged around the sodden and muddy estate, I suspected they regretted not having opted for boots and cagoules.

'This was all houses,' said Margaret, with a sweeping gesture. We had left their car for a walk around the derelict hulks of Cruddas Park, the sixties tower blocks rising from a landscape of lumpy lawns and car parks. Once rows of tightly packed terraced houses had led down the hill to the main road, now a busy dual carriageway. But it hadn't just been houses: 'There was a pub on every corner. There was *hundreds* of pubs right the way along, and of course all *that* side' – Margaret gestured towards the industrial estate turning its back on us across the road – 'was Armstrong's factory, and they made munitions and things.' In fact, the estate was named after the director of the Vickers Armstrong armaments works, George Cruddas. It must have seemed an unpromising place to start an exciting housing revolution.

'Rough area,' confirmed Ken.

'Notorious,' agreed Margaret. 'Like the Gorbals in Glasgow.'

Yet it was here in 1959, with the progressive demolition of the slums of Scotswood Road, that Dan Smith's vision began to be realised, with the construction of Haughton Court and King's Meadows, the first two modest 12-storey point blocks built by the Bovis subsidiary Leslie and Co. Along with the buildings rose an enduring cult of personality. One LCC architect who had moved north at this time commented that 'the most prominent councillors were just blustering, coarse, heavy men who were extremely ambitious – 60 percent proof personal ambition, to get knighthoods or hold the Mayor's mace!'[5] Dan Smith was ambitious too, but on a much grander scale than mere mayoralty. And he had the talent to match. Even his political rivals were in awe of his abilities, and it was generally held that 'he stood head and shoulders above the rest of the Labour group.'[6]

Soon Dan Smith had become a key player in Harold Wilson's great national plan, as chairman of the Northern Economic Planning Council. Over the years his renown steadily grew. By 1965 the *Observer* magazine was profiling him in the most gushing terms: 'It was his clearing of Scotswood, the decaying slum jungle at the west end of the city, that won him the name of "Mr Newcastle". One of the swiftest and most imaginative rehousing schemes in the country, it brought Dan Smith the leadership of the council itself.'[7] It had certainly been swift, but in fact there was nothing particularly imaginative about the housing scheme at Cruddas Park. The point blocks were exactly the sort of thing the 'soft' communist faction of the London County Council Architects' Department had long approved of, and had recently completed in the internationally famous Alton East development on the edge of Richmond Park.

After the first two 12-storey blocks, Dan Smith had promptly ordered a further eight, this time built by Laing and Wimpey.

These would be three storeys higher than the originals, with electric rather than gas heating, and under-floor heating in the lounge. 'We had to use multi-storey blocks that had been on the stocks for years and had not been built,' said Smith, 'but we were able to create around them the concept of open space.'[8] It was with these additional eight blocks that Dan Smith's plan for Cruddas Park began to diverge wildly from the LCC's Alton East estate. There were no plans for any modern low-rise housing to break up these high blocks, no effort here to create a 'mixed development'. Towers would have to do all the job of rehousing. Low-rise blocks and houses were being built around the estate and further along the Scotswood Road, but Cruddas Park itself was to be entirely a landscape of giants.

Ken and Margaret Denholm were there on the day the first of the 15-storey Cruddas Park blocks, The Willows, was officially opened.

'This was mother's house,' explained Margaret, as we trudged around to the front of the abandoned tower in search of her parents' old home. 'This was the first block which was occupied. Her and me dad were the first to move into the whole estate.' Margaret's father had been the caretaker.

'9 June 1962,' said Ken.

Five of the Cruddas Park blocks. © Jim Pickett

'Hundredth year anniversary of the Blaydon Races,' remembered Margaret. 'Her house was here.' She pointed to the boarded-up windows on the ground-floor corner of one of the towers, 'and this over here' – she gestured to where a number of other towers to the east of us now stood – 'was just big mounds of soil. There was nothing done with it. And then right in the middle, about where them seats are, was this monstrosity of a sculpture thing, you know.' (This 'monstrosity' was described by its creator Kenneth Ford as a 'powerful and satisfying image, transcending our frailties',[9], though a local art critic remarked on its unveiling: 'One hesitates to imagine what the inhabitants of the flats will think of it.'[10]) 'You couldn't make head nor tail of it, it was a modern thing, you know,' said Margaret.

Ken stepped in to clarify: 'It had a hole in the middle and it was the rebirth of Scotswood Road.'

'And it was Hugh Gaitskell that unveiled it and that opened the estate, and he even had a cup of tea at me mam's, as it was the only house occupied. And then they came out and stood just outside here and watched the parade go along Scotswood Road to Blaydon. And there was the Lord Mayor and everybody were all decked up in their garb of a hundred years ago, you know, on coaches and things, it was really good. And we had a bird's eye view, you know!'

The leader of the Labour party had been similarly impressed with this mixture of pageantry and progress, a classic Dan Smith PR coup. 'How Hugh Gaitskell enjoyed that day,' recalled the wily Newcastle councillor in his memoir. 'But the four-year housing slog which preceded this event was a trying period.'[11] Gaitskell was no stranger to launching major modern housing schemes – two years previously he'd been in Sheffield to declare the Park Hill flats open.

There were 980 flats in all when Cruddas Park was finished, with the 15-storey blocks given sylvan names suitable for the imagined 'city in the park' that was being built here: The Poplars, The Willows, The Beeches, The Hawthorns, The Larches, The Sycamores, The Pines and The Cedars. The towers follow a rather basic design, a mixture of concrete frame, red-brick walls and prefabricated steel frames holding what were, by the time I saw them, tangerine-coloured infill panels beneath generous windows. 'They were well-fitted, good flats,' said Dan Smith. 'They were a credit to their designers, and they were low in cost.'[12] The panels were now corroded, each one warped and stained, some bleached to pale yellow, some to lurid pink. Many of the lower flats had been boarded up, though the higher ones still displayed some faded relics of former inhabitants: ragged curtains, skewed blinds or sheets of yellowing newspaper at the windows.

Despite their shabby and slightly flimsy appearance, there was something plain and handsome about these towers, their simple forms and unfussy silhouettes a mild expression of their Swedish heritage. As in Park Hill, the sloping site gave the residents spectacular views over the city, the hill itself injecting a dose of rugged character to the estate. Clearing the terraces had allowed the landscape to show through. This was what Dan Smith meant by his 'concept of open space'. The landscape was supposed to be the 'hero' element of the estate, given the simplistic nature of the blocks themselves, yet 'park' was a generous term for the terrain on which the flats are situated. Once a free-flowing space between blocks, the area has long since been fenced off into a series of small bland hollows and uneven lawns where no ball games were allowed, with scrawny trees scattered in the voids between towers. This was no lushly planted garden city landscape. Even the sculpture had long-since vanished. And there had never never been enough parking spaces, with bays for five or six cars per block at the most. After all, this was an estate built not for the independent motorist but for bus users, for members of a socialist community bursting with the 'all in this together' spirit of the welfare state age.

'The people that lived here, the people that moved in were the people who originally lived here in the terraced houses,' explained Margaret. 'It was like a community, you know, and they moved out of the houses and into the flats and everyone knew everybody.'

Margaret and Ken were so taken with her parents' flat that in 1963 Ken applied to become caretaker in one of the original two 12-storey blocks, Haughton Court. After being chosen by a panel including T. Dan Smith himself (a fact that, as we talked, came as a surprise to Margaret), the all-consuming task he'd signed up for became quickly apparent.

'The second night we were in there was a party on the third floor I think it was, a lad's birthday party,' said Ken. 'We were in bed, and the noise from the party, oh! Now, I thought, *I'm the caretaker, you're disturbing the other tenants you know, the noise.* And she says, "You'd better go and see." So I had pyjamas on, I put my dressing gown on and up the stairs I went to the house with the party, knocked on the door. A lad comes to the door, and I says, "Could you keep the noise down, you might be disturbing the other tenants."' Ken made a face. '"Nah, we've asked the other tenants, he says, and they're all okay about it." He says, "Come on in anyway."'

'I didn't know whether they'd beaten him up or *what* happened to him,' said Margaret, 'and he was having a drink!' Ken still enjoyed the outrage in her voice 48 years on. As we talked, Margaret began to act more and more as his spokesperson. 'He got on with all the tenants. They used to knock on the door, if they'd locked theirselves out, could he help them get in? And of course you had to keep all the ground floor clean. And the lifts. There was a lift at either end. At nighttime you'd go to bed, ten, half past ten, and then you'd get woken up when they'd come home from the pubs, because they were drunk and they wanted to talk, or they'd locked theirselves out or something like that.'

'It finished me, didn't it?' said Ken.

''Cos he was on call 24 hours! Being a tenant was fine, but being a caretaker, well, you had a lot of tenants, and there's was always somebody wanting something doing, you know.' Margaret stopped and pointed at one of the ground floor flats in Haughton Court, its windows now hidden behind rusting metal grilles. 'That far corner there, that was ours.' It must have been strange for them to be looking at their old home over 40 years later, now so derelict and defunct. They seemed remarkably matter-of-fact about it all.

'The problem with that one,' said Ken, 'is, they're near the lift. Every time they went up they had to come down again automatically.'

'The door opened and shut, opened and shut.'

'Lying in bed you'd hear the lift coming down and then the doors, opening and shutting. You were just lying in bed, couldn't get to sleep.'

It's hard for us now to imagine the shock of moving to a flat high up in one of these brand new building types for those who had only ever known life in small terraced houses. As in the Gorbals, one group found high-rise life particularly challenging. In 1972 the *Newcastle Evening Chronicle* reported on the plight of young housewives trying to bring up small children on the estate. Shirley Meehan, mother of three children under six, lived on the top floor of one of the blocks: 'The flats are pleasant, and the view, if you avoid looking at the riverbanks, is beautiful. But there is nothing for the children.' Fellow resident Florence Douglas, living on the eleventh floor with two young children, also found the set-up far from ideal: 'I would prefer some kind of play centre for them. They cannot run around the corridors because they make too much noise.'[13] Along with their other duties, caretakers like Ken did their best to keep an eye out on behalf of these mothers ('the kids, if they were playing downstairs, they weren't supposed to be in the lifts by themselves. So they were forever ringing the doorbell, *can you take us up home?*') but negotiating rules in experimental dwellings was a difficult business.

Some local authorities, most notably the LCC, employed sociologists to report on the effect of their work and the lives of those housed in the new projects, but for most councils the focus was on quantity rather than quality: they needed to lift families out of squalor, and fast. They simply didn't have the time, the resources or the foresight to evaluate the effect of this massive shift in domestic life on residents. Emphasis was placed firmly on the delivery of units. Physical needs were catered for, and the psychological effects were assumed to be positive.

Yet despite the progress made at places like Cruddas Park, the drive to eradicate the slums of Newcastle was far from over. 'One in 12 homes unfit on Tyneside,'[14] was the headline in the local paper when in 1969 a survey by the Ministry of Housing and Local Government pinpointed that 69,000 homes on Tyneside still had no inside toilet, 45,000 no fixed bath and 71,000 no washbasin. Remarkably, these results were seen as a triumph, as they were significantly better than those of many local authorities. Dan Smith's crusade seemed to be paying off, and commentators were keen to give him full credit: 'Scotswood Road? Barren, broken Scotswood Road? A wave of Smith's wand and the long, black festering scar was gone,' reported *Northern Life*.[15] 1969 was also the year that the 10 brightly panelled point blocks, where Margaret's father was still caretaker, were joined by the prosaically titled Cruddas Park House, a slim and tough-looking 23-storey concrete slab that sat on top of the estate's much-needed new parade of shops, library and rent office. After her husband died, Margaret's mother remarried and moved into this new building, onto the thirteenth floor.

At 23 storeys, Cruddas Park House towers over the rest of the estate. © Jim Pickett

'She married a Chelsea Pensioner,' Margaret said, somewhat unexpectedly. They were left in no doubt of this because he dressed up in his uniform to meet the family. I didn't ask how he ended up there. 'She liked living here, she loved it, didn't she, Ken?' Ken duly nodded. Margaret then revealed a further connection to Cruddas Park House: 'My brother lives on the top floor.' I think I could have guessed his verdict: 'He loves it.' It wasn't just Margaret's family who'd enjoyed living here. Ann Malding, one of the original nineteenth-floor residents of Cruddas Park House, was interviewed in 1977 about her thoughts on the flat. When not chasing pigeons from her balcony it was the neighbourliness that she most enjoyed:

'We all know each other and everyone is willing to give a helping hand if they are in difficulties. I couldn't wish for better. There aren't many children in the block so it's nice and quiet. … I always wanted a home that was centrally heated and when the council offered me this flat I was really thrilled.'[16]

'You can get a good look over Newcastle from up there,' said Ken approvingly as we peered through the drizzle at the rough concrete panels. This from a man who used to enjoy climbing about on the roof of Haughton Court 13 storeys up to repair the lift, or hanging from the outside of the building to clean the curtain of glass that formed the stairwell windows.

Yet there was one member of Margaret's family who didn't enjoy tower block life at all: her father, caretaker of The Willows, was afraid of heights. It was a good job that Ken was on hand to crawl out of those fifteenth-floor windows with his bucket and squeegee. 'I used to clamber over the rail, hook my belt onto that rail and then come out and do the ones I could reach,' he remembered cheerfully, 'and then move on to the next floor and work my way down.' It may not have suited everyone, but some people were perfectly adapted for high-rise living.

Throughout the fifties and sixties, in a benign version of the Cold War arms race, the various opposing political and architectural factions continually boasted of their ideological supremacy, manufacturing prowess and technological superiority. As Labour and the Tories announced ever-greater targets for housing completions per year, the country entered an era that might be termed mutually assured construction.

In 1962, following the collapse of SuperMac's late fifties 'economic miracle', Keith Joseph, chairman of construction titans Bovis, was promoted to Minister for Housing and Local Government in Harold Macmillan's 'Night of the Long Knives' reshuffle. The new minister lost no time in pledging to build 400,000 council houses a year – 100,000 more than Macmillan himself had promised in 1951. As Joseph knew, something dramatic would have to be done to speed up the process of house building in order to make good on this promise. That something would be system building, a method that, in the words of *Concrete Quarterly*, had been 'well tried, and proved, in France, in Scandinavia, and in other countries'.[17]

As with the programmes pioneered by the Temporary Housing Act, and the Hills and CLASP systems for building schools, the new housing drive would depend upon the manufacture of large prefabricated components. These would not only speed up the construction of everything from bungalows to tower blocks, but would also, it was envisaged, cut the cost of building high flats. Many of the systems used in Britain were, as noted by *Concrete Quarterly*, either French or Scandinavian in origin: Camus, Sectra and Tracoba from France, and Skarne, Jespersen and Larsen Nielsen from Sweden and Denmark. They were rapidly adopted by building firms such as John Laing, Crudens and Taylor Woodrow-Anglian. The advantage of these systems over fifties' building methods was that, rather than the builders having to invent large besoke concrete components on site, as they had with Park Hill, contractors could build factories where entire walls or floors could be built for a number of different buildings and then shipped out to construction sites around the country. It was estimated that 2,000 'units' – or individual homes – would have to be produced to make any one system economically viable, and by the mid-sixties it looked likely that the government would approve 50 different systems for local councils to use in their housing drive. 'Nobody can doubt the absolute necessity for getting much of our building work off the site and into the factory' trumpeted a *Concrete Quarterly* editorial in 1965. 'Speed, economy, decent working conditions, precision building, modular coordination – these are only some of the reasons why precast concrete has a splendid future in front of it.'[18]

By 1964 a new regional drive, supported by central government, was underway to clear slums and build new homes. Keith Joseph was confident it was going to do the trick: 'We now have offices in Cardiff, Manchester and Newcastle to help local authorities accelerate their clearance programme. This means stepping up house production both by rationalisation of traditional building methods and by making use of industrial systems.'[19] But Joseph was unable to see through this vision: the new Conservative leader Alec Douglas-Home's beleaguered government limped to election defeat in 1964 off the back of that quintessential sixties sex scandal, the Profumo affair, and Labour found themselves in government for the first time since the dismantling of the Festival of Britain.

Richard Crossman was Joseph's replacement in the new technocratic government, and under him the system building drive continued apace. 'What is happening now is the beginning of major changes in the whole process of building and commissioning buildings, which will accelerate now through to the end of the century,' claimed A. W. Cleeve Barr, chief architect of Crossman's newly created National Building Agency. 'In a decade or so there will be far fewer men than at present working on building sites, and they will be producing a much greater volume of building, in very much shorter construction periods … In housing the better systems are 30 to 40 percent more productive in terms of man-hours per house than the better traditional builders, and these are twice as productive as the average house builder'.[20]

This would have been all well and good if local authorities had banded together as they had with the CLASP system for schools, so that components could be standardised and manufactured, and designs approved en masse. But despite the urging of Dame Evelyn Sharp at the Ministry of Housing and Local Government for councils to imitate the school programme, local authorities continued to insist on bespoke designs for their houses and flats, so that true standardisation across local authorities was never achieved by any of the major players. George Bowie, Crudens' first company architect, expressed the firm's frustrations with local councils:

> 'There never was a standard block! No authority ever came and looked at anything we did and said, "Can we have three of those?" There were always ifs and buts!' ... '"We do like it, but we'd like the following things, only tiny wee things, like a slightly bigger kitchen and different windows, Mr Bowie – and can we have a clothes drying area inside the block, and a play area on the ground floor?" – and so on and so on!'[21]

Despite the failure of local authorities to embrace the full advantages of prefabrication (or, put another way, their steadfastness in insisting on regional variation) the competition for the lucrative new contracts inspired a band of enterprising smaller companies to design their own systems. Kenneth Campbell, the principal housing officer of the LCC was unimpressed: 'Why, to be extremely rude, are so many firms now leaping on the bandwagon which they have watched pass them for some considerable time?'[22] The answer, of course, was money. With politicians and professional bodies advocating the adoption of building systems, it was clear that this was where growth was going to come from. 'A dynamic new local industry can be developed in the north-east,' announced Dan Smith in 1961, 'combining research into component design and production, factory component and frame production.'[23]

I met up with John Matthews, former chief buyer for building contractors Stanley Miller, in the café of Newcastle's gleaming new Central Library, to find out more about the systems building rush. John brought with him some terrific photos and documents going back to the early part of the twentieth century, which he had rescued from the receivers when the company went bust in 1991. A gentle bear of a man, John was full of boyish enthusiasm for the history of the company he once worked for. In the prewar period, Stanley Miller had overseen large civic building projects, such as Newcastle's art deco Paramount Cinema. By the early sixties they had begun constructing council flats using Britain's most widespread building system, Bison wall frame units, manufactured by the seductively named Concrete Ltd. But they were keen to free themselves from reliance on the Bison system. John Matthews described the company at that time:

'Very forward looking ... everybody knew that the Labour government at that time was trying to increase the amount of social housing – the likes of Harold Wilson were going around flying the red flag if you like. They did some research and they came up with MWM.' Miller, Wise and Mouchel, or MWM, was a system they developed with Douglass Wise and Partners (architects) and Mouchel and Partners (structural engineers) to capitalise on the demand for this new way of building.

It was at this point that John enthusiastically embarked upon an attempt to explain to me how MWM tower blocks were built. 'You have what's called a table,' he said, 'which forms your floor and the roof of each pod, if you like. Now the crane is adapted to lift the table into here,' he pointed to an old black and white photo of a Stanley Miller high-rise under construction, where workmen were toiling at the base as a tower crane hauled another slab into place above them, 'and the table is on jacks. The reinforcement is poured in.' The table itself was pre-greased with release oil, 'so the concrete doesn't stick'.

'It sounds like the construction of one of those very elaborate cakes on *The Great British Bake Off*,' I remarked.

'*Yes!*' agreed John rather to my surprise. 'The concrete had to be ready mixed and then taken up by tower crane to pour into the moulds. And then that would be struck, the jacks would be lowered – just tapped slightly – and then the crane would come in and lift the table out, leaving the floor cast. Obviously the verticals are done in a similar manner. And you literally go up like that.' He made it all sound very easy. I looked back at the photo: the builders looked so small, apparently fearless as they crawled all over the huge tower they were constructing. 'You'd be topping out and finishing out at the bottom. Very, very quick: that's why it became so cheap to do, because as soon as you put a few storeys up you were putting the windows, the panels on the bottom, and you were in the flats doing the second fix. So you could be halfway up the building with the flats almost ready to occupy when the rest was being built, cos it was all watertight. It's all good stuff!'

John beamed at me, proud of Stanley Miller's achievement – and with good reason. For this relatively small firm to have created such a successful system was an impressive feat: both technically and financially audacious. Other contractors produced specialised units for the likes of Stanley Miller, ready to be slotted into their blocks. John particularly remembers the company who used to deliver entire staircases for their buildings: 'General Concrete Products, who used to be in Gateshead – we spent millions with them. They came with a stairflight, a landing, with little anchor rings cast in for the crane.' This was more Duplo than Lego: a world where people could deliver huge precast chunks of a building on a lorry ready to be clicked into place.

Stanley Miller even turned their attention to developing their own finishes for the tower blocks they erected. One promotional document John showed me stated that for one tower block 'the gable modelling was designed by a sculptor after careful study of weather pattern-staining.' The accompanying photo showed a sheer rough concrete wall at the end of a slab block, its surface undulating like a sand dune rippled by a passing snake. It was not only out in the field that Stanley Miller embraced innovation. Back in 1959 an editorial for *Concrete Quarterly* had painted what at the time might have seemed a fanciful portrait of the engineers' office of the future: 'In recent years the phrase "electronic brain" or, more accurately, "electronic digital computer", has been increasingly used in scientific circles. ... Within the past year or 18 months civil and structural engineers have become interested in the possibilities of these machines in their own work.'[24] John vividly remembered the first computer system he saw:

> 'Stanley Miller were very innovative and brought in Honeywell to give them a computer system, a costing system, which was quite unheard of in construction in those days. This was 1969-1970. The computer room was the size of this café, it was *huge*, a bit like *Joe 90*, with the disks going round, you know? The invoice came in and then a punching slip had to be created. That would be sent to punch card operators – we had three of those – who would then transfer that information from the form into the digital format on a card which would then be put into the computer.'

It was like the paperless office in reverse, the computer not just generating paper but ingesting it too. I was reminded of the punch-cards Alan Turing's crypto-analysts were using for their proto-computers at Bletchley Park in their efforts to decode Enigma over two decades earlier.

Not all of Stanley Miller's experimental systems worked smoothly. The timber-framed windows were a weakness on the MWM blocks. 'A window on a two-storey house is subject to wind-driven rain at a fairly low level,' John explained. 'Stick the same window 28 storeys up and the same window doesn't perform very well at all. And it's not the window itself, it's the seals. So they had to experiment with lots of different seals. There was a period of going back to refit seals into windows which had leaked.' One particular memory, of his sister-in-law's family, turned John a little sheepish. 'When her father died they moved her mother to Harlow Green, Allerdine, which was another Stanley Miller development, and every time I saw her she would complain: "Can't you have another word with the people at your place, 'cos it pours through the window?"' He was actually blushing at this point. 'But they also had problems with the panels below the window, which tended to be an aggregate panel or a glass panel or whatever, again, with the mastic that was used. Again you're talking about cutting edge technology.'

Sometimes the innovations could have unforeseen tragic consequences. John recalled a sad story related to him by a former colleague, John Gunning.

> 'John was actually standing on one of the floor panels, the tables – and we don't know whether there were some chocks underneath the front edge, or whether someone had lowered the little jacks. But anyway, there's two of them stepped to one edge of it – and in those days although health and safety was important to the company, you didn't have any lanyards to tie you onto anything. Anyway, to cut a long story short, two of them slipped off. The table went with them. John managed to hold onto the table and swing himself into the floor below, but the guy he was with went off and he was killed. As far as I know that was the only fatality that they ever had.'

I thought back to the building site photograph we had been looking at – those tiny figures clambering about with ease all over the concrete frame of a tower block. Later I thought of Ken Denholm, climbing out of a fifteenth floor window to clean it. People had put so much trust in the safety of those experimental towers.

The tallest residential tower in the whole of Newcastle is Jesmond Vale, an MWM block built by Stanley Miller in 1966. The process of examining the Stanley Miller files in preparation for our chat had inspired John to do some investigations of his own. 'I actually went to

Jesmond Vale,' he said. 'I'd never been round till you contacted me.' He showed me a local newspaper clipping from 1969 which quoted a letter written by a Jesmond Vale resident to the council: *I am writing to thank you for the beautiful castle you have built me. In all my dreams of castles in the air I never imagined one like this … This is my castle and*

Jesmond Vale, in a 1966 publicity shot, showing off the MWM system. © Stanley Miller c/o John Matthews

I love it. John became animated once again. 'I thought, I should go and look at these places and see what they're like now. I happened to meet this delightful lady, Brenda – she's part of the residents' association. I explained my interest and I said, "I'm just keen because I have a letter written to the council about castles in the air, etc, and I just wanted to

know, all this time later, what do the residents feel about the building?"
And I was greatly surprised how much they love it. Because you get so
much negativity about blocks.'

At the eastern end of Cruddas Park four of the towers have been
completely renovated and re-clad as part of a regeneration scheme
for the area. Now covered in matt white render with cobalt blue
accents, they are unrecognisable. Jaunty balconies and windows
jut at irregular angles and intervals from the fascias in a complete
departure from the regularity of the original buildings. The stairwell
windows are now vertical slits, the glass tinted deep red. Each
building also has a large private car park at its base where once was
Dan Smith's 'concept of open space'. It is hard not to be impressed
at how luxurious they now appear, and how comprehensive the
transformation. One block is entirely devoted to flats for old people;
the others are for private buyers. The original idea had been to do all
of the estate, but the state of the economy has seen to that plan, and
now five of the blocks are facing demolition, including Margaret and
Ken's former home, Haughton Court. They didn't seem too sad about
the prospect, being much more excited by the transformation of the
regenerated towers. When their grandson Mark mentioned he was
moving to one of the swanky new blocks Margaret was incredulous.

'I said, "you're going back to Cruddas Park?" I said, "I can't
believe that!" I said, "that's four generations had a connection
with it, you know." Really, really weird. Our Leslie, he was
born here, and now his stepson has moved back in.'

It's no longer called Cruddas Park, of course. The stigma of what
eventually became a rough, run-down and neglected council estate
was too much for the developers to bear. They put forward three
alternative names, with locals voting to rebrand the area as Riverside
Dene. I remembered Shirley Meehan's comment in 1972 – 'the view,
if you avoid looking at the riverbanks, is beautiful' – and reflected

how fast cities and attitudes can change, and how alien recent history can seem. A new generation of residents is now moving into Scotswood Road. Some, like Margaret and Ken's grandson, are descendants of former council tenants made good; others have little or no connection to the area, or knowledge of its past.

5. 'A Contemporary Canaletto'

COLONEL SEIFERT'S OFFICE BLOCKS AND THE POST OFFICE TOWER (1956-75)

Arguably the biggest impact on the British skyline in the whole postwar period was made by a controversial, art-loving, Swiss-born architect who hid behind his round-framed spectacles – a tirelessly mercurial figure who even changed his name and nationality along the way. Not Charles-Édouard Jeanneret, who moved to France and famously reinvented himself as Le Corbusier, but instead, a curious figure, born Reubin Seifert, who fearlessly took our skyline and inserted into it some of our most notable, ambitious and controversial buildings.

When he moved to England almost a century ago, the young Reubin changed his name to Richard, but as his reputation grew he became widely known to his profession and to readers of *Private Eye* simply as 'The Colonel'. Colonel Seifert was the man behind literally hundreds of office blocks around the United Kingdom. His particular gift was his unequalled mastery of the manifold building controls the government and local authority planners sought to impose upon the developers who were buying up vast tracts of land all over the country. No one was more appreciative of the Colonel's skill than the startlingly young entrepreneur known rather incongruously as the 'daddy of all developers' – Harry Hyams. A shadowy, intensely secretive man, goatee-bearded, dapper, and with a taste for fast cars and luxury, Harry Hyams comes across in the few existing accounts of him as somewhere between Howard Hughes and the Roger Delgado version of the Master from *Doctor Who*. As the *Daily Express* wrote when profiling him in 2006, following an audacious multi-million pound robbery at his stately home in Wiltshire:

'Hyams never gives interviews, no recent newspaper photograph of him exists and the BBC admits that he is the only famous living person whose voice is not in their sound archive. You won't even find his name in *Who's Who*.'[1] Harry and the Colonel by no means worked exclusively together, but when they did collaborate, they produced spectacular results.

This is the story of postwar developers in the Harry Hyams mould, a breed of alpha-spivs whose careers were born out of the chaos of the war, and of the commercial architects they worked with, with their dogged pursuit of the sharpest deal and slimmest loophole. It reveals the impact of new communications and computing technology on what was built. Most of all, it traces how the arrival of big money, and a number of simultaneous major breakthroughs in science, radically affected the skyline of our island between the late fifties until the early seventies, whether in big cities, ambitious suburbs, or on remote wilds of heath, moor and down.

The developers ran riot in London. At its centre, marking the boundary between studious Bloomsbury and boozy Fitzrovia, runs Tottenham Court Road. Three striking structures near this road radically reshaped the city's skyline in the late sixties. At the south end stands Harry and the Colonel's most famous collaboration, and what was once the most controversial office block in the country: Centre Point, a tall, slender wafer with its distinctive, 'egg-box' concrete structure. To the north, across the hectic rush of the Euston Road, a massive cluster of squat blue-green mirrored glass boxes form the blank face of the Euston Centre. This was masterminded by developer Joe Levy, who had been Hyams' boss back in the fifties. And one street over to the west, in the heart of Fitzrovia, high above both of these gigantic office blocks, rises the cylindrical splendour of the BT Tower like a high-tech Nelson's Column, showing us just what the public sector could achieve when it came to planting a stake in our skyline.

Designing office blocks such as Centre Point or Euston Tower was not considered prestigious work by those architects who aspired to become the Le Corbusiers of Britain. Yes, Basil Spence's practice deigned to produce Thorn House near Seven Dials in London, a classic late fifties office slab perched on top of a low rise podium block, presenting the tower like a giant sculpture. And at around the same time Robert Matthew and Stirratt Johnson-Marshall consummated their architectural partnership with the design of New Zealand House, an embassy down the road in Haymarket, which also adopted the podium-and-tower approach. Even those daring iconoclasts, Peter and Alison Smithson, had a go with their early sixties offices for the *Economist* in smart St James's. The innovative brutalist design naturally rejected the mainstream craze for towers on podiums and instead created three small blocks with a plaza between them, a modern nod to the alleyways of old London from this history-obsessed couple. Yet on the whole, few of the MARS or CIAM elite in Britain troubled themselves with working for developers, the men usually behind the construction of the big office or shopping schemes that went up in the fifties and sixties. Generally they showed more interest in public sector projects such as housing or civic centre redevelopment, and tended to work within local authorities rather than private practices.

An exception was the Hungarian émigré Ernő Goldfinger, whose work at the Elephant and Castle I knew well. The multi-faceted offices he designed there, once home to the Ministry of Health, are now a luxury apartment block complex, rejoicing in the name of Metro Central Heights. I met one of Ernő's former colleagues, James Dunnett, who'd begun his career at the practice in the seventies. In the somewhat chaotic office in his beautiful Georgian home in north London, James fluctuated between pensiveness and bouts of nervous energy. He evoked the snobberies that lay behind the decisions of the big-name designers of the postwar period:

'Goldfinger was one of the few respected architects who was willing to work for developers. In those days the award-winning architects tended to work on universities or housing or possibly health buildings, but hardly any of them did any city centre development. It was thought to be practically *demeaning* working for developers in those days. The scene has completely changed now. Nowadays the top architects fall over each other to work for developers.'

For their part, the developers of the day were happy to ignore the highfalutin, unworldy – and more to the point, expensive – establishment architects. Instead they built up a sympathetic coterie who understood just what they were after – which tended to be a healthy return on their investments rather than philosophical correctness. One such successful commercial architect, Michael Rosenauer, in his 1955 book *Modern Office Buildings*, laid out the designer's two main challenges: 'one is the search for maximum economy in structural methods, the other is our growing awareness of the importance of healthy environment' – for the workers, he meant, rather than the planet.[2]

When the Conservative government scrapped a whole layer of regulations and red tape around building in the mid-fifties, a third, rather more basic consideration came to dominate these new boom developments: how to pack the largest possible floor space into the area the developers had bought, without blocking light from the surrounding streets. The eminent planner William Holford developed a calculation for the London County Council, known as the plot ratio, to determine the maximum square footage permissible on a given site. Developers were keen to exploit the plot ratio of their land as fully as possible, and their architects would become experts in playing the system to ensure that the greatest possible floor area was achieved, often well over what the LCC had originally intended. Loopholes were vigorously sought, inside information from the local authorities eagerly obtained. 'Although plot ratios were stated to be a maxima,' reported Holford wearily, 'in practice they have come to be regarded as a minima.'[3] By 1960, with the building boom in full swing, he was still convinced that Britain could avoid building town centres dominated by office buildings, even if he wasn't quite sure how that would be achieved. 'The fact that office rents bring the highest return (except perhaps for illuminated advertisements) is bound to mean an increase of tall, functional, cellular slabs and towers,' he told the Royal Institute of British Architects (RIBA) in his inaugural address as their president. 'What I imagine we shall not allow is their displacement of all other buildings of smaller bulk and greater individuality ... But to do this will require some hard thinking.'[4] Holford's own work, creating detailed plans for the rebuilding of the City of London, was not without controversy. His 1956 proposed layout for the Blitzed area around St Paul's Cathedral, for example, ran into a concerted press campaign to protect one of the country's greatest buildings from towering office blocks, a campaign that did not abate until said towers were demolished some 40 years later.

The relationship between planners, developers and their architects tended to operate at two extremes – cosy and collaborative, or hostile and suspicious. John Gyford, the avuncular former LCC planner I met in the Festival Hall café, recalled the battles they regularly faced with developers determined to maximise their floor space. 'On one occasion I attended one of these meetings between one of the senior officers and a developer's architect,' he said as we sipped our tea. 'They were dealing with a site at the very far end of Shaftesbury Avenue where it comes into New Oxford Street. And it was a slightly awkwardly shaped site, but the developer's architect had been as ingenious as he could to try to squeeze the maximum floor space out of it. The senior officer who was interrogating the architect was really not convinced that this scheme was going to meet the planning standards. And eventually the architect, in responding to this criticism produced what he may have thought was his clincher. He said, "But without what we're getting in this plan, the scheme won't be economic!" To which my senior officer replied, in his broad Yorkshire accent, "Well, it'll bloody well have to be *uneconomic*!"'

The Euston Centre, at the north end of Tottenham Court Road, furnishes a classic example of one of the most dominant forms of postwar office building: the glass curtain wall. This style had been perfected in New York in the forties and fifties: for instance in the United Nations Secretariat building, designed by the Brazilian rising star Oscar Niemeyer with interference from – and credit taken by – Le Corbusier; or in the deluxe curtain-walled Seagram Building on Park Avenue, designed by Bauhaus maestro Mies van der Rohe, the architect who came to be most associated with this approach.

In Britain the Smithsons had imported Mies' mode for their Hunstanton school, but it was the successful commercial team of Gollins, Melvin and Ward who in 1959 constructed Britain's first landmark office block in the curtain-walled 'international style' – Castrol House in Marylebone. There were painful teething troubles with these early curtain-walled buildings, as the Smithsons knew only too well. The steel mullions around the glass panels, for example, often corroded or buckled, cracking the glazing. Yet once the techniques were perfected, the advantages of glass curtain walls were many. Developers loved them because they were both cheap to prefabricate and slender, helping architects to maximise the floor-space within. For businesses keen to project a go-ahead image, they were ostentatiously modern. Architects of the Modern school approved of the fact that the structure was visible rather than being hidden away behind cladding or decorative detailing, while Michael Rosenauer noted admiringly that the mirrored surface presented, 'paradoxically, less the building it enshrines than the reflection of other buildings, clouds and sky'.[5] One final advantage from a planner's perspective may have been that they made the increasingly massive office developments, such as the Euston Centre, look less substantial and overbearing.

The business mastermind behind the Euston Centre was Joe Levy, who had started out as an estate agent shortly before the outbreak of the Second World War. Foreseeing that there would be a lack of office space in London after the Blitz, he took advantage of the rock-bottom wartime land values and snapped up sites all over London. For his sprawling Euston Centre, he spent years buying up little plots until he'd collected them all – like a football fanatic buying endless packets of stickers to complete his Panini album. This scheme for the Greater London Council was a triumph for his business, even though the resulting building manages to mangle Mies' elegant glass box aesthetic into a bulky cross-shaped lump of a structure. Still, it did help the council finance a much-needed underpass to relieve the choked Euston Road. Levy acted as mentor to several other notable figures in postwar development, including the mysterious Harry Hyams, who had worked for him as an estate agent, though he soon broke out to make a series of canny land deals of his own via his company Oldham Estates.

Richard *né* Reubin Seifert hadn't intended to be an architect. His plan had been to escape the family business of medicine by studying painting at the Slade, but in a fateful *Sliding Doors* moment in 1928 he enrolled instead for the Bartlett School of Architecture. He was posted to India as a Lieutenant Colonel in the Royal Engineers, and as for many of his generation, the war had changed his fortunes and his outlook: 'The Army is the greatest school of experience – particularly in the officer class – of all times. I certainly came back a person who had tremendous confidence.'[6] The newly ambitious demobbed Seifert bought a suburban semi for £300 in north London, and set about making a success of his little architecture practice, which started out modestly designing houses with a staff of 12.

The practice prospered, and Seifert began to pick up more sizeable commissions. One of his first notable office developments was the highly decorated, sturdy, stone-clad Woolworths' HQ in Marylebone, a florid collision of art deco, neo-Georgian and Festival of Britain styles built in the mid-fifties. However, before the decade was out he had started to echo the glass curtain-wall manner of the United Nations building, with a podium and slab development down the road from Woolworths. It was during this period that Seifert went into partnership with fellow architect George Marsh, whom many consider the genius of the outfit.

The first quintessentially Seifert and Hyams collaboration was Tolworth Tower in south-west London, which opened in 1964. Foreshadowing the work the pair would do together over the following decade, this was a slender, 22-storey slab of offices raised up on angled columns, the concrete gables at either end of the building in the shape of a thrusting arrow pointing upwards, like the smoke trail of a rocket. Given Hyams' peculiar fondness for naming his buildings after cosmological phenomena – Telstar House and Space House in London; Lunar House, Apollo House and Voyager House in Croydon; Astronaut House in Feltham; Planet House in Sunderland; Orbit House in Eccles – it is somewhat surprising that he resisted calling this one Rocket House, which would have suited it perfectly.

Tolworth Tower's rebellion against the right angle, so prevalent in the curtain-walled offices of the era, was prompted by Seifert's dislike of them, reflected even in his own boomerang-shaped desk. Even so, the design of Tolworth Tower bore the unmistakable mark of George Marsh, who would go on to design many of Seifert's most celebrated projects, taking the mild playfulness of this early office block and pushing it to create ever more 'pop' sculptural forms for his buildings.

Through the late fifties Harry Hyams was stealthily buying up land and properties around the junction of St Giles, at the bottom of Tottenham Court Road (while his former boss Joe Levy was doing the same at the top end for his Euston Centre). Meanwhile, the London County Council had also turned their attention to this busy junction, proposing a new roundabout to tackle the major traffic problem in the area. The two plans, developed in isolation, threatened to cancel each other out. But neither Hyams nor the LCC had foreseen that another, much smaller-scale, speculator held the trump card. Beatrice Pearlberg owned a key building on the site, and flatly rejected the LCC's statutory offer to pay a prewar price to buy the land from her so that they could build their roundabout. At this point Hyams' business instinct and eye for a sharp deal kicked in. He told the LCC that he would offer to purchase the building from Pearlberg at market rates and give it to them – as long as he got to build his office block on their roundabout. The LCC caved, as – eventually – did Pearlberg, and Hyams got his new favourite architect, Richard Seifert, straight onto the project: Centre Point.

In many ways Centre Point was the natural successor to Seifert and Marsh's triumph in Tolworth – constructed as it was from jazzily angled precast concrete components and elevated on mosaic-tiled, chevron-shaped columns. Le Corbusier had called such columns *pilotis*, and in the postwar period they became an essential ingredient of many commercial and city centre schemes, opening up space at ground level for pedestrians or traffic to circulate beneath the buildings. During

Centre Point under contruction.
© *Janet Gyford*

our conversation, James Dunnett described these as 'one of the key ideas of modern architecture really, that you lift the building up on legs, that you create space around it so you get transparency through and underneath the building'. I'd seen *pilotis* everywhere, from Park Hill in Sheffield to the Festival of Britain Lansbury Estate in east London. Central Croydon has *pilotis* like the Tower of London has ravens: if you took them away, the entire edifice would fall down. 'Various architectural and town planning effects are made possible by omitting parts on the ground floor – such as extending a street or plaza under a building,' Michael Rosenauer had explained in his book, although he was a touch sniffy about the craze, venturing that 'in many instances it is the sensation inherent in the fact that we can technically master the feat of putting a tall building on stilts that seems to make such a conception glamorous.'[7]

As part of Hyams' deal with the LCC, the slim tower and fountains of Centre Point would form a roundabout at this busy junction. The *pilotis* would allow cars to drive under a limb which connected the tower to a low-level slab block to the east of the roundabout. But after all the backroom dealing this idea was, in the words of planner Lionel Brett, 'outdated by a new circulation pattern before it was even finished' and dropped by the LCC.[8] This left the gangly tower and its sporadically spurting fountains oddly marooned on a not-quite roundabout, detached from the bustling shopping streets around it, and without even pavements to allow pedestrians past.

'There is a vulgarity about it.'

'It was all a bit of a mess at ground level, I have to say,' said James Dunnett, as he reflected on the accusations of bad taste that hung around some of Seifert's more expressive buildings. 'Centre Point was considered to have been pretty much unacceptable. And in a way there is a vulgarity about it. But then vulgarity is acceptable if it's in another country. Alternatively, if it's from another decade, from the thirties, like an Odeon cinema, or something art deco or whatever, then that also is acceptable. But looming over Fitzrovia and Bedford Square and so on, not far from the British Museum, this was felt to be an outrage.' He thought for a moment. 'And I used to hate it in a way, until I started to look at it in a different way. I used to hate that the lid on the top of it, the edge of it waves, along with all of the zigzag precast units. I thought, *that's really overdoing it. It doesn't need that. It could be flat, that top, it doesn't need that wavy edge.* And in a way I suppose I *still* think that. But I think the fun of it all is the *pilotis* at the ground level and the staircases. There was this rather splendid ramp on the island that went down into the garage, because the idea was that a chauffeur-driven limousine could come in there and drop off the chief executive at the foot of the steps that went up.' Except that for years there were no executives, chauffeurs – or indeed anyone at all – to use the carefully designed stairs and ramps, or admire the spectacular views of central London afforded by its 35 floors.

Centre Point remained unlet for a decade after its completion by Wimpey in 1966. The first people to lay claim to the building weren't quite the high-end clients Hyams had envisaged, but squatters, who in January 1974, invaded it to highlight the increasing problem of homelessness. Their protest immediately became front-page news. Two activists had infiltrated Burns, the tower's security firm, and opened the back door to let in 80 protesters: a mix of trade unionists, local councillors, teachers, lawyers and social workers, who proceeded to display banners and protest over loudspeakers against Hyams. Jim Radford, director of community centre Blackfriars Settlement, led the protest, announcing that 'we have occupied Centre Point because it is the symbol of everything rotten in our society. We could accommodate many of London's families in this building.'[9]

How had this happened? Centre Point may not have been everyone's cup of tea, but it wasn't so different from hundreds of other office developments of the time. Yet it was the sheer ostentatiousness of this empty 385ft block, situated as it was at the heart of one of London's busiest districts, that prompted people to question Hyams' motives. Public ire against the building was stoked by the Environment Secretary Peter Walker at the height of the early seventies housing bubble that left thousands priced out of London, and many of them homeless. Walker offered to buy it from Hyams for £5m (some £20m below the market rate) and turn it into flats, commenting sarcastically that he was 'very distressed to hear that such a charming man had been struggling so long and so hard to let Centre Point without any success'.[10] The developer stuck by his guns, insisting that he was waiting for a single client to rent the building, with deals with the British Steel Corporation, EMI and the soon-to-be disgraced Lonrho all falling at the last hurdle.

Hyams sued those who implied he'd deliberately kept it empty for years to make a killing on the vastly increased rents in the seventies, but for this secretive 'stealth developer', the public row and scandal must have come as a shock. Even Seifert refused to come to his rescue, rejecting the idea that the building was suitable only for a single occupant, and expressing his unhappiness that it had been left empty for so long. 'I do not like it and I have said so many times,' he told *The Times*.[11] But Centre Point was not unique: three other Hyams and Seifert office blocks in London – Telstar House, New London Bridge House and Space House – qualified when Peter Walker threatened to go over the heads of the developers and grant tenancies for office blocks over 50,000 square feet that had remained empty for over a year. To have one block standing empty may have been regarded as a misfortune, to have four looked like ruthlessness. In the end, Centre Point was let – in part, not in whole – in 1975; the early sixties Telstar House in Paddington was let to London Transport in 1974; and Centre Point's curvy cousin Space House in Holborn was let to the suitably aerodynamic Civil Aviation Authority in the same year, almost a decade after completion.

Space House is my favourite Seifert building. It's built with Centre Point-style precast concrete y-shaped units, and stands on similarly jaunty legs, but the resemblances end there. If Centre Point is an upended packet of bourbons sitting on a saucer, Space House is more a Hornsea Pottery biscuit barrel sitting next to a bread bin. This big, fat drum of a building is connected via a raised walkway to its other half, a super-cool, low rise slab, whose gleaming marble mullions are punctured with windows that look remarkably like a stack of marching Space Invaders. I studied at a night school opposite Space

Space House, my favourite of Seifert's buildings.

House and frequently found myself drifting off, distracted by this extraordinary structure, in much the same way that I had when I'd worked next door to Richard Rogers' Lloyds Building in the nineties.

John Gyford recalled the arrival of the plans from Seifert's office on his desk.

'An enormous amount of trust was put in us, as young development control officers, by the system. Particularly because with central London we were dealing with some quite major planning applications. Very often we were allowed to deal face-to-face with major architects and developers.'

One of these was the Colonel:

'I was allowed to phone him up personally and ask him to come into County Hall to discuss something with me. And he didn't bat an eyelid about this. I would find myself talking over the counter to Richard Seifert about why his planning application had too many floors on it. The one I always remember, if you go up Kingsway on the left hand side a couple of hundred yards there's a 1960s office block.'

I jumped in excitedly at that point, and asked if he meant Space House.

'Yes, that's right, Space House. He came in with the first drawings of this.' John used a napkin on the table to represent the slab block. 'And behind it was this drum.' He plonked down a pepper pot.

'Well, the first plans he produced didn't *have* a drum, they had a cross. We tested it against the daylight criteria and it contravened them. It threw shadows. It's surrounded by Peabody-type flats. And he came in and I explained the problem to him, and he said, *Oh, that's all right, I'll get them to design something different.* And they came back with the drum! Now there was always this view held by the planners that as far as Seifert was concerned, the only point of the external cladding was to keep the rain off the typists. That he didn't much care what it looked like. His job was to maximise the available floor space within what the planning system permitted. At that time he was very much given to using – and Centre Point is the classic example of this – those prefabricated reinforced concrete struts which were not only external cladding but a key element of structure. I don't think he did that because it was beautiful, it just worked.'

Space House under construction, planned by John Gyford at the LCC, and photographed by his wife. © Janet Gyford

Given my immoderate love for Space House, I had to bite my tongue.

'I never went to his offices myself but I know a colleague who did, and he said there were just these *rows* and *rows* of architects sitting at drawing boards. An entire great room of them! It was a bit like that scene in *The Apartment*, that Jack Lemmon movie, where there were all these guys sitting down at adding machines.'

What was Seifert like, I asked him.

'He was quite affable when *I* spoke to him, but on one occasion the mask slipped. He brought in the job architect to discuss a planning application, which I thought was proposing more office floor space than could be accommodated within the plot zoning for that site. The job architect insisted that they had not transgressed any limits so I went through page by page. I can't remember now what building it was, but I explained my calculations. At the end of it Seifert accepted my figures, that I'd got it right. He turned to his job architect and said, "*WELL*?" I felt for the guy.'

By the mid-sixties Seifert's firm had grown to 200 employees, and had made a dramatic impact on London's skyline. But the team weren't just transforming London; they were producing landmarks all over the UK and internationally too. There was George Laming's beautiful curved curtain-walled design for Gateway House, which opened in 1969, snaking its way to the doors of Manchester Piccadilly station. The mid-seventies saw the construction of the Elmbank Gardens complex above Glasgow's Charing Cross station, whose modular concrete components rivalled the complexity of those in his contemporaneous International Press Centre in the City of London. And despite the wealth of local architectural talent in Birmingham, Seifert's practice built a number of major landmarks there, among them the National Exhibition Centre.

Over the years the firm's designs continued to evolve: Seifert was determined not to be caught producing outmoded work. 'The increasing departure from traditional building methods,' he wrote in the *Financial Times* in 1971, 'spurred by the juxtaposition of economy and the more flexible use of concrete, with the added potential of reinforced plastic in building ... mark the future trend of city office design.'[12] By the mid-seventies the long horizontals, icy white mosaic and green glass of buildings such as the National Provincial Bank's 1957 HQ in Draper's Gardens were a thing of the past, replaced by the vertical accents, rough concrete earth-tones and deep brown glazing of King's Reach Tower – home of IPC magazines and, famously, Tharg, alien editor of *2000AD* and the young tyro journalists of the *NME* – and its giant cousin in the City, the NatWest Tower, which for a time was Britain's tallest building.

Interviewed by the BBC in 1977, Seifert reflected on his impact on the character of our cities. 'I lived in a time when monumentality was something which was considered to be something exiting and exhilarating and necessary. Canaletto painted the scenes of London with Wren's spires … We are taking [it] a few layers higher and we are creating almost a contemporary Canaletto, a skyline which has a remarkable effect on me personally, and I have no reason but to be very proud of it – at least, proud of our limited contribution.'[13]

One place that was changed beyond all measure by the postwar office boom, with the help of the Colonel, was my hometown of Croydon – so much so it inspired a new word: *Croydonisation*. The comprehensive development area legislation was all very well for the *coventrated* cities, but the process was too slow and bureaucratic for the 'managing director of Croydon', council leader Sir James Marshall.[14] When his original postwar development plan was rejected by the Ministry of Housing and Local Government, Marshall realised that the official centralised route was never going to work for him. Accordingly, in 1956 he pushed the Croydon Corporation Act through parliament, which allowed local authorities to compulsorily purchase land for redevelopment without the slow and interfering approval of central government. If the CDAs represented a socialist urge to bring great swathes of land back under central ownership and set them to work for the good of the people, the Croydon Corporation Act was an expression of pure capitalism, designed to encourage the rigorous commercial exploitation of land that was currently occupied by inconvenient schools and houses.

Croydon's status as the capitalists' dream town was in part an unwitting side effect of one of the most socialistic creations in British politics. Soon after sweeping to power in 1964, Harold Wilson's Labour party created a Department of Economic Affairs to sit alongside the Treasury. Its colourful head, George Brown, was tasked with creating an integrated Soviet-style National Plan for the economy. One of his first actions was to ban the construction of more offices in central

London, where there were acres of unoccupied floorspace, in the hope that it would boost the regions. The Brown ban took effect in November 1964. In *The Property Boom, Financial Times* journalist Oliver Marriott described how developers and architects invited LCC and corporation of London officials to last-minute parties in a venal scramble to get as many office developments signed off before the midnight deadline as possible.[15]

The main effect of the ban was to send office development out into the suburbs. In the south, towns like Woking, Swindon, Surbiton, Basingstoke, Slough and Reading all added stacks of office floorspace to attract overspill business from London. Croydon outpaced them all.

The passing of the Croydon Corporation Act had enabled Sir James Marshall's plan, with its 45 acres of town centre redevelopment to go ahead without fear of public enquiry. 'Having engendered the office boom,' wrote the academic Peter Saunders in his book on Croydon, 'Sir James and his colleagues sat back and watched with some amazement as their infant grew swiftly to elephantine proportions.'[16] The first office block to appear was Norfolk House, a rather tame 11-storey brick tower, in 1959. Within a decade a staggering 45 office blocks had been built in central Croydon – almost all wrapped in glass curtain walls. They were packed so closely together that, rather than reflecting the outside world as intended, they merely reflected each other in an infinite 'hall of mirrors' style regress.

Croydon highlighted the risks of doing without a comprehensive development plan. A panel of architects considered developers' applications in isolation, and were unable to judge the overall effect. 'Something more might have been done to encourage architects to work together in their respective schemes so as to integrate and develop the whole,' wrote the *Guardian* when visiting the town in 1962, at the start of the boom.[17] If they had been impressed with the ambition of the borough's plans, they were less keen on the reality: 'Unfortunately Croydon is getting a number of buildings where the chief design consideration has been the provision of the maximum lettable floor space.'

Borough Engineer Allan Holt's spurious desire for a landmark in the centre of Croydon twice the height of Norfolk House epitomises the ad hoc, unplanned nature of the area's development. This wasn't a plan, it was a craving, and it was fed by Ronald Ward and Partners with a 23-storey slab of Nestlé chocolate: St George's Tower. When the mayor opened this imperious block in 1965 he remarked that Nestlé 'could be excused for believing they own Croydon.'[18] Half a century later, in post-riots 2014, the company have vacated their famous tower. It feels rather as if they have sold the town off.

St George's Tower under construction in 1964. © Ian Steel

By the mid-sixties, after an 'everything must go' feeding frenzy, developers had bought up the whole of the town centre. On the site of Croydon Girls' School, Harry Hyams built Lunar House and Apollo House, soon to become twin homes to the Home Office's passport HQ. Richard Seifert's practice designed two quite different office towers near East Croydon station – delicate curtain-walled Corinthian House in the early sixties, and the chunky Jenga-like Noble Lowndes Tower, completed in 1970.

The Noble Lowndes Tower, known as the Threepenny Bit building: Seifert's landmark for Croydon.

Noble Lowndes Tower is Croydon's star building: 24 storeys of elongated octagons, covered in millions of the inevitable white micro-mosaic tiles, and placed crossways to the floor below to create a jerky, jagged, multi-faceted tower, known to generations as the Threepenny Bit or 50p building. Like Centre Point, it is built on an inaccessible traffic island, with car parking hidden beneath. It too suffered more than its share of construction hitches. In this case a resident of East Bridge House, which stood on one part of the Threepenny Bit's site, refused to move off when construction began. Here was the inevitable fallout from the gift James Marshall had given the town – redevelopment without consultation. It gave local authorities the power to kick intransigent residents out of their homes. Even when the tower was opened in 1970, East Bridge House was clinging to the site (it was eventually demolished three years later). Yet such hitches were glossed over by this most forward-thinking of councils. 'In sunlight the new centre appears as a glittering mass of white concrete and reflecting glass rising above the surrounding townscape,' enthused the Borough's official guide in 1971, adding, 'at close quarters it is equally impressive.'[19]

A trip to the top of the NLA Tower in 2010 gave me a skyscraper's eye view of the centre. The town made much more sense from that perspective. Seen from the ground, the blocks stood out like lanky boys dancing self-consciously at a disco. From up there their glass walls shimmered majestically like glitterballs in the autumnal gloom. Here was a different, more glamorous sort of town centre – one still waiting for *Jetsons*-style aerocars to be invented to make use of its fantastic skyscape.

'Even a Londoner without a head for heights might be persuaded to visit Croydon to see on the ground the kind of city all this commercial growth can make possible,' *The Times* reported in 1970. 'If there are faults of scale or design in the office towers, Croydon walkers follow the English habit of rarely raising their eyes at all. For those that do, there are unsuspected glimpses of strange and lofty angles of concrete and glass.'[20] Yet still the council wanted more.

'The demand for office accommodation in this large and forward-looking Borough has been beyond expectation,' reported the 1969 edition of Croydon's official guide excitedly.[21] With a staggering five million square feet of office space already either completed or under construction, it seemed incredible that another million square feet should be approved by the Greater London Council. Yet approved they were, and despite pockets of deprivation, such as New Addington, Croydon's council remained determined to favour business over social needs. In the spring of 1973 the council reduced projected expenditure on health, education and social services, while allocating a further £500,000 to the construction of a sixth car park.[22] The reason? The town chiefs were determined to have more multi-storey car parks than Birmingham. For all the talk of a more rational, scientific world, it was these heated inter-city rivalries that were often the basis for shaping the rebuilding of postwar Britain.

In 1974, with the economy in the grip of stagflation, Greater London Council announced that no further office development would be allowed in Croydon, even where a government permit to built had been granted. A decade after the Brown ban came its thundering echo, bringing the borough's boom to an abrupt and ugly halt.

Meanwhile, Birmingham had found a quite different use for its new skyscrapers: in 1973 the extraordinary Cliff Richard musical *Take Me High* was filmed around the Seifert-designed Alpha Tower. Cliff played a young corporate executive who thought he was being sent to New York but ended up in Birmingham, before embarking on a *You've Got Mail*-style romance with family café boss Debbie Watling. The film featured Cliff in Cuban heels and a grey suit singing upbeat songs with titles such as *It's Only Money* and *Winning* while driving round Spaghetti Junction, running enthusiastically across overpasses or staring up at newly built office blocks (*Concrete city / It can't slam the door in my face*). Sadly *Take Me High* bombed at the box office and became Cliff's final foray into film. It seemed that a musical about corporate rivalry in Birmingham lacked the appeal of, say, a romantic road trip across Europe in a converted double decker. Who knew?

Alpha Tower, Cliff's co-star in *Take Me High*, was built for ATV, the Midlands ITV franchise run by Lew Grade. By the late sixties office space was being reconfigured to accommodate not only humans but the latest in computer equipment. Here the Colonel's task was to create new studios fit for the colour television age. The site, formerly one of Birmingham's most famous wharves, had originally been earmarked for an exhibition centre to be designed by James Roberts, but this project was shoved aside to make room for Seifert's master plan. He envisaged a whole new cultural complex for the city: not just television studios and offices, but a hotel, two cinemas, a theatre and exhibition centre.

As the financial climate worsened after the devaluation of the pound in 1968, ambitions for the centre were scaled down. The theatre and cinemas were ditched, and the exhibition centre ended up somewhat squeezed by the office tower and studios. Even so, the most technically advanced studios of the day were opened by Princess Alexandra in 1970. Footage of the ceremony, captured in the brilliant documentary, *ATVLand in Colour*, shows rows of the great and the good – balding men, basically – sitting down to a celebratory lunch in the hangar-like Studio One. The vibe is more early seventies general election count than glamorous media launch.

ATV were soon broadcasting in colour, producing everything from *Crossroads* and *The Golden Shot* to *Tiswas* and *Spitting Image*. The design of the studio block was typical George Marsh, its flashy, irregular angles playing with the concept of the functional box. Construction of the offices, Alpha Tower, had lagged a couple of years behind the studios, and by the time they were finished ATV (not for nothing known as 'All Tory Values') had decided to rent them out in the midst of the Heath property boom rather than move in.

One of the advantages of the location of the new ATV studios was that they were very near Birmingham's new Post Office Tower, the gawky 31-storey telecommunications centre completed in 1966. This was just one node in a network of relay stations across Britain using the new technology of microwaves to beam television and radio signals around the country. The 1,000-foot high tower built at Emley Moor in Yorkshire in 1971 was another, and it remains Britain's tallest man-made structure, overshadowing even the Shard. Why did these structures have to be so high? Such were the limitations of microwaves as a telecoms technology that an uninterrupted 'line of sight' between towers was needed to send and receive information – hence the Birmingham tower's impressive 499-foot height, tall enough to see over the surrounding buildings and hills to the network of stations beyond. The developers who'd been granted permission for the construction of a tall new residential tower next door found it swiftly revoked when it looked as if this 'line of sight' was to be compromised – and so plans for yet another James Roberts landmark bit the dust.

The new relay stations were designed by the Ministry of Works, who had taken over a new office block above the Elephant and Castle Shopping Centre in London. The first one had been planned in 1956 and was slated to occupy the site of the Museum Telephone Exchange just west of Tottenham Court Road. The Museum Radio Tower, as it was initially known, was designed by Eric Bedford, the Ministry's chief architect. To Anthony Wedgwood Benn, Postmaster General in Harold Wilson's sixties cabinet, this project said everything about the 'white heat' of modernity their government stood for. 'Big Ben represents the fussy grandeur of the Gothic revival,' the *Daily Express* quoted him as saying in 1965. 'The Post Office Tower, lean, practical and futuristic, symbolises the technical and architectural skill of this new age.'[23]

Less than a year later, Benn announced the limited testing of colour television signals from the tower, starting towards the end of 1967 with a giddying four hours of colour a week on BBC2. When Geoffrey Moorhouse ascended the unfinished tower in a crane in 1964, he reported that 'at the moment it is bare concrete with a fringe of steel tubing. Then open air.' The weather was so bad that by the time the intrepid journalist reached the top, he couldn't see the ground below. 'At street level the air barely moves,' he wrote. 'Up here vicious gusts tug at coat tails and drizzle slashes at the

The Post Office Tower: 'lean, practical and futuristic'.

scaffolding. In gales of 90 mph the tower will twang like a tuning fork through 15 inches. On a still, cloudless day a movement of up to two inches will be induced by the heat of the sun.'[24]

This predicted sway had caused huge headaches for Eric Bedford and his team. In order to serve its purpose, the tower had to remain relatively rigid: if it deviated from the vertical by more than a third of a degree the microwaves that it fired out over miles of country would miss their targets. After various models were tested in the Teddington Wind Tunnel at the National Physical Laboratories, the slim, circular shape was finally chosen as the one that would most effectively minimise wind resistance.

A few months after Geoffrey Moorhouse's trip, Frank Goldsmith became the first member of the public to visit the tower. He'd escaped from nearby University College Hospital, where he was a patient, then evaded builders to enter the tower and climbed an astonishing 440 feet to reach the ledge of the aerial platform, from where fell to his death.

BT's records show how the opening of the tower was dogged with farce as much as tragedy, with more than a hint of Sir Humphrey Appleby and Jim Hacker. As I waded through boxes of fuzzy carbon copies, Roneos or fountain pen-written notes in the BT archive, I came across hundreds of letters and memos buzzing back and forth between Downing Street, Balmoral and the General Post Office (GPO). In 1963 Reginald Bevins, the Conservative Postmaster General, had written to the Director General of the GPO that 'I do not think we ought to delay the formal opening until the thing is completed both structurally and internally, but should do so as soon as the shell has been completed.'[25] The GPO's Public Relations Officer T. A. O'Brien took a dim view of this half-baked scheme: 'We would only make ourselves look silly if we tried to organise a ceremony which would have no meaning whatsoever.'[26] But by July 1964 others were beginning to understand the great PR opportunities afforded by the still unfinished Tower. 'Lord Mackintosh would like to arrange some special ceremony for the start of the Premium Savings Bond draw for November,' went an internal GPO memo. 'Lord Mackintosh would like to start the draw by someone pressing an appropriate button from the top of the Post Office Tower.'[27] To which, the reply was 'we are already receiving numerous enquiries from people anxious to hold parties on "top of the tower". A ceremony for [Premium Bonds] would only provide yet more enquiries. And every such enquirer must be told the Tower will not be open to the public until the end of 1965.'[28]

As the completion date for the building neared, the minutes of the Post Office Tower's project team from November reported on the key decisions taken: Muzak had been vetoed, coin-operated telescopes for the viewing platform were agreed, and Mr S. Horrox, the Chairman, expressed a desire that the public-facing staff should wear uniforms, perhaps of a striking red.[29] The name had posed a particularly thorny problem. In April 1962 the *Post Office Magazine* had run a Skylon-style naming competition, offering a generous £10 prize. The winner was announced as 'Telspire'. In the end, however, such florid pretensions were dropped and it came to be known as the Post Office Tower.

At first T. A. O'Brien was keen to enlist technophile Prince Philip to open the Tower, but this plan was derailed because of doubts about whether enough equipment to impress His Highness would have been installed by the July opening date. O'Brien's next suggestion was that Mrs Wedgwood Benn, the Post Master General's wife, should open it, but her husband had different ideas. He wrote to Harold Wilson in December to invite him to open the Post Office Tower, adding that 'it might furnish you with an opportunity for speaking about the scientific revolution in practice, and the part public enterprise plays in the process.'[30] As details of the opening were being thrashed out, O'Brien reported that 'PMG is most emphatic that the operational nature of the ceremony should be emphasised and not the sight seeing one.'[31] The date was finally set for 8 October. There followed a further panic about whether any links would be working in time for Wilson to demonstrate them to the world's media. It transpired that three transmitters would be working, but that only one, connected to Birmingham's Post Office Tower, would be using the new 'broadband' analogue channel. Also, only one lift would be functional by October. All in all, it seemed a very good thing that the royal visit had been postponed.

Then, as the big day approached, a modest proposal arrived from a Balmoral functionary: 'Her Majesty mentioned to me that she would be interested in due course to pay an informal visit to the tower.'[32] After another round of panicked discussions the idea was vetoed, and a second opening ceremony, this time a royal one, was hastily arranged for the following year.

I had an opportunity to experience Eric Bedford's design first-hand when I was given a tour of the building by BT's genial archivist, David Hay, while my friend Richard lurked around taking pictures. I was nervous about the full airport-style security check in the foyer, especially as my passport had expired the previous week. As we emptied our coins and phones and keys into the plastic trays provided, in the lobby beyond a group of business people waited to ascend. Presumably this is how BT make money out of the building, by renting it out to a select few corporate clients. When the Post Office Tower opened it had been a much more public affair. Sir Billy Butlin had won the tender to provide, on the thirty-sixth floor, the famously revolving Top of the Tower restaurant.[i] The public restaurant has long-since closed, but it still revolves three times a day for those lucky corporate clients.

We ascended in the super-fast lift, taking 40 seconds to reach T35, the viewing gallery – the level from which Frank Goldsmith had fallen back in 1964. The view was spectacular, giving a whole new perspective on London; a city of towers we might think it, but from up there it looked built on a very small, domestic scale – though the thought of confronting it without a protective layer of glass was terrifying. By 2013 six London buildings stood taller, but they were all huddled in the east: the nearby landmarks of Centre Point and the Euston Tower were dwarfed by this futuristic spire. The décor, however, was disappointing. Devoid of any period detail, it adhered to the kind of bland, neutral scheme favoured by television property developers looking for a quick sale.

---

i This famous London landmark had first revolved for diners in Ipswich, when managers at Ransomes and Rapier, who made and tested the revolving floor, had staged a lunchtime 'occupation' of it while it had stood in their construction shop.

T35: The viewing gallery of the BT Tower.
© Richard de Pesando

After a 30-minute question-and-answer session, David led us down in the lift to one of the most unexpectedly exciting places on my journey – T14, one of the equipment floors midway up the tower. No imagination was needed to picture what this would have been like when it first opened: all the original sixties equipment was still there. Towering racks of grey trim phones and stacks of multi-coloured plug boards filled the floorspace, and the Tower's central column was masked by the kind of black plastic matrix and once-white clip-on lettering more commonly seen on unrefurbished café walls. This was geek heaven. The floor had been more or less abandoned since the millennium, although we did startle one cheery engineer who had worked on this floor in the nineties, and who, it transpired, still popped into the abandoned office from time to time for sentimental reasons.

Technology from the sixties to the noughties rubs shoulders on Floor 14.
© Richard de Pesando

In the late nineties BT engineers were still using oscilloscopes and plug boards in the tower to beam, test and adjust signals. But as digital, mobile phone and internet bandwidth was progressively sold off to private companies, there was less and less for tower engineers to do. Now these floors stand quiet, dusty and abandoned. At one point I sat down at an antique grey metal desk with built-in acrylic buttons and an oscilloscope readout, and nonchalantly pressed a control. The entire desk sprang to life, lights twinkling, needles twitching on the read-out dials. I suddenly remembered the 1967 film *Smashing Time*, where two young women end up at the top of the tower at a happening party, and the revolve goes wildly out of control. I hurriedly switched the desk off.

Never touch antiquated equipment in the BT Tower.
© Richard de Pesando

I gazed around at the yellowing type-written instruction manuals; the fire drills and log books; the filing cabinets full of sticky vinyl folders; the Dymo tape informing technicians how to adjust the signals in case of adverse weather conditions; the eighties faxes; the seventies answering machines. The thick green glass windows were grubby, with vertical silver anodised aluminium blinds blocking out most of the view. The glass was a patented system of 9.5mm thick anti-sun glazing designed to minimise that curse of all glass-walled office blocks – solar heat gain. Somehow it wasn't a surprise when the startled engineer told us that, despite the crowded, cluttered, potentially claustrophobic space on these floors, the technicians had really liked working there, and missed it.

The final stop on our tour was the lower ground floor, known as The Pyramid for reasons that soon became obvious. To reach it we had to leave the building, and enter through an anonymous-looking door in the loading bay, which appeared as though it might lead to a broom cupboard rather than into the foundations of one of London's most recognisable landmarks. Hard hats on, we climbed straight down a ladder. At the bottom we stooped under some low-hanging bundles of cabling and drainpipes – and there in the damp, cold gloom we could make out the massive form of The Pyramid. It was a huge, rough concrete sandcastle built underground, with the core of the tower sticking out of the top like a flag. A narrow track ran round its perimeter. Here was the roughest of shuttering, concrete in its most brutal form – great grey beams of it that formed the walls and the floor and held up the roof. We could hear water trickling down the walls, and David informed us that no one had yet identified the source. He suggested we climb down from the gantry, along the precarious narrow planks of the makeshift walkway, and scramble to the foot of the steep concrete slope so we could walk round the base of The Pyramid itself. The trickling water had pooled on the floor, and splashing through this man-made cave in the gloom with our hard hats on felt more like a potholing expedition than a tour of Britain's most hi-tech sixties building. I hadn't thought to dress for an adventure in the underworld, and my new trainers were instantly ruined.

With The Pyramid rising above us, David explained the origins of the design. The heavy London clay made deep foundations impossible, so instead the building had to be supported on a wide, flat base that sprawls underground from The Pyramid. Essentially the Post Office Tower was designed according to the same principles as a standard lamp.

On the way back up I spotted that on one of the rough concrete beams someone had drawn stick men. Nearby was scrawled that quintessential sixties acronym: LSD. There at the base of this hi-tech telecoms tower was one of the oldest human forms of communication – cave drawings.

Underground, visiting the 'pyramid' beneath the tower.
© *Richard de Pesando*

The Post Office Tower was just one of a wave of atomic-age structures created to house new technology. In 1956 the Queen opened Calder Hall nuclear power station in Cumbria; situated next to the military nuclear processing plant at Windscale, it was the first in the world to provide energy for domestic use. The Engineering Gas Research Station, designed by architects Ryder and Yates to resemble a scaled-up laboratory bench of funnels and flasks, opened in 1967 in Killingworth, near Newcastle. The likes of Frederick Gibberd and Robert Matthew were called upon to design new airport terminals at Gatwick and Edinburgh to cope with the boom in passenger numbers. The magnificent Lovell Telescope at Jodrell Bank Experimental Station in Cheshire remains the largest steerable dish radio telescope in the world, and was completed in 1957. Then there was Antenna One, or Arthur, a parabolic dish built in 1962 at Goonhilly Downs in Cornwall, constructed to link with the telecommunications satellite, Telstar.

Most of these buildings were constructed on moors, heaths or downs, away from the general public. The Post Office Towers in London and Birmingham were the urban face of technological supremacism. The London tower rapidly permeated popular culture. Even before the it had opened, *The Eagle* comic was featuring it on the front page, as part of a 1964 Dan Dare story in which a dangerous alien had roused the bored teenagers of London into a revolutionary seizure of the tower. In 1966 it fell foul of another malign force, this time on television, when it was taken over by a giant computer called WOTAN, eventually to be defeated by a time-travelling alien on the BBC at Saturday teatime. Perhaps most memorably, in 1971 the entire tower was destroyed by a giant marauding kitten in *The Goodies* in one of the decade's classic television comedy moments.

That episode of *The Goodies* aired just two weeks after a real-life attack changed the fortunes of the tower for good. At 4:30am on 31 October 1971 security man Fred Graham was alone in the restaurant on the thirty-second floor when he heard a loud bang from the viewing gallery. 'Suddenly the floor heaved,' he told the *Daily Mirror*. 'My chair went up a couple of inches and I was on the floor. I thought, Christ, I've had it, this is my lot.'[33] A bomb had exploded on the floor above. Mustafa Bohour, who was watching from his top floor flat opposite the tower's entrance, described the scene: 'When I got to the window, debris was flying all over the place. Bits of metal were crashing onto the street outside. I could see my neighbour's car with its windscreen smashed and falling bricks had broken the roof of my lorry.'[34] Despite a warning the previous day, and a call claiming that the 'Kilburn Battalion' of the IRA was responsible for the bomb, a thorough investigation failed to identify the perpetrator.[ii]

The damage done by the bomb was soon repaired, but its effects were far reaching. Billy Butlin's revolving restaurant, a huge attraction since the time of opening, was informed that its lease would not be renewed, and by the end of the decade it had closed. Notwithstanding seasonal visits from Noel Edmonds for the BBC, and the frequent rebrandings of the privatised telecoms company which owned it, the tower began its long slide into seclusion and disuse. It remains a relic of an age where the state invested in industry and technology, a symbol of a lost vision of the future, of what was once possible, and the way we did things. It still towers on the skyline, but like some historic castle, it is devoid of function. Intended to demonstrate Britain's status at the vanguard of cutting edge innovation, it was completed at a time when the country's international influence was waning fast. Pretty soon all it seemed to add up to was a relay station for transmitting the cricket or regional adverts.

Even so, it's clear BT don't realise what they have here. Bursting with fascinating if outmoded technology, this temple of geek is a historic site of the communication world, like the huts at Bletchley Park. It contains the relics of the future – for some a haul as exciting as any number of crossbows, gold coins and pottery. In 2010 the

ii It wasn't the first time that windows had been replaced on the Tower. According to the *Daily Mirror* report: 'When the BBC "24 Hours" team took over the floor on the opening night, some of their more impulsive guests scratched some rude drawings on the glass.' The windows, which were on the observation deck, were hastily repaired.

management team was quite unprepared for the huge number of requests for tickets when they added it to the Open House Weekend programme, and they had to turn away most of the people who applied. The floors halfway up the tower are like a time capsule or a sealed tomb, just waiting for new generations to come, gasp with delight and set about cataloguing the incredible artefacts and hazard a guess at their meaning.

'British architects are well through the novelty phase of skyscraper building,' planner Lionel Brett wrote in 1961. 'Many are in fact alarmed at the effect on our old city silhouettes and open spaces of a proliferation of second-rate flat-tops with off-the-peg curtain walls.'[35] By the late sixties *Concrete Quarterly* was echoing his fears. 'The highly conventional "style" of international architecture is spreading a pall of monotony over the world's cities,' they reported, feeling it was time to 'introduce a more regional note into modern architectural design.'[36] Richard Seifert, Colonel of the curtain wall, had also become deeply critical of the standards reached by his peers. 'The complexities and functional problems have, for a long time, taken precedence over the aesthetic and architectural appreciation of design,' he wrote in the early seventies, 'thus derogating the appearance of buildings in our cities.'[37]

Appearance was one thing, but as time marched on and the pace of technological change accelerated through the seventies and early eighties, even the most modern-seeming office blocks of the previous two decades began to appear unfit for purpose. No sooner was the NatWest Tower finished, for example, than it was deemed to lack the trunking and cabling necessary for a modern bank with hundreds of desktop computers. Millions of pounds had to be spent converting it. Adapting to the needs of the digital age has been as tough on Centre Point and the Post Office Tower as it has on Georgian or Victorian buildings. From Croydon to the City of London, the mirrored towers of the fifties and sixties all became obsolete at the same time: the moment that Docklands could provide buildings native to the new technological age. Richard Seifert's humblebrag that 'future generations might be better judges of the exhilarating view of London's modern skyline,' was predicated on the notion that the modern skyline would still be there for future generations to observe.[38] But as many of his most recognisable buildings, from Telstar House to New London Bridge House and Draper's Gardens, are erased, the towering achievements of even this most prolific of architects may be returned to the obscurity that a largely disapproving and envious architecture profession would have wished on him from the very start.

6. 'A Village With Your Children in Mind'
SPAN AND THE PRIVATE SECTOR DREAMS OF NEW ASH GREEN (1957–1972)

'What was that place that used to make everyone laugh?' asked Jo Griffiths unexpectedly when I visited her and town planner husband Jim to talk about the new town of Cwmbran. 'Was it New Ash Green? Why did it make people laugh?' Jim was quick to deny that New Ash Green had ever made anyone laugh – and to point out the differences between it and Cwmbran, where they had lived.

'It was the private sector version,' he explained, 'and it was expensive and very small. Very nice, but *bijou*. Funnily enough, New Ash Green is nearer to the garden village model,' he said. We looked out of the window of their home in the quaint Edwardian garden village of Rhiwbina, with its cluster of Arts and Crafts style cottages. 'It wasn't a town.'

Two months later I was walking around New Ash Green to decide for myself just how funny it was.

It was late August when I took the train 25 miles out of London into the Kent countryside. From the train window I watched as clouds dragged their long shadows across golden, harvested fields. In ancient woodland, red and yellow leaves had begun to fall from the old oaks. I was travelling to the heart of the green belt, out beyond the creeping tendrils of suburbia. New Ash Green is a couple of miles from the nearest station, so I took a taxi, and could hear the quiet amusement in the driver's voice as I told him where I was headed. Perhaps Jo was right – even 40 years later, the novelty had not worn off.

I'd arranged to meet university lecturer Patrick Ellard. He lived in Knight's Croft, one of the earliest neighbourhoods. Like many postwar developments, houses weren't built along roadsides, but overlooked pathways instead, so as we drove through I peered out at anything that might provide a useful clue as to our whereabouts. The driver abandoned me as soon as he could, desperate to be out of the village's odd road system. I stood for a while trying to get my bearings among the quirky houses with their monopitched-roofs and the showily exotic foliage. There wasn't much for a stranger to work with, and the numbering system, supposedly based on the route taken by a postman, was almost impossible to follow. For some time I walked in what turned out to be entirely the wrong direction. It became clear almost immediately that even to someone who had managed to navigate Park Hill's streets in the sky, the underpasses of the Elephant and Castle and the baffling Dashes of Harlow, this was a formidable new challenge. I felt that I had entered a highly sophisticated but altogether alien landscape. Narrow paths, overgrown with shrubbery, led me deeper into the neighbourhood. This cluster of beautiful modernist houses hidden in the midst of dense woodland felt more like the setting for a Lars von Trier film than hop-growing country. Eventually I found Patrick's bungalow, in the corner of a square, where it sat stealthily clad in its black asbestos tiles. Large, glossy-leafed plants led up to the buttercup yellow front door, still proudly displaying its number in Eurostile, a squared-off sixties typeface.

I'd been told that Patrick was *the* go-to guy if you want to learn about New Ash Green. He'd lived there since he was four years old and had contributed to a book celebrating the developer, Span, and their mercurial architect, Eric Lyons. I was heartened to see that, although clearly a huge Span nerd and keen to retain as many original features in the bungalow as possible, Patrick's house wasn't a museum; it was a home. Duplo and Transformers showed that small children were at work. There were hints of his other obsessions, from the jazz playing in the background to the books on pop culture ranged along the walls. When he professed a fondness for Saint Etienne, I knew Patrick was a true renaissance geek. We sat in his lounge, with its glass wall opening out onto the garden. The Scandinavian obsession with teak was everywhere in evidence: a teak and glass floor-to-ceiling cabinet divided the kitchen and lounge; the floor was teak block; the doors were teak; and there were teak shelves in the kitchen. The ceiling sloped upwards to one end of the room, revealing a large spandrel panel beneath – in teak. A single steel beam crossed the room, solidly holding the light prefabricated frame together. It was a masterclass in lightness, efficient use of materials, and stylish mid-century living.

'We arrived here in autumn of 1969,' said Patrick, in his calm, unhurried manner. By 'here' he didn't just mean New Ash Green, he meant Knight's Croft, the neighbourhood he still lives in – as do his parents and sister.

'There were maybe about 200 other families here at the time, so not too many. But the first families started to move in in early '67. So there'd been enough time for a bit of a community to build up. And immediately we felt welcomed. I think it was very much due to what Span had put in place to promote the idea of a close-knit community. I think that was done through the physical embodiment of the village and the design, through to the position of the houses and really making it work on a pedestrian level.'

I chose not to confess quite how lost I'd been earlier.

'The paths were designed to be narrow, so that they would bring you into contact with your neighbours. And the residents' societies empowered people to have a say in how their communities were run so that brought people together again. Obviously my sister and I were quite young at the time, but it was the social life that was so important. As soon as you moved in people would be knocking on your door saying "how are you?" "where have you come from?".

Patrick's family had arrived from Birmingham, via Staplehurst. His parents were typical of the kind of young professionals that New Ash Green was attracting.

'He was an interior designer, she was a schoolteacher. They were the archetypal Span residents! People had come to New Ash Green to make it work, to participate in what many were describing at the time as a social experiment. It was fantastic. People were interested in people, and interested in the place as well. People coming here in the late sixties and early seventies brought their culture and interests with them so within months you'd have various societies being formed in people's houses. It was great, a wonderful place to live.'

Throughout our conversation Patrick was keen to impress how universal that enthusiasm had been back in the day.

'There was always something happening. Span set up shop in the manor house' – as had the Harlow development corporation, in Terlings – 'so the earliest societies like the film society held their shows in the manor house. And they put on parties. Every week there was a party to welcome the new residents. The parties were held in this exquisitely designed show hall, where there were scale models of the neighbourhoods, and scale models of the shopping centre, which wasn't built yet. Span even paid for a little temporary hut and some goalposts for the football club, and gave a bit of land so they could have their pitch. They were very benevolent.'

After a good nose around his house, and its original features – from the big white porcelain sink in the kitchen to the brushed aluminium door handles, the black ceramic tiles in the bathroom and the yellowing plastic light switches and power sockets – we went for a stroll around the village.

It was Span developer Leslie Bilsby who initially suggested that the company should branch out from building small housing estates to creating a whole town. He was eventually talked down to a village. When two adjacent farms in Kent – Newhouse and North Ash – came on the market in the early sixties, Span snapped up the 430 acres with an eye on building something more ambitious than just another suburban estate. It was a change not just in scale, but philosophy. 'We thought the village was exciting,' said Geoffrey Townsend, Span's other principal developer. 'It was trying to create a society for people; it wasn't just doing a spec-built job of selling houses.'[1] Eric Lyons, the architectural driving force behind Span, was in no doubt of the potential, remarking that 'this is the most exciting scheme I have ever undertaken.'[2]

Span were not alone in attempting such grand private projects. There was also Bar Hill outside Cambridge, whose developer Covell Matthews and Partners aimed to build 1,250 houses by 1965; and Vigo in Kent, just seven miles down the road, where Andrew Cunnison was set to construct 650 homes. The Observer suggested that these projects were 'sparking off a new trend, in an era when city centres are being torn apart, and redevelopment is becoming an OK word'.[3] Leslie Bilsby wholeheartedly agreed: '500 villages like New Ash Green could be built in the next five years,' he said, 'and 250,000 people housed in exceptionally pleasant and functional environments.'[4]

Yet Span soon discovered that private redevelopment wasn't an 'OK word' in the eyes of Kent County Council, who refused planning permission in January 1964. The train line was poor, they argued. And the project would interfere with their own new housing initiatives, such as the expansion of the nearby village of Hartley. Then there was the loss of all that premium agricultural land. And let's not forget this was the green belt, the council reminded Span. It was the new Labour Minster for Housing, Richard Crossman, who saved the project. He was convinced that Span's scheme and Eric Lyons' designs would 'show up what's wrong with the ghastly development in this part of Kent for the last 10 years.'[5] This was a direct knock at the sprawl of Hartley, and Dartford Rural District Council were furious. Labour councillor Leslie Reeves referred to the decision as 'Mr Crossman's unaccountable blunder' and offered to buy the unbuilt village for the council. The press were all over the story. 'Mr F. Sims, leader of the Conservative opposition group, told *The Times* that they gave unqualified support to protests against development at New Ash Green.'[6] To Sims' and others' dismay, Kent council finally passed the scheme in 1966.

By that time the Greater London Council had committed to buying 450 houses for council tenants moving out of central London. Here, then, was a mixed community of council and private houses built not by the state, but by a developer. In effect, it was a market-funded new town.

On a Sunday afternoon stroll with Patrick along the 'wents' – the old Kentish word for paths – it became clear how Span thought people would live back in the late sixties, and how much has changed

Span houses overlook the 'minnis' in New Ash Green.

since then. The impression was of green space punctuated with the odd row or cluster of houses – pretty low density for a private development. Buildings were grouped in small terraces, angled in staggered 'saw-toothed' layouts. Gardens were designed with steel hook fencing to allow the residents to look straight out onto the 'minnis' – the old Kentish word for open spaces. And people could look back in too, over the lawns and low fences, through the picture windows and glass doors. Span's New Ash Green was all about relaxed informality and openness. Today most of the gardens have been hemmed off with tall fences, and the householders have turned their backs on the communal green spaces. Not only that, the Span homes in New Ash Green are now vastly outnumbered – five to one – by those designed and built by Bovis in the eighties. This hugely expanded modern village now features hundreds of red-brick *Brookside* houses, and cars and pedestrians were no longer separated: roads ran directly in front of all the houses, in whose driveways fleets of 4x4s were parked. And the small windows of the new houses no longer 'let the outside in', giving instead a mean, fortress-like element to the estate. Span's original village, with its calm Scandinavian-style beauty, was perhaps the most beguilingly lovely place I'd visited on this tour. But something had clearly gone very wrong in paradise.

Eric Lyons' successful architecture practice, which was based in his garden, grew up in the fifties. His first job had been working for modernist maestro Maxwell Fry and his eminent – if short-term – colleague Walter Gropius. During the mid-thirties they designed and oversaw the construction of Impington Village College in Cambridgeshire, the Bauhaus master's only major British work. 'I don't believe that I emulate Gropius architecturally,' Eric was later to say, 'but his rational discipline was something that I needed. I'm basically irrational.'[7] A fellow architect described Eric as 'the most amusing *ex tempore* speaker I know, slightly satirical, poking fun at everybody, including himself'.[8] The shrewd architectural critic

Ian Nairn, who would later present a BBC documentary on him, found Eric 'a robust extrovert ... whose forthrightness might well puzzle the earnest sophisticates who on average seem to represent the typical Span-dweller ... There is no Corbusian arrogance ... each new housing scheme represents a different problem and may need a different solution'.[9] Lyons, self-deprecating as ever, was less kind: 'I am a rehasher,' he said, 'and I believe in rehashing, although I call it an evolutionary process.'[10] He would design all sorts throughout his career, from cinemas to tower blocks, but it was his work for Span that would define him. His 'evolutionary' approach, testing out ideas over time in subtly different estates and developments, was brilliantly suited to the exploration of new ideas in building homes, and Span allowed him to experiment. 'Few local authorities have, like the LCC, seen their housing problems as a great challenge to be met with new ideas for creating a new domestic environment,' he wrote in *The Times* in 1961. 'Few speculative builders, indeed, see housing as anything but an old business made tricky by changing architectural style, to which they sometimes must pay lip service.'[11]

Rather than sticking to the tried and tested methods of building homes, Lyons and the team at Span were always looking for new angles and approaches to the problem – from the layout of the estates they planned to the means of construction. He was keen to incororporate elements of prefabrication and standardisation: 'People dream of their special house because they do not like the ready-made articles available, but there is no reason why needs should not be satisfied by ready-made houses any more than by ready-made cars or refrigerators.'[12] He was also a fan of designing terraces, squares and courts, patterns more familiar to Georgian architecture than modern estates with their neighbourhood clusters and precincts of towers. 'We need grouped houses, not only for the sense of community they impart, but for economic and sensible use of land and to enable us to use modern building techniques by repetitive design.'[13]

The kind of modern design Eric and Span were championing was somewhere between expensive architect-designed villas for the rich and rational large-scale council developments for the working class. These were viable replacements for the mock-Tudor suburban semis that had come to define the middle classes around Britain's cities. Selling them to that most cautious and status-conscious of constituencies was as much of a skill as designing them. Placing show houses at many of the Ideal Home-style exhibitions was a trick Eric and Span had learned early. In 1957 they had constructed a home from their Blackheath estate at the second *House and Garden* 'House of Ideas' show, and received rave press reviews. 'There is no doubt at all that this is an enchanting little house,' enthused the correspondent from the *Manchester Guardian*, although 'the housewife in me would rather not dust that staircase where wooden treads meet iron angles.' Still, she concluded 'anything that succeeds in bringing this kind of house to the middle-income groups is a good thing.'[14]

The Span name was first used in 1957 at Parkleys, their estate in Ham Common, west London. Here Eric's updated versions of terraces and courtyards, complete with communal gardens, were built to a standardised but flexible design. Robert Matthew, the increasingly eminent former LCC chief architect, was swift to praise the estate. 'These housing groups are obviously congenial to those living there that it becomes the more difficult to understand why the techniques used by the private developer have for so long remained almost static in a world of great change.'[15] A further accolade came the company's way when in 1959, a Span development was selected to represent a milestone in postwar building. 'The Minister of Housing, Mr Henry Brooke, yesterday handed over the one millionth house built by private enterprise since 1945 to its owners, Mr and Mrs L. Saunders. The house chosen for this honour was at Corner Green, the latest project by Span Developments at Blackheath Park, London S. E.'[16]

I'd visited Parkleys the week before heading to New Ash Green, and met up with Oliver Childs, who lived in one of the flats and ran a vintage furniture restoration business. There was a great deal more regularity in the design here than in bespoke New Ash Green. Almost 200 flats were designed in what Oliver described as 'a sort of Georgian square idea, so you've got these lovely courtyards.' One thing that was consistent with Span's later village was the astonishing variety of beautiful planting around the estate. The design of the flats and courtyards encouraged a free-form ramble through the backs and fronts rather than the oppressive 'keep off the grass' regime favoured by local authority schemes. But the most recognisably Span detail, above all others, was the

Classic tile-fronted Span flats at Parkleys.

tiled fronts. For the most part Parkleys is two storeys high, and all the way round the top floor was fronted with terracotta tiles, hung flat against the prefabricated panels. It's this slightly Arts and Crafts detail on these otherwise recognizably modernist flats that gives them so much distinctive charm.

I walked through the glass-fronted stairwell and up a flight of stairs to Oliver's flat, and rang a suspiciously ancient-looking doorbell. Some time later, after a bit of tapping, I heard barking, and

Oliver came to the door with his excitable Parson Russell terrier, Rufus. Slim, pale and dressed immaculately in the manner of a fifties man about town, Oliver looked rather as if he'd been cryogenically frozen at the opening of Parkleys and defrosted for the occasion. Like his dog, he was sometimes breathlessly quick and eager, and at other times quietly observant.

'The doorbell's intact,' he informed me later, proudly. 'It doesn't work at the moment, but nothing's been added to it.' His flat was, as I'd expected, full of marvels. A long Robin Day sofa ('his take on a Chesterfield') divided the room. There were a couple of beautiful austerity-era chairs made by Remploy ('found in a skip') and a colourful painting by Anthony Frost on the wall. But the dominant presence, as in Patrick's house in New Ash Green, was the huge picture window, looking out over a verdant courtyard and the back of a now rather tatty row of shops, also built by Span.

'The minute we got the chance to buy I knew I wanted Span,' he said, perched on the edge of a Remploy chair, 'and we couldn't have a house, unless we looked for a real run down wreck.' What was it that made him want to live in a Span house in particular? 'Initially it was New Ash Green. I remember seeing a postcard. A guy used to come into a shop I used to run and he dropped off a postcard when the New Ash Green website had first been set up.' I imagined a network of like-minded vintage furniture fans tipping each other off about the latest teak sale. 'I'd never even heard of it before then. Ultimately, the tiled fronts, aesthetically – just that Span tile – is what I like about these. I'm from Old Amersham, a very little cottagey place, so I always thought as a kid I wanted a little cottage on the high street, and I see these as cottages. It's a realistic version of where I thought I'd be when I was 14. The idea might have been to buy a bigger one eventually, but now I'm of the opinion of still trying to get that cottage, but keeping this one. I don't ever want to get rid of this.' It was clear that Oliver, in his Span flat surrounded by beautiful mid-century Scandinavian furniture, was living the dream.

It wasn't an easy dream to maintain. The twenty-first century had a way of intruding. Oliver gestured towards the large black television sitting incongruously in the corner of his sitting room.

'The awful thing is that if you want to be in 1957 little things like tellies and fridges get in the way. If I could afford it I would have a reconditioned little fifties fridge.' His kitchen was a work in progress. After eight years the mismatched furniture had yet to settle into a state of vintage bliss. 'I won't have a toaster because they're new,' said Oliver. 'It's hard to find the balance between literally trying to be in 1957, as I am, and …' He didn't have a chance to finish the thought, because we were distracted by a stack of old books on the floor; they turned out to be the minutes from the earliest residents' meetings in Parkleys, which Oliver and his wife Lisa had rescued from a clear-out of the neighbourhood office. They told the story of a thousand local disputes stretching right back to the beginning. 'Milton Court, at the back, was the last to be landscaped,' he explained as I browsed through the yellowing pages, ''cos all the stuff from this end of the estate was just dumped at Milton. For about a year the arguments went on – *when will we get some grass, when will we get turf.* And Eric Lyons chaired the meetings, just trying to calm everyone down.' The rapid spread of new technology in the fifties was another contentious issue. 'In the early days there was one aerial on the estate for telly, and the arguments about people not getting the right reception! And so they decided in the end to go with individual aerials. The idea that they just put one aerial in that everyone plugged into! But that goes back to the social aspect of the era, because it was television for a start, in 1954, and there were a lot of people getting tellies – certainly a couple of years later.' Eric Lyons wasn't above designing the odd stick of furniture himself. He'd exhibited two chairs and a table at 'Britain Can Make It' in 1948, and Oliver was as much fascinated by Lyons' furniture design as by his architecture. 'We bought this chair here when it was still thought to be Eric Lyons,' he said, indicating a beautiful blond wood armchair, 'and we've since found out that it's not.' (Some months later, scanning Oliver's rantings on Twitter at the *Antiques Roadshow* expert misidentifying one of these as Lyons' work brightened up an otherwise quiet show.) 'I have got an Eric Lyons chair in the study,' he continued. 'This is quite aesthetically pleasing; Eric Lyons' is quite clunky. He did quite a few products – he did heaters and radios – and it wasn't very fine design, it was quite logical, in the same way that Span wasn't refined. It's quite a simple idea: lots of light in a box.'

Glimpses of Parkleys reminded me of an opulent version of Fieldway, the sixties estate in my home town of New Addington. It was that Span tile, hanging on the frontages of modern, part-prefabricated houses. It was what I'd felt in Welwyn Garden City when looking at those red-brick Arts and Crafts cottages: a rush of 'here's what you could have won!' Much as interwar house builders had aped the garden city style, so huge building contractors such as Laing or Wates developed mass-produced systems that brought elements of Span's instantly recognisable language to much wider attention. 'There's no doubt he inspired me,' Neil Wates once remarked of Eric Lyons.[17]

'These were built by Wates,' explained Oliver at Parkleys. And he'd noticed how the building contractor, like so many others, had gone on to be much inspired by Span. 'In Ham there's a massive Wates estate, which basically looks like these, only they're town houses. You can see in the detail that it's not as well thought out as Span, there's a bit more clunkiness to them. But essentially Wates 10 years later tried to do their own version.' It wasn't only the middle classes that private developers targeted with their designs. Cheaper, smaller versions of Eric Lyons cropped up all over the country too, in council estates and sixties infill. Where Parkleys was well maintained by a gardener and workmen – for a fee – and at ease with its pretty middle-class take on modernism, Fieldway, designed and built by Laing, had always looked cramped. Like so much of New Addington, it felt abandoned by the council. The green space between the homes had been done away with, and the meanly proportioned houses were crammed together, separated only by the width of an alleyway. Here was a version of Span that had shrunk in the wash.

'Happiness is an adopted frog,' announced an advert in *The Times* in June 1969, a month before Apollo 11 landed on the moon. 'Come home to New Ash Green.' The blurb was persuasive – invasive, almost. 'Span is building a village with your children in mind.'[18] The advert campaign was pure *Mad Men*, slick and shameless. 'A complete village, entire in itself, with a choice of 18 brilliantly designed "homes for all seasons"' went another. 'You'll come home to a warm, cosy, bright and airy, centrally-heated "place in the country", with every mod con, and then some.'[19] The cons may have been mod, but they were nothing less than the executive class being wooed to the Kent countryside would expect. The social and self-improvement aspects of this space-age village were also trumpeted. 'One mother told the researchers that she now realised that the village offered more than a detached house,' reported *The Times*. 'It is part of a healthy trend to be rid of the standoffishness of the suburban Englishman's semi-detached castle, and accept that people, especially mothers with young children, need each other.'[20]

'We seemed to be doing all the right things at that moment in our social history,' said Patrick Ellard, thinking back to the early days of New Ash Green. 'All of those baby boomers had been given the chance to go to university for the first time. There was a whole pop explosion – *youthquake* – new fashions, new music, new attitudes to life, and I think New Ash Green encapsulated that. You weren't just moving to a new place, you were moving to a new lifestyle. It quickly became a delightful, friendly, welcoming place to be.' As in the new towns, forming social groups was essential at the beginning. 'Dad was a founder of the cricket club, rugby club. Mum was a member of the amateur dramatic society. I think I even appeared in some of those productions as a munchkin or an elf or something like that!' But life in New Ash Green was a mixture of these traditional pursuits and a more modern, almost spiritual vision of society – a step towards utopia.

'All the publicity was talking about providing an environment for a new forward-thinking community. The vast majority of people came here because they wanted to participate in this roly-poly 1960s experience. And because you were coming to the middle of nowhere it was a concerted decision. *I don't want to live in the suburbs or whatever, I want to try out this new lifestyle.* I even met one of the managing directors, Geoff Townsend, and he said it was about what we saw as creating a new society. I suppose in the 1960s there were a lot of things that went wrong. This idea of imposing an architecture style, which later became known as the deterministic approach, dictating *this is how you will live, you will adopt the high-rise, you will use the streets in the sky* – it never felt like that in New Ash Green. Clearly there was a strong sort of aesthetic to the place, but I don't think it was deterministic. I think people embraced it and created their own lifestyle. Undoubtedly the physical arrangement of the place encouraged that, but at no time did we think we were having an alien lifestyle imposed upon us. It was great times. People were amenable to new things, whatever it might be – mind-altering drugs, men growing their hair, outlandish fashions.'

The would-be residents were so keen, that even before they had moved in they were creating a record of the place.

'I've collected photographs taken by residents who came to watch their houses being built,' said Patrick. 'Walking through the shells of their houses before the first fix. I've got all these fantastic photos taken by people who would later go on to become our friends, walking round these half-built houses. But people wanted to get in.' The village was officially opened in 1967 by Sir Keith Joseph, former Minister for Housing and part-time building magnate. It was reported that '10 percent of the houses for sale were intended as first homes for couples, where the husband was still in his twenties. The aim was to achieve a balanced community, including older or retired people and newly married couples as well as established and prospering families'.[21] Fears of creating a 'pram village' were clearly on Span's mind, yet in other ways, Span's ambitions were remarkably close to those of the new town planners, even to the extent that they invited the Greater London Council to buy a quarter of the village's proposed 2,000 houses. It was a canny deal, ensuring both a hefty pay cheque from the council and an easy rejoinder to folk who accused Span of building yet another exclusive estate for executives.

'Essentially those early Span developments were very middle class,' said Patrick. 'But with New Ash Green the original concept was to be more of a social mix. The GLC at the time had a policy of encouraging people to move out to the country, whether it was to Essex or to Kent. So we did have people from south London coming to New Ash Green who weren't necessarily architects, designers or teachers, so I think we *did* have that social mix, and there *was* a variety of accents.' I must have looked sceptical, because all of a sudden he sounded slightly defensive. 'I wouldn't say there was an air of snobbery or elitism at all,' he said.

What Patrick had said about New Ash Green reminded me of Jo Griffith's half-remembered antipathy. In Coed Eva, the neighbourhood Jo and her husband Jim had lived on in the new town of Cwmbran near Cardiff, the social mix had been encouraged by the development corporation, who'd built houses for both council tenants and private buyers. 'Below the school field it was development corporation,' remembered Jo, 'and above that it was private.'

'In the end you want your social mix,' explained Jim. Before the development of Coed Eva in the late sixties, the new town had embodied a much more traditional postwar socialist model of building, with little or no private ownership. 'There was an awful lot of public housing. It's mixed now, but it wasn't then. It was all housing for rent.' But then among the thousands of council houses landed smaller estates of private housing: by 1978 over a fifth of all Cwmbran's houses were privately owned. 'They were worried then about creating a different sort of ghetto. It was a mixed social experiment. They were nervous about having lots and lots of large council estates,' said Jim. He sat back, attempting to conjure up some kind of context for me. 'By the end of the sixties Jane Jacobs had written her book in America' – he was referring to the unlikely bestseller, *The Death and Life of Great American Cities* – 'and there were lots of texts about "social engineering" it was called, steering people into these places. The town planning world was getting nervous about endlessly building council houses.'

'It's funny, when you come from renting somewhere in London to renting somewhere here it didn't seem like a big issue to me,' Jo recalled with a shrug. 'But a lot of people wanted to buy. They were *desperate*.'

'A lot of people came with mortgages and they wanted to buy into the market,' confirmed Jim. 'Some rented for one year and then went into private sector.'

'But they ended up just *there*,' said Jo, shaking her head at the thought that the difference between the private and council houses in Cwmbran was often only as narrow as the width of a hedge. 'Their kids were at the same school, and they went to the same shops.'

Jim took me on a drive out to Coed Eva in Cwmbran to see the house they'd moved to from London in 1969. Jo had found the idea of New Ash Green funny, but I think Jim was aware just how close Coed Eva had become to Span's modern village. Sure, in many ways it was a classic new town neighbourhood unit, houses clustered near their communal car parks and surrounded by wide child-friendly lawns. But the houses themselves weren't the sort I'd seen in the early estates in Harlow or Cwmbran. They had big picture windows, flashy mono-pitch roofs, and black timber panelling front and back. There were small rows of terraces, pairs of semis, as well as the odd detached house, all grouped inventively around greens that were planted with large trees and shrubs. On the bigger houses the windows were dotted playfully around the façade, breaking up the shape from the outside, and the brickwork was a warm yellow on the gable ends – although Jim was quick to point out that on the later, privately owned houses the brickwork was paler and cheaper. The gardens still had their original fencing of horizontal planks too. The paths and clusters of houses were plotted on curved lines and irregular patterns, conforming to the hilly landscape all around. 'Efforts have been made to avoid the monotonous street enclosed by continuous façades of houses,' was the verdict of Frederic Osborn's opus *New Towns* in 1977, which praised the 'siting of houses so that they often appear at different angles and unusual groups in relation to roads, paths and surrounding spaces.'[22] A stream wound its way through Coed Eva and old hedgerows from the farmers fields broke up the lines of houses. Here was a new town development corporation adapting the newly fashionable idiom of Span – modern Scandinavian-style design, large windows, timber or tile cladding, mono-pitched roofs – to the gently irregular language of new town layout that had existed since Frederick Gibberd had planned Mark Hall North in Harlow in the late forties.

Jim's verdict on New Ash Green – very expensive and very small – neatly summed up the reasons for the spectacular collapse of Span's grand project at the end of the sixties. 1968 had seen a national financial crisis, resulting in a devaluation of the pound and Harold Wilson's empty promise to the electorate that the 'pound in their pocket' would not be affected. By May 1969 the GLC were mired in a huge financial crisis of their own – partly because they had been lumbered with the unforeseen £3 million cost of strengthening their estate of multi-storey system-built flats following the partial collapse of Ronan Point in Newham (of which more in the first chapter of the last section of the book). Faced with a huge bill from Span for their 450 houses in New Ash Green, the council made their excuses and left without paying, and the developers found themselves perilously exposed. 'The decision was forced upon the housing committee by the parlous state that the GLC finds itself in,' said Horace Cutler, their beleaguered chairman.[23]

'They lost about £1 million in income,' explained Patrick, 'and that contributed towards their demise.' The attitude of Britain's building societies hadn't helped either. Because of the experimental steel 'A'-frame used in the construction of the houses, the lenders refused to ratify mortgages in the village. Some 226 people were turned away by building societies after putting up deposits for New Ash Green homes.[24] Struggling with £2 million of debt, Lyons decided that the game was up, and left Span in December 1969, with developers Bilsbury and Townsend following soon after. It was headline news. 'It's a wrench of course,' said Lyons to *The Times*. 'There have obviously been differences of policy, and difficulties, but I feel that in the end I'd reached the end of the line. It comes too from my own unrest. I feel I've got a lot more to give. I want to find myself expanding into new fields.'[25] He remained much in demand, designing the Shawbridge neighbourhood for Harlow development corporation, and Worlds End on the Chelsea waterfront, with its surprising mixture of brick tower blocks and low rise flats. And there was also work at the more executive end of his portfolio. Back in the sixties he'd been one of the designers working on developments at Weybridge – 'the Beverley Hills of England' as historian Elain Harwood has it – and such exclusive schemes continued to crop up.[26]

Patrick Ellard still feels the effect of the collapse of Span's New Ash Green dream keenly. 'I've seen some of the drawings of the architecture still on the drawing board,' he told me, 'and there was some fabulous architecture still to come.' These new designs had been borne out of close collaboration with the residents' society as well as Lyons' own team of designers. Yet this process of 'continual evolution' that Lyons so prided himself on was brought to a premature end. In 1971 Bovis paid £3 million for the development rights to New Ash Green.

Patrick had followed the ensuing saga between New Ash
Green's hippy-yuppies and their new masters through the residents'
association magazine. 'The early issues were dominated by the
conflict between the Span pioneers and Bovis,' he explained. 'It was
warfare. What Bovis did was bring in a more conventional style,
just going to brick cavity walls instead of prefabricated panels and
steel frames, and they cut down on the size of the greens, how much
they were prepared to spend on the planting. There were various
wooded areas that would have been retained by Span which Bovis
tore down, and built in much higher density. And built more
houses than Span had intended. The irony was, that brought the
community together.' But ultimately, they saw it atomised too. The
1971 study by the Centre for Environmental Studies on New Ash
Green held that '10 years later, when their children are older and
more independent [the residents] may welcome the prospect of a
detached or semi-detached house with walled garden or private
back and front, to insulate them from the incursions of another
generation's small children. They may want to opt out of that
community because, now more mobile, they have other recreational
and social interests.'[27] This turned out to be an uncannily accurate
forecast of the shift that occurred in the eighties, not just in New
Ash Green, but across Britain, a place where Margaret Thatcher felt
that there were individual men and women, but there was no such
thing as society. And in New Ash Green the Bovis estates, soon to
become four fifths of the housing in the village, accelerated that
switch from community to privacy.

In New Ash Green Patrick lives in the fragment of the
village built as Span and Eric Lyons had wanted, and lives with
the encroachment of a less generous developer's will on the
environment. In Parkleys, Oliver has looked on as some of the
other residents attempt to transform the listed estate with all
manner of unsympathetic modernisations. 'If you go round there's
a lot of really *bad things* that have occurred,' he declared darkly.
For example? 'A woman over there has got a lion doorknocker on

her door.' It might not sound much, but such incongruous details rankled with Oliver. 'In theory the doors are listed as well. Luckily the doors themselves have never been changed.' He told me the story of a former neighbour who'd rebelled against the restrictions placed on Parkleys' residents by English Heritage. 'He decided to get the estate de-listed so we could put plastic windows in. And the amount of people who were with him! We came home from that meeting and I literally opened a bottle of wine and I could have cried. Luckily not enough people were, but the fact that there were people *whooping* at the idea of getting plastic windows in... When he failed to get it de-listed he sold up and moved. Luckily the estate was listed before anything major happened.' These might sound like relatively minor, if depressing incidents, but Oliver affirmed that things have occasionally taken a more worrying turn at Parkleys. 'I nearly got run over by a resident the other day,' he said, 'because she genuinely *hates* me. She was on the pavement, driving along, and I was chatting to a friend of ours, and she beeped, and I just gestured where the road was, and she put her foot down. And *that's* when it gets a bit Midsomer.'

The starkest example I saw of seeing people working against Span rather than with it was not initiated by the residents, but the town council. New Ash Green's shopping centre had been designed by Lyons and later expanded by Bovis. It might have lacked the charm of Span's houses, but it still demonstrated that celebrated eye for detail. The design was irregular, with the heights and frontages of the buildings varying along a snaking path. These days, though, the place was desolate: shop units stood empty all the way along. Much of the brickwork on low walls and slopes was missing or had been dislodged. The first floor gallery has been worst hit. Patrick and I came to a halt at an abandoned, grilled-off arcade. He was shocked by the signs of recent vandalism. The grille had been bent and ripped up, all the doors had been jemmied, fresh graffiti was scrawled over the woodwork and broken glass lay deep as snowfall on the walkway. The local authority had long since given up on promoting or protecting the centre, keen to sell it off and see the lot bulldozed.[i]

'We did have our fair share of celebrity residents,' Patrick recalled. 'Whenever there was a Village Dance, where they'd close off the shopping centre and turned it into a huge nightclub, Tim Blackmore' – a Radio 1 producer – 'would invite his mates – David Hamilton, Noel Edmonds, Emperor Rosko, Tony Blackburn – they would come down and do the village dance! We had – it seems rather quaint now to mention these names – but Chickory Tip, who did have a big hit in 1973.' Thin Lizzy's manager lived a couple of doors down from Patrick and he remembers their big, noisy parties. Elton John's manager lived in the village too, and Elton himself played the summer party the year *Rocket Man* came out, arriving in a Rolls Royce Silver Ghost, and dressed in a fur coat. As we stood in the shopping centre on a raised brick platform, a kind of modernist bandstand, Patrick remembered how DJ Emperor Rosko had played his set from up there, bringing over 4,000 people to the little village for a party. He recalled the colours, the clothes – the kaftans and Ossie Clark dresses – and the brilliant summers of 1971, 1975 and 1976 that made it feel like they were on holiday all the time. 'Noel Edmonds so enjoyed his experience of doing the dances he decided to live here. When we had a Village Day there would always be a celebrity to come and open it. 1977 – or '78 – we had David Prowse – *Darth Vader! The Green Cross Code Man!* And he arrived by helicopter.' I told Patrick about the obsession with heliports I'd discerned in the postwar plans. 'Well, seventies DJs …' he said, 'it was the only way to travel. Span did spend a lot of money of helicopters because they brought architects to visit New Ash Green from across the world.'

After all these years Patrick is still in New Ash Green, still loving it, and occasionally waxing nostalgic about its glorious past. The most

---

i A year later I heard from Patrick that they had suddenly seen the potential of it – and applied for one of the government's Mary Portas grants. The application was not successful.

A village day, New Ash Green, in the early 1970s © Peter Copping Family Archive.

emphatic moment of our interview came when he leaned forward to ensure that my phone would catch his words: 'Most people who lived here between 1967 and 1984 would say this was the greatest time of their lives,' he said. If that was the case, what happened to them all? Did that generation of long-haired, Ossie Clarke-wearing progressives sell out as the sociologists had predicted, and seek a less communal way of living in the Bovis developments, where their cars were a status symbol and the garden walls ensured that no one could see them going about their lives?

In Parkleys, Oliver dressed the part as the fifties husband, and rescued fragments of the estate from destruction, while his wife Lisa organised community days in the gardens, as Span had back in the day. Here in New Ash Green, Patrick might have been hiding his tie-dyes and beads under a convincingly sober exterior, but his passion for the dreams of a bygone age was just as strong. Yes, Span's architecture has endured, and it becomes more desirable by the year. But perhaps more surprisingly, and despite all the changes in Britain over the last few decades, pockets of the Span lifestyle have endured too.

7. 'A Veritable Jewel in the Navel of Scotland'
CUMBERNAULD AND THE SECOND WAVE OF NEW TOWNS (1955-72)

Fenella Fielding hopped down from her helicopter, resplendent in a coat of shocking pink feathers, to be met by a pair of hit men and a safari-suited professor. Soft disco-funk played.

'Cumbernauld!' she cried to a group of townsfolk who'd turned up apparently dressed as characters from the board game *Guess Who?*. 'Tomorrow already here! A town *festooned* with awards for community architecture, a veritable *jewel* in the navel of Scotland.' She could barely suppress her delight – or her theatrically raised arms – as she announced the real reason for her visit: 'Ladies and gentlemen – we're going to hijack Cumbernauld!'

Of all the new towns, Cumbernauld is the one with the most unassailable pop cultural credentials. To start with, there's Scotland's greatest rom-com, *Gregory's Girl*. Then, in 1967, the town featured in the very first international live-by-satellite television show, *Our World*, sandwiched between items from Australia, Canada and Europe, and starring Picasso, Maria Callas, and most famously, The Beatles, giving the first public performance of their latest single, *All You Need is Love*. There's also *Cumbernauld Hit*, an extraordinary low-budget thriller backed by the development corporation, which may not have featured the nation's favourite romance or the world's greatest artists and musicians, but still managed to be artistically the most ambitious film shot in the new town. Eschewing the mundane public information documentary format favoured by the likes of Harlow, *Cumbernauld Hit* instead looked to *Dr No* and *The Italian Job* for inspiration. After all, the town boasted the nearest thing to

Ken Adam's brilliant Bond villain lairs built for real anywhere in the world.

'It was deliberately different,' said Ken Davie, one of the pioneer architects at Cumbernauld, when I interviewed him at the local golf club. For one thing, the new towns had been an overwhelmingly socialist project. Of the 32 new and expanded towns built under the Act, Cumbernauld was the only one to be designated by a Conservative government, a decade after the pioneers at Cwmbran or Harlow. It had been forced upon them by Glasgow's persistent and acute overcrowding as rebuilding work proceeded slowly in areas such as the Gorbals.

Ken confirmed how much J. M. Richards' 'prairie planning' critique of the first wave of new towns had shaped the vision of Cumbernauld's original chief planner, Hugh Wilson. 'There was a move towards a more compact town,' he explained. 'The designated area was the smallest of any new town, at just over 4,000 acres. The site dictated it. It had to be.' Garden city ideals were out, dense urban planning was in. This unpromising windy ridge to the north-east of Glasgow was expected to house almost three times as many people per acre as fellow new town East Kilbride. Four fifths of the population were due to come from the overcrowded areas of Glasgow, prompting *Guardian* journalist Mary Stott to comment in 1965 that 'presumably they will not mind being packed as neatly and carefully into this small space as sardines into their tin.'[1]

Yet it wasn't the housing that bore resemblance to sardine tins; it was the central area megastructure. Condensing all of the activities of a town centre into one huge building suited Hugh Wilson's super-tight plan just fine. And in addition to its practical advantages, it was seen as a unique opportunity, after the perceived loss of nerve of the first wave of new towns, to implement some of the most daring concepts of the age. Wilson had two highly imaginative deputy architect-planners, Derek Lyddon and Geoffrey Copcutt; one was to take charge of housing, the other to tackle the town centre. According to Copcutt, the two men decided their roles on the toss of a coin. Of the results of that chance outcome Copcutt later ruefully declared: 'Those to whom it may seem the toss was a poor deal for the centre can be consoled that the rest of the town was spared my attentions.'[2]

Geoffrey Copcutt certainly couldn't be said to have been lacking in vision. In a 1963 article for *Architectural Design* magazine he described the megastructure as 'citadel-like', being 'half-a-mile long, 200 yards wide and up to eight storeys high.'[3] Relatively low-level but sprawling across the A80, the central area was to house 'most of the commercial, civic, religious, cultural and recreational' activities for the projected town of 70,000 people, being the 'largest single employment source, traffic generator and land user'. There would even be a twin row of penthouses on the top deck of the building.[i] Copcutt put a great deal of himself into the project, later commenting that 'the paper prototype passed from passion to obsession.'[4] His somewhat megalomaniac description of the project might have seemed purple even as part of Fenella Fielding's dialogue in *Cumbernauld Hit*: 'And all the while, like a jeweller fashioning precious metal, I hammered the cross-sections and shaped landscape, to forge an urban morphology.'

One young architect, fresh from college with a thesis on entertainment provision in new towns, was John Knight, who was interviewed in 1964 to join the growing team at Cumbernauld. I met John in a vegetarian café in Edinburgh, where his anecdotes on life in the development corporation were delivered with the witty turn of phrase of a Ned Sherrin.

'They said, "You'll obviously want to work in the town centre group," explained John, 'and I said, "Yes I did, actually." I think construction started in about '62. But of course there was a huge amount of under-building required for the megastructure. I remember my first view of it when I came out in a bus from Glasgow. You saw the hilltop, and there were these three cranes.

---

i The fixation with 'decks' was a hangover from the early modernist mania for ocean liners – though in its rugged grey masculinity Cumbernauld Central Area resembled less the Queen Mary than HMS Ark Royal.

You couldn't actually see any construction because it was about the height of this table.'

It may not have looked impressive, but Copcutt's vision was in its infancy. With the instinct of a sci-fi writer, Copcutt had suggested in 1963 that 'in the extreme future, if particular central area functions decline ... the centre could become a gigantic vending machine through which the motorised user drives to return revictualled.'[5] It's safe to assume that neither in Harlow nor in Cwmbran had the planners anticipated a future where their town centres would become giant vending machines. *The Times* speculated that 'closed-circuit television might be used by the police; and the cleaning of floors might be performed by automatic vacuum cleaning machines.'[6] Other architects may have been content to solve the problems of today; Copcutt was anticipating those of tomorrow. It's something of a surprise that the producers of *Cumbernauld Hit* settled with making a spy thriller to advertise the town: science fiction might have been a more appropriate genre, especially as, after phase one had been completed, the central area bore a close resemblance to the star destroyers from that other classic 1977 film, *Star Wars*. 'I think the thing that finally settled me on trying for Cumbernauld rather than some of the nearer new towns like Skelmersdale,' said John, 'was the fact that *Architectural Design* in May 1963 produced this wonderful edition on Geoff Copcutt's town centre. When I read that there was no choice, I had to go there. It was a Damascene conversion. I'd spent all my life in London or thereabouts, and I thought, I've got to fly away.'

Another young architect who had his head turned was Tom Reilly. I met him and his former boss Ken Davie in the red-brick, varnished wood and brass-fitted function room of the Dullatur Golf Club in Cumbernauld. We were looking at old promotional prints of outline drawings of the central area produced by Mike Evans in the early sixties, well before construction began: drawings showing people busy pushing prams, pulling tartan shoppers or gazing down at the cars gliding through the centre of the structure on the A80.

They had that jarring, off-key quality all images of the future from the past have, bizarrely evoking a *Blade Runner* cityscape peopled by characters from a Gary Larson cartoon.

'These were published in *Architectural Review*,' recalled Tom. 'I was at Strathclyde University at the time and these seemed absolutely fantastic.' Tom was softly spoken but expansive, some years younger than Ken, but twice his size, and dressed formally in a dark lounge suit. Ken was a wiry old gent, cautious, sharp-eyed and gravel-voiced, who'd arrived in his car coat, clutching a carrier bag full of old documents, brochures and drawings from the CDC. He'd started work for the development corporation straight from university in 1957, and taken the job as chief architect and planner for Cumbernauld in 1970.

'This is a walk down memory lane for me,' Ken said wistfully at one point. As with almost all of the surviving members of the development corporation, both men lived locally and were active members of the Rotary Club. 'The first phase was only one fifth of the total concept,' he pointed out as we examined Copcutt's plan. 'But then things changed. Copcutt had in mind that things would "clip on". Churches, offices, buildings and suchlike. As time went on it wasn't as easy as that.' The town grew, and the needs for the centre kept evolving. As Ken pointed out, the residents 'were looking for other things,' undreamt of by Copcutt in his masterplan. And the problem with locating everything in a single structure was that it had to be pretty future-proof, so that great chunks of it wouldn't be rendered redundant, and large areas wouldn't continually need to be added.

'I worked with Doug Stonelake, who was group leader on phase two of the town centre,' explained John Knight. 'Phase one was in the next room, and I would rather curiously look through the door.' Copcutt had gone by this time, and John recalled the legend of his departure well.

'He had completely blotted his copybook by that time. Phase one was behind, it was over budget, all those things ... The development corporation were getting very frustrated and were saying, "We really have to see something of phase two." Because his initial concept was along the entire spine of the hilltop. Phase one was just a slice of the cake. And they said, "We need to see what's going on at either end." And he just wasn't interested. It wasn't happening. As I understand it, he was given a deadline by the development corporation – by Mr McGill, the general manager – and he was told to produce for the next board meeting the plans for phase two. And apparently he'd sketched something out more or less the night before, put them in a dustbin, and the dustbin I believe was carried into the board meeting. He took the lid off and produced the plans. It was just a lot of doodles and sketches.'

Alone on the crest of the hill rather than surrounded by other large buildings, the central area after its first two phases was both dramatically dominant and painfully exposed. Frank Schaffer, former head of the new towns division of the Ministry for the Environment, associated with the mild early phase of Harlow and Stevenage, was sceptical of the hill-top location, questioning 'whether mothers will take kindly to pushing prams up the long ramps, with its rough grey concrete and lack of trees and grass … and, above all, whether the high cost of building and maintenance will ever be fully met from the rents.'[7] Yet the town had friends in high places. Dame Evelyn Sharp, permanent secretary at the Department of Housing, for example, was contemptuous of the genteel early new towns. 'She loves Cumbernauld,' recorded her minister, Richard Crossman, in his diary, as the pair swept through on a flying visit of the sort Fenella would have approved.[8]

'There were four of us working on phase two,' said John Knight.

'The problem was that Copcutt had established the grid for the first phase, because it all had to be modular and gridded right the way across … There were two floors of car parking that had to be built before you even started. And that was its final undoing, because no developer said, "I'm willing to to stump up for two floors of car parking that I have no control over." And on top of that I had to fit entertainment buildings into this grid. Of course it didn't work. I fell out with Doug Stonelake who was the group leader, because he said, "You Have Got To Work To The Grid." And I said, "This is a nonsense Doug. You can't have a cinema with columns coming up the middle of it." It was as stupid as that. I said,

'Whether mothers will take kindly to pushing prams up the long ramps.'
© *North Lanarkshire Archives (ref: UT/178/1/171)*

"The grid's got to blossom into the areas you need for a dance hall, a skating rink, etc." We never saw eye to eye on that. In fact, we talked about it a fortnight ago and he said, "I really gave you a bad time." I remember one day he came with a sheet of tracing paper – I'd designed a nice cinema – and he just spread this sheet of tracing paper over the top and drew these heavy lines right across. The grid!'

'The trouble was,' said Tom, 'it was multi-storey but it wasn't enclosed. It was open.' I looked again at the drawings and realised

that the folk staring down from walkways outside the shops at the
cars below weren't behind glass, but leaning on open balconies. It
seems incredible that such a huge structure, built on an exposed
Scottish ridge, with a shopping centre at its heart, was designed to
be open to the elements. Tom shook his head in bewilderment at
Copcutt's apparent oversight. 'The wind came in at one end. Modern
shopping centres after this were enclosed and centrally heated and
warm. If this had continued and had been enclosed properly and
had been heated it would have made a difference.'

In Edinburgh, John Knight was equally nonplussed:

> 'There's no way you could have a tunnel shopping street in
> the highest hilltop town in Scotland short of Dalwhinnie,
> and people would want to shop in it. It was all raw concrete
> because everybody thought that was the thing to do at the
> time. And, of course, they couldn't get shops, that was the
> other big problem. There was a temporary shopping centre
> at Muirhead which had started off as temporary buildings
> but had got a supermarket and whatever, but none of them
> wanted to move into this megastructure because it was going
> to cost them so much money to fit out the units. But some of
> the photographs from when it was first built … It does look
> pretty good. That wonderful dog-leg ramp thing that comes
> up from the south. Nothing was ever worked out for either
> end of it, of that I'm pretty sure.'

So hard was it to let shops on the upper floors of the centre – a
problem familiar to developers at the Elephant and Castle – the
decision was taken that they would have to abandon planning for
these decks, and go back to developing on the ground. 'So what you
got was escalators taking you down to the ground,' said John, 'a total
admission of failure.'

It turned out that the wind whistling through the centre was not the
only serious problem. Many other issues stemmed from the futuristic

ambitions of its designer coming up against the corner-cutting workmanship of the day. Water penetrated the concrete and some seriously shoddy finishes were built by the soon bankrupted building contractor, who, outrageously, entirely failed to leave records of the infrastructure buried beneath the concrete. Copcutt's vision of an endlessly flexible construction proved illusory, as later architects and developers found their plans for additions to the largely unrealised central area thwarted by the structure's intransigence: like a spoilt child it stubbornly refused to play nicely with the other developments. In the end the much-vaunted 'megastructure' existed largely in the minds of a handful of architectural critics and academics, with the central area never reaching a size that merited the name.[ii]

'The thing that annoys me,' says Ken, 'is that there were problems with the town centre, but very often it's Cumbernauld as a whole that gets the criticism, whereas there's a whole lot of excellent housing. There was a series of programmes, Channel 4 was it?' He mimes teeth. Janet Street-Porter, I say – the show in question being 2005's *Demolition*, a week-long series where the public were asked to nominate buildings they wanted demolished. 'There was one shot of her on Central Way [the A80] saying "I don't know how to get into the town centre." Now, of course, she should never have been there.'

'Because of the pedestrian separation,' nods Tom grimly, referring to one of the basic tenets of the town, that wherever possible cars and pedestrians should be completely separated.

'These sort of things stuck in the throat a wee bit,' says Ken, who had been a paragon of gentle tolerance for the rest of our conversation. And it's hard not to agree that this sort of willful misrepresentation didn't help anyone. 'It's easy to criticise the town centre but it did provide innovation for a lot of things. Parking your car underneath and going up, which is quite normal in many shopping centres now, was frowned upon initially.' Later I discovered a clipping from *The Times* in 1972, a decade after Copcutt's plans were revealed to

---

ii Copcutt himself had never used the term 'megastructure' to describe Cumbernauld's central area.

the press, where a journalist got Ken to admit that with hindsight, he would have designed the town centre rather differently.[9] This enormous building must have been rather a millstone for him all these years. Architecture critic Ian Nairn gave a 'half term' report on the centre in 1967, declaring that the one fifth of Copcutt's design so far built was 'worthy but leaden, with none of the high spirits of schemes like the Tricorn at Portsmouth'.[10]

'I keep saying to people who pass judgement on Cumbernauld,' said Tom patiently, 'that you've got to go back to the time it was designated and what was happening in the world and the UK at that time. You're talking 50 years ago. Things were quite different, car ownership was quite different. There were virtually no supermarkets at all, and in the town centre Cumbernauld had the second largest one in Scotland – now disappeared.'

'But now they've sold the whole central area to private development,' he said, a note of quiet outrage in his voice, 'which means a development company owns all of the land there. So it means if you come to build a new office block in Cumbernauld there's no public land, you'll need to go to the developer there to get ground. Before it was all planned, but now it's all handed to the developer.'

This warning didn't serve to lessen the shock of actually visiting the central area itself. I don't know what I'd expected to see: a decaying hulk of concrete isolated on barren land between two huge road interchanges, perhaps. Something vast and tragic, for sure; the crumbling wreck of a crashed spaceship on the rugged Scottish hilltop. Instead, the central area has all but vanished. A huge section of phase one and all of phase three were demolished in the nineties, and a new shopping centre, the Antonine, has been tacked onto the side of the remains of the old one, like a parasitic plant strangling its host. In turn, a vast Tesco shed buts up against the Antonine Centre. Ground level car parks have replaced the internal ones from the original design. The penthouses (once optimistically referred to as the 'sun deck') can still be discerned from a distance, their black spine the only original feature still visible. Ironically, the whole central area now resembles an out-of-town shopping mall rather than the centre of anything; from one of the most recognisable places in Scotland it's been converted into a non-place.[11] It's only when driving on the road that cuts through what's left of the centre that the original structure reveals itself. A valley is formed by irregular concrete walls stained with algae that rise above on either side, and rusting pedestrian bridges decay high above the road. This is where all the ducts, vents, service entrances and loading bays front onto the road. Here security guards stand around puffing cigarettes by back doors, IT professionals park up with new components for old retail equipment, and reps hurriedly eat sandwiches in their cars between appointments.

Inside the Antonine Centre are vast walls of crisp matt white, giving it an unfinished nineties air. The minimalism attempts to counteract the complex arrangement of escalators, stairs and levels leading off from it. When we eventually reached the old central area

The remaining section of Geoffrey Copcutt's Central Area megastructure, seen from the road that passes through it.

shopping levels high above, it was clear that almost all of the shops have long-since closed, including a beautiful wooden-clad bookshop called Span. A few ancient cafés and opticians shops still cling to life, but the gleaming decks illustrated in Mike Evans' line drawings have become shabby and dark. Copcutt had been saddened that the finished structure had been shorn of so many of the features he'd intended, such as 'the mosaic of sites' he had intended for flea markets, as well as 'countless minor delights' that were 'not so much "simplified" as simply missed'. Now time has cruelly granted him his wish: the entire centre feels like a flea market. Consequently, it has that quality that designers try so hard to build into environments, but which only grows over time: it has developed *character*. The lack of chain stores, the irregularly shaped paths between the shops, the brown and orange wall tiles, the internal ramps – they all give the place a quirky, independent feel, especially when placed next to the apologetic blankness of the Antonine Centre.

Very little of Copcutt's design was built as intended, yet odd glimpses remain: the long slopes and staircases tucked away from the shops; the walls of stained net glass that look out at the penthouses, pedestrian bridges and flat roofs of the remaining structure. They are reminders, however imperfect, of Evans' pristine line drawings from 50 years ago, ghostly sightings of the space age we've consigned to history.

The drawings are not the only ghosts that haunt Cumbernauld. There's also Hook.

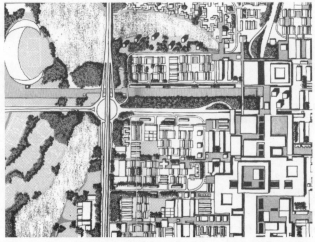

From the Hook book,
the layout of the central area of the town that was never built.

Planned in the mid-fifties by the London County Council rather than an official government-sponsored new town, Hook was meant to create urgently needed housing for 100,000 people, mostly former Londoners. After much scouring of land around the capital they chose to site the town in fields around Hook, a village in rural Hampshire between Basingstoke and Farnborough. Chief planner Oliver Cox and team churned through detailed reports on everything from suitable industries for the town (a propelling pencil factory was among the proposals) to the number of homes that would be needed for an average family of 3.2 people 50 years after the completion of building work. Delegations were sent to study the other new towns, particularly cutting-edge Cumbernauld, and the planners set to work designing future-proof housing schemes, shopping centres and road networks.

In an audacious move, Cox employed his very own visionary to rival Copcutt: Graeme Shankland, a young and controversial London County Council planner who had got into all sorts of trouble as a leading light in yet another modernist splinter group – this one called SPUR. The Society for Promotion of Urban Renewal had frightened the residents of Boston Manor in London when the BBC showed their plan to demolish the entire district and rebuild it as a futuristic landscape of towers and walkways. Several prominent members of SPUR went on to design the Barbican. Yet Cox was adamant that Shankland, despite his bad boy reputation, was the man for Hook, refusing to take on the job without him.[12]

After a year's work by Cox and his team, the authorities decided that it would be quicker and cheaper to expand the nearby towns of Basingstoke and Aldershot, and the Hook scheme was abandoned. Yet although the town was never built, the team's work was not altogether in vain: they produced an extraordinary book, *The Planning of a New Town*, which detailed exactly what it was they had planned, and why. Given its technical subject matter, large format and pages of dazzling stats, The Hook Book, as it became known, was not an obvious bestseller, but it became a surprise worldwide hit.[iii] Oliver Cox later speculated that 'one reason why the Hook book was the only bestseller that the LCC ever produced is that it did contain a summary of what we found interesting in the other new towns that were being built.'[13]

The Hook Book is a wonderful snapshot of an optimistic moment in British history, with the planners rightly seeing themselves at an important crossroads in modern history. 'Ten years ago there was a shortage of consumer goods and many items, including petrol, were rationed,' they noted, pointing out the decline in cinema attendance and the rise in television viewing as important signs of the way in which family life was evolving in the postwar world.[14] Their solutions were state-of-the-art for 1960. First, there was the urgent need to separate pedestrians and cars. Hook's planners predicted that in the future most families would own more than one car, and designed the central area to cope with 8,150 vehicles under the pedestrian platform level at any one time. At the same time, they maintained that, 'the whole system should be designed to encourage pedestrian movement and so reduce or obviate the need to use cars for as many journeys as possible.'[15] The footpaths, away from the road network, 'would form a new kind of town "street". They would become the focus of activity and outdoor social life.'[16] Naturally, as a town of the future, Hook was to have its own heliport 'designed to meet the requirements of an inter-city service'.[17]

Like Cumbernauld, Hook would have a vast central area: a mile-long platform suspended 20 feet off the ground from which buildings would sprout above and below, as if from a huge hyacinth vase. With cars, buses and lorries segregated beneath the deck and pedestrians happily shopping, socialising and working above, this would form a gigantic megastructure at the heart of the town. The tight site would mean that the houses would need to be built much more closely together than in previous new towns, with the Hook plan envisioning flats built right next to the central area, and smaller houses on the outskirts. A network of raised walkways through the

iii My own copy is stamped University of Wisconsin.

residential areas would bring pedestrians effortlessly up to the deck of the central area rather than to the subterranean world of car parks, roads and industrial hoists below. 'At last, we were to see an English new town which had shaken off the dead hand of the Garden City formula,' wrote Edward Carter, then head of the Architectural Association.[18] Like Cumbernauld, this was a town that promised to be the fulfillment of the postwar modernist dream on all fronts, not only in its wealth of innovative details but in its conceptual audacity.

The Hook team acknowledged their debt to Cumbernauld, but they were also critical of their Scottish counterpart. Their central area had been carefully sited in a valley so that the raised pedestrian deck could sit 'like a lid', in contrast to Cumbernauld's rearing conspicuousness on the crest of the hill. 'Such a site would save excavation for roads and car parks needed at the lower level, and would enable pedestrians to walk down or along into it instead of having to walk upwards as would happen with location on a hill-top site.'[19] 'We were right about that' maintained Oliver Cox in a later interview, remarking that 'taking a centre and placing it on top of a hill was totally wrong.'[20]

In fact, an alternative site for Cumbernauld's central area had been proposed: at the foot of the hill where the train station now sits. 'Tests on the traffic showed this wasn't feasible,' said Ken, still sensitive to the Hook team's accusations. But when Copcutt's scheme became a notorious wind tunnel, it became increasingly hard to ignore the predictions of the Hook planners that 'retailing trends in the future are likely to favour enclosed, centrally-heated and serviced shopping centres.'

The Hook team's criticisms were forgotten when a delegation from the American Institute of Architects visited Cumbernauld in 1967 as they scoped out potential entries for the R. S. Reynolds Memorial Award for community architecture.

'To our amazement we were on the shortlist with Stockholm and Tapiola,' said Ken, his delight still plain to see for all his efforts to conceal it, 'and we then won!' The award was announced in Washington on 10 May 1967, the *Financial Times* reporting that the jury chose it as 'the western world's highest achievement in new urban design for modern human needs'. A month later at the award ceremony in Scotland, Richard Reynolds, whose metals business sponsored the prize, claimed that 'Cumbernauld has set the standard for the world ... some of the most expensive buildings in the history of architecture have been the ugliest. In Cumbernauld you have, to your credit, combined outstanding design with reasonable cost.'[21] It was the biggest international prize given to any of the new towns.

'It meant a lot to the prestige of the town, there's no doubt about that,' confirmed Ken. Even Bison, the contractor who built Cumbernauld's eight 11-storey tower blocks in a record 15 weeks, placed adverts in the national press congratulating the team on the award – and proudly boasting that 'much of Cumbernauld is being built with Bison wall frame' because of 'its smooth-working industrialised building system.'[22]

More recent prizes have been less kind: Cumbernauld's town centre topped Channel 4's *Demolition* poll in 2005, and came second in the 2003 edition of *The Idler's Crap Towns* vote, with many agreeing heartily with *New Society* journalist Nicholas Taylor's 1973 description of the building as a 'dirty, windy megalith of piled-up shopping ledges'.[23] Of course, fans of visionary modern architecture see it quite differently: Miles Glendinning describes it as 'one of the key monuments of postwar European architecture, and the most important postwar work in this country'.[24]

'You still get architects from all over the world coming here,' said Tom. 'There's a Berlin school of architecture that are still very interested in Cumbernauld, they've brought students along.'

The central area was not Cumbernauld's only innovation. Every aspect of the job contained new ideas. This was attested in detail by a thick A4 book Ken Davie pulled from his carrier bag; in it, a former colleague had filled pages and pages with lists of technical firsts. Yet one of the most remarkable innovations was not technical; it was a

new way of working. There was, Ken told me, 'the strong desire to
mix all of the professions. So you didn't have an engineers' office, an
architects' office, a planning office, we were all mixed in teams with
all of these disciplines.'

'It was very cohesive,' stressed Tom. 'There was a great atmosphere
in the office. People are still friends. We've kept together. There's a
stack of people who came to Cumbernauld to work on the town
whose families are still here in the town.' Was this really different
from the nearby comprehensive development areas in Glasgow?
Tom was convinced. 'If you worked in Castlemilk – say you were
housing management or an architect – you'd stay in Bearsden or
Milngavie or some desirable area and Castlemilk was your *job*. In
Cumbernauld it was part of the *life*.'

John Knight enjoyed the working conditions too: 'We were all
based in Cumbernauld House, which was wonderful. A William Adam
building, sadly in a parlous state now.' And like Terlings in Harlow,
the old house was gradually surrounded by huts, 'a series of prefab
offices that were actually very good. We were all there, everybody was
there. The architects, the engineers, the estate side, we were all there
together, so you were mixing all the time with these people.'

As John and I sat and chatted, he dropped a bombshell. 'Where I
was so extraordinarily fortunate in the end,' he said, 'was that I lived
in one of the penthouses that I'd worked on.' The penthouses sat
on top of the megastructure. They were the Bond-villain lairs, the
ultimate in postwar futuristic design, the Concorde of twentieth-
century town planning. It hadn't been easy for John to persuade
the authorities to grant him one of the flats: 'For some reason
the housing officers decided they didn't want me to live there. But
eventually the housing manager overruled his staff … it was all very
petty. So I selected the one that I wanted to live in, and it was the
most exciting house I'll ever live in. It was fantastic … I had the
most fantastic 18 months there.' This even managed to put my envy
of those Span-dwellers I'd met in the shade. It was like talking to
someone who'd once owned a Tardis.

'You went in at a half level,' he explained, 'and you went down to the single bedroom and the bathroom, you went up one level to what was an open living area, huge windows facing south, up another half level to a large open kitchen, with windows looking northwards to the hills, and then finally another half-flight took you up to a little roof terrace. And of course, one was young, so could run up and down stairs all day! But the biggest break of all was that we won the Reynolds award, and suddenly we were inundated. We'd always had a good flow of visitors, but suddenly you couldn't stop them. And not only that, we were getting celebrities. And, of course, they all wanted to see the town centre penthouses. I was living in the show flat!' John had clearly been in his element. 'What would happen was someone in housing would ring up and say, "Oh John, we've got so-and-so coming, could they visit your penthouse?" … The most, I suppose, important celebrity I had was Prince Claus of the Netherlands. He had a certain notoriety because he'd been in the Hitler Youth. He led a delegation to Cumbernauld and had to see a penthouse. But because he was a semi-crowned head of Europe, I had to leave the house, even though I had the whole place inspected from top to bottom by Strathclyde Police. I had to stand outside my own flat!'

The entire experience sounded bizarre and exciting. 'Strangely, I was the only development corporation employee who lived in one,' he said. 'They were all Glasgow commuters.' The revelations didn't end there. It also transpired that John played a role in a promotional film in 1970, one that was a rather more conventional older brother to *Cumbernauld Hit*. 'Films of Scotland decided to make a film of Cumbernauld,' explained John. 'I think the development corporation decided its time was almost up and it needed to be recorded, what had been achieved. It was called *Town for Tomorrow*. And this starts in the penthouse! With a silly kind of scenario to illustrate how well situated Cumbernauld is for the country. They said, "Well John, the scenario is that we film you in the penthouse" – I was given a token wife at this point, a model called Angela, which was amusing – "and because it's a lovely day you're going off for a picnic in the hills. We want to show how Cumbernauld is so wonderfully situated with such gorgeous countryside. So what you do is, she's making up the picnic in the basket, you're reading the paper, and you go down and get the car out of the" – well, there weren't any garages in the town centre, so it had to be filmed somewhere else, me reversing my Spitfire out. And Angela doesn't come, and Angela doesn't come, and Angela doesn't come, and eventually she comes teetering along with her picnic basket and I have to give her a row, you see. It's all silent, but all this goes on. She says a few rude words to me, dumps the picnic basket in the back and off we drive. And the first bit was to go through the town centre, then do all sorts of exciting things round the interchange, and whizz off northwards. And this was all filmed from helicopter: quite adventurous for the time.'

In keeping with the mood of the times, helicopters featured large in the story of Cumbernauld. 'Robin [the director] comes out and says, "Disaster." I said, "I did what you told me!" He said, "Yes, but the problem was, as you drove off, the helicopter banked and the sun just caught the camera, so you'll have to do it again. And this time you'll have to drive the wrong way round the interchange." I said, "WHAT? What if a police car comes up?" He said, "Just do it!" By this time they'd got in the helicopter and taken off. You can see it on the film. I drive the wrong way round the interchange and they reversed the film, so the sun is shining from the north. And amazingly there was no other traffic.'

He sat back demurely and sipped his tea.

Hugh Wilson's eager young team separated road traffic and pedestrians on a far larger scale than had been achieved before.

'We planned for the car,' Tom Reilly confirmed. 'And therefore we planned for this vehicle/pedestrian separation. That was part of the concept. So that people – the women – could walk to the main shopping centre, any place on that hilltop there. You could walk and you could go through an underpass without crossing a road. Children could walk safely to school.' In 1967 road traffic figures revealed that Cumbernauld was afflicted with a mere 22 percent of the national average of road accidents, prompting another barrage of positive PR following the recent Reynolds Award win. 'This staggering reduction in accident figures must largely be due to the segregation of traffic and pedestrians, together with the advanced road design of the town,' MacGill, the general manager of Cumbernauld development corporation, was quoted as saying in *The Times*.[25] Here, as in Birmingham, the underpass was the hero, sending people underground while cars drove overhead.

However, the planners at Cumbernauld were soon noticing what was to become a universal truth. 'Women were a bit wary of going down an underpass,' acknowledged Tom, 'so when it came to the extension area we didn't have underpasses. We controlled the speed of the traffic by the shape of the road and had traffic islands at certain places so you could safely cross the road.' It's certainly a town of roundabouts, cul-de-sacs and pedestrian bridges, the latter made famous in *Gregory's Girl* ('Do you know that at least twelve tons of cornflakes passes under here every day?') and now painted a lurid cyan to draw attention to their existence rather than mellowing into the background.

'People are not sent to new towns,' remarked the Hook book, 'they are attracted to them.'[26] Copcutt's view of Cumbernauld was somewhat more prosaic: they 'were building a cheap town in severe conditions for a lengthening queue of Clydesiders'.[27] And with the siting on a bleak, windy ridge, and 80 percent of the future inhabitants coming from Glasgow, mostly from the old tenements, there was no doubt at all about two-thirds of his analysis. But was Cumbernauld building a town on the cheap?

Tom was quite ready to point out the low standard of the build quality of the housing. 'In Carbrain, you'd three ply felt, timber, a roof joist and then plasterboard, that's what was actually spent on the roofs of those houses ... The windows were minimum windows ... Here it's a very low standard.' This critique had come quite unprompted, and I was taken aback by such a bleak statement from one of the town's own architects. 'We'd to do so much, after the war the problem was so big. People had to take it on and build new homes, new towns quickly. But no one was really saying quality.'

'I think we built to last,' interjected Ken. 'There was no notion that it was a temporary thing. We're now coming up to some of them that are 40 years old.' He was at pains to point out some of the more successful and innovative housing built by the corporation: Seafar, for instance, in the north of Cumbernauld, designed by Harry Eccles who went on to work in Warrington and Milton Keynes. 'These are popular houses,' he said, tapping a drawing of a Seafar house in a book. 'They are very innovative in that you go down to the bedrooms and up to the living accommodation. They're upside down, so you had views over the top.' Yet despite all of the new thinking on layouts, roads and the town centre, most of Cumbernauld's new housing was surprisingly traditional for a place that has such a radical reputation.

'They looked at traditional Scottish construction,' explained Tom, 'low density roughcast, and the colours, and everyone worked to the same kind of pattern. You didn't as an architect go in and say, "We're going to have a red roof here and a green roof there."'

'Perhaps they're not everyone's cup of tea, the initial ones,' admits Ken, 'but it was an attempt to establish Cumbernauld as a desirable place to invest a lot of private housing money, and that did happen.'

Like the central area, Seafar won awards for design, and is considered by some 'Scotland's most significant ensemble of postwar urban architecture and planning'.[28] In the words of planner Lionel Brett, it is 'drily described by the Scots as "popular with architects"'.[29]

Later, my friend Kirsten and I drove around streets that the sixties Housing Minister Richard Crossman had described as having homes of 'a tremendously austere, exhilarating, uncomfortable style'.[30] The

big shock after the megastructure was just how *unshocking* these
areas were. Cars and pedestrians had been separated by that most
traditional of materials: cobbles. With the pale grey roughcast
everywhere, the small, cottagey houses, the steep hilly landscape
and gulls screaming overhead, I kept expecting to see the sea round
the next corner. No wonder Sir Robert Grieve, then Chief Planning
Officer at the Scottish Office, described it as looking 'like the little
fishing village ... tight, against the wind'.[31] Long, low 'pram steps'
were crumbling everywhere, a hangover from the days when the
average age of a Cumbernauld inhabitant was mid-twenties and
starting a family. The fabric of the place – Abronhill, Kildrum,
especially Carbrain – was falling apart. Many of the kerbs, steps,
roads and pavements were subsiding, wonky and in need of
replacement. People had tarted up their houses and many of those
seemed to be holding up, but the communal spaces had suffered
since the winding up of the development corporation in 1996.

Back in the sixties, people began moving into these houses while
construction work on the town was still going on.

'The early pioneers had to suffer a lot,' said Ken, echoing the
experience of everyone I'd met in Harlow. 'It was the muddiest town
in the world. It was pretty hard going.'

'The first thing I did,' recalled Janice Scott Lodge, a Cumbernauld
resident writing in the *Guardian*'s women's page in 1965, 'was step
out of my car and flat in the mud.' And while the mud haunted her,
invading her home, she found that 'the only place it never seemed to
encroach was our garden, which appeared to consist of solid concrete
and resisted every attack made on it.'[32] The comprehensive nature of
the development in an area like Kildrum meant that early residents
were plonked in an entirely new district, with amenities so new that
no one knew how to work them, and left to get on with it. At the
time Janice pointed out the poor transport connections to nearby
towns, noting that owning a car was essential, and that the local
shops traded on their monopoly by charging way over the going rate
for goods and services. 'Most of these drawbacks should disappear,'

The cobbles of Kildrum.

*The roughcast houses on the steep slope
'like the little fishing village … tight, against the wind.'*

she remarked, 'but at the moment they cause so much frustration, even real hardship, that many newcomers are disheartened and return to the cities at the first opportunity.'

Journalist Sheila Black found plenty of these discombobulated new residents when she visited for the *Financial Times* in 1967: "'It's lonely," says one. "It's dull." "I want to go back to what they called the slums.'"[33] As these newcomers left, and the builders moved onto the next muddy bit to start all over again, hardy souls like Janice remained to tough it out. She described those that remained as 'a vigorous, far-sighted nucleus, who are prepared to lift their eyes from the mud to see the stars'. A survey sponsored by the development corporation in 1968 revealed that '74.6 percent of the respondents claimed they had bettered themselves by going to Cumbernauld' with 'better housing' emerging as the most popular reason for the claim.[34]

'There was a tremendous sense of community in the early days,' said Ken, and Janice's experience seemed to bear this out: 'Life is difficult, certainly, without the amenities our standards have led us to expect – but life is fun,' she wrote. 'It has challenge and a purpose.'

'And not everyone got in,' Tom reminded us. 'The housing department would actually go out and see people in their homes. Interview people.' My friend Kirsten's family was one of those interviewed, and they passed the test. Having spent much of our trip lamenting the current state of the town, she began to recall those early days with great fondness – much to her surprise.

'I lived in Cumbernauld between '78 and '83,' she said. 'The great thing about Abronhill, which I think was replicated everywhere else, was the play areas. Obviously the kids would congregate, so the parents would come to find them and speak to each other, and the relationships really started to build. It was a fantastic place. The branding of Cumbernauld was brilliant for the residents. *I'm a Cumbernauld Kid* – and I was! You could have cut me in two and it would have said Cumbernauld all the way through.'

Back in 1965, Janice Scott Lodge had found that making new friends on the estate wasn't quite so easy for all the new residents, re-

Houses in Abronhill, where Kirsten grew up.

porting that 'the planners and architects of the new town have heavily accented privacy in their housing designs, perhaps too much so. The result is houses whose windows overlook none of their neighbours, or, in the instance of my present home which is built around an individual courtyard, no outer windows at all.'[35] Yet the residents interviewed by sociologist Peter Willmott painted a much more complex picture than the press. 'I think the houses are too close together,' said a housewife in Carbrain, 'but surprisingly enough it's very, very private. It's been very cleverly done. None of our windows look into other people's.'[36] Nevertheless, the sheer proximity of the homes meant that privacy could easily be compromised: 'When you walk along the path, you're conscious you can see in,' said a housewife in Kildrum. 'I feel sometimes that I've no right to be there. You feel guilty because you can't help looking in.'[37]

Ian Nairn wasn't convinced by talk of the uniqueness of Cumbernauld. To him it was 'simply the old kind [of new town] moved closer together.' He discerned three main faults in the design: the vehicle/pedestrian separation had been overdone; the pedestrian paths simply followed 'the pattern of the industrial revolution slum with its street and back lane, given a modern architectural dress'; and there was a woeful lack of protection from the elements around the central area.[38] He ended his critique on an ominous note – that Cumbernauld had to have been built to stop similar mistakes being made elsewhere. Perhaps after all Hook had had a lucky escape.

Tom had a different perpective. 'You felt as if you were really doing good, it was better than being in politics. If you wanted to do good in politics you had far more power if you worked in a development corporation because you were providing people with new housing. The pleasure of a woman coming out to see a brand new house and handing it over was fantastic. If you were spending money that was a good way to spend it.'

And Ken agreed: 'We felt that this was a good place to live, a good place that we've created.'

Part 3
NO FUTURE

TOWER BLOCK HIGHS AND LOWS (1968-74)

The news from 1968 records a world in turmoil. A year had passed since the summer of love, and student and hippy protests against the Vietnam War had spread from the US to London's Grosvenor Square, outside Eero Saarinen's monumental sixties American Embassy. Martin Luther King was assassinated in Memphis, and the medallists of the 200 metre race at the Mexico City Olympics had displayed the Black Power salute. Meanwhile, in Birmingham Enoch Powell raged against the tide with his infamous 'rivers of blood' speech. In the Soviet bloc, moves towards reform and democratisation in Prague had been crushed by an invasion by Warsaw Pact troops. A million students marched in protest against De Gaulle's government in France. Civil rights demonstrators in Londonderry were violently repressed by the Royal Ulster Constabulary, sparking a new era of 'Troubles' in Northern Ireland. And 1968 was also the year that the decade-long boom in high-rise flat building across Britain came to an abrupt and tragic end.

Welcome to Balfron Tower,
Ernő Goldfinger's baby.

324 CONCRETOPIA

Yet the year had started on such an upbeat note for the high-rise. In February one of its most redoubtable champions, Ernő Goldfinger, moved into a flat on the twenty-fifth floor of a 27-storey slab block he'd designed in Poplar, east London. Balfron Tower had been completed the previous year, a distinctive building whose main slab of flats was connected to the separate lift shaft tower by a series of walkways. Built in rough concrete poured on site rather than with a system of pre-cast panels, there was something hyper-masculine and provocative, almost warlike, about it. The lift tower was topped with a series of concrete ventilation pipes that gave it the look of battlements; the concrete had a gritty, stubbly feel to it; and its strange asymmetrical silhouette, with the ladder of walkways dividing the flats from the service spine, was designed to create maximum impact on the skyline. 'I want to experience at first hand,' said Ernő when he moved into flat 130 Balfron Tower, 'the size of the rooms, the amenities provided, the time it takes to obtain a lift, the amount of wind whistling around the tower, and any problems which might arise from my designs, so I can correct them in the future.'[1] He was thinking of the future because he planned to build more towers in this form. 'All architects should live in a home they have designed for themselves,' he told the *Guardian* in 1969.[2] Although he did live for two months in his East End landmark, Ernő quickly retreated to his real home, a large detached pad he'd designed in leafy Hampstead. Ursula, his wife, told the press when they left Balfron after their brief stay that 'we aren't eligible tenants for this one and there isn't a private one built by my husband.'[3] There would, however, be a bigger one. Trellick Tower, commissioned by the Greater London Council in 1966 for a site in west London, would be four storeys taller than Balfron when it opened six years later.

James Dunnett worked for Goldfinger in the seventies and well remembered the fallout from these two huge social housing projects. 'I went to work for him when I left Cambridge,' he told me as we sat in his office in north London. 'I was thought to be a lunatic really. And anyway I was told I wouldn't survive *days* because he was

famous for sacking people and so on.' New recruits were known to
have resigned by lunchtime on their first day, or else sent packing
for the most minor of infractions. Ernő was even reported to have
sacked someone who didn't work for him, a man who had happened
to be waiting in reception when the arch-modernist had been in one

Ernő and Ursula Goldfinger lived for two months in flat 130.

of his rages. 'Of course he was a volcanic man, and he was dangerous
and difficult to work for,' conceded James. 'But then I didn't expect
anything less. I thought that anyone who designed buildings with
that amount of punch in them is not going to be a sop.' James joined
Ernő's team in 1973. 'Trellick had just been finished. The second

phase was still being built. He'd moved his office to the tower by that stage, and it was brilliant. It was brand new, it was superb. It still seems to have power over people despite its mutilated, ill-maintained state,' he remarked pointedly.

James continued on the theme of Ernő's personality. 'He was never cold, but he was volcanic. I think he got on best with people like [architect] John Winter or [critic] Gavin Stamp, people who were quite big, pugnacious people themselves. I think he was a bit of a bully, I think I have to say that. If you were nervous he would exploit that really. But beneath that he was discerning and kind … He was riveting company. Because there was a sense of danger. You never thought you knew what was going to happen. He'd leap several points ahead of you in an argument then turn around and berate you for not having caught up with him.' Goldfinger's attitude to women was another controversial point. Jane Drew, one of the early modern movement's stars, who'd worked with Le Corbusier in Chandigarh, India, wrote that 'he was always pawing you. And if you didn't like having your bum pinched and slapped, it was rather off-putting.'[4] Yet the architect was no more popular with the men he employed. As his biographer reported darkly: 'One site agent was heard to mutter, "One day he will fall off a roof."'[5]

'I only worked for him for a year and a half,' James told me, 'because they had no work. The whole thing was deflating. He'd never had a big practice. He was totally unknown really. Insofar as he was known, it was only about his personality really. He had a heyday when he was thought to be fashionable, around 1960–63. But things were moving away from the kind of work he was doing even then.'

If Ernő's heyday was brief, the work he produced in it was remarkable. As well as the designs for Balfron, there were the buildings in the Elephant and Castle – cinema, health service offices, flats – that had added a touch of flair to the otherwise flawed scheme. For the flats in Draper Street, he explained to the *Observer* the rational basis behind his work. 'Two feet nine,' he said, 'is the width of a door and its jamb. It is also the width of a man standing comfortably with his hands on his hips. Make a square out of this dimension and multiply it by six and you have a grid 16 feet 6 inches either way that I lay down on my site before I even start designing. Into this grid fits the building. Its guidance gives me a complete integration of structural proportional control of all the outside and inside spaces.'[6] He was echoing Le Corbusier, whose rational scheme of human proportions, the 'Modulor' – on which he'd based his Unité – had influenced a generation of architects. And as in Park Hill, the shadow of Le Corbusier's great design fell across Goldfinger's most famous buildings, from the access balconies that led off to three floors to the rough concrete used to mould the form.

I've visited Balfron Tower a couple of times. The first was as part of Open House Weekend, where one of the top flats was open to the public and was exhibiting the work of local artists, many of whom were based in the building. I remember pushing open a kitchen window and leaning out over the sheer drop, finding it both thrilling and terrifying. The second time was to visit Katharine Hibbert, author of *Free: Adventures on the Margins of a Wasteful Society*, who was one of the beneficiaries of the housing association Poplar HARCA's decision to rent out unlet flats in the tower to writers and artists. Well spoken, sunnily disposed, well informed and distinctly bohemian, Katharine talked about Balfron Tower life from both a political and personal perspective.

'I've rarely lived anywhere I've liked as much,' she said as we sipped tea and ate homemade cake in her sparsely decorated flat. From her front room the view was truly spectacular. London was spread out before us: the shiny towers of Canary Wharf to our left; the bristling spires and skyscrapers of the city centre ahead of us; a scattering of point blocks and slabs to our right. 'I love the views,' she said. 'I love how spacious it is. I mean, we're lucky being just two people in a two bedroom flat.' At the time Katharine lived there with her boyfriend and a cat called Awol. But what was spacious for them would have felt cramped to many of the families living round and about. 'It's not so popular with council tenants because, almost by definition, they're gonna have a family. And if you've got a family then you've almost certainly got more than one child. So you're looking at four people minimum in a flat like this, probably more. So you're going to be really crowded, aren't you?'

The bridges of Balfron Tower connects the lift shaft and 'services' to the main body of the flats.

But for two, it was luxuriously large, especially by comparison with the mean proportions of more modern builds. To enter Katharine's flat I'd taken the macho industrial steel lift up to her balcony level. The lift landings in the service tower were a little grim: buzzing circular flourescent light fittings illuminated a rather unsavoury, mouth-like space lined with yellowing, stained and cracked enamel. The tiled floors were patched with black where the linoleum had been trashed, and the concrete walls unevenly painted. But the trip across the bridge from service tower to residential block, high above the city, was exhilarating, with all of London laid out behind sturdy net glass. Then, once in the main building, the run of front doors was busy, friendly and humanising. 'I think that the arrangement of corridors works really well,' said Katharine, 'because you've got three floors of flats feeding onto each corridor. So it's far more likely that there's going to be someone there. And there's a lot more people who are your neighbours, as it were. So I know Jules, who lives upstairs, and I know Simon, who lives above that, and various other people all along the corridor. Jules and Simon were people I'd have never met if we were all on our own corridors.'

We went through the door to Katharine's flat and immediately descended a terracotta-tiled staircase to reach the living space, which gave it an incongruous, subterranean feel, even though we were almost 100 feet above the busy east London streets below. 'Although there are lots of things you might not like about the area,' said Katharine, making reference to the poverty that still pervades the East End, 'the fact that it's mostly council flats means that people are here for the long term. Unlike other bits of town I've lived, you don't get the sense of people just moving through. Everyone is remarkably friendly in the lift and stuff, and it shouldn't be surprising. But it's really noticeable how much people, for instance, hold the door for you when they see that you're coming, or check that your button is pressed in the lift. Of course you should expect it, but people are pretty polite and pretty friendly.'

It isn't just the area, the people and the atmosphere Katharine likes about the tower. 'I like it as a building,' she asserted. 'My mum always said about Harlow that when you were at school, everyone lived in the same houses. There was no issue about what kind of house you lived in, everyone was just the same. Some people had slightly nicer than others, but basically everyone's really just the same. And I like the feeling that you get here, that it was made to be good houses, as good as you need.' Katharine may have grown up in Oxford, but her mum was raised in Harlow, among other folk who'd been cleared out of the East End as part of Patrick Abercrombie's plan for London. This was an added attraction of Balfron for Katharine. 'It feels a bit more like Essex than most of London. Like, there's two pie and mash shops in the Chrisp Street Market. And there's also a seafood stall where you can get your cockles and your whelks at the weekend. Those were the things we used to get when I was a child. And I like the fact that it's got a town centre.'

I asked Katharine how her friends and family had reacted to her moving to the tower. She was quick to contrast her friends' reactions with what her grandma, who had grown up in the area but moved away before the redevelopment, was likely to say when she visited. 'All my friends are like, "how cool, how exciting." My grandma will be like, "this is exactly what we left the East End to get out of! Another bloomin' concrete tower block." I think when you're living it the first time, and people reappropriate it, that's a little bit weird.' She pauses for a moment to consider not just her grandma's situation, but that of all the council tenants still dotted about the tower. 'Having your own self reappropriated is a bit weird.'

Ernő Goldfinger moved out of the flat in Balfron Tower on the 16 May 1968. The very next morning, a mile and half to the east of Balfron, a story broke that would completely change the fortunes of Britain's postwar rebuilding programme, and would become one of the biggest stories of this big news year. At 5:50am, in a system-built high-rise of the sort Ernő was contemptuous, Ivy Hodge, a 57-year-old cake decorator, got up to make a cup of tea. 'I remember filling the kettle but the next moment I was on the floor,' she told a reporter. 'I remember coming to and staggering to the landing door and shouting for help. I can't remember anything after that.'[7] She was lucky to be alive. Gas had leaked into her eighteenth floor flat in Ronan Point and, as she lit the hob, her kitchen had exploded.

Night watchman George McArthur was in a hut 15 yards away from Ronan Point when the explosion occurred. 'I heard cracking and banging and I saw concrete flying around. I ran like hell,' he told the *Daily Mirror*. 'A whole wing of the building came down like a pack of cards.'[8] Ivy's neighbours on the eighteenth floor, John and Jean Bruns and baby Samantha, were faced with a frightening scene. 'Our front door and front wall had gone and I had to remove rubble

The morning of 16 May 1968: the Ronan Point flats in Canning Town, walls blown out by a gas leak.
© *The Telegraph Group*

with my hands to get to the staircase so we could escape.'[9] A man on the fifteenth floor had improbably slid all the way to the ground on a slab of concrete as the floor collapsed beneath him, escaping relatively unscathed. Lower down the block on the seventh floor, James and Beatrice Chambers told reporters that their 'bedroom wall fell away with a terrible ripping sound. We found ourselves staring out over London, our heads only a matter of two feet away from an 80-foot drop. Furniture plunged past us. Suddenly we heard screams. I grabbed my wife and we got out quickly. I had to put my leg on first.'[10] Brenda Maughan, in flat 65 on the thirteenth floor, was widely thought to have had an even more miraculous escape. Asleep in a chair in her living room, she had a violent awakening as she was thrown from her seat. 'Virtually the whole of the living room floor had fallen away,' noted the report of the public inquiry, 'and Mrs Maughan was standing on a narrow ledge, her feet and legs covered in rubble, clinging on to the upright of the door frame.'[11] Her husband who'd been asleep in the bedroom managed to grab hold of her through the door and clear away the rubble so she could escape, albeit with broken bones and teeth. Amid the chaos, rescue teams still found time to arrest a first-floor resident, who'd been tooled up for house-breaking. Tragically, four people died as a result of the explosion and collapse. Amazingly, Ivy Hodge, whose flat had exploded, suffered only minor burns and shock.

What exactly had caused such devastation at Ronan Point that spring morning? The gas explosion had been of such magnitude that it had lifted the top four floors from the rest of the tower. Not only that, the blast from Ivy Hodge's kitchen had travelled outwards to the living room next door, which stood at the corner of the tower. When the top four storeys fell back in place, the load-bearing walls in the corner of the sitting room began crashing down onto those below, all the way to the ground. Ivy's early morning routine had undoubtedly saved lives – if the explosion had occurred any later in the day many more people would have been up and about in their living rooms directly below hers; as it was, most were still in bed. The report into the collapse, following a public enquiry, showed pictures of the wreckage inside the block. One photograph presented a scene of almost abstract devastation: a room of rubble and shapes heaped up on each other, labelled with the most sardonic of captions: 'Miss Hodge's gas cooker showing the flexible hose,' it read.[12] It takes some moments to connect the caption to the photo.

The explosion had come only two months after the blocks had been finished. It may have been a lone accident in Newham affecting just the 260 occupants of a single high-rise, but it quickly became a national scare, with the finger of blame pointing at the construction firm, the local council and ultimately the government for encouraging the boom in system-built high-rise flats. This particular block had been constructed using a 'large panel system' – big factory-made pre-cast slabs bolted together on site. Taylor Woodrow-Anglian, the contractors, had manufactured the panels in a factory in Lenwade, Norfolk. At the time of the explosion over 30,000 dwellings in blocks over six storeys had been built using similar systems. *The Times* reported that on the morning of the disaster Harry Ronan, the local councillor, in whose honour the tower had been named, had visited the scene, 'an area in which he had lived and became well known, and met the Borough Architect, Thomas North, who was in tears. "He, like me, had been saying that the blocks were our answer,"' Ronan told them.[13]

Harry Ronan may have seen him crying, but North told the *Express* bullishly: 'There is nothing structurally wrong with the building. The undamaged flats could be occupied tonight if we could persuade people to go back in.'[14] Thomas North's stiff, patrician exterior, covering his private humanity and deep belief in social equality, was typical of the postwar era. But with rioting and the rise of protest movements in the late sixties, the establishment was to be challenged as never before. And as we'll see in the following chapters, the role of the lofty expert would be diminished both by a distrusting media and a failure among those experts to adjust to a new climate of openness and sometimes hostile debate.

Larsen Nielsen's large panel system, which had been used to build Ronan Point and eight other blocks in Newham, had been developed in Denmark in 1948, and by the sixties it was being used in 12 countries. Within 26 years 6,000 homes in Britain were either built or in the pipeline using Larsen Nielsen. Contractors Taylor Woodrow-Anglian had licensed the system from the Danes.

Here was a chain of large businesses coming together to make the building of systems as cost effective as possible. Taylor Woodrow were a huge construction conglomerate, now merged with Anglian Building Products, whose speciality was the manufacture of concrete components – 100,000 tons of them each year. Together they were a highly efficient team, able to manufacture and construct buildings quickly and cheaply. All they needed were buyers.

Since 1959 Thomas North had been scoping out the best system for the area. After all, West Ham had lost a quarter of its housing in the Blitz, so he and his team had to make a difference, and fast. A postwar record for a London borough was set when by 1968 almost 15,000 new dwellings had been built in Newham, the new borough created from the merger of East and West Ham. And yet their job was still only half complete. There were still 9,000 slums to be cleared in the area.

North and his deputy Kenneth Lund had been to Liverpool and Woolwich in search of a system suited to build the nine tower blocks planned for the comprehensive development area of Clever Road. The area had been marked by Patrick Abercrombie as far back as 1944 as a site for towers. Camus, a French system, had been used in Liverpool, but Kenneth dismissed it as 'a terrible, crude design, there was no possibility of changing it, you either took it or left it,' which left Larsen Nielsen, the system they'd seen in 10-storey blocks in Woolwich. Here was a system where Thomas felt 'you could have some aesthetic input!'[15]

The panels certainly were large: eight feet high, nine feet wide, made from solid concrete over six inches thick. The architects managed to fit 66 one-bedroom and 44 two-bedroom flats into each tower. At 210 feet high and 22 storeys, these were the highest towers to be built in Britain using the system, but they came with the assurance that Danish designers Larsen and Nielsen had personally approved the plans. As well they might, with a £5 million contract in the offing. Then there was the crew of 10–12 builders constructing each block, whose pay depended on their speed. There was a great deal invested in the swift approval and construction of the scheme for all parties concerned. What did it matter that the Larsen Nielsen system had only been designed for buildings of six storeys, and was being thrown up by a workforce of largely unskilled labour, for whom speed was the main concern? Or that 260 people would end up living there, unaware that corners had been cut during construction and that the hastily cobbled together tower was vulnerable to the slightest structural change. The worst might not happen; probably people would never find out. Only they did find out. That morning.

Here was a tower that had been built 16 storeys higher than its construction system had been designed for. Each of its large panels had been affixed with just two bolts, which started rusting as soon as water permeated the structure. Where cement, mortar or concrete should have been used to securely fix the tower's panels together, voids were stuffed instead with newspaper, or left open. As Lynsey Hanley so dramatically describes in her book *Estates*, local architect Sam Webb 'tested the size of the gaps between the floor and wall panels by dropping coins and pieces of paper through them: they fell, he said, "as if going into a slot machine"'.[16] And for the want of a nut the tower was lost: it was substandard gas fitting equipment that led directly to the leak that blew apart the building. That morning each of Ronan Point's failings were laid bare for all to see.

It wasn't just building systems like Larsen Nielsen that were causing alarm. By the mid-sixties another problem was emerging with new concrete buildings. It would lead to the collapse of the assembly hall roof of Camden School for Girls in June 1973; the disintegration of the roof beams of the Bennett Building at Leicester University that same month; and a year later the same thing at the swimming pool of Sir John Cass's Foundation and Red Coat Church of England Secondary School. The cause? High alumina cement: a new form of cement that in certain circumstances underwent conversion to crystalline state, making the buildings unstable and the concrete liable to crack. One man emerged as the self-appointed scourge of high alumina cement, an engineer called Geoff Scott, who described its use as 'a mistake of horrendous proportions'.[17] Scott was quite sure how the error had occurred: 'One can fully appreciate the attitude of a site operative who adds more water to the mix to avoid time-consuming vibration when the amount of money in his back pocket on a Friday night depends on the volume of concrete poured.'[18]

Neither was it only this new kind of cement that was causing problems. CLASP, the prefabricated system used in many schools around the country, was found to be prone to devastating fires: Fairfields old people's home in Nottingamshire, and Usworth Comprehensive School in County Durham both burned down in 1974, to be joined the following year by Yarborough High School in Lincoln. The link between the three was found to be voids in the roofs and vertical wall cavities – spaces that were in effect huge flues within the structure of the buildings, perfect for the incubation of fires.[19] And then there were the great concrete cooling towers that collapsed in high winds. In November 1965, 85 mph winds howled through West Yorkshire, felling three out of eight new cooling towers at Ferrybridge 'C' Power Station. Less than a year later the biggest cooling tower in Scotland, at ICI's Ardeer Nylon Works in Ayrshire, collapsed during a ferocious night-time storm due to cracks in the concrete.

Then from the final comprehensive development area to be completed in the Gorbals, Hutchesontown-Polmodie, known as Hutchie E, came a tale of low rise system built disaster to rival the high-rise one at Ronan Point. Approved in 1969, and opened in 1972 by the Queen, Hutchie E was built using the French Tracoba system. The resulting estate featured 759 flats, housed in a couple of 24-storey towers and 12 seven-storey blocks. They were constructed by Gilbert Ash, an offshoot of Bovis, who had a lot of experience in the field: they'd even built Britain's very first tower block, The Lawns, in Harlow back in 1951. That had been a bespoke design built in brick and concrete, but Hutchie E showed the difference a couple of decades of technological advances in prefabrication and system building could make. It was large panel all the way.

Within months of the Queen's visit, tendrils of black mould began an insidious attack on the blocks. 'A painter who worked on the job told me that as he put the wallpaper on it just fell off,' wrote Phil McPhee, who chronicled the saga in his essay *Hutchie E – A Monument to Corruption, Stupidity and Bad Planning.*[20] The reason was pure Stephen King: Hutchie E had been built over some old, abandoned mine shafts, long since flooded by water from the Clyde. Workmen struggled with flash floods, and water cascading down the newly built walls. 'Ludicrous excuses were made,' McPhee recalled, 'such as: the tenants' heavy breathing, gas heating, sleeping with windows open, condensation.'[21] After a decade of spirited resident action and protest, the unfortunates housed in Hutchie E were moved out, and the deck access blocks were demolished in 1987. They were the first of the new comprehensive development area buildings to bite the dust. In a few short years, modern construction techniques and materials had ceased to be viewed as marvels of hi-tech engineering. Instead they were the scourge of modern living: not just ugly in the eyes of many, but lethal too.

Three months after the explosion at Ronan Point, Anthony Greenwood, the Minister of Housing and Local Government, set in motion a structural survey of all large panel system blocks in England and Wales, with Scotland following suit soon after. Over a third of the 162 blocks in Scotland to be re-evaluated were in high-rise Glasgow. Sociologist Pearl Jephcott, in researching that city for her book *Homes in High Flats*, remarked that the Ronan Point collapse 'did not seem to peturb these tenants about their own safety. Nor did Clydeside's furious gale of January 1968, although some high flats had their windows sucked in, people saw their furniture moving across the bedroom, and in some flats the lights and lifts went off.'[22] Yet it certainly perturbed Eileen McConnachie, an ex-eighteenth floor resident of the city's towering Red Road flats, a scheme which, like Goldfinger's Balfron Tower, had eschewed building systems. Eileen told the *Herald* that 'on one particularly windy night my husband found that the wardrobe had moved four inches because of the tilt of the building.' Not for her the stiff upper lip displayed by Jephcott's subjects: 'I was delighted to get out of a multi-storey.'[23]

The problems Pearl Jephcott encountered were of a social rather than architectural nature. Tenants of the tower blocks she visited complained predictably of lawlessness, of drunks vomiting or pissing in the lifts, but also of the heavy-handed management style, with negative notices posted everywhere, from *No Loitering* to overbearing instructions concerning rubbish disposal. A young mother living on the nineteenth floor of one block told Jephcott that 'the lifts are quite often off. Once or twice I've had to walk up. They are a bit better now. The kids have started to paint on the walls which annoys me.'[24] The sociologist noted that 'the highly artificial character of the layout of the multi-storey estate demands extra careful upkeep.'[25] And when such upkeep broke down, vandalism bedded in. On one estate Jephcott found railings had been broken down, telephone equipment torn out, handles wrenched off fire doors, and lights on the estate's Christmas tree broken. As far back as Christmas 1962 the *Herald* was reporting on a 'catalogue of complaints at Glasgow skyscrapers' at Roystonhill, where 'tenants have complained of lifts jammed with delivery men's milk crates, of common rooms used as rubbish dumps, of broken windows in the laundry rooms, of refuse disposal chutes used as bowling alleys for empty beer bottles; and of noise.'[26]

By the seventies, local papers across the country were brimming with shocking stories of high-rise vandalism, deprivation and despair. 'A 26-year-old mother plunged to the ground from the eleventh floor of a Birmingham tower block holding her two-year-old baby son,' the *Newcastle Journal* reported in 1977, 'because her skyscraper flat was a prison.'[27] The *Evening Chronicle* had also followed the story, and asked some Newcastle residents for their tower block experiences. Doris Cuthbertson lived in Shenfield House, built by Stanley Miller, and told a reporter: 'I don't feel at home here. After

I've been out for a couple of hours it feels like I'm going back to jail.'[28] Cruddas Park, once so proudly looked after by Ken Denholm, was in a parlous state by the eighties, beset by glue-sniffing, graffiti and vandalism. One grim report for the local paper followed a glue-fuelled rampage in the Sycamores. 'The door entry system is out of order, there's urine on the floor, graffiti in the lift and human excrement on the stairs ... Older residents say it used to be a joy to live in.' The two journalists visited the top floor flat where the door had been kicked in and there was vomit on the floor. 'We meet a frail, elderly woman and ask her if she knows what happened but she is terrified of being seen talking to us. She says, "I'm terrified. I'm just shaking. I've lived here for 13 years and the past few weeks is the worst I've ever seen."'[29]

In 1964 over 27,000 high-rise flats were approved by the government. Following the explosion at Ronan Point there was a sharp drop, and as the financial crisis deepened, construction slowed almost to a standstill. By 1978 only 37 new flats in high-rise buildings got the go-ahead. Between 1956 and 1967 the government had run a scheme to subsidise the building of high-rise flats. This subsidy increased in line with the height of tower. When the scheme ended, Ernő Goldfinger was just one of the people who attacked the government for their decision. 'I am appalled,' he told *The Times*. 'It is a ridiculous attitude that will put us back 30 years.'[30] But the man who'd overseen the design of Park Hill's streets in the sky in Sheffield was rather less bothered. 'Unless you have a bad land shortage, I don't think there is much of a case for them any more,' Lewis Womersley told the *Guardian*. 'If more are to be built, they will have to be special designs with extra amenities – like interconnecting decks for children to play in, with easy access to the ground. A lot of the bad name which high flats have got is because the needs of the occupants were forgotten.'[31]

'High-rise flats. A great idea at the time.'

Eddie McGonnell, former resident and cheerleader for Basil Spence's blocks in the Gorbals, has had more experience of them than most. 'And then people began finding, maybe it's not such a good idea. We might want people to get houses with a back and front door and a garden. But at the time ... there was no option, that wasn't on the table. You were coming from this tenement where you never had a bedroom, you never had a bath, you had to go to the toilet outside, where everybody was using it, but going to the Gorbals it was like mardi gras, that's what it was like.'

People who criticised Eddie's beloved Queenies were 'thinking about the Basil Spence flats at the end, the way they ended up. They became dilapidated, which happens when you're not getting investment from the city council. If they'd had investment the people that were in them would have maybe have taken more pride in them as well.'

How had he felt when the blocks were demolished in 1993, after two floods and a crime wave, less than 30 years after they were opened?

'Very sad. It felt as if part of your life was being taken away. I remember seeing a programme on the telly with the Queen. She was crying over Britannia. You never see the Queen showing emotion. That's the way we felt when we seen that happening. That was our childhood, we grew up there.'

The crime levels, the dirty corridors, broken-down lifts and smashed lights ... Eddie was sure of one thing: it wasn't the architect who was at fault, rather a lack of investment in the upkeep of the buildings. 'I think Spence was a visionary, but he was too far ahead of the culture. He was the scapegoat, the whipping boy. It was the council that was to blame.'

This official insouciance endured, tragically, to the very end. When the Queenies – Alcatraz, Barlinnie and Sing-Sing – were blown up by demolition specialists, their failure to use the correct amount of explosive or sound a warning horn led to one spectator being killed by flying rubble.

'It felt as if part of your life was being taken away ... That was our childhood, we grew up there.' The demolition of Basil Spence's Queen Elizabeth flats in 1993.
© *Simon Chirgwin*

By contrast, in 2011 when I went to visit Katharine Hibbert in Ernő Goldfinger's east London block, Balfron Tower, it was having a facelift.

'Because this block is listed they're doing massive renovations,' she told me. 'You can see the cranes and everything. They're really snazzing the whole place up. This being listed, they can't knock it down which is what I think they'd have liked to do because I don't think it's very popular with the council tenants ... So instead they're gonna tart it all up and then sell it off ... They're gonna put in new lift shafts, new rubbish chutes, all the windows are gonna be new. Carradale House' – the low rise block in the cluster – 'is going to carry on being social housing, but this one isn't. And in a way I think that makes sense because if people in social housing almost inevitably are old or have children this is not a suitable place, whereas your yuppies who want to live in a brutalist classic ...' She gestured around the room. It was certainly all here for them, those concrete fetishists. 'It'll be interesting to see who moves in because it's never going to be a posh area – unless they changed *all* the housing. It's never going to be that much different from how it is. And I just think that if you were driving a Porsche and working in Canary Wharf, even if it wasn't true, you'd just *feel like* you were going to get mugged. You wouldn't feel good living somewhere like this. I think the trouble will be if they sell them all off and they get sold to buy-to-let people and it's less well-off people living in them but still really transient, so you don't have the benefit of it being council tenants where at least they're permanent, at least they've got a stake.'

Yet it was hard not to conclude that, as in Park Hill, a degree of social cleansing was in operation here, with the tenants squeezed out of precious council housing at a moment in time when such homes were desperately needed. Had the gentrification already begun?

'The thing is you can't really tell that easily because there's a whole lot of artists wandering around who almost by definition sort of *are* middle class. I know there's at least one guy on this corridor who bought his flat because it was stylish rather than because it was cheap. So I guess he's a gentrifier. And there's a couple of others that are renting flats – I assume they're renting them from people who used right-to-buy to buy them – but they're trendier than your average. I'd be really interested keeping an eye on what happens here after they finish doing it all up in 2014. I'd move back in like a shot! Yeah, totally! Absolutely! I *really* like it!'

What of Ronan Point, the block that in effect ended the sixties high-rise boom? You might have thought it would have been knocked down after the explosion back in 1968, but you'd be wrong. Instead, something unexpected happened. The block was repaired and along with its seven sisters it was strengthened. Gas was removed from the towers, and electric boilers installed in its place. And in 1973 Ronan Point was re-opened.

'They are lovely flats,' said Selina McCambridge, one of the original residents, as she moved back into her fourth floor flat.

'From the day we left we said we would be back.' She was carrying a card and flowers from councillor Harry Ronan, the building's namesake, when *The Times* interviewed her. Sheila Attreed, mother of 20-month-old Amanda, told the press that 'it was one of those disasters which happens once in a lifetime. You don't stop going on planes because of an air crash.' William Watts, chairman of Newham Housing Committee talked the project up. 'This is a fine building. There has been no pressure on anybody to move here,' while Patrick Davies, Newham's director of housing, was even more forthright: 'Nobody has refused a place in Ronan Point because it is Ronan Point.'[32] There were local petitions that disputed that. The reconstructed tower stood for another 13 years, before fatal structural weaknesses led to it finally being demolished: the bolted-together structure had been wrecked by the strong winds that tall towers were liable to attract. Its rubble was used as hardcore for the runway at nearby City Airport.

Yet most strange of all, even Ivy Hodge herself, the very day after the explosion that had left her unconscious and her flat destroyed, had been unexpectedly positive about her experience in the tower. 'I liked it on the eighteenth,' she said. 'I would not mind going back to live there, I was quite happy.'[33]

2. 'A Terrible Confession of Defeat'
PROTEST AND PRESERVATION (1969–79)

*'What the Ministry is concerned with is the environment
(horrible word)'* Dame Evelyn Sharp.[1]

In the mid-sixties, architect John Knight had been living the sci-fi life in a penthouse in Britain's most futuristic building, the megastructure that formed Cumbernauld's town centre. By the end of the decade he'd fallen out of love with his profession, and drifted to Edinburgh in search of new challenges.

'In 1970 we had here a major conference on the conservation of Georgian architecture,' he told me over lunch in Edinburgh's New Town. 'Now this was Robert Matthew, who comes into the picture now big time. He obviously had a similar body swerve here, because suddenly, from doing pretty major developments like the Gorbals or whatever, he suddenly starts down this conservation route. And he realised that unless someone picked up the cudgel on behalf of the Georgian New Town here in Edinburgh it was a goner. Because it was really beginning to give out – had been built up to 1860, and 100 years later it was beginning to fail. It was his inspiration to have the conservation conference here. I sat in the back row of the top tier looking at all the great and the good, like John Betjeman and others, talking about how what we had here in Edinburgh was unique. I thought, *You've got to get into this. This is the future.* And I did.'

The drift of modernists to what was known at the time as preservationism had been going on for some time. John Betjeman was an early convert: he was a founder member of the Victorian Society, a group formed to fight for the conservation of nineteenth-century architecture – a wildly unfashionable cause at the time.

Gavin Stamp, then both a student and a self-confessed young fogey, was one of a younger generation who joined the society in reaction against the redevelopment that had been ongoing since the war. 'We need to remember that not only was so much of the architectural production sheer rubbish,' Stamp wrote, of the sixties boom, 'but that architectural ambition, when allied to the utopian mania for comprehensive redevelopment, could be arrogant to the point of megalomania. Indeed, by the end of the decade, Modern architecture had become a form of *terror*, a systematic assault on city after city, which drove many people like me into an uncritical hostility and into conservation.'[2]

It was fair to say that feelings on the subject were running high. Young architectural historians Dan Cruikshank and Colin Amery, in their short, sharp shock of a book, *The Rape of Britain*, described the redevelopment of towns such as Worcester, Bath and Hereford as 'an officially sponsored competition to see how much of Britain's architectural heritage could be destroyed in 30 years.'[3] They were echoing a cry from across the Atlantic. Jane Jacobs' 1961 book *The Death and Life of Great American Cities* had become, in its own way, as influential as Ebenezer Howard's *Garden Cities of To-morrow*. In it she railed against the visions of modern life championed by Howard and Le Corbusier, and their 'dishonest mask of pretend order, achieved by ignoring or suppressing the real order that is struggling to exist and to be served'.[4] Instead she advocated a return to the bustle of traditional street life, before comprehensive development schemes and neighbourhood planning had simplified towns to death with their pedestrianised precincts and wholesale disruption of old street patterns.

Old street patterns had started to preoccupy John Knight too, after his damascene conversion at Robert Matthews' Edinburgh conference. 'I moved to Fettes Row,' he said. This was one of the yellow stone Georgian streets in the New Town, a couple over from the one I'd been staying in as I shuttled to Glasgow and back interviewing former Gorbals residents and exploring the library there. Other than admiring its beauty, I'd not really paid much attention to it, but suddenly this 200-year-old new town seemed to have become central to my postwar story.

After moving to Fettes Row, John could view at close quarters the dangerous dilapidation of the entire area. 'The east side managed to hang on by its toenails to a little bit of elegance, I think, but the west side was just disappearing. One reason being it was built in very inferior stone, because our famous Craigleith had already run out and was too expensive even for the New Town. So the stone was beginning to sheet off.' He soon found himself at the forefront of a pioneering conservation scheme. 'I project managed – we'd now call it – the first project in the New Town: 23-24 Fettes Row. What we had to do was brigade a group of very difficult and quite recalcitrant owners together, who were living in a building that was ripe for demolition.' Thanks to some quick calculations by Robert Matthew, they were able to provide figures for the cost of repair; it ran to £15 million for the New Town, and they were able to apply for grants to cover it. 'The stone was done for, but we were able to reface it and keep the buildings in occupation at the same time – the flats were so big that the owners could move to the back. We scoured the front off and put a new stone front on, and it still looks all right today.'

Robert Matthew's involvement in this project seemed rather baffling to me. I'd encountered him as the big-thinking moderniser behind the Festival Hall and the riverside Gorbals scheme. 'I am frequently charged with being on the one hand, a dyed-in-the-wool preservationist,' he said in 1972, 'and on the other a callous destroyer. I plead guilty to both, for choices have to be made. The world cannot become a vast museum, with the living population relegated to marginal and temporary shanty towns.'[5] And so this esteemed modernist managed to secure the Georgian heritage of Edinburgh's New Town. Here, suddenly, was a viable new model, driven by an alliance between the preservationists and concerned local residents – whose views were now being taken more into account. 'We have learned one lesson,' Matthew told a conference in 1974, after being named conservation advisor to the Secretary of State for Scotland. 'Buildings are infinitely more adaptable than we have hitherto been persuaded to believe … there are many ways of using these solid structures today, or any other day.'[6] It was the message that had resonated across the Atlantic from Jane Jacobs and her book on the life of America's old city streets. Many would call Matthew's conversion to the conservation movement a betrayal of his earlier modernist principles. But Matthew himself would argue that his vision had never wavered; what he wanted to create and what he wanted to protect were one and the same: buildings of quality.

By the mid-seventies arguments about modern planning and architecture had moved beyond the textbook or special interest groups like the Victorian Society. If you'd happened to tune into a classic 1973 episode of *Parkinson*, for example, you'd have seen *Carry On* regular Kenneth Williams deliver a tirade against 'the dreadfulness of the Elephant and Castle, which used to be a place of humanity and warmth and people, and is now just a concrete desert and a mess and an absolute disgrace'. And there was fellow guest John Betjeman to garnish the outburst with a characteristic 'Frightful!'

School kids were getting similar instruction. In May 1976, a touring theatre-in-education company took their transit van to the Welsh new town of Cwmbran to perform two plays to the residents. The first was a right-on production called *Newtopia*, aimed at junior school children. It opened by involving pupils in a town planning roleplay and ended with them singing protest songs against the town they had just planned. Their other play – *Confessions of a Town Planner* in everything but name – was aimed at young adults. *Round the Bend* was the tale of Mr Crutch the planner and his dream of imposing on the wretched people a new kind of town, given the delightfully dystopian name of Futurepoint 80.

It seemed that the tension between modernisation and heritage had finally caught up with everyone.

The great divide between modernisation and heritage was felt, at the sharp end, by millions of council tenants around the country. Many had been moved out to new estates and premises, and were delighted (or not) with the improved amenities they found there. But for many more, the thought of leaving beloved homes and communities was a dreadful prospect. 'If only they'd let us stay. No one wants to go. We are not young and he (the informant's husband) will only last five years. That's what he says, "If only they'd let us stay".'[7] In Sunderland, sociologist Norman Dennis aimed to get a snapshot of local opinion on proposed slum demolition and redevelopment in the late sixties. 'I went to the Town Hall about it,' said one resident who was set to move because of rebuilding work, 'but they want it, so that's the end of it. There's nothing more we can do. It seems as if they are stuck on it, they said word had come down from London that they had to come down.'[8] One local government official in Sunderland Council dealing with the slum clearance programme sounded like a character from *Round the Bend*: 'All houses built before 1914 can and ought to be cleared in the next 10 years,' he told Dennis. 'We ought to have plastic houses that we can throw away after 20 years. Good God! We will be on the moon in 2000 and these houses were built when Charles Dickens was writing his novels.'[9]

Funny, feisty former planner Jo Meredith, who I'd met in Sheffield, took me through the challenges she'd faced. 'I was involved in slum clearance in Manchester, in the early seventies, because there were still *huge* areas,' she remembered. 'And of course this was the seventies – the love affair with tower blocks had gone.' Despite that, there was still a lot of redevelopment being planned. 'At that time in the late sixties and early seventies local government was actually *doing* things. You were building things: you were building housing, you were building sheltered housing for older people, you were building public buildings. Local authority design departments were very fizzy places to be.' But she also remembered less happily the change that occurred when the tide turned against these redevelopment schemes. 'It was also the beginning of the conservation period which in a sense

I thought totally grew like topsy and got out of hand. So by the time
you got to 1980 anything more than 50 years old had got to be kept
because it's *wonderful*.' She rolled her eyes at the 'heritage' they'd
inherited. 'There were some awfully bad buildings built, you know.'
And she didn't mean the modern ones.

Jo Meredith's career straddled the period when, in the fag-end
of Wilson's sixties government, thinking on building and planning
suddenly changed. Comprehensive development areas were out,
and with it the bold, free-thinking style of planners like Patrick
Abercrombie. Instead, the onus would be on local councils to
improve existing buildings, as in Edinburgh's New Town, rather than
to redevelop. The accusation was levelled that homes were being
mislabeled slums by planners in order for them to push through
redevelopments, and that some simple adaptations might have saved
these houses from being knocked down in the first place. There
was 'planning blight' too, that suffocating syndrome caused when
a future scheme was unveiled and threatened to put a district to
slow death by the creeping poison of compulsory purchase orders.
Professor John Gold, in the introduction to the first of his series of
books on modernism in Britain, recalled what happened to his home
town of Ilford in Essex when a major redevelopment scheme was
announced in 1962. 'Houses were boarded up and the slates removed
from their roofs to keep out squatters,' he wrote. 'Once they were
suitably derelict, they could be cleared piecemeal, leaving islands of
uninhabited dwellings surrounded by dereliction masquerading as
temporary car parks. Street repairs halted and infestations of mice
and other vermin were experienced.'[10] He also recalled how a local
councillor had appeared on television and dismissed terraces of late-
Victorian houses as slums, to the anger of the residents. John had seen
the original plans for the scheme in the local library when they had
been first announced, and had loved their futuristic functionalism.
In the end Ilford's plan was abandoned due to lack of funds, and the
area was rebuilt in dribs and drabs, losing any sense of coherence and
community in the process.

The government began to alter its stance on redevelopment. Robert Matthew's company RMJM carried out a study in the late sixties as part of the development of the romantically named Central Lancashire New Town. *New Life in Old Towns*, the resulting book, features interviews with residents of Nelson and Rawtenstall, two towns in north-east Lancashire; the same point is made by the residents over and over again: 'Keep them standing and improve them. They've knocked down far too many good old houses already.'[11] Residents, Matthew's researchers found, 'overwhelmingly supported the idea that the two study areas be rehabilitated rather than redeveloped.' Where once RMJM's employees would have angled for work in a comprehensive development scheme, suddenly they were the preservationists' friends. 'The choice for the foreseeable future lies not between rehabilitation and redevelopment,' wrote their researchers, 'but between rehabilitation and continuing neglect.'[12]

Yet rehabilitation was no easy task. A Ministry of Housing and Local Government study estimated that there were still almost two million slum dwellings left in England and Wales, and 4.5 million homes in need of substantial repair. Almost a fifth of houses in England and Wales still had no inside toilet or washbasin.[13] These may feel like descriptions of life in bygone centuries, but it's salutary to remember that this was no longer the age of austerity and bomb-damage: it was 1967, the year of the summer of love, when the Beatles released *Sgt. Pepper* and Sean Connery starred in his fifth James Bond film, *You Only Live Twice*. London, at least according to popular myth, was swinging, but housing conditions were still primitive and grim for millions who lived around Britain.

The latest revolution in planning would soon start to have tangible effects. Heath's government encouraged building societies to make mortgages easier to come by, and that engendered an early seventies boom in home ownership – and in do-it-yourself. There followed a flurry of gentrification as homeowners began to do up houses in seedy London squares in Islington, Notting Hill and Lambeth. These were the kinds of places that until recently, private landlords such as racketeer Peter Rachman had been dividing up into tiny flats in order to charge extortionate rents to poor tenants. These potentially ideal homes had to be reclaimed from criminally neglectful and greedy landlords – and their exploited working class tenants – and often dragged up from slum conditions before they could become the havens of the demographic known today as the 'chattering classes'.

The more I read and researched, the more I came to realise that many of the most exciting and ambitious schemes of the postwar era can't be visited, because they were never actually built. The ghosts of London's failed attempts at modernisation, for instance, are everywhere. One of the most extraordinary examples is at Piccadilly Circus. Although Patrick Abercrombie had diagnosed it as an urgent case for treatment as long ago as 1943 because of its notorious traffic jams, the fifties passed by without any coherent new scheme emerging to salvage it. Developers' models came and went, only to be dismissed by the London County Council and the government as being unsuitable for such an important historic London landmark. One developer even brought in Walter Gropius to add credibility to the design of a major new building – only to have the elderly Bauhaus founder suggest that there was no point designing a single structure because the entire junction had to go. In 1960 the London County Council hired eminent planner William Holford to come up with a rescue plan for Piccadilly Circus. As in every town centre rebuild since the fifties, developers sensed a killing and moved in, only to be frustrated by the London County Council's slow progress. 'The land should have been compulsorily purchased years ago, so that the planning authorities could organise the logical combination of sites,' developer Joe Levy told the *Architects' Journal*, recommending 'flyovers, underpasses and extensive underground garages'. He finished with a weary flounce: 'As it is, I doubt I shall ever see it completed.'[14]

Yet the saga dragged on. 'Something must be done if Piccadilly Circus is to remain the hub of the West End,' Holford told *The Times* in 1966. 'Otherwise it would become like the centre of Los Angeles

– an abandoned area given over to traffic. One must try everything to keep Piccadilly a place where people want to go to, particularly in the evenings. Otherwise it would be a terrible confession of defeat.'[15] Eight months later he unveiled a new megastructure for the site: the London Pavilion. 'With pedestrian thoroughfares and services underground, police and traffic control rooms under the deck and open and covered concourses above, the new London Pavilion would be a public building to an even greater extent than the Royal

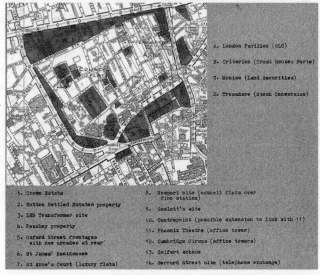

The 1972 plan for the rebuilding of the West End, including the key landowners at Piccadilly Circus. © John H. Hutchinson

Festival Hall,' he told *The Times*. Monico, the famous neon-clad building, would be linked to this new pavillion by a pedestrian deck, moving Piccadilly Circus' colourful street life up a floor and burying the 'services' and cars beneath, on ground level. On the deck would be shops and restaurants, with the offices above clad in illuminated signs. The Trocadero would be rebuilt as a 140-foot high hotel. 'It is envisaged that ultimately the pedestrian concourse and deck should be extended by means of walkways throughout the circus, possibly up Regent Street, into Soho, towards Leicester Square and eventually as far as Covent Garden.'[16] The newsreels covered it, and it was a big story in the press. It was even hailed as 'the biggest breakthrough in planning since Ebenezer Howard developed the garden city.'[17] Not by redoubtable architectural critic Ian Nairn, who was frightened by the plan. 'Can you imagine, on their present performance at Hyde Park Corner and at the Elephant and Castle, just what the GLC entrances to that upper level will look and feel like?'[18] The government was equally gloomy. 'He would be a rash man who tried to guess when the planning process will end and redevelopment will begin,' wrote Dame Evelyn Sharp from the Ministry of Housing. 'The general public is all too likely to simply want it to go on looking much as it does at present.'[19] Wandering round Piccadilly Circus these days is a dispiriting experience, as you try to navigate its semi-pedestrianised muddle, mustering the courage to cross from one side to the other, only to disappear into the crush of pedestrians funneled into tiny pavements. It's clear that none of Abercrombie's valid criticisms from the forties were ever acted upon, let alone any of Holford's space-age sixties plans. The best hasn't even been made of a bad job.

'What, one wondered, had this beautiful bronze slab to do with the City of London, its grey wintry vapours and bowler hats?' was the response that greeted the unveiling of Mies van der Rohe's model for a glass-walled office block for Lloyd's Bank. And that wasn't the response of the *Daily Telegraph*, but of *Concrete Quarterly*.[20] The preservationists weren't keen either, to say the least, having seen much of the City's Victorian architecture razed by developers since the war. When I interviewed architect James Dunnett, he made an interesting observation about the hoo-ha that surrounded Mies' project at the time: 'Neither he, but certainly not the opponents, talk about conditions inside the tower for one minute. They're not interested. The whole thing is talked about in terms of the pedestrian walking along, the picturesque views or whatever. But that wasn't what it was for. The idea was a building like that was designed to improve the conditions of office workers. And it's for the office workers that the buildings are being built … The conditions inside the buildings are the key to understanding what modern architecture is about, which for some reason the generation who came to fruition in the fifties and early sixties understood, but then they were suddenly forgotten about by everybody. Because people were traumatised by the disruptive effect on the fabric of the cities.' In the event, Mies' design was dropped, and Lloyds eventually moved into a fantastic deconstructed building by Richard Rogers some streets away.

Yet the outcry surrounding Piccadilly Circus and Mies's Lloyds building paled to nothing beside that provoked by the redevelopment of Covent Garden. Firstly, to relieve traffic congestion, the ancient fruit and vegetable market had been moved from its home in central London to the run-down back-streets of Battersea, south of the Thames. Then, as mentioned in the Piccadilly Circus plan, Greater London Council planned to redevelop the grand old market site and a fifth of the West End with it. There would be a gigantic shopping centre, a hotel, an international conference centre, as well as ring roads, car parks and flats. Unfortunately, the seventeenth-century piazza, nineteenth-century neoclassical market building and many other icons of post-Great Fire development stood in the way. Protests from residents' groups began in 1971: the alarm had been raised by Brian Anson, Greater London Council's community liason planner who'd met the residents and gone native. The protesters were a strange alliance of politicians and hippies, local residents, theatricals, market traders and, of course, the preservationists. In 1973, facing the conundrum of how to protect the piazza while also making positive noises to the planners, Secretary of State for the Environment, Geoffrey Rippon came up with a solution straight out of *Yes Minister*. He gave permission for the scheme to go ahead, while at the same time listing hundreds of buildings in the area, which rendered the redevelopment impossible. Instead, the area was regenerated, as Edinburgh's New

Town had been. Soot and grime were scrubbed from buildings and cobbles, and the twee stalls of the re-opened market hall played host to street theatre performances while the ghosts of the long-gone market porters looked on. When the right-to-buy policy came along in the eighties those former council residents who'd fought to save the area sold up and moved on.

Perhaps the most drastic piece of replanning that never came to pass in London was the inner ring roads. Abercrombie had proposed four arterial ring roads: radiating outwards from an inner ring feeding the centre of the city to a distant orbital road circling the outer suburban sprawl. What later became known as the 'motorway box' was the smallest of the rings, but also one of the most destructive, knocking its way through densely populated boroughs like Brixton and Islington. The nearest London got to the 'box' was the Westway, a raised section of urban motorway constructed in west London during the late sixties. Even this one relatively small scheme lay waste to great chunks of old housing, uprooting numerous communities in the process, and leaving those who found themselves suddenly living in the shadow of the flyover bitter and resentful. It crops up as the setting for local resident J. G. Ballard's stunning 1974 novel *Concrete Island*, wherein the protagonist, a rich architect called Robert Maitland, crashes his Jaguar and ends up marooned on the central reservation at a motorway intersection. Far bigger redevelopments had happened to east London in the fifties, but this was different: since the early postwar years politicians and experts of all kinds had suffered a huge drop in credibility, with a new wave of satirists and an ever more critical media feeding on a plethora of political scandals. Ordinary people were coming to believe that their opinions mattered as they never had before. It's also fair to say that the Westway affected more middle class communities than the East End rebuilding ever had, people who were more confident, vocal and influential than their working class equivalents. And even though the Westway protesters were not in the end successful, they did help inform those fighting against the motorway box.

Not that anyone knew about the plans at first. It was only in 1964 when Battersea Borough Council couldn't get planning permission to build a swimming pool, and with no reasonable explanation from London County Council forthcoming, that people began to suspect that something odd was going on. 'The fact came out under persistent questioning,' reported *New Society* magazine, 'that the then London County Council was sitting on plans for a vast network of motorway rings round London, a section of which would sweep through the site where the baths might be.'[21] As befitted the mood of the day, there were protests from the hastily formed London Motorway Action Group, soon joined by highly organised residents associations across London.

Yet it was the Land Compensation Act of 1973, which gave compensation to home owners if new road building lowered their property values, that really put paid to schemes like the motorway box, which came to be seen as liabilities of monstrous proportions for the cash-strapped councils involved. In a time of financial hardship this and most other comparable schemes all over the country, from Glasgow to Croydon, bit the dust. Today only the 'barrier block' in Brixton, with its hostile speak-to-the-hand design, and the Westway, with its eggbox-grey concrete marching on sturdy legs through Paddington, are there to remind us of what might have been for what soon became London's gentrified core.

Most town and city planning departments faced the fallout from this heady mix of public protest and expert fatigue in the early seventies. One of the most spectacular meltdowns occurred in Newcastle, where T. Dan Smith had been working his magic since the fifties to transform the city into 'the Brasilia of the north'. The plans were monumental: skyscraper hotels, rapid transport systems and town centre 'streets in the sky'. Early developments such as Cruddas Park had been concerned with rehousing the poor from notorious slums. By the seventies it was about luxury flats in the city centre. Bewick Court, a 21-storey tower block built straddling a road in the heart of the city centre, sought to attract a new class of young urban professional – 'doctors, civil servants, business executives, retired couples and young swingers' – rather than the working-class families housed in most of Newcastle's blocks.[22]

Bewick Court's original residents were interviewed for the *Newcastle Journal* in 1972, in what is probably my favourite of all the newspaper articles I read during my research. Their answers revealed the new lifestyle to which the city's young elite aspired – and it bore little resemblance to the communal fun and games that had characterised the early days of Cruddas Park. 'I was the second person to move in,' said resident Suzanne Burke. 'I wanted the impersonal bit, the prestige of living here. Everyone loves a good address. I don't want to know about Mrs Smith's cake that hasn't come out of the oven properly. If I bought some fish and chips but had no salt I'd go without. I wouldn't borrow it off neighbours. I want to keep myself to myself.' Kay Nicholls, 25, was if possible even more blunt. 'We moved out of a new housing estate deliberately. We don't really like knicker parties and coffee mornings, which is all you seem to get there. So we came here and we're pleased.' She added: 'We've sold our car because there was nowhere to park it and it kept getting broken into.' A young mother who'd escaped life in a pit village told the reporter: 'In the village everyone knows everyone else's business. I couldn't go back to that.' And then there was Alan Black, a young executive from the Department of Trade and Industry. 'I could imagine that living here can be quite horrible,' he said. 'But I've escaped what I wanted to escape from.'[23] Bewick Court wasn't run by the council, but by a housing trust who, in a move no doubt designed to flatter the wallets of this generation of aspirational young executives, doubled their rent within a year.

These thrusting young business types needed somewhere suitably ritzy in which to spend what was left after the rent, and city architect Ken Galley had just the thing to offer them: a shopping mall in the heart of the grand old Georgian town centre. 'We are determined we can do better than any other British city,' he told the friendly folk at the *Newcastle Journal*. 'The ideas we have been developing for four or five years were confirmed strongly by our visit to America' – by which he meant urban motorways, malls, walkways, and flats such as Bewick Court in the centre to keep the city alive at night.[24] Newcastle's plans didn't go unnoticed in London. In 1970 the *Illustrated London News* interviewed the *Journal*'s cheerleading editor, Ian Fawcett, who told them that the new developments 'could reverse the traditional north–south flow of people looking for a life with better prospects'.[25] Fawcett's influence can be felt on many of the *Journal*'s articles from this period, with their sunny glass-half-full attitude. 'It looks as if Newcastle's years of waiting will all have been worthwhile,' he wrote in 1970. 'The shopping centre planned for the city is nothing less than magnificent. … Only the passing of Eldon Square gives any major cause for tears.'[26]

Eldon Square was an instantly recognisable landmark: the centerpiece of the city's Georgian plan. By the end of the sixties it had been partially demolished to make way for an American-style mall, a partnership between the council and developers Capital and Counties Property, and for the construction of a towering hotel, to be designed by Danish modernist master Arne Jacobsen. Yet in the midst of all this activity it suddenly became apparent that Newcastle City Council and Galley's team had hugely underestimated the strength of affection among the city's population for this grand landmark. Alan Brown's letter to the *Newcastle Chronicle* in 1969 reflected a widely held view that Eldon Square was 'being devastated to make way for a skyscraper hotel and shopping precinct … a hollow, meaningless showcase, a Brasilia, a little Los Angeles, a drive-in for motorway enthusiasts'.[27] Architectural historian Bruce Allsopp was in the vanguard of the battle against Galley's plans for Newcastle's centre. At a noisy public meeting he told the shellshocked planner that 'the demolition of Eldon Square was a slap in the face of public opinion throughout the country'.[28] A protest group, SOCEM (Save Our City From Environmental Mess), was set up, and Galley found himself and his work roundly pilloried in the press and in public. 'It would have been much better if the great debate had taken place at the planning stage rather than now at the implementation stage,' he ruefully told the still sympathetic *Newcastle Journal* in 1972.[29] A few months later he vented his frustration further. 'Just imagine how many would come to a planning meeting in Jesmond tonight. No hall would be big enough to hold them.'

Galley came from a generation of officials used to proceeding with their plans regardless of public opinion, in the unquestioned belief that they were right, and he was not alone in finding the adjustment to these new, more democratic times difficult. 'Sometimes in moments of despair,' wrote that expert of all experts, Dame Evelyn Sharp, 'one wonders, in the Ministry, whether planning is possible at all, or at least whether it is worth the effort – and the abuse. But of course it is; if we didn't have it we should have to invent it.'[30]

It wasn't just protests that were doing for plans like Ken Galley's. In a decade of global financial crises, strikes and IMF bailouts, the writing was on the wall for other city centre shopping malls. 'With Nottingham's Victoria Centre, Manchester's Arndale and Market centres and London's Brent Cross, Eldon Square represents an image of massive regional comprehensive shopping redevelopment unlikely to be repeated in the foreseeable future,' wrote the *Guardian* in 1976. 'It is a concept fallen out of fashion even before its results are realised.'[31]

While Eldon Square was being mauled in Newcastle, Arndale were building their massive flagship centre in Manchester. For this major scheme they had taken what was for them the unusual step of appointing a firm of big name architects – Wilson and Womersley, comprising the once great local authority talents of Hugh Wilson, Cumbernauld's original chief planner, and Lewis Womersley, the futuristic brain behind Sheffield's postwar transformation. Almost a decade in the building, the mall, covering acres of the city centre – and clad with thousands of beige and brown ceramic tiles – was instantly dubbed by locals as the largest public lavatory in England, and the developers and architects found their names had become dirty words.

Kenneth Shone, one of the job architects, did not take their criticism lying down. 'I'll readily accept the comment that to take 13 acres of land out of commission for five years is rather inhuman,' he told the *Guardian* in 1978. 'Right – but it was an inhuman scale problem that people gave us to solve ... I think it's a bit rough now for people to start knocking Chippindale or us because in the meantime the tide has turned. Conservation has become the in-thing, as if conservatism and redevelopment were mutually exclusive.'[32]

However, there was one group conspicuously loving the huge new mall, with its heating and seating. Journalist Gillian Linscott found that elderly people were 'sat in the arcade all day because it was warmer and more companionable than being at home.' The mall had become a winter garden. '"It's warm, and you meet a lot of people," said one woman by the miniature waterfall.'[33]

The crises of 1973 brought an end to these huge developments more effectively than any protest could. After a face-off between the Arab oil-producing states and the west, the taps to supply Europe and the USA were turned off. As energy prices soared, inflation boomed and the UK economy slipped into recession: 'stagflation' was born. Things were already looking bad, but when a disastrous round of pay negotiations between Edward Heath and the National Union of Mineworkers broke down, Britain's domestic production of fuel was also cut. A three day week was introduced, where commercial consumption of electricity was confined to just three consecutive days each week until the energy crisis had passed. The modern British way of life had not looked so shaky since the dark days of the Blitz.

The Arndales, like the rest of Britain, were forced to keep strange hours, without light or heat for four days out of seven. Robert Waterhouse, a *Guardian* journalist channeling the dystopian writers of the day, speculated on the role of these huge new shopping centres in the coming social apocalypse. 'If the worst does happen,' he wrote, 'and the social economy of the nation breaks down, these centres will be part only of a much wider disintegration of urban services'. But he saw instead a more likely 'slow war of attrition experienced by all the developed countries'. If that was the upshot, it wouldn't necessarily mean the end for these giant shopping malls. After all, 'hundreds of thousands of square feet of glass and concrete are not going to be wished away merely because they are no longer profitable. The challenge will be to see how they can be brought back into productive use.'[34]

In the context of these wider economic catastrophes, the ideals of developers, planners and protesters became somewhat moot. The simple truth was that Britain couldn't afford to maintain the pace of redevelopment of the previous two decades, even if it had wanted to. Geologists can pinpoint global extinctions and climactic events by pointing to lines in the strata of rock, where the geological record abruptly changes; an analogous hiatus occurred in our town centres, between the frenetic activity of the fifties and sixties, and the mid-eighties, when widespread building began again. By that time styles had changed so much that the edifices of the postwar period seemed like relics from a distant age – a foreign country where they did things differently, where plans to demolish Covent Garden, put Newcastle on stilts or plough urban motorways through London's most desirable districts seem like alien curiosities, at which we can only scratch our heads in wonder.

3. 'As Corrupt a City as You'll Find'
UNCOVERING THE LIES AT THE HEART OF THE BOOM (1966–77)

'*We have the best police force in the world. We have the greatest local government. We have the most wonderful press. Whatever it was it was inviolate, it was achieving great things, it ran perfectly.*'

If Britain at Christmas 1973 was facing meltdown, 1974 would prove to be nothing short of apocalyptic for the established order. Two general elections in eight months kicked out Edward Heath's troubled government and replaced it with one led by an increasingly doddery Harold Wilson. In November two IRA bombs exploded in pubs in Birmingham, including The Mulberry Bush at the foot of James Roberts' new Rotunda, and killed 21 people. In a wave of terrorist attacks, a coach was blown up on the M62, killing 12, and there was an explosion in the Tower of London, where one person died.

The other big story of the year was corruption. In America, Richard Nixon finally left the White House on 8 August. In Britain a crooked trail led from an architect's office in west Yorkshire all the way up to Heath's Home Secretary. Its exposure laid bare a network of unscrupulous businessmen, dishonest officials and immoral politicians, and discredited an entire generation of public figures. On the back of the collapse of Ronan Point and widespread popular protests against many new development schemes, this very public unmasking of the corruption at the heart of Britain's architecture and planning community completed a perfect storm from which the professions have never quite recovered.

At Leeds Crown Court in February 1974, John Poulson, who had been quietly running Europe's largest architectural practice from the West Riding town of Pontefract, was convicted of fraud. In April, 'Mr Newcastle', T. Dan Smith, was found guilty of corruption in the same courtroom. Both men, along with sundry accomplices from civil servants to local councillors, were jailed, as the law finally exposed a pervasive web of illegal deals, dodgy contracts and widespread bribery. This was the system and these were the people who had rebuilt British cities, especially those in the north of England, motivated not by the high ideals they often professed, but by a greed for profit and personal gain that trumped all other considerations. For their sensational unmasking we have one man to thank, a dogged young journalist who in the late sixties was working for the *Bradford Telegraph and Argus*: in this *All the Architect's Men* tale, both Woodward and Bernstein are played by a man called Raymond Fitzwalter.

When I visited him just before Christmas 2012, Ray was living in a cosy stone cottage on a hill overlooking Manchester, as though he were still policing the north. The trimmings of a successful life in journalism surrounded him. Two BAFTAs sat on a sideboard, surrounded by shelves of books covering all aspects of news and current affairs, from the sixties to the present. Still remarkably boyish in his steel-rimmed glasses and black v-neck, he answered questions with the fiery and incisive spirit you'd expect from a man who'd been one of the country's most respected journalists.

It hadn't been an easy ride for a young journalist on a small local paper, trying to investigate a whole strata of society: the people who ran Britain. He described a complacent world of long lunches, jollies and conferences in grand hotels, where pompous folk in local government and business met to slap each other on the back. Police, politicians, press, business: it was the crème de la crème.

'The Masonic influence was strong,' Ray told me in his rich, narrator's voice. 'Much stronger than now.' I knew that John Poulson had been a big Mason, and his trial had helped to drag much of that secretive world out into the open too. Yet by the time details of the corruption infesting this world of privilege and power began to surface, in many cases it was too late for the police to prosecute. 'They described it as cutting the top off the pyramid,' said Ray. 'It'd gone on for so long, so much, some of them had died before we could get at them.'

John Poulson, the founder of a huge and corrupt architecture empire. © Bridget Howard

Although many successfully evaded discovery, the number rooted out as a consequence of Raymond Fitzwalter's investigation and Poulson's bankruptcy hearing was still breathtaking. A snapshot of some key figures reveals the insidious nature of Poulson's network. There was Graham Tonbridge at British Rail, who helped him get contracts such as the rebuilding of Cannon Street Station in London, while in return one of Poulson's staff drew £25 from the bank for him each Saturday morning. There was Billy Sales of the National Coal Board, for whom Poulson designed their £1 million northern HQ, Coal House in Doncaster, while paying the mortgage for Sales's large house in Doncaster and sending him on a number of luxurious holidays. Sir Bernard Kenyon, the influential clerk of West Riding Council sat on the board of Poulson's construction company, Open Systems Building, among others. And while he was never dragged through the courts like so many of Poulson's other contacts, the former local government cabinet minister Richard Crossman was at his most waspish while claiming to be surprised to read that Keynon 'for the last three years before his retirement managed a number of Poulson companies although Mr Poulson had contracts with the council.' He remarked with heavy irony:'I suppose it is possible to believe in the Immaculate Conception of county clerks.'[1]

And there was Bill Shee, who as secretary of the Leeds Hospital Board fiercely championed Poulson's tenders for hospital projects in the city, and who immediately on retirement became a consultant for Poulson, claiming sizeable commission on fees the architect received for winning two large Manchester hospital contracts. The architect generously paid for renovations to the house of south-west region Metropolitan Hospital board secretary George Braithwaite, who in turn ensured three lucrative hospital contracts in the district went Poulson's way. Andrew Cunningham was helpful to the architect for his many contacts, not only as a Durham Alderman and chairman of the local Labour party, but also as chairman of the Newcastle airport, police and river authorities. Cunningham pushed a £2 million housing scheme Poulson's way, a job that never even went out for tender, as well as three schools and a technical college. Both he and his wife had been kept on retainer by Poulson as consultants.

Then there was William Pottinger, an ambitious Scottish civil servant, who worked on Poulson's giant Aviemore tourist centre and received free holidays for his trouble. A typical letter from Pottinger to Poulson read: 'Thank you for your letter about the Italian holiday. I need not say again that we are quite overwhelmed by your kindness. Having said that, I have set out a note of what we would really like.'[2] This was typical of the way Poulson operated. Ray recalled that upon meeting the mayor of Bradford, the property tycoon had remarked: "I think you look a bit peaky. You need a good holiday, lad." A few days later tickets arrived for a foreign break for the mayor and his wife. Of these figures, Pottinger, Braithwaite, the Cunninghams and Tonbridge were all arrested and charged with conspiracy by the police, and all were sent to prison, except Mrs Cunningham and Mr Tonbrige, who served suspended sentences.

Yet in his heyday, with all these contacts and many more eager to shove lucrative contracts his way in return for favours, Poulson's business had expanded from a turnover of £20 million in 1958 to five times that within a decade. Jo Meredith, the ebullient ex-planner I interviewed in Sheffield, remembered the growth of this unusual practice well.

> 'Poulson's main British office was in Pontefract, of all unlikely places! And it was the largest employer of architects in Europe in the sixties. I was in Leeds then doing my planning degree, and he was notorious for employing all the foreign architecture students to do their architecture there. We're talking sixties, and we're still talking a lot of discrimination. And he would employ all of the Asian and African architects that came to study, at really cheap rates. It was amazing, because there in Pontefract was this multi-storey office block full of architects working for Poulson, with huge racial mix, which you just didn't get in West Riding towns in those days!'

This was no utopia, however: 'He ran the place like a bully,' Ray told me, 'and he was a very, very difficult man to deal with.'

The Pontefract office churned out a huge amount of work. For Arndale, Poulson designed the Crossgates shopping centre in Leeds,

Poulson's staff, photographed in the grounds of his house, Manasseh, in the 1960s.
© *Bridget Howard*

and his busy practice also designed the Leeds International Pool, whose Olympic-sized baths gained the unfounded reputation that they came in a few inches short of the required 50 metres, causing a fuss of 'wobbly bridge' proportions. No matter, because he moved swiftly on to specialise in hospitals. At least, his talented staffer Paul James did, designing among others Airedale Hospital near Keighley, St Luke's in Huddersfield and St James in Leeds.

James Dunnett, architect and stout defender of Richard Seifert, hemmed and hawed over Poulson when I mentioned him. 'I think that even Poulson wasn't totally devoid of merit,' he said. 'I was just reading a thing about hospitals. His firm designed the first of a new kind of hospital built up there. But I've never seen anything that had real architectural distinction that came out of his practice … There was this euphoria at the time, so a lot got built that wasn't very good.'

Whether his buildings were good or not, the service Poulson offered certainly sounded impressive, as *Building* magazine gushed at the height of his success in 1967: ‘Quantity surveying, planning, interior design, structural engineering, electrical, heating and ventilating engineering, he has them all.’[3] Some of his work even won awards from the government. The contracts may have been generated through nefarious means, and some of the constructions may have been of dubious quality, but by the end of the decade John Poulson’s business was a huge success.

Poulson’s unravelling began in Bradford in 1969, where a young Ray Fitzwalter was working as deputy news editor on the *Telegraph and Argus*. The paper had reported a local corruption scandal in the town hall, where four of the city architect’s staff were sent to jail and the architect, W. Clifford Brown, was fired for passing on building contracts to local businessmen who had bribed them. Ray’s editor, Peter Harland, was convinced there was more to the story, and in his spare time the rookie reporter began to investigate.

‘It was seemingly quite straightforward,’ Ray explained, ‘because what the police had done in their prosecutions was they had got the man who had given the bribes to turn Queen’s evidence. He was a local contractor, mainly electrical – fairly small stuff. And he was gabby. I managed to persuade him to meet me, which he did – at midnight, in a room with no lights on!’ He laughed at the absurdity of it. ‘It was his offices. He was very forthcoming. “Look, you don’t understand,” he said. “These kind of rackets operate on three levels. There’s small fish like me bribing junior engineers and whatever. There’s a middle ranking sphere of bribery that operates on a regional level, not a city level, where larger firms take the big contracts worth quite a lot of money. And there’s a top level where jobs into the millions are ripped off.” Then he asked: “Have you ever looked at that man Poulson?” And I said: “Who the hell are you talking about? Never heard of him.” Poulson was not from Bradford, he was from Pontefract. And that was outside our circulation area. But my editor encouraged me to go further. Normally you were lucky if you got your bus fare anywhere.’

It soon became clear that Ray's investigation would require resources far beyond the means of a small local paper, even one prepared to pay for unlimited bus fares.

'The significance of what the briber had told me was: "There's a multi-million pound city centre development scheme coming off. They're going to demolish the old Victorian covered market, right in the middle, and they're going to redevelop it. It'll be in the millions. Poulson is at the back of this, he's going to get the core work controlling that." And I said: "How do you know?" And he said: "Because I've been talking to one of his staff. I met him at a building exhibition and he was on Poulson's stand. Poulson has a building company." I said: "That's unusual. He's an architect. If you're an architect you're not allowed to control a building company." And he said: "Nobody knows he controls it. There's a reference to his wife in it." I said: "Well that's very interesting!" And we were off, as it were. We had a tangible evidential lead.'

He paused for a sip of tea. I was on the edge of my seat.

'I went to Companies House in London, looked up the building company and it was like opening a treasure trove. It had been registered by a man whose name was illegible. Because I couldn't read it properly I left that and went on, and going through the file was absolutely amazing. I found Reginald Maudling [the former Conservative Home Secretary] was a director of the company. This was a seemingly small operation based in West Yorkshire! I found Maudling's son. I found the clerk to the county council. The clerk to the county council was the chairman of a building company! I found William Sales, who was the director of the National Coal Board for the north-east. An *amazing* array of names, and I thought, this is a very strange company. It was called Open Systems

Building – and it was a building company that didn't own a
wheelbarrow. I began tracing Poulson people and asking them
all sorts of things. And everyone I talked to on his staff who
knew about it talked about bribery one way or another. And
then I went back to this name that was at the beginning of the
file, and I recognised the address rather than the name. It was
very unusual, it was Spital Tongues, Newcastle – and that's
Dan Smith's address. And at the other end of the file I find
Mrs Poulson, who's a director, and the offices were Poulson's
offices, so we had the two of them tied together and Maudling
in between. It was an absolutely *amazing* thing!'

How had 'Mr Newcastle', T. Dan Smith, the hero of Cruddas Park,
become mixed up in all this? If Poulson was an outsider, his name or
business rarely if ever cropping up on the national stage, Smith was a
master communicator, a man who ran his own public relations firm,
and who revelled in being seen to be at the centre of things. By the
early sixties he had been named Man of the Year by the *Architects'
Journal*; been chosen by Colin Buchanan to sit on his *Traffic in Towns*
government committee; and was close friends with that formidable
champion of local government, Dame Evelyn Sharp of the Ministry
of Housing. In the midst of all this high flying and good work, Dan
Smith met John Poulson in 1962. They immediately clicked.

'When I first came across the Poulson outfit, as a housing man
it looked like manna from heaven,' said Smith.[4] The architect was
quick to put Smith's Town Planning Advisory Organisation on a
retainer. 'Dan Smith mesmerised me,' he wrote in his autobiography,
while he in turn tried to impress Mr Newcastle with his snow-white
dreams of 'rescuing our city centres'.[5]

From what, it is not quite clear.

Letters were written between Smith and Poulson, as they worked
out who would work which levers in which council. Smith later
wrote that he was taken with the idea of building up a regional
power base, using local firms such as Poulson's to increase the

independence of his beloved Newcastle. Whatever the justification, by the late sixties Smith's companies had received £155,000 from Poulson, while the architect was reckoned to have made a cool £1 million from Smith's contacts.

Poulson was not the only dodgy customer with whom Smith would deal. In 1963 he told Bovis offshoot Leslie and Co. that he could put work their way if they paid him as an advisor. He made good on the deal, omitting to mention this particular conflict of interest when Leslie and Co. were awarded the tenders for the building of new flats in Newcastle. Then there was Crudens, the Scottish construction firm. Smith represented them through his PR company with one hand, and awarded them big contracts with the other: as chairman of Peterlee new town development corporation, for instance, he had presided over the building of 1,000 houses built with the system used by Crudens. Dan Smith shrugged off the ever more frequent accusations of corruption. 'I had many temptations from prominent people in Newcastle,' he told the *Evening Chronicle* many years later. 'I resisted and rejected them all. I didn't get my son a job in the town hall. I didn't get a house. I got nothing.'[6] After all, he told the *Guardian*, 'getting things done is not synonymous with pulling a fast one.'[7]

By the mid-sixties Smith's influence had spread far beyond Newcastle. There was Wandsworth councillor Sidney Sporle, for example, a kind of south London chip off the old block, whose work included redeveloping the area where my parents had grown up. 'Mr Newcastle' wangled Sporle a lucrative place on the board of Poulson's construction company Open Systems Building in 1966; shortly afterwards, Sporle hired Smith's PR company to represent the council. A local councillor got wind of the affair, and soon the pair of them found themselves in court.

Meanwhile Ray Fitzwalter, investigating Poulson in Bradford, realised he had to get up to speed on the Newcastle councillor's shady past too. 'Dan Smith had already been prosecuted in Wandsworth, and acquitted in what can only be described as disgraceful circumstances,' he told me, disgust still evident in his voice. 'He ought to have been prosecuted successfully. He wasn't because the trial was fixed. It was as bad as that. He was tried by a judge who knew him. They were old political colleagues in the Labour party. Dan Smith had campaigned for him, can you believe it? I also know for a fact that Dan Smith was tipped before the trial that he would be acquitted.'

The discovery of so much corruption had been a shock to the reporters on the *Bradford Telegraph and Argus*. 'You can imagine,' said Ray, 'we're a small local paper, with a local solicitor giving us advice ... you didn't *do* things like this.' And yet they decided to push on. 'The thing that I was also aware of,' he added, 'was that Poulson's empire was extremely shaky. He was in deep financial trouble.' To keep the wheels oiled in this complex machine, Poulson had need of a great deal of ready cash to bribe potential contacts, but despite all of the business the practice was winning, cash was short. 'He'd not gone over the edge,' said Ray, 'but he was vibrating.' At this point Lord King, Poulson's brother-in-law, stepped in to prop up the business with some much-needed capital. But the situation remained fragile.

With the evidence piling up, the paper decided this was the moment to take a risk. They published a profile of Poulson under the ironic headline 'The Master Builder', including a series of coded nudge-nudge hints about the nature of Poulson's business. Then they waited to see if he'd sue – or if anyone else with more clout would take up the story. To their dismay something worse happened – the story sank like a stone. Even when *Private Eye* took it up, printing an article entitled 'The Slicker of Wakefield' in April 1970, none of the national press was interested. More than a couple of articles, it seemed, were needed to clear the miasma of complacency from the upper echelons of Britain's establishment.

Two years later Ray was working for ITV's investigative programme *World in Action* when Poulson filed for bankruptcy. The reporter immediately grasped the significance of this development for his dormant story: the architect's financial papers would be released by the courts. Soon he was drawing up a master chart of the complex affair that covered a whole desktop in his office at Granada's studios in Manchester.

'It was almost unravelable ... all the people who were connected with it, and all the different layers, starting with small county councils and then the Coal Board and the nationalised industries, and big county councils. Sir Bernard Kenyon [Chief Executive of West Riding county council] was right in the frame, and right up to politicans, and right at the top – Maudling. I said, "That is what we want to put on the screen. It looks complicated, but we need interviewees who can explain it." By that stage this was a bang-bang national scandal that everyone knew about but nobody understood.'

Unfortunately for Ray and the *World in Action* team, the Independent Broadcasting Authority banned their film. Ray was in no doubt as to why. 'Four members of the IBA had connections with people who were right in the middle of the frame!' His indignation was still much in evidence. 'One of them was outrageous, and that was Dame Evelyn Sharp. She was the principal civil servant at the Ministry of Housing. She'd appeared as the only witness at Dan Smith's Wandsworth's trial.' She also had 2,000 shares in Bovis, Keith Joseph's construction firm. A subtly re-edited version was finally broadcast some months later, after a stormy IBA meeting. 'Dame Evelyn Sharp said in direct hearing: "If this comes out it'll ruin Dan." Completely partisan!'

After the broadcast, the emboldened journalists began to push harder at what suddenly felt like an open door. A sister programme followed, putting Reginald Maudling, the Home Secretary, in the frame. Maudling had become involved with Poulson in the oddest of cirumstances. His wife Beryl Maudling's dream had been to build a ballet theatre in East Grinstead, but by 1965 the project had run out of money. Poulson stepped in, offered Maudling a role as a board member of Open Systems Building in 1967, and stumped up £22,000 to keep Mrs Maudling's dream alive.[i] Thereafter Maudling found himself ever more deeply involved in Poulson's expansionist schemes which, helped immeasurably by the backing of a politician of such standing, now reached far beyond Britain's shores.

'It was a step-by-step unraveling of the greatest corruption imaginable,' said Ray of their second documentary. 'The day after, Maudling got up in the Commons and said, "I'll sue everyone connected to this programme!" – and he didn't. That was his way of frightening everybody. We had him banged to rights and he knew it.' *Private Eye* ran a cover on 14 July 1972, with the headline 'Poulson Affair – Govt's. "Grave Disquiet"', and a picture of Maudling leaving number 10 to Heath's cry, 'All right Reggie, you can look into it,' and the Home Secretary's response: 'I shall leave no stone unturned.' There was little doubt that the corruption reached the heart of government. 'He sued everyone in sight apart from us and the *Daily Mirror*,' recalled Ray. 'And then he died, with a liver two and a half times its normal size.' Poulson was arrested in June 1973 and eight months later was sentenced to five years in prison for fraud. A couple of months after that Dan Smith was tried at the same court and sent to prison for six years. Thanks to the dogged efforts of Raymond Fitzwalter and his peers, an era of institutionalised corruption had been dramatically uncovered.

In the mid-sixties the *Guardian* had described local government as 'the biggest and potentially the most important of all big businesses'.[8] This, of course, was why companies were so keen to hang onto their contacts – whatever it took. 'I've seen conveners of housing committees almost crawling up the stairs at night, being stroked and patted on the head by builders!' claimed one onlooker attending the annual Scottish National Housing and Town Planning conference in Peebles.[9] The prosecution in Poulson's case described

---

i Sadly her dream remained unrealised, and the people of East Grinstead have had to manage without a ballet theatre.

the method as 'by the back door – by using a fifth column within the local councils and not openly, but stealthily and secretly and for reward'.[10]

One of the more notable cases of corruption in the story of Britain's postwar rebuilding was that of Alan Maudsley, city architect in the mid-sixties in Birmingham, England's most go-ahead modernised city. As with Poulson, *Building Design* magazine lauded Maudsley to the skies, hailing this energetic fellow in an article titled 'Forward with Maudsley', in which he was quoted as saying that he 'couldn't point to any other city where private architects have had a greater opportunity … Architecture is a business. I set out as a businessman and the fact that I'm qualified as an architect is incidental.'[11] Birmingham's industrial revolution had made it a town of engineers, but Maudsley was determined to wrest control of the budget and the glory from the city engineer. 'Why does Maudsley want to get involved in "more important" schemes like the projected concert hall, the central magistrates courts and an expanded airport?' asked *Building Design*. 'He doesn't say, but the reasons could be many.'[12] As it turned out, one reason was less than noble. At the start of 1973 a story broke in the *Birmingham Mail*: local architects James Sharp and Evan Ebery were charged with offering Maudsley bribes, the architect with accepting them. All three were sent to jail that Watergate summer.

Smith and Poulson apart, perhaps the most shocking British case was uncovered in 'the Chicago of the north' – Dundee. The city had undergone a vigorous postwar rebuilding programme: by 1970 their housing output was a staggering 88 percent higher than even the power-crazed Alan Maudsley had achieved in Birmingham at the height of his regime.[13] The standout scheme was Whitfield, a massive estate of 5,000 homes, over half of which were deck-access flats built in hexagonal honeycomb formations, made from Skarne system-built units. Like Newcastle and Birmingham, the city appeared to be a model of postwar modernisation. Then Ray Fitzwalter at *World in Action* was called in to clean up the town.

'I got a telephone call from a councillor,' he recalled. '"We have terrible trouble in Dundee. Terrible. It's as corrupt a city as you'll find and we can't solve it. Will you come and have a look?"' Ray was not one to turn up the chance of a good story. 'The police had had a significant go at it. The local villains had a party in the town hall the night the police investigation was written off. They were that strong. Nobody seemed to be able to touch them.' Ray and team descended on Dundee and it didn't take them long to uncover some leads. 'We very quickly identified that there were three people in the frame. One was the Lord Provost, one was the chair of the planning committee and the other was the leader of the Labour group. What we found in essence was the most explicit, overt corruption I've seen in Britain. I don't know how they thought they were getting away with it.' It transpired that each of these three key figures owned companies such as electricians or demolition specialists, and 'each one of them was taking contracts from committees that they controlled. It was straightforward!'

In the course of his investigation, Ray ploughed through seventeen years' worth of council minutes, checking them against property records and Companies House, but some of the team's research methods were not quite as above board. At one point Ray decided to set a thief to catch a fraudster. 'A very valuable contact I found burgled a safe for me. He knew what I was doing and he knew what I was looking for, and he had a safe of one of these villains – not the three I've mentioned, but an integral associate – opened and he had the documents inside photographed, and he gave me pictures.' The safe contained a series of invoices for sums up to £20,000 from developers who'd seemingly had no connection to the projects. Vast sums of money were being siphoned away to line the pockets of corrupt businessmen.

The ensuing 1980 trial was the longest criminal trial in Scottish legal history up that point. It was known as the 'Dundee Dossier' affair, after the *World in Action* film. 'And the police got only one of the three.' Ray still looked crushed by this turn of events. 'They got the leader of the council; he went to jail. We tried to interview him and he jumped up halfway through screaming, "You're trying to suggest I'm a Scottish T. Dan Smith!"' Ray laughed now, but it had been a frightening case to work on. 'Dundee was a mafia town … They set fire to businesses if they didn't get what they wanted – not the three councillors, others. There were people there on the council who robbed the poor box. There was a terrible incident where the Lord Mayor, who was the innocent party, in his robes, had a fight in public with another councillor. This guy assaulted him because he knew the Lord Mayor had been helping us. He grabbed him by the testicles! The Lord Mayor turned round and got the car door open and jammed the guy between the car frame and the door. Literally there they were, brawling in public. It symbolises what Dundee was like.'

'T. Dan Smith: Saint or Devil?' asked the *Newcastle Journal* in 1970 in the wake of one of his court cases.[14]

Perhaps it was a little more complicated than that. Like many others, ex-planner Jo Meredith didn't see these scandals in black-or-white terms. 'I know there was a lot of controversy around bribery and corruption,' she said. I mentioned T. Dan Smith and she interrupted at once: 'Did a *huge* amount of good! You can see the good of it and the bad of it. T. Dan Smith in Newcastle, he was *doing* something, he was changing the face, he was doing what people wanted to be done.' She went on: 'I don't think people in those days were cynical like they are now. I mean, now we assume that everyone is corrupt!' Wasn't that partly because of all these scandals back in the seventies, I suggested. As we spoke, the Murdochs were being quizzed about their media empire by a committee of MPs; the spirit of T. Dan Smith seemed to be in the air again. 'Fifty years ago, we were so naïve. We still believed in social good.' She checked herself. 'Some of us still do!'

The corruption scandals that broke in the postwar decades characterise the era as vividly as the Profumo scandal, the Suez crisis, or Enoch Powell's 'rivers of blood' speech. These were crimes committed by people so arrogant they thought they could never be caught, because this was the way the whole world worked for people with power. Poulson's words at his trial showed the power-crazed tendencies beneath the surface of this deeply unpleasant north Yorkshire businessman, and others like him: 'I have been a fool surrounded by a pack of leeches,' he declared. 'I took on the world on its own terms, and no one can deny that I once had it in my fist.'[15]

MILTON KEYNES, THE LAST NEW TOWN (1967–1979)

In the midst of a decade riven by corruption, protest and financial collapse, one huge postwar project kept the flag flying for progressive modernisation – even if it did seem at odds with much of what had been achieved since 1945. It was to be a new city, larger than any of the new towns so far conceived. It turned its back on the high-rise, favoured houses over flats and stuck two fingers up to the 'all in it together' idealism of earlier projects. Instead its mantra was freedom of choice. 'Milton Keynes sounds like Los Angeles in Buckinghamshire,' went the editorial in *The Times*, on 17 March 1970. 'If Milton Keynes can reproduce what people favour in the Los Angeles environment while avoiding its acute inconveniences there is much to be said for the resemblance.'[1]

An older generation of architects and planners may have hated the thought of Los Angeles in California, let alone in Buckinghamshire, but since the sixties the city had begun to fascinate some of the more rebellious factions in Britain. *Reyner Banham Loves Los Angeles*, for example, was an eye-popping 1972 BBC documentary, following the middle-aged, bearded English hipster around the city as he marvelled at its epic suburbia, vast freeways, golden beaches and seedy strip clubs. What comes across most is his wonder at the freedom of it all – how people were living the lives *they* wanted, rather than kowtowing to the do-gooders faced by British estate-dwellers. In Los Angeles there was none of the Presbyterian sensibility of Lord Reith, that arch-patrician who'd shaped Britain's new town movement as he had the BBC a generation before. Instead the city demonstrated a free and easy attitude to planning, perfect for California dreaming. Here people had the space and privacy to live their lives how they wanted. So what if everything was a car-ride away? At least the roads were wide and the city centre wasn't jammed. After all, as an incongruously bow-tied Reyner told his students at one point in the film, 'you can build a city any shape you like as long as it works.' And in Milton Keynes, that little LA in the heart of England, this idea was tested to the max.

Yet at first it didn't feel very Californian – in fact, it felt very much like any other new town. That much was clear from talking to Peter Barry, one of the pioneers, who moved into his home in the estate of Galley Hill in Milton Keynes in 1972, at about the same time Reyner Banham was tripping around LA. His house, a groovy Scandinavian-style red-brick semi with a steep-pitched roof, faced onto a square, where a simple climbing frame on a grassy courtyard acted as the centrepiece for 20 or so houses. A big, silver-haired man in his seventies, Peter welcomed me into his home with a huge smile. He had been recently widowed, and his front room was full of pictures of his wife Gillian and their children and grandchildren. With the mildest of Welsh accents, this natural raconteur seemed to relish the opportunity to talk about how he and his wife had ended up in the new city. Like the Harlow pioneers I'd spoken to, whose fathers had all been builders, Peter was exactly the kind of person this embryonic new city must have needed: he worked in management for Mixed Concrete, one of the few companies supplying the grey stuff to construction sites all over the UK. And Mixed Concrete wanted him to work in Milton Keynes.

'I came over and wandered through the neighbouring court and met the Milton Keynes Development Corporation lady in the show house,' he recalled of his first visit to the few half-built homes that constituted the start of a new city. 'And she said: "If you want to come here you can have one of these houses within a month." And I said: "Oh!" And she said: "It'll be like this one, four bedroom." I said: "Okay. Are you here on the weekends?" She said: "Yes." So I said: "I'll bring my wife over because she won't believe me ." We knew that if we went on the housing list in Abingdon or Oxford we'd be on there for three years.' As Peter had predicted, Gillian was initially reluctant, as they'd already had to move several times for work. 'I said: "It's your decision, but I want you to come to this new place, Milton Keynes, with me. There's a lady I want you talk to." I brought her over, and I said: "This is the lady. Now tell her what you told me, and I'm going outside!" I took the kids out for a run round the court, and she came out with this dazed look on her face.'

Peter and Gillian Barry and family, photographed in 1972 on arrival at the estate of Galley Hill.

Some 41 years later here I was sitting in the living room of the house they'd bought. The couple had felt guilty at first, moving into such a nice new house when there was a housing shortage locally. 'It was very unjust that all these houses were not made available to the local people, which caused a lot of ill feeling. There were a lot of young couples in Stony Stratford' – one of the small towns swallowed up in the new city – 'who could not get one of these houses. We were coming in from all over the place and just walking in.' Not that he was complaining. 'When they were built these places were called ugly because of the monopitched roofs. Well, they are utilitarian to look at, but the estate has matured with all the trees and everything and it's lovely. You come through here in the summertime when all the trees are in leaf and I love it.'

If the homes, at least to start with, were classic new town social housing, it was the roads that suggested Los Angeles wish-fulfilment. Instead of the increasingly ubiquitous tangle of orbital motorways, urban flyovers and clogged streets, the Milton Keynes plan had specified that the whole city would be based around a formal grid of horizontal and vertical dual carriageways. These formed kilometre-square blocks, into which estates such as Galley Hill fell. The car is king here.

Retired planner Jim Griffiths had studied in the sixties under Richard Llewelyn-Davies, who helped provide the initial master plan for Milton Keynes development corporation. We pored over a map of Buckinghamshire before Milton Keynes had been built, showing the old villages and towns contained within it. The planners' map showed a grid of roads superimposed onto the area, and this grid would form the basic layout of the town. Existing villages and towns would be contained within this strict road network. Jim traced the lines of the plan excitedly. 'If I invited you to draw a grid on that which didn't hit anything, you'd be quite a long time and you wouldn't end up with something far away from that.' I could see what he meant – it was remarkably neat, helped by the fact that, unlike Cumbernauld, this part of Buckinghamshire was very flat. He called the ideas behind this road network 'The Los Angeles Model'. 'Los Angeles is the grid with no centre at all,' he explained. 'You just have McDonalds at every junction and away you go.'

At Peter's house in Galley Hill we got to talking about his career, which helped to give a sense of scale to the work required to turn these roads from concept to concrete. Having left Mixed Concrete to work on the sites, which at the time were 'a license to print money', as he put it, he built roads like the A5 dual carriageway.

The ravine for the A5 had already been cut when they first arrived, but he recalled having 'to be careful driving along there because suddenly the road ended and there was a 30 foot drop! No barriers or anything, because you weren't meant to be on there, because they were private roads.' Pretty soon Jim found himself working to finish this major A-road himself. 'I was the foreman of the site batching plant which supplied all the concrete for all the bridges from the bottom of the A5,' he explained. It was incredibly hard work for the young family man. 'To be honest, for two years I didn't really see the family. The uprights for the bridges, they were all done on what they called a "controlled pour". Because it was shuttered, the concrete was only allowed to rise at a certain rate because the weight would burst the shuttering. A 200 cubic metre pour would take all day. You'd get in at five o'clock and they wouldn't be ready. You'd be pissing about till lunchtime.' It wasn't until 2 pm that they'd be ready to start pouring the concrete, and once that process had started they couldn't stop. Working past midnight was not uncommon. 'You'd come home get something to eat, fall asleep and be back there at five the next day. And this went on for two years, seven days a week!' Building railway bridges was, if anything, even more demanding, and he wouldn't go home at all over those weekends. 'You slept on the job.'

For a while these grid roads were simply known by their horizontal or vertical number, such as the V5 or the H7, but in more recent years they have all been given more traditional names. The V4, the section of the A5 that passes through Milton Keynes has now reverted to Watling Street, after the pre-Roman track that led from Dover to Holyhead. I asked Peter how he felt about the grid system once it was finished.

'Love it,' he said without hesitation. 'I can't understand why people complain about not knowing how to find their way around, because it's *so easy*. Being involved in the building of it I still know all the roads by their V and H designations. Half of the roads I don't know the names of.' More famous even than the city's grid system became the nodes that held the grid together: the roundabouts. Milton Keynes has 130 roundabouts, by some way the most per square mile

of any city in the UK. They keep the speedy dual carriageway traffic
flowing, even though they do lopsidedly wear out car tyres on one
side. In a place where all the buildings are screened from the roads
by thick layers of trees, the roundabouts act as useful landmarks,
especially now that each is clearly named. Bottledump and Pagoda,
Yeomans and Fenny Lock, Furzton and Cricket Green: these are the
roundabouts of Milton Keynes, with their brick-built arrows and
tall evergreen trees. These days you can even sponsor them, which
gives you an idea of the kind of town Milton Keynes has become.

This LA-like dependence on the car went completely against
the original concept for the city. Milton Keynes was first mooted
by Fred Pooley, an ambitious local Buckinghamshire planner, back
in the early sixties as an overspill town for the overcrowded south-
east. His proposed city was designed not around a grid road for cars,
but around a monorail. 'All shops – except "corner shops" in the
housing areas – would be built in the city centre, as well as all the
civil, cultural and public buildings,' reported the *Guardian* in 1964.
'There would be multi-level separation of pedestrians and traffic,
and car parking would be provided below the pedestrian deck.'[2]
Pooley's plan was essentially an even more space age Cumbernauld
– complete with a monorail. 'Cars were not rejected, since it was
accepted that everyone living in the new town would own one. On
the other hand, by providing a monorail service of great convenience
and excellent aesthetic quality it was planned to take a considerable
load off the roads.'[3] It was not to be. A year later the government
performed a land grab, stealing the site Pooley had selected,
between the Buckinghamshire towns of Bletchley, Stony Stratford
and Wolverton, and tearing up his plan. The only thing they kept
was his projected capacity for the city: a quarter of a million people,
far more than had been attempted in any of the other new towns.
Harlow, for example, houses about a third of that.

Milton Keynes was to differ from Harlow and its ilk in many other
respects too. From the outset, at least half of the houses would be
for private ownership. 'In Galley Hill they wanted 60 percent home

ownership and 40 percent rental,' recalled Peter. And that was just for starters. 'Those of us that had moved in as tenants were almost immediately offered mortgages arranged through the development corporation, which we took advantage of, obviously. And because of that, it always had a little bit of exclusivity.' The development corporation hoped to encourage private developers to build many of these private houses. 'The city is designed to encourage variety by the mixing of land uses and densities, housing types and tenure, building forms and development over time,' went the super-flexible plan drawn up by Richard Llewelyn-Davies and team for the development corporation, and published in 1970.[4]

The thinking behind the city was set out in bold, if rather vague terms: 'The purpose of our future cities, for which Milton Keynes could be the prototype, must be to provide a setting for learning, for the development of imagination, and for the exchange of information.'[5] The plans met with a luke-warm reception from the media, who were still obsessed with the ghost of the long-scrapped monorail.

As they built up momentum, Richard Llewelyn-Davies and his planning team junked more and more of their new town baggage. Gone was the emphasis on neighbourhood and community: communication, freedom and public consultation were the new watchwords. 'There is an increasing demand for participation in public decision making,' wrote Llewelyn-Davies.[6] Derek Walker, the dynamic and artistic young planner who was brought in by the development corporation to flesh out the initial ideas, expressed in 1980 his sense of the need for a new kind of urban configuration: 'A village or a neighbourhood in a city had a social relevance at a time when physical nearness was the only possible basis for social contact [but] in the light of this new view of the way that society now organises itself, the attempts by British planners in the fifties and sixties to structure social groups by physical arrangement seem a misstatement of the problem, and their failure is explained.'[7] He went on: 'You cannot get a village by pushing a few houses together, or a neighbourhood by isolating a critical number of dwellings.'[8] Walker was planning a town for a different age, when the television, the phone and the car were transforming family life across the country. Milton Keynes was his 'vision of a city which is an open matrix for selection, by the individual, of opportunities for social contact, recreation, education and the rest.'

I've spent a great deal of time in Milton Keynes. My partner lives there, in a district that encapsulated the spirit of innovation the plan had sought to foster. When it was built in the early eighties its name was Energy World, but it has been renamed Shenley Lodge in a classic example of how the futuristic optimism of the plans gradually became domesticated and suburbanised. All the original Energy World houses were built with features such as solar panels and experimental gas and electric systems, including a wind turbine (which never quite worked) and the streets are all named after famous scientists. As far back as the newly environmentally conscious late sixties, the potential to experiment with energy had led people to speculate that Milton Keynes might even have become 'the world's first totally electric city' but this, like many other ideas, never came to pass.[9]

'Compromise is not really a word that should describe the design and construction of a new city,' mused Derek Walker, 'but in the end that unfortunately is what it's all about.'[10] Not that they'd junked all of the idealism of the original plan, but that it had been tempered, both by the pressure from the government to build this city at three times the speed of previous new towns, and by the unfortunate timing of the recession. Back in the early seventies a younger Derek had been more hopeful: 'Its prime quality,' he said of the city plan he'd inherited, 'is ambiguity and one could make it up as one went along.' This was in spite of 'the more sinister aspects of economic pressure, the dilemma of the British cultural climate, and the constant "lemming charge" to mediocrity'. Milton Keynes, he said, 'offered hope in a morass of greyness'.[11] That hope lay with the people he'd worked with to design and create the city. Time and again

Walker is on record claiming his primary achievement in Milton Keynes was employing so many talented and challenging people – even if their independence did occasionally create problems. 'In teasing out people to actually produce varied design solutions,' he told *Architectural Design* in 1973, 'one invariably went outside one's own personal taste.' Despite the tensions, he was fiercely loyal to his young team: 'It's surprising how incredibly attached you do become to people who are with you on the project, and it's equally surprising what lengths you will go to protect and support them.'[12]

As one might have expected from such a vast and complex project, there were failures. Some of the early estates – Netherfield, Coffee Hall and Beanhill in particular – suffered from problems beyond the corporation's control. Before the crash of 1973, the construction boom was putting huge pressure on building material supplies, and the shortage was compounded by a national brick-makers' strike. Fred Lloyd Roche, building manager for the development corporation described their predicament succinctly: 'We were trying to build a thousand houses per annum and the materials and labour just weren't available.'[13] Government funding relied on them hitting targets, so the corporation found itself squeezed between the need to build the new city, and fast, while lacking the desirable materials or workers to do so.

These early estates can come as a bit of a shock, even to other Milton Keynes residents. With the hedgerows, trees and planting all along the H and V roads, Milton Keynes residents simply never glimpse many of the housing areas in their city, even from a distance. One cold and rainy winter's day, my partner Adam took me on a tour of these districts. We were both somewhat surprised by what we saw. At the estate of Coffee Hall, breeze blocks had been used in place of brick in the construction of the long terraces of small bungalows and houses. Later estates favoured curved cul-de-sacs and irregular clusters of houses, while here in Coffee Hall the roads were straight and long – and the tall oak paling fences erected in front of low bungalows meant that you couldn't really see any of the houses. The lack of human activity in evidence gives Coffee Hall the atmosphere of an abandoned prefab estate, almost a shanty town.

Beanhill, the neighbouring estate, had fared little better. Here, rising star Norman Foster had designed long streets of bungalows with pitched roofs, but the lack of brick and tile meant they were largely constructed with corrugated metal and wood. Netherfield, not to be confused with Mr Bingley's estate in *Pride and Prejudice*, had been originally designed for brick construction, but instead continued the corrugated metal theme. Terraces of three-storey town houses, all built for rental, stand divided by sturdy concrete pillars, their walls formed from ridged aluminium and timber. Even the original flat roofs had been aluminium. These days, paint peels from colourful frontages on some of the streets, while others are as grey as any of the harled homes in Cumbernauld.

Caught between impossible cost issues, a lack of materials and the pressure to build at super-speed, it's a wonder that Derek Walker's team ever got beyond these early disasters to build a whole city, let alone a successful one. 'By ingenuity and a little rule bending,' Walker recalled, they 'tried to produce the best possible housing with lower cost allocations. In the early years this meant disappointments.' Fred Lloyd Roche was still in defensive mode a decade later when he said that 'if you look at the quality of houses from 1975 onwards when the situation became much easier, on the whole we've achieved a quality of housing as good as, if not better than, any other community throughout the world in the last 30 years.'[14] This was great for the later residents, but tough on the people who had to put up with the leaks, the condensation and the cracks in the three early estates. Those buildings now come with an urban myth attached: that they were only ever temporary houses erected for the builders.

It wasn't long before success stories began to outweigh these early failures. Simpson, one of many villages swallowed up by the new city, had been a hamlet of a handful of beautiful thatched cottages. With the arrival of the city, these cottages were joined by clusters of super-modernist blond brick houses with big picture windows. While the atmosphere of the sleepy village where everyone knew your name – and your business – was clearly obliterated, the result was something unique and rather brilliant: a sort of mash-up of St Mary Mead and New Ash Green. Then there was Peartree Bridge, built along the Grand Union Canal, whose sharply modern three-storey town houses overlooked the water. Yes, it's a bit run down these days, but, with ducks waddling about in front gardens, canal boats drifting by beyond the weeping willows and a hippy art triceratops guarding the estate, it remains an idyllic little haven of modernism, even if it does need a little TLC. It reminded me of Newcastle's amazing Byker estate of the same vintage, with its long walls of flats and houses, unapologetically modern balconies, detailing and sense of friendliness.

Ralph Erskine, Byker's architect, did in fact contribute to Milton Keynes. His estate, Eaglestone, brings many ideas from Sweden's welfare state and the Byker Wall, with its emphasis on green space, an abundance of communal street furniture, and an almost total separation of housing and cars. By the time Energy World was being built in the eighties, that era of creative welfare state architecture was all but dead in Britain. It hadn't taken long for the privately owned red-brick pitched-roof houses I'd seen in the Bovis areas in New Ash Green to become the norm across the country for new builds. Milton Keynes came to epitomise the Thatcher era boom in estates by developers such as Wimpey, whose off-the-shelf designs were so wickedly satirised by Hilary Mantel in her novel *Beyond Black*, with its catalogue of house types, named 'the Belvedere' and 'the Trafalgar'.

When I interviewed ex-planner Jo Meredith, she'd helped put the house building of the seventies, before the arrival of those Belvederes and Trafalgars, into context.

'My parents grew up in a little terraced house on a colliery housing estate. After my father retired they got old persons sheltered housing – a brand new bungalow. This is early seventies. I remember going to see this with my parents after they got the key, and me with my sniffy architect's eyes, looking at it and thinking: *Oh my god, this has been designed by the local building department, and it's no more got any sense of design about it than fly.* And I remembered standing there with my mother in this bungalow and the sun was coming through these huge windows, and the sun was on the far wall. And I remember my mother standing there and saying: "Just look at that," and looking at the sun shining on the wall. And me suddenly realising it was the first time she'd had a house in all her life where the sun came through the window! Because she'd lived all her life in small terraced houses with hardly any light. And for her to be in a house with a huge picture window with the sun blazing through was an absolute delight. And I just felt so humble. I just thought, forget your sniffy attitudes about design, this, for her, is wonderful. That it was light and it was airy. It was just an example of what people got from living somewhere like that.'

Milton Keynes was casting a similar spell on its new residents, if press reports from the time were anything to go by. An *Observer* journalist, visiting in 1974 reported that 'nobody I met was other than pleased and excited to be part of what's happening. Statistics say a mere three percent of residents think they'd like to leave.'[15]

Peter's wife Gillian had been a mother helper in a playgroup in Abingdon, and when they moved to Milton Keynes she and a like-minded neighbour formed the Galley Hill Playgroup. 'She ended up playgroup leader,' he said proudly. 'Her progression in Milton Keynes was fantastic! It was the best thing that happened to us as a family.' Peter's memories of the early days reminded me of the other new town pioneers I'd met, in Harlow, Cwmban and Cumbernauld. 'When we first came here there was nothing, there were no shops, there was no community centre. So everyone made their own entertainment. We would have a house party and it was all of us getting together. Young couples in their early thirties, and all the kids were put to bed in their own beds when the time came, and then every 20 minutes two of the guys would walk out on "chalet patrol". And if they heard a disturbance, one guy would stay put and the other would come over here and get mum.' He paused. 'Hence we got the reputation of being a wife-swapping community – but that was rubbish. There was nothing happening!' Swinging or not, there was precious little in Galley Hill to keep the new residents amused. 'There was no cinema, no theatre, no pubs, apart from going into Stony.'

Milton Keynes Development Corporation was aiming higher than simply providing a few decent houses for the residents. They were selling a vision of the future too. As befitted the home of Alan Turing and the Bletchley Park brainiacs, Milton Keynes was all for embracing the latest in science and technology. The original development plan from 1970 paid the usual lip service to 'changes in office work as a result of the use of computers' but then went further: 'The video-phone is already in use experimentally in the United States of America and could well be in use in Milton Keynes in the 1980s.'[16] Much excitement was generated by the development corporation's idea of installing cable into every home: a 1972 edition of *The Times* featured 'Mrs 1990' dialling 'her shopkeeper on her audio-visual telephone' or 'using her two-way TV' – as well as possessing 'her own lightweight electric car for shopping'.[17]

Channel 40, the town's own cable station, was launched 1976. After a couple of years the channel had built an audience of 13,000; it consisted mainly of live phone-ins, educational programmes and news shows focussing on community affairs. 'Channel 40 was a breakthrough for local broadcasting in this country,' said one of the programme makers, Dusty Rhodes, 'although it's been happening in America for a long time. We did all kinds of things: election specials where we'd courier video tapes about on motorbikes so we could go out almost live. We did a rock show once from a youth club which was a real riot.'[18] By the early eighties this ground-breaking experiment had fizzled out, becoming a local radio station instead. Like Croydon, Milton Keynes has taken more than its fair share of *Crap Towns* ire and bad stand-up gags. Peter Barry was convinced that the flak was caused by jealousy. After all, this city was not only the birthplace of computing and the home of cable television; it could also boast Britain's first recycling plant, and its first multiplex, The Point, which hosted the UK premiere of that quintessential 1985 sci-fi blockbuster *Back to the Future*. Perhaps most excitingly for me was the discovery that by Furzton Lake, a few hundred yards from Adam's house, there lies that most quintessentially modern symbol of all: a real-life helipad. After all of the promises in plans the country over, at long last I had found one. Not that it is ever used.

Yet Milton Keynes embodied a vision of the future that went far beyond domestic technology and high-tech amenities. The 1970 plan had cited among the major reforms and innovations of the postwar era the 'vast expansion in education, particularly further education'.[19] It was in the sphere of adult education where the new city broke all of the rules. Harold Wilson had conceived of a remote-access university, the University of the Air, back in the early sixties. A decade later the Open University, as it became known, was putting down some very terrestrial roots in Milton Keynes. The initial outcrop of buildings were designed by the studio of married couple Maxwell Fry and Jane Drew, the eminent prewar modernists who had worked with everyone from Le Corbusier to Walter Gropius. This complex in the east of the city housed all the administrative and planning facilities for the experiment, including the studios from which BBC television broadcast their lectures.

The new university was an immediate hit. By 1973 it already had more students than any other UK university. Yet at first the city did not embrace the new arrival with great enthusiasm. 'They don't like us much in Milton Keynes,' remarked Clive Fewins, editor of the

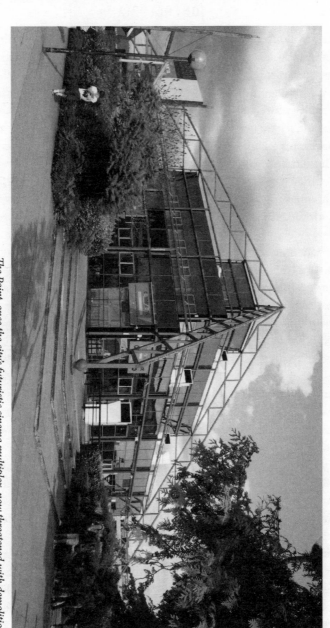

The Point, once the city's futuristic cinema multiplex, now threatened with demolition.

staff's in-house magazine in 1975. 'They think we don't do anything.'[20] Perhaps this was an inevitable problem given the lack of students on campus. Yet pretty soon Milton Keynesians were warming to these bright young academics and unconventional thinkers – especially once the university had become the largest employer in the city. 'The university does attract energetic and able young people,' said Ray Thomas, head of the OU's own new towns study unit, keen to point out how the staff were making a difference at a local level in community groups, 'so in that respect Milton Keynes is better off than other new towns.'[21]

Milton Keynes' booming economy wasn't all down to state investment in education and building. Pretty soon the development corporation, as in so many new towns before it, was going out of its way to attract all sorts of companies to the area. One such was VAG, the Volkswagen and Audi specialists. Jerry Latham, the company's relocation project manager, explained his decision to move the business. 'To us, Milton Keynes was ideally located. We found a site of the right size with enough room for expansion.' Not only that: when VAG put an advert for staff in the *Milton Keynes Gazette* in 1977, they were overwhelmed by the response. 'By six o'clock there was a queue half a mile long. ... The quality of people applying was far higher than we might have anticipated too.' Like those at the OU, Jerry put this down to the town's pioneering spirit. 'They were people who wanted to become involved, wanted to get stuck in.'[22]

Factories of all shapes and sizes were springing up in the city. Unlike in the early new towns, efforts were made to place factory estates and business parks regularly throughout the plan rather than in isolated specialist areas. At Kiln Farm, the factory units were made from brightly coloured plastic-coated steel panels. 'The factories may be colourful,' *The Times* reported in 1972, 'but in style overall the architecture is not trendy bravura. Critics might call it negative, or anti-style. It is certainly against the new brutalism.'[23]

Early Milton Keynes was full of these glossy, curvy, modular structures – forms that were starting to be described as a new architectural style: high tech. Even the less showy buildings looked cleaner, sharper, less reliant on traditional materials such as brick or concrete to maintain their shape. The offices surrounding the railway station and the town centre shopping mall, for example, reminded me of the Smithsons' school in Hunstanton, designed back in the forties, with their sheer glass walls and long low profiles – yet without the school's tough yellow brick and blokeish factory chic. High tech was glossy, flawless and expensive-looking: shiny disco glitterballs to brutalism's down and dirty Marshall stacks.

Work started on the town centre in the late seventies. 'Critics who had already denounced the new town as being over-committed to the private car and private choice will no doubt take the designs for the centre as further proof that the city will effectively become a middle-class ghetto,' reported *The Times* in 1975.[24] Yet despite the shopping centre's size (it was the largest in Europe when it opened) there was a curious modesty about it. This was due to Derek Walker's in-

The Mies van der Rohe-inspired train station (pictured) and shopping centre adhered to the principal that no buildings in the city should be above the height of a mature tree.

sistence that it should remain relatively low rise. 'It is expected that the mature plane trees will eventually be higher than most buildings and that the pedestrian scale will predominate,' he wrote in *Architectural Design* magazine.[25] A decade on from his christening of the flyovers of Birmingham for the film *Take Me High*, Cliff Richard was back at the vanguard of modernist Britain, recording the rollerskates and walkman-themed video for his 1981 hit *Wired for Sound* in the new shopping centre by some palm trees outside John Lewis.

One element of the town centre that has continued to fascinate me are the 'porte-cochères' – small porches, painted black, placed next to roads to delineate pedestrian crossings, and forming the entrances to many of the buildings. Together with the rows of identikit trees, gleaming glass surfaces and wide boulevards that wouldn't be out of place in Welwyn Garden City, these polite little black porches suggest a civilised, sensible life for the citizens of Milton Keynes – the life intended by the planners back in the late sixties.

'*Porte-cochères*' – *positioned at crossings and entrances in the town centre.*

What could be more civilised than the green spaces plotted in a 'linear park' running throughout the city? In Milton Keynes, £5 million worth of trees were planted during its first 20 years. Not that existing residents in the old villages were impressed when the city moved in. 'Everything is spoilt around here now,' one resident near the OU grumbled in the mid-seventies. 'You used to be able to go for miles on lovely walks, but now the birds are disappearing, the road has been widened and we might as well be living on the M1.'[26] Of course the new towns took up land, as any development must, but here an effort has been made to plant things in an attractive and exciting way. At first each district even had its own distinct flora, although this exotic plant zoning was gradually phased out as the city grew. And the great H and V roads are screened from the estates by the most dense and dramatic planting, spectacular in spring with kilometre-long walls of flowering shrubs, and then again in the autumn, as the leaves burst into vibrant reds, yellows and browns.

Perhaps the most impressive feats of landscaping I'd seen in any of the new towns were the many large lakes built in Milton Keynes. Not all were created solely for aesthetic or recreational purposes: some were needed to balance the water levels of the Great Ouse, the river that flows from the Midlands all the way to the North Sea. An enormous effort and cost was involved in excavating these areas, filling them with water, and planting them to look and act naturally. 'The great lakes and engineering structures, the large scale housing and employment areas now have a rawness that grates,' wrote Derek Walker in the early eighties. 'They await the patina of the second-hand, the lived-in look.'[27] These days it's beginning to happen: the tall reeds provide homes for coots and moorhen; lichen and moss decorate mono-pitched roofs and concrete weirs; shrubs and trees provide secluded walks and a peaceful sense of place. A couple of decades later Milton Keynes' lakes are populated not only with windsurfers and fishermen, but with grebes, heron, swans, ducks, geese and the like.

Yet one of the more beloved leisure facilities in the new town, Calverton End Adventure Playground – known as 'The Boat' – has vanished. Built in the early seventies, it was designed by those arch-pranksters of sixties architecture, Archigram. By the time they received their commission from Derek Walker, this loose collective of young architects with their trippy newsletters had been bugging the terribly serious postwar British architecture scene for over a decade. For the most part their ideas were outrageously impractical: cities that walked, or could be thrown away, or moved and plugged into a grid. Their architectural drawings look more like the covers of prog-rock albums than serious proposals for actual, physical buildings: somewhere between Philip K. Dick and Monty Python. Yet Archigram did build two things in Britain: the playground in Milton Keynes and a swimming pool for Rod Stewart. The playground was part DeLorean car, part cruiseliner. A half-sunk concrete building formed an indoor activity area, its entire front and back formed from giant garage doors that swung up and over. The structure was topped by a couple of funnels and some low railings, a throwback to thirties modernism's most ubiquitous reference point, the ocean liner. It was knocked down by the council in 1988 and replaced by a more conventional playground, but is still fondly remembered as the most eccentric and exciting playground by all who sailed in her.

'By the end of this century,' wrote new towns central planner Frank Schaffer in 1972, 'one out of every seven people in Britain will be living in a new town.'[28] This was a large overestimate, certainly, but by 2007 2.5 million people – or four percent of the population – were living in new towns: one in 24 Brits. And a tenth of those were in just one of them: Milton Keynes. In 1976, Labour housing minister Peter Shore took the decision to divert the new towns budget into the failing inner cities; and with that decision this huge postwar project drew to a close. With the completion of Milton Keynes, Britain's new towns story was over. Since then, some new towns have been used by their councils as giant sink estates in which to dump the poor, while others have seen so many of their houses bought by the tenants that they have become middle-class ghettoes. Milton Keynes was big enough that both things have happened in different areas of the city.

As a whole, the new towns allow us a view of a brief moment in history where planners challenged the way our towns and cities worked, and were given the opportunity to test out new ideas. They are bubbles of optimism, steps towards a future we have long since abandoned. As I was leaving Galley Hill, Peter looked out through his nets at the darkening square and remarked that living in that house had been a form of time travel. At first it had all been young families, and then people grew up, moved away, died. Now the young families were there again, and kids were back playing in the square as they had been in 1972.

5. 'A City within a City'

THE LATE FLOWERING OF THE BARBICAN AND THE NATIONAL THEATRE (1957–81)

It may seem odd to end this book – and this journey – at two places whose origins were much earlier than the late seventies. In the case of the Barbican, I could have placed its story anywhere from 1945 onwards. After all, here is a tale of Blitz reconstruction right in the heart of the burned-out city, with plans drawn up in the fifties, building commenced in the sixties, and residential communities flowering in the seventies. The origins of the National Theatre are even older. A National Shakespeare Theatre was first dreamt of in the mid-nineteenth century, yet it was Patrick Abercrombie's wartime suggestion that arts centres should be central to the regeneration of the derelict south bank of the Thames that kick-started work in earnest.

So why end up here? Well, the buildings seem to me a last push to create exciting and experimental public spaces, before responsibility for these kind of projects shifted decisively away from public and into private hands. Also, I love both of these places: they feel epic, imaginative and alive. Since my teenage years I've spent so many hours hanging around in their concrete foyers and balconies, theatres and bars. I've heard people describe both the Barbican and the National Theatre as cold, impersonal, ugly and dystopian. To me they are quite the reverse: comfortable, welcoming – in a non-threatening, low-key way – stunningly beautiful and entirely life-enhancing. So it was very exciting to go behind the scenes of both of these places, to find out how and why they'd come to be built, and what it had been like to create such inspirational and enjoyable environments.

These days the Barbican may be famous for its high-rise millionaires and swanky arts centre, but for 1,000 years – until the Blitz razed the place – it was, as Peter Ackroyd wrote, 'best known

The remains of London Wall in the foreground, and the high-rise towers of the Barbican beyond: an area traditionally 'best known for its dirt and its squalor'.

for its dirt and its squalor'. This ancient City of London district, with its Roman city walls, was 'the centre of a thousand different infections, and a miasmal neighbourhood that threatened the whole of London.'[1] The 1960 documentary short *Barbican Regained* showed the enormous hole in the City where the Barbican had once stood: churned-up waste ground, overgrown and overshadowed by the steel and glass office blocks of London Wall. By then plans were already well advanced for the resurrection of the neighbourhood. I had the chance to speak to one of the architects, John Honer, who worked for the firm of Chamberlin, Powell and Bon from the fifties to the eighties. I was rather nervous before meeting this eminent figure who'd helped design such a world-famous structure, but this

Taken from the Golden Lane estate's tower block, Great Arthur Tower, looking over the derelict site of the Barbican. Office block City Point is shown under construction on the left of the picture. © Janet Gyford

gentle, genial, round-faced and white-haired man couldn't have been more delightfully friendly and charming. I'd travelled to his home in Cambridge, a stylish modern conversion of an old stone building, where he made us a cafetiere of coffee and produced some posh chocolate biscuits before we got down to business.

'I've probably become more aware of the history since working on it than during that process,' he told me in his beautifully modulated tones. 'Of course, the Barbican site is only a fairly small proportion of the area that was totally destroyed. The destruction went all the way down from Finsbury all the way down to the river.' For John there was a personal as well as a professional angle. 'My father was in a volunteer fire brigade, and he was up there during the Blitz. And my grandfather had a business in Golden Lane!' Three generations of his family, each with connections, however different, to the same place. 'My grandfather was in the clothing business. He was typical of many working in that area. It was the centre of the cloth trade – the rag trade they used to call it. He produced the sort of children's clothes with velvet collars and Harris tweed that sold at Harrods. Very upmarket!'

By 1951 there were only 48 people living in the Barbican, eking out a wretched existence amid the ashes, dereliction and opportunistic rats and weeds. Holden and Holford were brought in immediately after the war to work out what to do with this devastated district. They envisaged a mighty double decker road snaking from Holborn in the centre to Aldgate in the east. 'Because of economic and administrative difficulties,' wrote William Holford, 'this proposal came to nothing.' This hadn't stopped them producing reams of plans, and I was delighted to discover that they hadn't been able to resist the lure of the helipad, suggesting that the corporation of London should 'reserve Moorgate Station and its surroundings for a helicopter landing ground and a two-decked car park.'[2]

The 1944 *Greater London Plan* demanded that the area be turned over to commercial use. Between 1952 and 1956 numerous proposals along those lines were submitted. In 1954 ambitious architect Sergei Kadleigh produced a plan which included offices, warehouses, parks, shops and homes, all contained within terraced four-storey maisonettes . At the planning enquiry for New Barbican, Sergei was bullish about his scheme. The new trade hall would become the 'historic future focus of business activity' and the area would become 'in effect, a twentieth century forum on the site of a Roman fortress.'[3] According to John Honer, the single advantage of Sergei's scheme was a spine road that would have helped people orientate themselves in the rebuilt landscape. But it was eventually thrown out, just as Sergei's plans for High Paddington, a high-rise city in the sky for 8,000 people above the west London station, had bitten the dust in 1952. In fact, none of Kadleigh's grand schemes were ever built in Britain.

In 1956, Duncan Sandys, the Minister of Housing, kicked off a search for a new plan for 'a genuine residential neighbourhood, incorporating schools, shops, open spaces and other amenities, even if this means foregoing a more remunerative return on the land'.[4] The City desperately needed its own population to bolster its independence: the sheer lack of voter power in the immediate postwar years put them at risk of being absorbed into the mighty bulk of the London County Council. The City corporation's intention was to build 'a small new town within an ancient city'.[5] Not that there was much ancient city to work with other than a few bits of the old Roman wall and a church, St Giles. John remembered the inspiring sight that greeted them. 'If you see photographs of that site it's staggering: it was just a pile of weeds, old railway tracks and so on.'

The architectural practice of Chamberlin, Powell and Bon was formed in 1952, by three lecturers from Kingston Polytechnic. 'I was a student of theirs at Kingston,' explained John, 'and joined them a year after they set up practice.' The trio had founded the firm on the back of Geoffry Powell's victory in the Golden Lane competition to build a residential estate just over the border from the City, adjacent to the Barbican site. 'Competitions were all the rage then, and this was the second major housing competition, the first being Churchill Gardens, won by his namesake Philip Powell – no relation. As students Philip and Geoffry used to share digs, just to confuse everyone. So then I joined the practice, partly qualified, and my first project was Great Arthur House, the 16-storey block of Golden Lane. It was my initiation as it were.'

At this stage John insisted I have coffee, and as he was being so hospitable I didn't have the heart to tell him that I loathe the stuff, and that this would only be the third cup of coffee I'd had in my life.

'I should think we were about 15 staff,' he continued, 'including partners and secretaries. Quite small. As soon as they gained an international reputation they attracted people from all over the world. There was a great influx from Australia, I seem to remember … New York, India … It was a very, *very* exciting and cosmopolitan office. It was like a studio. The atelier system, master and apprentice sort of relationship. The great benefit of working with them was that staff were made responsible for buildings from initial design to final account. So one went through the whole stage. It was exciting, particularly for someone like myself, who was brought up in the London suburbs and was not at that stage the least bit urbane. Naïve. Green.'

He had grown up fairly near my home in south London, and I could easily imagine the clash of cultures between the suburban boy and both the sophisticates and artisans he was working with: 'We were thrown into the deep end. I had to conduct site meetings, and we'd go to a site office, which then were absolutely *full* of smoke. You were sort of choking away and you were doing your best to either explain the design or administer the contracts. When I think back I don't know *what* the builders made of me, because I knew virtually nothing.'

I asked him to describe his bosses, the famous trio of Chamberlin, Powell and Bon. 'Chamberlin could have been a barrister, he could have been a high flyer in almost any field. He studied PPE – Politics, Philosophy and Economics – at Oxford and he didn't complete his degree because it was during the war and he was called up, and he was a conscientious objector. I think the war interrupted his studies. Because of his very broad interests he was able to communicate with the businessmen in the City at their own level. He was not at any disadvantage in that respect. He was a brilliant architect. He was a multi-faceted renaissance man. He was immensely interested in the theatre. Theatre, cinema and the visual arts generally was his passion.' John still sounded a little overawed by him after all these years. 'Geoffry Powell was an *entirely* different sort of person. He was a family man, the only family man of the three. He was perhaps less fanatical about architecture but perhaps more intuitive than Chamberlin and Bon. They were both products of the public school system, and that gave them the edge with the City. Geoffry went to Wellington and Chamberlin went to Bedford. Geoffry didn't go to university, he went to the AA.'

John took a deep breath. 'And then there was Christoph Bon. Architecture to him was a sort of fanatical cause. He was *infuriating*, he was almost impossible to work with – well, I found him impossible – but I also recognise that he was highly talented. He wasn't as mature an adult as the other two … He was extremely dogmatic … He was a bit like *The Man Who Came To Dinner* – he came and was given a bed in Chamberlin's flat and never left for 30 years. He lived with them. And, in fact, after Joe Chamberlin died he married Jean Chamberlin.'

This was all a long way from suburban south London, that was for sure. 'So, they were very different as personalities, but there was a lot of mutual respect. And they complemented each other, that was the thing. I have to say that it is my opinion that although it was on the basis that Geoffry Powell's winning them Golden Lane that the practice was set up, Chamberlin was the dominant personality. He had more energy and had a broader scope of interests. He just naturally came to the surface. There was some resentment, particularly amongst wives, I think, about that.'

Winning the competition to design the Golden Lane estate, which sat next to the derelict Barbican site but over the border from the City of London, would be the firm's ticket to success. It was designed to house the people needed to keep the businesses in the City running – not the bankers and the bosses, but the caretakers, nurses and dustmen.[i]

'At the time that Golden Lane was being built and extended there was a vast amount of exploratory activity concerning the Barbican

---

i It wasn't any old working-class people the corporation wanted in their brand-new estate: in order to keep out large families they demanded that the flats were mostly one bedroom.

site,' recalled John Honer. 'There was pressure to provide housing
not just for the caretakers and the police and the nurses, but for
workers with a wide scale of incomes within the City boundaries.
And that was the basis of the Barbican scheme.' The difference
between the subsidised housing of Golden Lane, just outside the
City boundary, and the private enterprise scheme for middle class
people within the City walls, is striking. But Chamberlin, Powell
and Bon were interested in providing more than simply housing
in either development. 'At Golden Lane – subsidized housing –
there were all sorts of communal facilities. There's a community
hall. There were sports facilities. There was a pub. There were shops
and so on. And the same idea was proposed for the Barbican site,
that it should incorporate schools. And then of course gradually
the brief for the arts centre evolved.' This idea had initially come
about because the City's prestigious Guildhall School of Music and
Drama needed to be rehoused in the area. At first it was thought the
school's theatre and concert halls could be shared by the Barbican's
new residents. In the end they became home to much bigger fish
– the London Symphony Orchestra and the Royal Shakespeare
Company.

Meanwhile, across the Thames, a decade after the Festival of Britain
had been dismantled, its planner, Sir Hugh Casson, lamented the
lack of progress of Abercrombie's scheme to regenerate the South
Bank, with the suggested overspill offices for Whitehall and arts
centres to adjoin the lonely Festival Hall still on the drawing board.
The area had fallen into decline. 'The Festival Hall looks as if it
has the hump,' he wrote in the *Observer* in 1961. 'The Shot Tower,
decapitated and bolted up, clearly knows it is under sentence
of death … The pools are cracked and empty, the fountains
dismantled, the sculpture removed. Flaking paint, rusting wire,
temporary fencing, discouraging notices, twist and wriggle and
spout in all directions.'[6] That same year, the Chancellor, Selwyn
Lloyd, refused funding to build a National Theatre on the South

Bank, prompting an impatient Laurence Olivier in 1963 to found the National Theatre instead at the Old Vic, a Regency-era theatre near Waterloo.

Olivier's move coincided with a government change of heart. They now looked to build a new National Theatre and Opera House on the site of the long-dismantled Dome of Discovery, next to where the London Eye now stands. Die-hard modernist Denys Lasdun, who had been designing large-scale buildings since before the war, was chosen to plan the scheme, and by 1965 he revealed his idea. The National Theatre and Opera House buildings would face each-other across a plaza, constructed in a style that Lasdun would make his own, with long horizontal balconies, platforms and walkways, from which large almost cubist blocks jut and sprout. He liked to think of his buildings as landscapes: 'public places, public domains … an extension of the city'.[7]

Yet as with many of the buildings in this book, a new regime scuppered all of Lasdun's plans. In 1966 the new Labour government axed the Opera House, although funding for a new National Theatre building for Olivier's company, still playing at the Old Vic, remained in place. Suddenly half of the building Denys Lasdun had designed was redundant. I spoke to Paul Jozefowski, who joined the National Theatre in the early eighties, and who had been researching the history of the building. Paul was now head of NT Futures, the project to adapt the building to a new millennium.

'The building was originally designed as a theatre and an opera house together,' he said, 'as a symmetrical building. When the opera house fell away it was more or less cut down the middle, moved along and attached to Waterloo Bridge.' This new site, known as Prince's Meadow, was offered to Olivier by the new Greater London Council. For Lasdun, Waterloo Bridge was 'the umbilical cord', tethering the theatre to the rest of London. 'It was hoped most people would come down from the bridge that way onto the terraces,' said Paul, 'but I remember when I first used to come here I used to get frustrated trying to find my way in or around.'

The balconies of the National Theatre: 'public places, public domains ... an extension of the city'.

As with the Festival Hall, the builders and engineers had a hell of a time trying to turn marshland into habitable space. 'The theatre is built on a series of concrete rafts and sits on marsh land. And you can, if you look down the foyer just there,' he said, pointing into the shadows as we sit near the ticket booths, 'you can see some expansion joints. There are bits where the building has to be allowed to move. We're constantly pumping out water from underneath because of the water table. But at certain points there are pressure release valves in the car park. If the water level goes so high they will spurt out and flood the car park to stop the whole thing lifting up. If the river really rose up – and hopefully we'll never test it – but technically if the water table really rose the building would just float.' Which is a good tip for Londoners, given our increasingly unpredictable climate.

It was no mean feat to get projects of the scale of the National Theatre or the Barbican up and running. For Chamberlin, Powell and Bon, chatting up the City Corporation was a key element of the Barbican job, and the partners took it very seriously. 'During the gestation period, Chamberlin took several members of the Court of Common council on a tour of Europe,' explained John Honer. 'They went to see, for example, some of the German concert halls and German theatres that were being built. But they also went to Venice. It may sound fanciful, but Venice provides an excellent example of a city with segregated traffic and pedestrians. The traffic, which is all on water, is at one level, and the pedestrians are all at another level. So it provided a ready-made example of what we were exploring in terms of pedestrian/traffic segregation in the Barbican.'

I wondered whether there was also a more obvious inspiration for the design: Le Corbusier. 'I think there was,' agreed John. 'Almost every architect of that period was influenced by Le Corbusier … Where I think we are indebted to Le Corbusier is firstly in the use of concrete, but also in the planning of some of the flats. The sort of open planning, the abandonment of the usual circulation spaces within a flat which are wasteful – an entrance hall, staircases and so on. Both in Golden Lane and in the Barbican, several of the staircases connect the living room with the upper levels. Now, this was something that Le Corbusier had explored and we were fully aware of all that. Yes we did owe a lot to him, but then we did owe a lot to the other pioneers of the modern movement.'

It was industrial action, more than Venetian waterways or Le Corbusier's circulation plans, that preoccupied those who were actually building the Barbican. In September 1965 when three carpenters refused to attend the mass meeting of a union to which they were not affiliated, 380 men walked out on strike. The resulting violence between the strikers and the non-strikers became known in the press as the Battle of the Barbican. Journalists made much of a possible racial element to the violence. Many of the builders were either Irish or West Indian, and according to a *Financial Times* report 'the air is thick with Irish voices making remarks like: "this thing started from nothing and bombshelled into a snowball". The journalist clearly relished a national stereotype: 'It seemed quite in character when two men began their speeches to an afternoon strike meeting by apologising for having drunk too much at lunchtime.'[8]

I'd asked builder Danny Gill about what the teams of builders were actually like on those big schemes. 'It would be about 55 percent Irish,' he said. 'The shuttering carpenters, they were mainly Irish. You had the London lads. Then you had about five percent Scottish. Then you had about three–to–five percent black people.' He was remembering the early seventies, when a climate of race hate was growing across Britain. 'In those days racial prejudice was bad,' was Danny's recollection of site work. 'The black people was kept down.' And if they weren't, as in the case of a Jamaican friend on the Heygate being promoted to site agent, many of the white men were outraged. 'At that time it was unheard of, you know. And I thought it was good.'

At the Barbican, it seemed that as soon as one strike ended,

another began. In 1967 the construction firm Myton attempted
to reopen work on a site there that had been closed by industrial
action for almost a year. Their attempt to get work going again
ended in running battles between the police and strikers, with one
unfortunate builder telling the press, 'I ran down Aldersgate Street
after an inspector had shouted "grab him" ... they threw me on the
floor and started to kick me. In the process they fractured my arm.'
It wasn't just pay and conditions that the workers were angry about.
Roger Raikes, the contracts manager of beleaguered Myton sent a
letter to Chamberlin, Powell and Bon in August 1966, claiming that
their labour relations problem 'had been greatly aggravated both by
the complicated and non-repetitive nature of the design and also by
the repeated changes and alterations ... these factors had affected
both the earnings and morale of the operatives.'

By 1972 the situation had escalated to the point where there
was a national building strike. Danny Gill, working on subsidised
housing in the Elephant and Castle, remembered it well.

'Most jobs in London were actually picketed,' he told me.
'And that was something similar to 1974 when you had the
three-day working week. You had pickets on the gate, with
flying pickets or whatever you want to call them, and they
had pickaxe handles. They made it quite plain that if you were
going on a job you'd be getting battered ... I was between
the North Peckham and the Heygate and I was ducking and
diving. One of the strikes I went on, and the pickets said:
"Right, if you cross this picket line we're gonna attack you." I
said: "Hold on boys, all I'm doing is picking my tool bag up
to level up and then I'm coming home" – and I went off to
Glasgow for a month's holiday. So I done that, and I always
remember the site agent saying to me as I crossed the picket
line to get my tools, he said: "You're not going to let a few
pickets frighten you, are you?" I said: "Too bloody right I
am!" In the building trade strike, I forget what it was they

were striking for, I think it was £1 an hour, £1.50 an hour, something like that. They never got it. Some of the jobs stayed open 'cos some of the subcontractors were giving the strikers a backhander.'

Architect John Honer remembered working with the heads of these great building firms. 'We talk about building *contractors*,' he told me, 'we don't generally talk about *builders*. And there's a vast difference. And I don't know enough about the history of the building industry to know when the contractor was first introduced. But the contractor is like a speculator. He's a money man. He doesn't necessarily know a lot about building ... And that is a very unsatisfactory situation.'

When judging the Barbican or the National Theatre, the method by which they were constructed is as important as the design. Louder than any other buildings I visited, they shout concrete. Inside and out, the surfaces that make up the National Theatre hold

Experiments at the Barbican with different finishes to the concrete.

the crisply cast impression of wooden shuttering – the planks that formed the moulds for the concrete. And the Barbican's rugged pick-hammered surface is in its way as rare and handmade as the gold leaf on the frames of portraits in the National Gallery.

'As you know,' said John Honer wryly, 'architects of that period were all grouped under that silly label "brutalist", but we were all in our different ways experimenting with the different uses of concrete. Lasdun frequently used the shutter board to give some character to the surface. Others went for the pure sheen; others were painted. In fact the corporation began to paint the surfaces of the Golden Lane concrete to disguise some of the rust stains, which I don't think is a very suitable or appropriate finish to concrete.'

But – a key question – why concrete? When materials such as marble and Portland stone were available for these big-budget projects, why did the architects go instead for the raw, uncompromising roughness of concrete? For Denys Lasdun, the National Theatre he'd designed 'could only be made in reinforced concrete. It is a very difficult material concrete, very intractable, not always loved. But I wanted the theatre not to be a flossie affair … When it is lit up, carpeted, softened, it can be very beautiful, rather like stone. I didn't want to cover it with anything. That is what it is and that is what is shown. It will weather, it will streak, it will become part of nature. It will probably get lichen from the river.'[9]

'We were more inclined to build in reinforced concrete than we were in steel,' John Honer told me. 'There were one or two steel schemes, but steel was in short supply, so it seemed natural to work in reinforced concrete. We therefore tried to develop a way of using concrete without cladding. In other words, concrete was the exposed face. And initially we were using ordinary gravel aggregate within the concrete, and then we began to tickle the surface with this pick or bush hammer, to give a kind of rugged feel, but it wasn't entirely satisfactory. The gravel didn't respond too well to that sort of treatment. And, even though it's river gravel, there are iron particles in it which cause the rust staining. That is not staining from the reinforcement, it's from iron pyrites. So eventually, and throughout the Barbican, we used a granite aggregate, so we're really building in cement and stone, and a stone which is long, long lasting. Although it stains in the weather, I think that gives it a bit of character – though that may just be self-justification.'

This bush hammering didn't come cheap. But then neither did Lasdun's obsession with displaying the board marks at the National Theatre. It was by no means easy to achieve the quality needed to show the wood grain to its best effect. 'We paid great attention to the quality of the concrete,' Lasdun told *The Times*. 'There are special mixes. The men who actually handled it for McAlpine's have done a superb job, absolutely wonderful. A lot of one's reaction to concrete is prejudice, because it is often used or made very badly. Here it is used with poetry and made with great feeling … The grain of wood that is used for doors and panels is not unlike the grain from the shuttering against which the concrete is formed, so there is a great sympathy between wood and concrete.'[10]

The board marks of the rough shuttering used as the concrete moulds for the National Theatre's structure: 'Here it is used with poetry and made with great feeling'.

Even the colour of the concrete used was selected to go with the tone of Waterloo Bridge. It was made from coarse aggregate of marine dredged ballast with fine aggregate of Leighton Buzzard sand, and two types of waterproof cement – essential both due to the climate and to the theatre's marshy setting. All the rough stone texture gives the theatre the feeling of something archaic, in contrast to the machine-age slickness so popular in the glass and steel boxes being designed for corporate clients the world over.

Yet in the case of the National Theatre, even concrete's greatest advocate, *Concrete Quarterly*, was in two minds about whether Lasdun had overdone it. 'Boardmarked concrete can look superb inside a building, as in the National Theatre,' wrote George Perkin, reviewing it for the magazine. 'Outside it is surely, to say the least, questionable, particularly in our damp grey climate.' Still, Perkin had nothing but praise for the interior. 'Concrete is a hard, grey, matt, rather primitive material. To show it off at its best it needs the contrast of soft, colourful, sparkling, rather sophisticated materials.'[11] And that's what the National Theatre got. There were those, however, who found concrete interiors a little disconcerting. 'Imagine a beautiful woman in evening dress with bare shoulders leaning against a concrete wall,' said Peter Shepheard, President of RIBA. His point was that concrete might look impressive when used well, but it was uncomfortable to the touch.[12]

For Paul Jozefowski, working to update the theatre, anti-concrete feeling was not necessarily rational. 'Some people just don't like concrete,' he told me. 'When we were doing the presentations for NT Future, people kept saying: *Can you get rid of the concrete*?'

The extraordinarily sophisticated silhouettes of the Barbican and the National Theatre were made possible by the decision to use concrete. Even John Betjeman, that dogged critic of postwar modernism, was moved to write to Denys Lasdun, full of praise for his South Bank building as it neared completion. 'I gasped with delight at the cube of your theatre in the pale blue sky and a glimpse of St Paul's to the south of it,' he wrote. 'It is a lovely work and so good outside, which is what matters most. Your theatre looks so good from so many angles ... It

has that inevitable and finished look that great work does.'[13] When
it opened in 1976, the *Guardian*'s redoubtable theatre critic Michael
Billington was similarly enthusiastic. 'A superb piece of sculpture,' he
wrote, 'inside which it is possible to watch a play or walk and talk in
the lobbies without feeling dwarfed by one's surroundings.'[14] A feeling
of friendliness and intimacy within the huge building were very
much part of the idea. Peter Hall, director of the National Theatre,
told *The Times* in 1974: 'I do want it to be a place where anyone would
enjoy being, whatever their mood, whatever their age and interests,
whatever their income. They can come in dinner jackets or jeans;
they can call in at the National at any time just for a stroll around for
free, or to have coffee, a sandwich or a meal.'[15]

In 1977 John Langley was one of the first wave of staff to join the
building, while he was still a student. Shy, a little self-conscious and
in possession of some delightful old-school manners, John told me
how he had started coming to the National partly because it was a
good place to read the *Evening Standard*'s small ads while he was flat-
hunting. 'I thought two things,' he said, of his first impressions. 'One
was, this was an amazingly civilised place for a theatre, and the idea
that it was open from half past ten in the morning and you could buy a
coffee and sit here, or even if you didn't buy a coffee you could simply
sit here and read a newspaper ... It just seemed like an incredibly
pleasant place to come. I was also struck by the hideous complexity of
the booking system. The scheme was intended to be democratic, but it
was also intended to get people here early. So you never bought a seat,
you bought a voucher, and that voucher was exchangeable two hours
before curtain up ... I just couldn't get my head around it.'

Paul, who had joined the lighting department in 1982, had
similarly warm feelings about the building from the start. 'I always
loved the building,' he told me. 'I live in central London, just down
the river, and I watched it being built. I used to come down here and
get excited, and I always thought it was a wonderful space, a
wonderful structure. Always liked it. Always fascinated by it.' After
beginning to work there, he soon realised that what you could see

'An incredibly pleasant place to come.'

from the outside in the public spaces was only the half of it. 'What was wonderful about working backstage is that you got to see so much more of it. And it's a labyrinth backstage. It's not particularly pretty, but it's quite an exciting space. There was no money expended, I'm not even sure how much he was interested in the look of the back areas. It's such a complex building. I appreciate that now working on the refurbishment. I don't know how they managed to visualise it without computer-generated plans. It was all drawn by hand. It's fascinating, the level of detail and the complexity.'

'It's very confusing,' confirmed John. 'I think by the time I started it was already *notoriously* confusing. So you went in with the preconception that it was confusing and actually if you found your way round that was something of a triumph. There were all sorts of stories about actors ending up on the wrong stage. Apparently Beryl Reid made an entrance in completely the wrong show one night. The point is, I didn't really know any different.'

Yet plenty of people who had transferred from the National's previous home at the Old Vic *did* know different, and there was no consensus on whether it was an improvement or not. 'There were two schools, really,' said John. 'There was the school of the dressers and costume people who were close to the actors, who, my memory is, really loved it, because they were all in the same building for one thing, and there were wonderful new facilities. And then there were all the stage crew and the backstage staff who were having to get used to completely different working conditions, and completely different requirements, including the pay structure, which is why there was so much industrial unrest.'

I took a trip backstage, and even though I'd been visiting the building for 20-odd years I was greatly surprised by what went on behind the rough-shuttered walls. To say that this was a no-frills, ultra-functional and startlingly unromantic environment might be to glamorise it. The spaces feel more like a factory floor than a theatre – except that where in a traditional factory there might have been crates of mass-produced products, here there were severed heads, fake ham sandwiches and Roman costumes. Beyond the immediate backstage areas there are huge workshops which house a paint shop, and wood- and metal-working units. A forklift truck was gliding below the skylights, carrying a pallet onto which was strapped great chunks of a kitchen. The exposed brick walls, single-glazed glass roof, metal hangar-doors and bare concrete floor of the workshops make them notoriously cold in winter. The aesthetic was that of an art classroom on an industrial scale.

'The concept of having everything on site has been hugely successful,' said Paul. 'We're probably one of the last surviving major factories in central London.'

And then there are the offices, rehearsal rooms and dressing rooms, which are arranged round a courtyard. Laurence Olivier, who was heavily involved with the design of the building, had made sure it was a fit place for his actors to work.

'He had this wonderful company of actors,' said Paul, 'and the building was designed around it. It was about the actors when it opened. They've got good facilities … In the centre of the building there's a dressing room block, there's four floors of dressing rooms for 140 actors. It's like a mini hotel really. All of them look on a central well, so there's four floors of windows, and they can all see each other, so it creates a real sense of company. They shout across at each other, throw water bombs, smoke out of the window even though they're not supposed to. It's a bit of a school in a way, it's got that sort of feel. It's a very friendly space.'

If backstage is like a budget hotel/factory mash-up, front-of-house is far from cold and institutional. In fact, Lasdun's interiors have a rather cosy aesthetic. 'The lighting was very dark,' recalled Paul. 'Everyone complained about it. I spoke with Richard Pilbright who did the original lighting. He wanted to make it brighter, but Lasdun didn't want it. He wanted a cave looking-out effect.'

I mentioned that I'd always been struck by the number of small, intimate spaces within this huge building. Spaces, perhaps, that you stumble across rather than visit by design.

'That's probably its biggest failure I would say,' said Paul, 'The complexity. It aggravates or annoys or frustrates people who don't know it or don't come in very often.'

'Also,' said John, who was getting quite worked up now, 'it was the inaccessibility of it. It was a long time before the DA [Disability Act] and the accessibility lobby. But it's always struck me as odd that an architect learning his trade in postwar London, when there must have been so many disabled people, could have come up with a building that was so inaccessible. How many floors were inaccessible?' He did a quick count. 'Two of three on the Lyttelton side are inaccessible, and two of the five on the Olivier.'

'They put a lift in for goods,' said Paul, 'but not for the public.'

I asked them whether they'd ever encountered Denys Lasdun around the building back in the day.

'He regularly came to these guest night things,' recalled John. 'He always had notes that he wanted to pass on – he was incredibly observant and proprietorial. Whoever was the house manager on a guest night, Lasdun would come up and say: "Can I just tell you that such and such is wrong in lighting," or something like that. I remember him having something to say about where the sales desks were and things like that. He had a real eye for detail. And then there were things that we wanted to do to the building that he didn't always like.'

But then, the building has subtly evolved since it was conceived, and continues to do so. One aspect it initially shrank from emphasising was its location.

'It doesn't make the best use of the river that it really should,' said John.

'When it was designed I suppose the river wasn't a destination place,' said Paul. 'There was a road that went all the way round the building. So you could stand outside the building and not see the river.' In the late nineties they did away with the road and created a plaza at the front of the building for outdoor theatre events in the summer. By the noughties the National's 'Watch This Space' festival had become a staple London tourist attraction.

I thought back to Cruddas Park, and how the early residents had turned their gaze away from the Tyne because of its unsightliness. Across Britain new marina developments are springing up and waterfront flats have tempted 'urban professionals' to move back into the heart of their home towns. I'd seen on my journey how, from Glasgow to Plymouth, cities have begun to fall back in love with their once neglected riversides. Regeneration of the waterfront has undoubtedly been one of the major changes to our cities.

By 1966, the National's big sister, the Barbican, was taking shape on the skyline. Colin Buchanan, prophet of the motorcar, described the place as 'a revolutionary reconstruction. Already the pedestrians are circulating on walkways and platforms 20 feet above the level of the traffic, and at this level the shops, banks and restaurants are appearing.' Never one to pass up an opportunity to expound his theories on the separation of people and cars, he continued: 'This is only the beginning. In a few years time it will seem incredible that this simple, obvious principle for gaining circulation space and for solving the bitter conflict between pedestrians and vehicles should have taken so long to be applied.'[16]

The Barbican flats were designed to bring life back into the heart of the City of London.

The first flats were completed in 1968. I watched a promotional film shot the following year, *Barbican – A Concept for Bringing Life Back into the Heart of a City*, at a screening at the London Metropolitan Library. The aim, according to Frank Harvey's fruity commentary, was 'to build a city within a city' in this 'square mile of cats and caretakers'. The film vividly evoked sixties luxury: flats were filled with white plastic moulded chairs, and G-plan furniture, all resting on the kind of intense red, gold, dark blue heavily patterned carpet we might now associate with Indian restaurants. There were glancing shots of glossy kitchen cabinets, Garchey waste disposal chutes (as at Park Hill) and extractor fans. But there were people too, flesh-and-blood incarnations of those figures on architects drawings: a girl playing with a hoop; a naked woman having a shower, briefly flashing the viewer as she wrapped herself in a towel; a fat, hairy banker speaking on a golden phone from his bath tub. The Barbican of the film was a utopia: both safe and sexy, luxurious and practical. After all, as Frank the commentator put it, 'a modern home is nothing if it does not set us free to live our lives fully.' By 1968 there were already 1,000 applicants for the first Barbican flats.'[17]

'The early residents had a hell of a time,' said John Honer. 'They lived on a building site until the arts centre was finished.' This took 15 years.

The London County Council, as the planning authority, had the final say over what could or couldn't be built on the site. And they were quick to cause a fuss over Chamberlin, Powell and Bon's designs for the Barbican flats.

'There was a stage when they objected to internal kitchens in the residential blocks,' recalled John, wearily. 'They weren't so cut off from natural light or air that they were like closed cells. Although they weren't given external windows, they had plenty of borrowed light, and of course they were artificially ventilated.' The council's objections to these kitchens had held up the scheme for a whole year, to the great frustration of the architects. 'If the kitchens had not been designed internally we could not have possibly accommodated the required number of flats on that limited site, because the frontages of each one would have had to have been larger.' One day John happened to pick up an architecture magazine and see that London County Council themselves had designed a housing scheme with internal kitchens. 'I rushed up to Chamberlin and said: "I know you're having problems with the LCC – what about these?" He just rocked with laughter and explained to me that *of course* in the big organisations the left hand never knew what the right hand was doing. And that the left hand, in this case, had realised the benefits of internal kitchens.'

Shakespeare Tower, one of the three identical skyscrapers built as part of the estate.
© *Richard de Pesando*

The flats are just the sort described by J. G. Ballard in his darkly brilliant 1975 novel *High Rise*, the follow-up to *Concrete Island*. Essentially a *Lord of the Flies*-type fable set in a luxury block of flats, it depicts a world in which brutalised executives turn on each other in a war of territory and dominance. I'd read it as a teenager, and since then a part of me had always imagined that was what Shakespeare, Cromwell and Lauderdale, the three Barbican high-rise towers, were really like. It seems, however, that the reality is somewhat less sinister.

The Barbican: somewhat less sinister than Ballard's High Rise.

'What the Barbican demonstrated,' said John, 'was that if you're going to pile people up like that they've got to be properly managed. You've got to have permanent staff at ground level, you've got to ensure the lifts are continually working, and if they're being repaired then you've got to provide an alternative.'

What about crime?

'Actually, from a security point of view, I'm told there are relatively few problems. Now, of course it's unfair to compare the Barbican with some of the subsidised estates, particularly the current estates, the Barbican owners have established middle class values and there's very little crime and very little sign of vandalism.' John went on to mention a crime syndicate who rented a flat for a short time and caused some, but as yet the Barbican has escaped a Ballardian social apocalypse. Instead it has gained an ageing population of retired civil servants and bankers, installing country-style kitchens in their modernist paradise, while the ripped-out original features are respectfully stored by the estate management for future inhabitants.

In 1971 the Corporation of London debated one of the biggest departures for the development – creating an arts centre to rival the new one that was agglomerating on the South Bank. The *Financial Times* reported that voting on the arts centre displayed 'all of the essentials of a traditional battle between culture and Mammon'. There was senior Alderman Sir Edward Howard, for example, who argued that 'the City is essentially a business centre and to try to graft in a concert hall and theatre seems to be alien to why it is there.'[18] For their part, the residents were keen to see more facilities for recreation. Eventually the corporation gave the go-ahead and the arts centre finally opened in 1981.

Throughout the process, the corporation had continued to suggest alternative uses for the arts facilities, insisting that they double up as conference venues. 'The cinema was designed as an experimental cinema,' recalled John, 'and in the end that had to be altered so that it could if necessary be used as an extra hall as well as a cinema.' Initially the designers had planned to place the screen on a diagonal that faced down onto the room, with the projection coming up from the floor, and seats ranging from upright to almost horizontal depending on their position in relation to the screen:

'That would have been fun to play with, but of course it would have been totally unsuitable for conferences!' Although what's not to like about a conference where the speaker dangled on wires above the delegates, many of whom were lying down?

Unlike so many buildings of its era, the Barbican has always been largely accessible for people with disabilities. My mother was confined to a wheelchair for most of her adult life, so this was important to me. We used to hang out together in the Barbican, watching films and plays, or drinking tea by the ponds. It still feels very calm and quiet there – unlike the South Bank where the crowds are now heaving even on the wettest Wednesday. Even so, by 1973 this huge bush-hammered concrete complex was beginning to look part of the City's furniture. For H. A. N. Brockman in the *Financial Times*, it had 'already achieved the indefinable attraction of a castle which has matured over the centuries'.[19]

Not everyone has warmed to the building. 'The English are a funny bunch ... As a piece of architecture it's not *over*-enthusiastically received, I don't think, by the English.' I asked John whether he liked the Barbican, whether he thought it worked. He took a moment before offering a non-answer. 'The priorities of our society today are different from those of 25-30 years ago. The Barbican caters for a different world.' John took a deep breath. 'So I'm not comfortable about going back there because I don't understand the twenty-first century and its values. I'm too much of a dinosaur.'

He sounded like a man battered by decades of dismissive and vicious criticism of people who don't like concrete, high-rise flats or complex planning. Or perhaps he was just having a bad day. I hope he can see that at the Barbican he had helped create an ambitious, social and skyscrapingly civilised version of what our future could be, an experiment which, decades later, we are only just beginning to appreciate.

THE DREAM HAS GONE BUT THE BABY IS REAL

The sleet was icy and the wind was gusting as I made my way to my brother Ian's flat in New Addington, in the dead days between Christmas and New Year 2012. I'd recently watched the Channel 4 show *The Secret Millionaire*, where Indian businessman Bobby Dudani spent eight days in New Addington, ostensibly filming a post-riots documentary, meeting local kids and community workers. Despite the requisite uplifting ending, it painted a bleak picture of life for the young: teenagers with nothing to do taking over the estate's streets at night, shouting their mouths off about robbing and drug taking. As Bill, a local youth boxing coach put it: 'Give them nowhere to go and they will burn down these huts, they will smash our windows, they will draw their names everywhere. They need places to go.' It was a reminder that not much had changed since I was a kid.

Walking the half mile from the tram stop, I saw much that reminded me of my journey around Britain and the things I'd learned. There were vast lawns: those early new towns prairies, strange municipal areas of green that people still felt reluctant to colonise. There were the few remaining British Iron and Steel Federation prefab houses from the late forties, their corrugated metal cladding painted bright colours. There was the John Laing estate at the foot of the hill, reminding me of the tile-fronted Span houses I'd seen at Ham Common, only here shunted together tightly with none of the expert landscaping. Further up the hill were the developers' little red-brick flats, in a variety of styles from modest point blocks to pitch-roofed tenements and flat-roofed slabs, their bright infill panels framed beneath windows in what I now knew was the Scandinavian manner. Like the Laing houses, these flats were packed too tightly together, a reminder that the council had failed in their bid to expand the estate outwards into Patrick Abercrombie's green belt. And finally, at Ian's door, here were the red-brick houses and maisonettes I'd grown up with, these poor relations of the handsome Arts and Crafts-style cottages in garden cities and villages like Welwyn and Rhiwbina.

As I stood there in the sleet I finally felt I understood the estate I'd grown up in – how it had come to be built, and why it had always seemed so baffling to me. The politics were now transparent. Here was a monument to slum clearance and the *County of London Plan*, bearing the scars of the scramble for numbers between Labour and the Tories. It also reflected commercially canny Croydon Council's outsourcing to developers, their dogged pursuit of the lowest tender. Unlike the new towns, New Addington wasn't the story of planning – it was a tale of expediency. The hotchpotch of buildings crammed together was not the result of some kind of utopian experiment, a study in contrast by great architects to showcase the best in modern thought. Rather, it was a have-a-go attempt at whatever was fashionable to fill in the gaps: a bit of garden village here, some system building there, a muddle of prefabs, point blocks and 'keep off the grass' signs, chopped and changed because of lack of funding and loss of nerve. It didn't have what all of the successful developments I'd visited, from Coventry to Milton Keynes, had: an infrastructure to support it. Isolated on a remote hill, clustered around the weakest of civic centres, there was no attempt to create a new town here. With no development corporation to nurture it, no arts or culture for people to get involved in, few sports facilities for the increasingly rowdy youth, this wasn't community building, it was a holding camp.

The centre of Croydon struck me the same way. On that cold winter day, long after the riots had passed, the concrete monoliths were stained black in the rain and the lights were out in the office blocks. They presented a colossal silhouette between East and West Croydon – giants huddled together in the wind. In central London,

Richard Seifert's towers had long been seen as the poor relation to those designed by more 'respectable' architects; the Smithsons, Goldfinger, Spence. Yet in Croydon his two buildings are without doubt the star turns, surrounded by 43 less adept versions of Mies van der Rohe's glass box: the little black dress of modern architecture. This was what *Croydonisation*, the private, unplanned attempt at city building, had added up to. Even the town's attempt at an urban motorway conks out, going nowhere but squeezed back into single lane traffic with little warning. Above the shopping centres, the urban motorway and the office blocks looms the Nestlé building. Like many of its less distinctive kin, it has lost its purpose: the food giant has announced plans to move from the offices it has occupied since the mid-sixties, leaving just the company's logo rendered in concrete, that suddenly ironic nest with a bird feeding hungry chicks, suspended high above the town. Perhaps the riots had marked an end of an era, a time where Croydon felt confident and showed every affluent sign of growth. By early 2012 over 1,000 business premises, or one in eight, stood empty. Many grand building projects to build ever taller towers had been long abandoned. Were the riots a sign of the managed decline of a town gone awry? If so, following that with the most Croydon Council move of all time, namely flogging the libraries off to a building contractor (Laing, who in turn immediately sold them on) was never going to help. Naturally, by 2014 there were yet more ambitious plans for a new shopping centre, while the office blocks had been hopefully rebranded as Tech City.

Dereliction and abandonment was something I'd seen all over. Since I started writing this book in 2010, Gateshead's *Get Carter* Trinity Car Park has been demolished, and the remainder of Cruddas Park flattened, as have a further group of Gorbals slab blocks. The Heygate Estate in the Elephant and Castle is deserted and awaits the bulldozer. The Excalibur Estate in Catford, where I began my journey, has been condemned and only six of the 187 Uni-Seco prefabs will be preserved. New Ash Green's Span-designed shopping centre failed to get Portas Pilot money from the government to help regenerate it, so looks set to sink further into dereliction and disrepair. Cumbernauld's megastructure has been so nibbled-at that it's now barely a building, and there are even plans to plonk a glass box over the rough concrete of the South Bank Centre, to evict the skaters from the colourful undercroft. Even Harlow Museum has been shut, its content merged with a science park, the services of expert curator David Devine no longer required. And then there's that third of Park Hill which has suffered the least sympathetic makeover since Ally Sheedy was tarted up in *The Breakfast Club*. Which is infinitely better than Glasgow's thankfully abandoned plan for the Red Road flats, shops, pubs and 1,000-seater underground bingo hall: all were to be blown up in a grotesque statement of self-mutilation as part of the opening ceremony of the 2014 Commonwealth Games. In other good news, Preston's much-admired brutalist bus station has been listed, thanks to a spirited international campaign to save it.

One late surprise I encountered was Elizabeth House. This huge early sixties office development stretches along the southern boundary of the old Festival of Britain site by Waterloo station, and includes a glass- and tile-fronted tower and a long black marble and Portland stone-clad slab. I'd taken for granted that this must be some celebrated post-festival landmark, and I'd always admired it whenever I used the station. For years I'd also watched as sheets of tiles fell in chunks from the front of the office tower, until half the frontage had become exposed mortar. The entire complex is now scheduled for demolition, and another link to that grand Abercrombie-era redevelopment scheme bites the dust. Perhaps its architect would not be too bothered: John Poulson built very little in London, and like his career, his other landmark, Cannon Street Station, has already been torn down. I was amazed to discover that the most corrupt architect of the age had come so close to the site of the Festival of Britain, that very pinnacle of the British modern optimism and achievement.

Today, while the government dismantles the welfare state under the dubious banner of 'austerity', Britain has begun to reconnect with its postwar heritage. The Mid-century Modern Show, for example, is a touring fetish club for people into postwar furniture and furnishings. Held at Dulwich College, it has become a biannual fixture of the local scene, the busy crowd easily categorised into groups: the wide-eyed enthusiast, gasping with excitement at every sputnik-legged table or anglepoise lamp; the monomaniac, ruthlessly patrolling the rooms like a shark on the trail of prey (*It's* fake *Eames darling, come away*); the kitsch-collector, giggling wildly with delight at hand-painted Midwinter pots, orange globe television sets or Tretchikoff-print coasters; and the bored partner, dragged along under pressure, forcing buggies of grizzling tots violently through every bottleneck, and wishing for a minor earth tremor to wipe out every fat lava pot in the postcode. These shows have become increasingly popular in the last decade, helped hugely by television. Perhaps the trinkety boho chic of Sarah Jessica Parker's character in *Sex in the City* helped kick it off, and the retro charms of *Life on Mars*, *Mad Men* and *The Hour* have kept it going. In the early decades of the new millennium the resurrection of mid-century Britain is all around us, from biopics of the early days of Margaret Thatcher, Fanny Cradock and *Coronation Street* to Amy Winehouse's beehive, as she recreated mobster funerals and girl-group angst. Not to mention the unstoppable rebranding of second hand as 'vintage'.

Yet architecture has been late to the party, or in many cases not invited at all. While a few emblematic structures – Park Hill, Centre Point, the Festival Hall – have been rebuilt from the inside out, many more – the Tricorn Centre, Basil Spence's Gorbals flats or the Bull Ring – have been erased. While you'd be hard-pressed to find anyone who didn't like London's lofty Post Office Tower, Liverpool's glorious Metropolitan Cathedral or the exuberant Toast Rack in Manchester, many of the era's most famous buildings – hard-faced Trellick Tower, gritty National Theatre, Cumbernauld's complex central area – are as polarising now as they were when they were built. Ownership of

Britain's urban landscape has changed utterly since 1979, seen as clearly in ex-council estates as in former municipal town centres. We've moved from the postwar nationalisation of land to build new towns or motorways, into an era where almost everything we think of as public space is actually private land, and where public housing has been sold off for a long-elapsed economic kick.

For my obsession with the postwar rebuilding of Britain I partly blame Martin Parr's collection of *Boring Postcards*, published in 1999. It triggered something in me, a desire to reconnect with something I'd long suppressed: my interest in my home town. I found in it page after page of delight and wonder. Parr's collection showed pristine new town centres, 'contemporary' lift lobbies and gleaming airport lounges – the Britain I recognised from my childhood. Ever since the early days of the twentieth century, photographers have been accused of peddling a deceit about modern architecture, while architects were accused of creating buildings for the photographers rather than the end users; best seen, or snapped, untouched, unpeopled and in black and white. The Smithsons are the classic example of this, demanding their Hunstanton school was photographed with no sign of children. But the *Boring Postcards* are different: they are gaudily tinted, with shoppers thronging pedestrianised precincts and diners packing out octagonal motorway service station restaurants. They present a friendly image of the modern world, a mild, diluted version of *Mad Men*-era advertising photography, removed from the dystopian images we're used to. Perhaps in their own way they're as unrepresentative of these places as the cool architectural photos, but they offer as intoxicating a vision of our futuristic past as any footage of sputnik, a Concorde fly-past or jet-pack test flight.

Did the towns and cities I visited live up to these postcard images? Of course not. Sure, Coventry Cathedral and the Barbican have remained as spotless as the days they were opened by the Queen, but they are in the minority. In some cases they were a tired and dingy, but recognisable ghost of the promotional shot; in others the buildings and landscapes had changed beyond all recognition. Above all it was the first-hand testimonies from the people I interviewed that brought these scenes to life. Eddie McGonnell's enthusiasm for a childhood spent in Basil Spence's Gorbals flats was infectious, as was ex-caretaker Grenville Squires' passion for the secret side of Park Hill. There were the four generations of Ken and Margaret Denholm's remarkable family housed in Cruddas Park, and the three generations of Barbican architect John Honer's family who'd had connections with that ancient district in the City of London. Then there were the planners: Ken Davie's fiercely protective attitude to Cumbernauld, Jo Meredith's insider's tales from the collapsing discipline in the seventies, and John Gyford's vivid memories of the Festival of Britain. I'd followed John Knight on his conversion from modernist to conservation expert, and Ray Fitzwalter through his exposure of a network of corruption across the country. Then there were Bob and Irene Chaney, who'd shown their love of Coventry Cathedral from its earliest days. Oliver Childs and Patrick Ellard had both spoken with fierce pride of their Span homes. And there were the many new town pioneers, everywhere from Harlow to Cwmbran, muddling through in lousy conditions until their neighbourhoods were built. Their stories were as bright as the fresh concrete on those postcards, as varied as the patterns on the curtains, and as startling as the models' clothes.

These people have given me cause to re-evaluate my difficult relationship with New Addington, and with Croydon too. I now understand them a little more, and condemn them a little less. My home town wasn't brilliantly thought out, or, as any visit to New Addington will show, successful in practice either. It's not the work of big-name planners like Abercrombie or architects like Gibberd. But so what? It was an attempt to make the most of what was at hand in that moment of postwar plenty, often with new materials and new ways of building that would have boggled the minds of those even a generation before. They built for a boom time, and never dreamt of the succession of crises that have wrecked its chances of continued growth and success. The planners and builders in Croydon hadn't lead the way with innovation by any means, but they were still part of an ambitious experiment to force the future on a country that perhaps always feels more comfortable looking backwards, eulogising an imaginary past.

Such is the eeyorish nature of our national culture that you might be led to believe that the period between 1945 and 1979 was simply a mess of austerity, financial collapse, strikes, corruption, decay and diminishment. Yet those few decades after the Second World War saw the creation of much that Britain is rightly proud of: a roll call that includes the foundation of a welfare state and National Health Service; breakthroughs in computing and genetic science; daring engineering feats in aero and car design; and an unrivalled explosion in creative talent across art, fashion, film, music, television and theatre.

The architecture and planning of this period is generally seen to fall on the debit side of the argument: the rise of systems building and the collapse of Ronan Point; the corruption trials of John Poulson and T. Dan Smith; the demolition of Victorian 'treasures' and the erection of concrete *monstrosities*; the perceived inhumanity of high-rise estates and streets in the sky. Many of these criticisms are retrospective and anachronistic. In the fifties very few people would leap to the defence of a Victorian terrace or town hall, while many more were inspired by the visions of the future that architects were offering. By the eighties the thought of visiting parts of Cruddas Park, Park Hill and the Gorbals projects would have filled all but the hardiest of us with dread. But many of their original inhabitants had loved them, not just for their futuristic triumph over the slums they'd replaced, but for the communities they'd created.

It's clear to me that any postwar roll of honour should include the achievements of rebuilding. These include the peerless monumentalism of new brutalism, a national style with truly global influence. The demolition of the much-missed and mythologised Festival of Britain, whose Skylon, Dome of Discovery and eccentric pavilions matched our recent Olympics for spectacle and grandeur, has cast a long shadow. Then there was the invention of landscape architecture as a discipline, so that much of what was built in this period – the Span estates, say, or Harlow and Milton Keynes – was not just grey, but also green and blue. Of course the high-rise has had its problems, but it's easy to forget the success stories, from posh Barbican to working class Trellick Tower, where real communites were created, and pride taken in the shared environment. And towering above them all are those remarkable new towns, built from scratch to house over two million people – an unimaginable achievement in our age of housing shortages and timid NIMBYism.

I write these words as I sit beside the man-made lakes at the Barbican, listening to the rush of the fountains and surrounded by some of the tallest concrete residential towers in the world. People of all ages are enjoying the late spring sunshine, reading the Sunday papers, amusing their kids, or watching the world go by. It reminds me that I'm not alone, that other people are glad there's more to urban Britain than endless tudorbethan semis, made-over terraces or poky *Playschool* houses. There are echoes here: ghosts of the Roman walled city, the bustling medieval markets, the infernal flames of the Blitz, so hot that the very stones of buildings exploded. To me the bricks underfoot and the rough concrete above seem far from hypermodern or jarringly new. Instead they hold the soul of something that connects us to centuries gone by. Perhaps this is true of all the great postwar projects: whatever their original purpose, these futuristic visions all tell us something about our history, our landscape, our climate, our people. In many cases, that message is one of continuity of progress and expression, of a deep pragmatism laced with inspired optimism and innovation.

Concrete itself is made from our oldest construction materials – sand and rock – and in the structures it was used to create in the twentieth century there are echoes of some of our most ancient building traditions – castles, catacombs, cathedrals, monasteries, walled cities, watch towers. The Barbican feels like all of these things, and older structures too: the three vertical towers and the horizontal slabs remind me of a gigantic concrete henge.

I am lucky to have seen and scaled and explored some of the most exciting places ever built in Britain, from the Post Office Tower to Coventry Cathedral, New Ash Green to Cumbernauld. I've tried to see them on their own terms, not with the baggage of received wisdom and hindsight. I thought I might hate what I saw, and what I found out. In some cases, of course, I did. But on the whole I have returned full of admiration for the people who kick-started this revolution, and the pioneers who gave living and working in these new environments their best shot. And rather to my surprise I find that, far from having become sated and disillusioned, I'm even more in love with the world, this 'Concretopia', they tried – and in many cases failed – to build.

ENDNOTES

INTRODUCTION:
'Concrete Jungle Where Dreams are Made'

1 Rev. F. J. Nixon, *Croydon Advertiser*, 10/3/35
2 Gavin Stamp, *Britain's Lost Cities*, p3
3 Alice Coleman, *Utopia on Trial*, p176

PART 1: SO DIFFERENT, SO APPEALING
1. 'A Holiday Camp All Year Round': The Temporary Building Programme and Prefabs (1944–1951)

1 Donald Gibson, *Midlands Daily Telegraph*, 5/12/40
2 Nicolas Bullock, *Building the Post-War World*, Routledge, 2002, p173
3 *The Times*, 24/2/45, p5
4 *The Times*, 27/6/44 p5
5 Seco ad, *The Times*, 29/10/45, p3
6 Advertisement, *The Times*, 27/11/52, p7
7 Uni-Seco ad, *The Times*, 30/9/52, p3
8 Steve Humphries and John Taylor, *The Making of Modern London*, Sidgwick and Jackson, 1986, p144
9 Greg Stevenson, *Palaces for the People*, Batsford, 2003, p55
10 Stevenson, p103
11 Ros Anderson, *Guardian*, 28/12/2012
12 Cleeve Barr, chief architect NBA, *The Times Supplement on Industrialised Building*, 21/3/66, piii
13 *Guardian*, 14/2/61, p6
14 Ros Anderson, *Guardian*, 28/12/2012
15 Greg Stevenson, *Palaces for the People*, Batsford, 2003, p56
16 *Daily Herald Modern Homes Exhibition in Dorland Hall, Lower Regent St, Spring 46*, Mass Observation, p3
17 *Second Report on Modern Homes Exhibition*, Mass Observation, 8/4/46, p10
18 *Second Report on Modern Homes Exhibition*, p11
19 *Guardian*, 28/12/2012

2. 'A Decent Start in Life': Garden Cities and the first New Towns (1946–51)

1 Ena Elliot, secretary, in Gibberd, Hyde Harvey and White, *Harlow: The Story of a New Town*, Publications for Companies, 1980, p30
2 *Harlow Journal*, 1/5/53, p7

3 Frederick Gibberd in Gibberd, Hyde Harvey and White, p11
4 Ebenezer Howard, *Garden Cities of To-morrow*, Dodo Press, Second Edition, 1902, pvi
5 Frederic Osborn in Gibberd, Hyde Harvey and White, p5
6 Silkin in Frank Schaffer, *The New Town Story*, Paladin, Second Edition, 1972, p11
7 Norman Mackenzie, *Harlow Citizen*, 1/5/1953, p6
8 Silkin in Frank Schaffer, p12
9 Public meeting in Frank Schaffer, p47
10 E. M. Forster in David Kynaston, *Austerity Britain: A World to Build*, Bloomsbury, 2008, p163
11 Godfrey Arkwright, letter to Eric Adams, Sept 53, in Gibberd, Hyde Harvey and White, p31
12 Frederick Gibberd in Gibberd, Hyde Harvey and White, p43
13 Roger Berthoud, *The Times*, 16/12/77, p14
14 Frederick Gibberd in Gibberd, Hyde Harvey and White, p32
15 Gordon Logie, *The Urban Scene*, Faber, 1954, p142
16 Frederick Gibberd, *The Design of Harlow*, Harlow Council, 1980, p18
17 Frederick Gibberd in Gibberd, Hyde Harvey and White, 1980, p22
18 Frederick Gibberd in Gibberd, Hyde Harvey and White, p107
19 *Observer*, 22/7/51, p7
20 Lewis Silkin, *The New Towns Act 1946*, (annotated), Sweet and Maxwell, 1947, Foreword p5
21 *Manchester Guardian*, 16/5/57, p5
22 Jim Cattle in Steve Humphries and John Taylor, *The Making of Modern London*, Sidgwick and Jackson, 1986, p149
23 Frederick Gibberd in Gibberd, Hyde Harvey and White, p69
24 *Harlow Citizen*, 1/2/57, p17
25 *The Times*, 5/5/71, p2
26 *Guardian*, 23/10/59, p2
27 Derek Senior, *Manchester Guardian*, 4/6/57, p18
28 Frederick Gibberd in Gibberd, Hyde Harvey and White, p210
29 Marriott, p79
30 Roger Berthoud, *The Times*, 16/12/77, p14
31 Gordon Cullen, 'Prairie Planning in the New Towns', *Architectural Review*, July 1953, p34
32 J. M. Richards, 'Failure of the New Towns', *Architectural Review*, July 1953, p31
33 Cullen, *Architectural Review*, July 1953, p36
34 J. M. Richards, *Architectural Review*, July 1953, p32
35 Peter and Alison Smithson, *Ordinariness and Light*, Faber, 1970, p25
36 Smithson, p26
37 Lewis Mumford in David Kynaston, *Family Britain*, Bloomsbury, 2010, p345

38 Frederick Gibberd in Gibberd, Hyde Harvey and White, p112
39 Roger Berthoud, *The Times*, 16/12/77, p14
40 Frederick Gibberd in Gibberd, Hyde Harvey and White, p6

3. 'A Real Effort to be Jolly': The Festival of Britain on London's South Bank (1951)

1 *Daily Express*, 18/4/51, p3
2 *Daily Mirror*, 15/10/48, p1
3 Patrick Abercrombie and J. H. Forshaw, *County of London Plan*, Macmillan, 1943, p130
4 Abercrombie and Forshaw, p12
5 Robert Matthew in Miles Glendinning, *Robert Matthew*, RIBA Publishing, p86
6 Stuart Matthew, in Miles Glendinning, p93
7 Leslie Martin in Nicholas Bullock, *Building the Post-War World*, Routledge, 2002, p62
8 Hugh Casson in Nicholas Bullock, p70
9 Basil Spence, *Phoenix at Coventry*, Geoffrey Bles, 1962, p13
10 Spence, p13
11 Hugh Casson in Bullock, p70
12 H. T. Cadbury-Brown in Charlotte Mullins, *A Festival on the River*, Penguin, 2007, p48
13 Laurie Lee in Barbara Hooper, *Cider with Laurie*, Peter Owen Publishers, 1999
14 Jean Symons, *Royal Festival Hall: Concert Hall Notebook*, Festival Hall, 2000, p4
15 Symons, February 1950, p7
16 Symons, p4
17 Glendinning, p106
18 Jean Symons, July 1950, p11
19 Hugh Casson in Mullins, p49
20 Philip Powell in Kenneth Powell, *Powell & Moya*, RIBA Publishing, 2009, p33
21 Jacko Moya in Kenneth Powell, p34
22 Margaret Sheppard Fidler in Powell, p36
23 Barry Evans in Turner, pxx
24 Jean Symons, p4
25 Jean Symons, p12, July 1950
26 Le Corbusier in Glendinning, p108
27 Le Corbusier in John McKean, *Royal Festival Hall*, Phaidon, Second Edition 2001, p10
28 John McKean, p61
29 *Picture Post*, 5/5/51, p11
30 Clough Williams-Ellis in Glendinning, p107
31 Jack Godfrey-Gilbert in Barry Turner, p170
32 Abercrombie and Forshaw, p4
33 Abercrombie and Forshaw, p9
34 Frederick Gibberd, in Turner, p174
35 Robert Matthew in Glendinning, p117
36 Turner, p53
37 Frederick Gibberd in Barry Turner, p172
38 Basil Spence, *Phoenix at Coventry*, Geoffrey Bles, 1962, p3
39 *Daily Mirror*, 26/6/51, p2
40 *Daily Express*, 18/4/51, p3
41 Vere Hodgson in David Kynaston, *Family Britain*, Bloomsbury, 2009, p7
42 *Picture Post*, 5/5/51, p13
43 *Picture Post*, 5/5/51, p15
44 Dylan Thomas in Mullins, p63
45 *Architectural Review*, November 1951, p283
46 *Manchester Guardian*, 1/10/51, p7
47 *Daily Express*, 8/12/51, p3
48 *Observer*, 6/6/52, p4
49 *The Times*, 23/7/74, p9
50 Gerald Barry in Kynaston, p8
51 Leslie Martin in McKean, p61

4. 'An Architect's Dream!': Rebuilding Blitzed Plymouth and Coventry (1940–62)

1 *Coventry Standard*, 30/11/40
2 Percy Johnson-Marshall in Keith D. Lilley, 'Urban futures in early postwar Britain', in Iain Boyd White (ed), *Man-Made Future*, Routledge, 2007, p147
3 Jock Colville, secretary accompanying Winston Churchill, 2/5/1941, in Juliet Gardiner, *Wartime Britain*, Review, 2005, p421
4 Viscount Astor, Lord Mayor of Plymouth, in Patrick Abercrombie and James Paton Watson, *A Plan for Plymouth*, Underhill, 1943, pv
5 *Picture Post*, 15/5/54, p44
6 Percy Johnson-Marshall in Bullock, p268
7 Percy Johnson-Marshall in Boyd White (ed), p126
8 Donald Gibson, *Midlands Daily Telegraph*, 5/12/40
9 Donald Gibson in Iain Boyd White (ed), p126
10 *Manchester Guardian*, 22/11/40, p4
11 Donald Gibson, *Midlands Daily Telegraph*, 5/12/40 (talk on Wednesday of that week, report is from Thursday)
12 Bullock, p276
13 Wilfred Burns, *British Shopping Centres*, Leonard Hill, 1959, p73
14 Unnamed interviewee in Boyd White (ed), p155
15 Abercrombie and Paton Watson, p28
16 John G. Winant, US Ambassador to Britain, in Abercrombie and Paton Watson, piii
17 Abercrombie and Paton Watson, p9
18 Abercrombie and Paton Watson, p66
19 Abercrombie and Paton Watson, p11
20 Abercrombie and Paton Watson, p87
21 Patrick Abercrombie in Jill Craigie (dir), *The Way We Live*, 1946
22 *The Times*, 6/7/46, p7
23 *Observer*, 1/6/47, p5
24 *Observer*, 22/6/47, p6

25 Giles Scott of his Coventry Cathedral plan in *The Times*, 9/2/44, p2
26 *Coventry Cathedral Architectural Competition*, October 1950, p17
27 Spence, p5
28 Spence, p6
29 Spence, p14
30 Spence, p12
31 Spence, p16
32 Spence, p19-20
33 Spence, p25
34 *The Times*, 16/9/52, p8
35 *The New Coventry Cathedral* (from 2 articles in *Coventry Evening Telegraph*), Baynard Bress, 1944, p11
36 *Evening Herald*, 11/1/51, p4
37 *Evening Herald*, 9/1/51, p2
38 *Observer*, 2/9/51, p5
39 *ibid*
40 Harold Macmillan, *The Macmillan Diaries* (1950-57), Pan, 2004, p185, 24/9/52
41 *The Times*, 13/7/54, p9
42 *The Times Supplement on Coventry Cathedral*, 25/5/62, pii
43 *ibid*
44 *Coventry Evening Telegraph*, 5/7/56
45 *Coventry Evening Telegraph*, 31/12/58, p1
46 *The Times*, 7/11/61, p6
47 Jean, in Boyd White (ed), p154
48 *Picture Post*, 15/5/54, p45
49 *ibid*
50 *Picture Post*, 15/5/54, p46
51 *The Times*, 26/5/62, p6
52 *Spectator*, 22/6/62
53 *Coventry Evening Telegraph*, 26/5/62
54 *ibid*
55 *Spectator*, 22/6/62

5. 'A Touch of Genius': Herts, minds and Brutalism (1949-54)

1 Stirrat Johnson-Marshall, *The Times*, 'The Architect in Britain Today' supplement, 3/7/61, piii
2 David Kynaston, *A World to Build*, Bloomsbury, 2007, p28
3 *Manchester Guardian*, 5/4/54, p10
4 Maurice Lee in Miles Glendinning, *Modern Architect*, RIBA Publishing, 2008, p206
5 Stirrat Johnson-Marshall, *The Times*, 'The Architect in Britain Today' supplement, 3/7/61, piii
6 C. H. Aslin, *Manchester Guardian*, 5/4/54, p10
7 Andrew Saint, *Guardian*, 14/4/09
8 Stirrat Johnson-Marshall, *The Times*, 'The Architect in Britain Today' supplement, 3/7/61, piii
9 *Observer*, 16/4/50, p5

10 *Observer*, 20/2/55, p8
11 *ibid*
12 *Manchester Guardian*, 9/10/54, p2
13 Mark Girouard, *Big Jim: The Life and Work of James Stirling*, Chatto and Windus, 1998, p54
14 Magda Cordell in Girouard, p54
15 Mary Banham in Girouard, *p54*
16 *ibid*
17 J. G. Ballard in Kynaston, 2009, p653
18 Peter and Alison Smithson in Bullock, p101
19 *Architectural Review*, December 1955, p357
20 *Architectural Review*, September 1954, p148
21 *Architectural Review*, December 1955, p356
22 Theo Crosby, *Architectural Design*, 25 Jan 55, p1
23 Nikolaus Pevsner, *Pevsner on Art and Architecture: The Radio Talks*, Methuen, 2002, p298 – 'The Anti-Pioneers', 3/12/66, BBC Third Programme
24 Theo Crosby, *Architectural Design*, 25/1/55, p1
25 Sir William Holford, *The Times*, 'The Architect in Britain Today' supplement, 3/7/61, pii
26 Guardian, 26/2/63, p3
27 K. Feakes in Miles Glendinning, *Modern Architect*, RIBA Publishing, 2008, p237
28 Lionel Esher, *A Broken Wave*, Pelican, 1983, p57

PART 2: SHAKE IT UP, BABY NOW

1. 'A Flying Saucer Taking You to Mars': Glasgow, King of Comprehensive Development (1957-65)

1 *Herald*, 1/7/1961
2 Patrick Abercrombie and Robert Matthew, *The Clyde Valley Regional Plan*, HMSO, 1946, p341
3 Abercrombie and Matthew, p2
4 Miles Horsey, *Tenements and Towers: Glasgow Working Class Housing 1890-1990*, HMSO, 1990, p32
5 *Herald*, 21/11/1958, p6
6 *Herald*, 23/3/1961, p11
7 John Maclay, Secretary of State for Scotland, in the *Herald*, 9 Feb 1957, p5
8 Elizabeth Williamson, Anne Riches and Malcolm Higgs, *The Buildings of Scotland*, Penguin, 1990, p507
9 *Herald*, 11/9/1957, p9
10 *Herald*, 12/1/1946, p2
11 Letter from 'Town and Country Planning', *Herald*, 29/1/46, p2
12 Leader, *Herald*, 15/1/46 Jan 15, p2
13 Colin MacFarlane, *The Real Gorbals Story*, Mainstream, 2007, p228
14 Pearl Jephcott, *Homes in High Flats*, Oliver and Boyd, 1971, p64
15 Williamson et al, p518
16 *Herald*, 24/11/62, p7

17 Robert Matthew, *The Times*, 'The Architect in Britain Today' supplement, 3/7/61, pxxiv
18 *Gorbals Riverside Newsletter*, Spring 2006, Glasgow Community Health And Well-Being Research And Learning Programme, p4
19 Williamson et al, p519
20 *Herald*, 11/2/61
21 Horsey, p39
22 Glasgow Housing Committee Minutes for 19/12/58
23 Miles Glendinning and Stefan Muthesius, *Tower Block*, Yale University Press, 1994, p224
24 W. A. Allen, *The Times*, 'The Architect in Britain Today' supplement, 3/7/61, pxv
25 Jephcott, p60
26 MacFarlane, p226
27 David Gibson, addressing the 1962 Annual Housing Inspection, in Horsey, p46
28 Jephcott, p59-60
29 Jephcott, p63
30 Leader, *Herald*, 15/1/46, p2
31 MacFarlane, p229
32 Jephcott, p48

33 Jephcott, p51

2. 'A New Dimension Added to the Street':
Sheffield's Streets in the Sky (1957-61)

1 Geoffrey Moorhouse, *The Other England*, Penguin, 1964, p158
2 Jack Lynn, *Sheffield*, p58
3 John Partridge in Elain Harwood and Alan Powers (ed) *Housing the Twentieth Century Nation*, The Twentieth Century Society, 2008, p116
4 Frederic Osborn at CIAM 8 in David Kynaston, *Family Britain*, Bloomsbury, 2009, p12
5 Jack Lynn, *Sheffield*, p61
6 Geoffrey Moorhouse, *The Other England*, Penguin, 1964, p158
7 *The Times*, 15/9/61, p19
8 *The Times*, 10/11/69, pVI
9 David Kynaston, p344
10 Alison and Peter Smithson in *Architectural Design*, June 1955, p185
11 Alison and Peter Smithson, 'Team 10 Primer' in Charles Jencks and Karl Kropf (ed), *Theories and Manifestoes of Contemporary Architecture*, Wiley, Second Edition 2008, p219
12 Peter and Alison Smithson, *Ordinariness and Light*, Faber, 1970, p52
13 Denys Lasdun in John Gold, *The Practice of Modernism*, Routledge, 2007, p209
14 Michael Young and Peter Willmott, *Family and Kinship in East London*, Pelican, Revised Edition, 1962, p198
15 *The Times*, 8/9/80, p17
16 Kynaston, p344
17 Lynn, p69

3. 'A Wild and Romantic Place': Arndales and Urban Motorways (1959-65)

1 *Guardian*, 13/10/72, p20
2 Frank Price, *The New Birmingham*, West Midlands Press, 1959, p9
3 Abercrombie and Forshaw, p11
4 Abercrombie and Forshaw, p48
5 *Preston By-Pass* official opening brochure, 5/12/58, Ministry of Transport and Civil Aviation, p7
6 Figures from James P. McCafferty in Miles Glendinning (ed), *Rebuilding Scotland*, Tuckwell Press, 1997, p76-83
7 Colin Buchanan, *The Times* 'Survey of the Architect in Britain Today' supplement, 3/7/1961, px
8 Professor Colin Buchanan, *The Times*, 19/9/66, p9
9 Wilfred Burns, *British Shopping Centres*, Leonard Hill, 1959, p74
10 Burns, p73
11 *Guardian*, 22/10/59, p4
12 Colin Buchanan, *The Times* 'Survey of the Architect in Britain Today' supplement, 3/7/1961, px
13 Burns, p74-75
14 R Furneaux Jordan, *Observer*, 5/2/56, p9
15 Esher, p55
16 Sam Chippindale, *Architects' Journal*, 19/1/61, p97
17 Dominic Sandbrook, *White Heat*, Abacus, 2006, p118
18 Arnold Hagenbach, addressing the AGM of Arndale Property Trust Limited, July 8, Bradford, *Guardian*, 9/7/64, p12
19 Sam Chippindale, *Architects' Journal*, 19/1/61, p97
20 *Guardian*, 8/6/73, p25
21 G. A. Jellicoe, *Motopia*, Studio Books, 1961, p95
22 Burns, p74-75
23 *Guardian*, 20/4/72, p21
24 *ibid*
25 *Guardian*, 8/6/73, p25
26 Esher, p54
27 A. L. Lloyd, *Picture Post*, 8/1/49, p10
28 Lloyd, *Picture Post*, p13
29 Sir Isaac Hayward, Feb 1956, in Oliver Marriott, *The Property Boom*, Pan Piper, 1969, p248
30 'Elephant and Castle – Redevelopment and Road Improvement', LCC Press Release, 2/2/56, p2
31 *South London Press*, 13/12/46
32 *South London Press*, 8/5/59

34 *South London Press*, 23/11/62
35 *Guardian*, 9/9/64, p19
36 *Guardian*, 9/9/64, p19
37 'The Elephant and Castle Shopping Centre: A Willett Development' brochure, p6
38 'The Elephant and Castle Shopping Centre: A Willett Development' brochure, p10
39 *Guardian*, 9/9/64, p21
40 *South London Press*, 15/7/60
41 Graham Shaylor, *Developing Birmingham: 1889–1989*, Birmingham City Council, 1989, p90
42 Neville Borg, Birmingham Chief Engineer in John Holliday, ed, *City Centre Redevelopment*, Charles Knight, 1973, p49
43 Frank Price, *The New Birmingham*, West Midlands Press, 1959, p9
44 *Bull Ring*, 1961 brochure promoting the Bull Ring to businesses, Laing, p25
45 *Bull Ring*, 1960 brochure promoting the Bull Ring to businesses from John D. Wood and Company (London) and Chesshire, Gibson and Company (Birmingham)
46 Professor Colin Buchanan, *The Times*, 19/9/66, p9
47 Geoffrey Moorhouse, *The Other England*, Penguin, 1964, p93
48 Joseph Minogue, *Guardian*, 27/3/62, p8
49 Rodney Gordon in John Gold, *The Practice of Modernism*, Routledge, 2007, p115
50 Rodney Gordon in Elain Harwood and Alan Powers, *The Sixties*, The Twentieth Century Society, 2002, p78
51 Rodney Gordon in Harwood and Powers, *The Sixties*, p75
52 *Guardian* 3/11/77, p18
53 George Perkin, *Concrete Quarterly*, October-December 1970, p40
54 Sam Chippindale, *Architects' Journal*, 19/1/61, p97
55 Diana Rowntree, *Guardian*, 29/5/64, p10
56 Jan Morris, *The Times*, 15/1/76, p13
57 Neville Borg, in Holliday, ed, p49
58 Colin Buchanan, *Guardian*, 28/9/70, p7
59 Colin Buchanan, *Traffic in Towns*, Penguin, 1964, p37
60 'Must Britain be a Mess?' 4, *Observer* 19/6/60, p19
61 *ibid*
62 W. Konrad Smigielski in Holliday, p154
63 Buchanan, p32
64 Peter and Alison Smithson, p66
65 Burns, p105-6
66 G. A. Jellicoe, *Motopia*, Studio Books, 1961, p12
67 Jellicoe, p11
68 Jellicoe, p143

4. 'A Natural Evolution of Living Conditions': Newcastle Gets the System Building Bug (1959–69)

1 Dan Smith in Chris Foote Wood, *T. Dan Smith*, Northern Writers, 2010, p56
2 Kenneth Galley in Holliday, ed, p228
3 T. Dan Smith, October 1958, quoted in *Evening Chronicle* 21/10/86, p8
4 *Guardian*, 4/4/62, p8
5 Glendinning and Muthesius, p166
6 Liberal Alderman William McKeag in Foote Wood, p56
7 *Observer Magazine*, 21/2/65, p14
8 T. Dan Smith, *An Autobiography*, Oriel Press, 1970, p62
9 Kenneth Ford, *NE Arts Review*, 1962, p18
10 P. S. Rowson (curator from the Gulbenkian Museum of Oriental Art and Archaeology, *NE Arts Review*, 1962, p16
11 Smith, p65
12 Smith, p62
13 *Newcastle Evening Chronicle* 15/9/72, p17
14 *Newcastle Evening Chronicle*, 19/9/69, p3
15 June Hulbert, *Northern Life*, 18/8/77, p52
16 *Newcastle Journal*, 2/8/77
17 *Concrete Quarterly*, July-September 1963, p37
18 *Concrete Quarterly*, April-June 1965, p1
19 Keith Joseph, *Journal of the Town Planning Institute*, March 1964, p91
20 Cleeve Barr, Chief architect NBA, *The Times Supplement on Industrialised Building*, 21/3/66, piii
21 George Bowie, in Glendinning and Muthesius, p203
22 Kenneth Campbell in Glendinning and Muthesius, p203
23 Dan Smith in Foote Wood, p75
24 *Concrete Quarterly*, April-June 1959, p1

5. 'A Contemporary Canaletto': How Office Blocks Transformed our Skyline (1956-75)

1 *Daily Express*, 4/2/06, p34
2 Michael Rosenauer, *Modern Office Buildings*, Batsford, 1955, p19
3 Marriott, p44
4 Sir William Holford, inaugural address as President of RIBA, *The Times*, 2/11/60, p6
5 Rosenauer, p75
6 *Telegraph*, http://www.telegraph.co.uk/news/obituaries/1360803/Richard-Seifert.html
7 Rosenauer, p31
8 Esher, *A Broken Wave*, p55
9 *The Times*, 19/1/74, p1
10 *The Times*, 29/6/72, p3

11 *ibid*
12 Richard Seifert, *Financial Times*, 21/6/71, p26
13 Richard Seifert, *The Listener*, 27/10/77, p554
(interview for *Arena*)
14 Marriott, p217
15 Marriott, p212
16 Peter Saunders, *Urban Politics*, Hutchinson and
Co, Third Edition 1983, p301
17 *Guardian*, 3/7/62, p10
18 Saunders, p299
19 *Croydon Official Guide*, London Borough of
Croydon, 1971, p43
20 *The Times*, 11/9/70, p3
21 *Croydon Official Guide*, London Borough of
Croydon, 1969, p72
22 Saunders, p303
23 Tony Benn, *Daily Express*, 9/10/65, p5
24 Geoffrey Moorhouse, *Guardian*, 21/3/64, p7
25 Letter from Reginald Bevins to Sir Ronald
German, 6/11/63
26 Letter from T. A. O'Brien, 15/1/64
27 Letter from A. W. C. (Bill) Ryland (Director of
Inland Telecommunications) to K. H. (Kenneth)
Cadbury (head of mechanisation), 16/7/64
28 Letter from Kenneth Cadbury to Bill Ryland,
23/7/64
29 Minutes of the Post Office Tower Project Team,
5/11/64
30 Letter from Anthony Wedgwood Benn to
Harold Wilson, 17/12/64
31 Letter from T. A. O'Brien to Kenneth Cadbury,
16/7/65
32 Letter from Edward Ford (Balmoral) to Sir
Ronald German, 20/8/65
33 Fred Graham, *Daily Mirror*, 1/11/71, p16
34 *The Times*, 1/11/71, p1
35 Lionel Brett, *The Times*, The Architect in
Britain Today supplement, 3/7/61, piv
36 Editorial, *Concrete Quarterly*, October-
December 68, p1
37 Richard Seifert, *Financial Times*, 21/6/71, p26
38 *ibid*

6. 'A Village With Your Children in Mind':

Span and the Hippy Dreams of New Ash Green (1957-1972)

1 Townsend in Barbara Simms (ed), *Eric Lyons &
Span*, RIBA Publishing, 2006, p74
2 Lyons in Simms (ed), p73
3 *Observer*, 1/12/63, p27
4 Bilsby in Simms (ed), p79
5 Crossman in Simms (ed), p74
6 *The Times*, 21/1/65, p6
7 Lyons in Simms (ed), p23
8 Caroline Moorehead, The Times, 21/7/75, p5
9 Ian Nairn, *Observer*, 17/9/67, p26
10 Lyons in Simms (ed), p87
11 Eric Lyons, *The Times* 'Survey of the Architect
in Britain Today', 3/7/61, pvi
12 *ibid*
13 *ibid*
14 *Manchester Guardian*, 28/5/57, p5
15 Robert Matthew, *The Listener*, 23/10/58, p644
16 *Guardian*, 8/12/59, p7
17 Caroline Moorehead, *The Times*, 21/7/75, p5
18 Advertisment for New Ash Green, *The Times*,
13/6/69, p9
19 Advertisment for New Ash Green, *The Times*,
7/2/69, p8
20 Tony Aldus, *The Times*, 13/4/71, p3
21 *The Times*, 22/9/67, p4
22 Frederic Osborn and Arnold Whittick, *New
Towns*, Third ed, 1977, Leonard Hill, p461
23 *Observer*, 15/6/69, p3
24 Simms (ed), p92
25 *The Times*, 9/1/70, p8
26 Elain Harwood in Simms (ed), p60
27 Tony Aldus, *The Times*, 13/4/71, p3

7. 'A Veritable Jewel in the Navel of Scotland':

Cumbernauld's Curious Megastructure (1955-72)

1 Mary Stott, 'New Town Life in Scotland',
Guardian, 8 October 1965, p10
2 Geoffrey Copcutt in *Rebuilding Scotland* edited
by Miles Glendinning, Tuckwell Press, 1997, p92
3 Geoffrey Copcutt in *Architectural Design*, May
1963, p210-11
4 Copcutt in Glendinning, p89-90
5 Geoffrey Copcutt in *Architectural Design*, May
1963, p210-11
6 'Concept of New Town "In Advance of Any
Yet"', *The Times*, 30 November 1962, p8
7 Schaffer, p142-3
8 Richard Crossman, *The Diaries of a Cabinet
Minister, Volume 1*, Hamish Hamilton and
Jonathan Cape, 1975, p159
9 Tony Aldous, 'Scotland's New Towns Come
Down to Earth', *The Times*, 26 August 1972, p12
10 Ian Nairn, 'Half Term at Cumbernauld',
Observer, 23 April 1967, p36
11 Schaffer, p142
12 Oliver Cox in John R. Gold, *The Practice of
Modernism*, Routledge, 2007, p152
13 Oliver Cox in John R. Gold, p154
14 *The Planning of a New Town*, LCC, 1965 fifth
impression, p16
15 *The Planning of a New Town*, p84
16 *The Planning of a New Town*, p86
17 *The Planning of a New Town*, p89
18 Edward Carter, *The Future of London*, Penguin,
1962, p56

19 *The Planning of a New Town*, p29
20 Oliver Cox in John R. Gold, p155
21 'New Town a "Standard for All the World"', *Guardian*, 20/6/67, p3
22 'Congratulations to Cumbernauld', *Financial Times*, Wednesday, 24/5/67; Edition 24, p241
23 Nicholas Taylor, *The Village in the City*, Temple Smith, 1973, p17
24 *Rebuilding Scotland* edited by Miles Glendinning, Tuckwell Press, 1997, p172
25 'Traffic Segregated Town Safest', *The Times*, 3/8/67, p3
26 *The Planning of a New Town*, p45
27 Geoffrey Copcutt in Glendinning, p89
28 Glendinning, p171
29 Lionel Esher, *A Broken Wave*, Pelican, 1983, p58
30 Crossman, p158
31 Sir Robert Grieve in Gold, p150
32 Janice Scott Lodge, 'The Gum Boot Society', *Guardian*, 8/12/65, p8
33 Sheila Black, 'Happiness Comes Only Slowly', *Financial Times*, Wednesday, 29/11/67; p12; Edition 24,401
34 'Life is Friendly in Cumbernauld', *The Times*, Tuesday, 10/9/68; p3
35 Lodge, *Guardian*, 8/12/65, p8
36 Housewife, Carbrain, in Peter Wilmott, 'Housing in Cumbernauld', *Journal of the Town Planning Institute*, May 1964, p199
37 Housewife, Kildrum, in Wilmott, p200
38 Ian Nairn, 'Half Term at Cumbernauld', *Observer*, 23/4/67, p36

PART 3: NO FUTURE

1. 'A Pack of Cards':
Tower Block Highs and Lows (1968-74)

1 Ernő Goldfinger, *Guardian*, 14/2/68, p5
2 Ernő Goldfinger, *Guardian*, 8/3/69, p7
3 Ursula Goldfinger, *Guardian*, 15/5/68, p5
4 Jane Drew in Nigel Warburton, *Erno Goldfinger: The Life of an Architect*, Routledge, 2004, p136
5 Warburton, p132
6 Ernő Goldfinger, *Observer*, 16/12/62, p25
7 *Daily Express*, 17/5/68, p1
8 *Daily Mirror*, 17/5/68, p4
9 *ibid*
10 *Daily Express*, 17/5/68, p4
11 Hugh Griffiths, Sir Alfred Pugsley, Sir Owen Saunders, *Report of the Inquiry into the Collapse of Flats at Ronan Point, Canning Town*, HMSO, 1968, p15
12 Griffiths, Pugsley and Saunders, plate 7
13 *The Times*, 11/1/73, p5
14 *Daily Express*, 17/5/68, p1
15 Glendinning and Muthesius, p219

16 Lynsey Hanley, *Estates*, Granta, 2007, p109
17 Geoff Scott, *Building Disasters and Failures*, The Construction Press, 1976, p88
18 Scott, p93
19 Scott, p19
20 Phil McPhee in Farquar McLay (ed), *Workers City: The Real Glasgow Stands Up*, Clydeside Press, 1988, p46
21 McPhee in McLay (ed), p45
22 Jephcott, p48
23 *Herald*, 19/11/74, p12
24 Jephcott, p59
25 Jephcott, p61
26 *Herald*, 27/12/62, p6
27 *Journal*, 9/9/77, p7
28 *Evening Chronicle*, 26/7/77, p5
29 Clare McCarren and Brid Fitzpatrick, *Evening Chronicle*, 21/10/86, p8
30 Ernő Goldfinger, *The Times*, 8/8/68, p2
31 Lewis Womersley, *Guardian*, 13/8/68, p4
32 *The Times*, 18/4/73, p4
33 *Daily Express*, 17/5/68, p4

2. 'A Terrible Confession of Defeat':
Protests and Preservation (1969–79)

1 Evelyn Sharp, *The Ministry of Housing and Local Government*, Allen and Unwin, 1969, p11
2 Gavin Stamp in Elain Harwood and Alan Powers (ed.), *The Sixties*, The Twentieth Century Society, 2002, p135
3 Colin Amery and Dan Cruikshank, *The Rape of Britain*, Elek, 1975, p10
4 Jane Jacobs, *The Death and Life of Great American Cities*, Vintage, 1961 (Vintage Edition 1992), p15
5 Robert Matthew in Miles Glendinning, *Modern Architect*, RIBA Publishing, 2008, p461
6 Matthew in Glendinning, p476
7 Norman Dennis, *People and Planning*, Faber and Faber, 1970, p297
8 Dennis, p346
9 Dennis, p330
10 John R. Gold, *The Experience of Modernism*, Spon, 1997, px
11 Robert Matthew, Johnson-Marshall and Partners, *New Life in Old Towns*, HMSO, 1971, p66
12 Matthew, Johnson-Marshall and Partners, p74
13 Matthew, Johnson-Marshall and Partners, p57
14 Joe Levy, *AJ*, 19/1/61, p100
15 William Holford, *The Times*, 13/1/66, p5
16 *The Times*, 5/8/66, p10
17 Peter Hall, *London 2000*, Faber, Second Edition, 1969, p210
18 Ian Nairn, *Observer*, 7/7/68, p25
19 Sharp, p183
20 *Concrete Quarterly*, October–December 68, p33
21 *New Society*, 1/8/68 in www.cbrd.co.uk

22 *Evening Chronicle,* 3/6/71, p14
23 David Durman, *The Journal,* 3/6/72, p11
24 *Journal,* 11/12/70, p9
25 *Illustrated London News,* 28/11/70, p16
26 Editorial, *Journal,* 22/1/70, p8
27 Alan H Brown [letter] *Evening Chronicle,* 31/10/69
28 *Evening Chronicle,* 29/10/70 p3
29 *Journal,* 14/3/72, p4
30 Sharp, p184
31 *Guardian,* 5/3/76, p6
32 *Guardian* 16/10/78, p8
33 Gillian Linscott, *Guardian,* 2/1/73, p6
34 Robert Waterhouse, *Guardian,* 22/12/73, p9

3. 'As Corrupt a City as You'll Find': Uncovering the Lies at the Heart of the Boom (1969–77)

1 Richard Crossman in Clive Borrel and Brian Cashinella, *Crime in Britain Today,* Routledge, 1975, p90
2 Letter from Pottinger to Poulson in Martin Tompkinson and Michael Gillard, *Nothing to Declare,* John Calder, 1980, p33
3 Tompkinson and Gillard, p17
4 T. Dan Smith in *You (Mail on Sunday),* 10/5/87, p82
5 Poulson in Foote Wood, p109
6 *Evening Chronicle,* 10/5/77, p6
7 *Guardian,* 9/7/71, p11
8 *Guardian,* 24/9/65, p2
9 Glendinning and Stefan Muthesius, p215
10 *Guardian,* 25/4/74, p3
11 Alan Maudsley in *Building Design,* 5/11/71, p10
12 *Building Design,* 5/11/71, p11
13 Glendinning and Stefan Muthesius, p251
14 *Journal,* 30/9/70
15 Poulson, in Dominic Sandbrook, *State of Emergency,* p512

4. 'A Little Bit of Exclusivity': Milton Keynes, the Last New Town (1967-79)

1 *The Times,* 18/3/70, p11
2 *Guardian,* 7/1/64, p4
3 *Guardian* 18/5/65, p3
4 Llewelyn-Davies, Weeks, Forestier-Waker and Bor, *The Plan for Milton Keynes,* vol 1, Milton Keynes Development Corporation, 1970, p16
5 Judy Hillman, *Observer,* 2/2/69
6 Llewelyn-Davies, Weeks, Forestier-Walker and Bor, p10
7 Derek Walker, *The Architecture and Planning of Milton Keynes,* The Architectural Press, 1981, p8
8 Walker, p9
9 *The Times,* 15/2/67, p3
10 Jane Turner and Bob Jardine, *Pioneer Tales,* People's Press of Milton Keynes, 1985, p12
11 Derek Walker, *Architectural Design,* June 1973, p351
12 Walker, *Architectural Design,* June 1973, p352
13 Turner and Jardine, p16
14 *ibid*
15 *Observer,* 26/5/74, p26
16 Llewelyn-Davies, Weeks, Forestier-Waker and Bor, p11
17 Peter Evans, *The Times,* 'Milton Keynes – City of the Future supplement', 24/3/72, pI
18 Turner and Jardine, p29
19 Llewelyn-Davies, Weeks, Forestier-Waker and Bor, p9
20 *The Times,* 28/8/75, p12
21 *The Times,* 28/8/75, p12
22 Turner and Jardine, p28
23 Peter Evans, *The Times,* 'Milton Keynes – City of the Future supplement', 24/3/72, pI
24 Robert Maxwell, of UCL – *The Times,* 28/8/75, p12
25 *Architectural Design,* June 1973, p363
26 Timothy Boutwood, resident of Walton, *The Times,* 28/8/75, p12
27 Walker, p73
28 Schaffer, p15

5. 'A City within a City': The late flowering of the Barbican and the National Theatre (1957–81)

1 Peter Ackroyd, *Barbican at 25,* City of London, 2007, p29
2 Sir William Holford, *Manchester Guardian,* 17/09/57, p6
3 *Manchester Guardian,* 20/1/56, p7
4 *Barbican at 25,* City of London, 2007, p18
5 Sir William Holford, *Manchester Guardian,* 17/09/57, p6
6 Sir Hugh Casson, *Observer,* 23/10/60, p17
7 William J. R. Curtis, *Denys Lasdun,* Phaidon, 1994, p108
8 *Financial Times,* 8/10/65, p11
9 *The Times,* 24/3/75, p10
10 *The Times,* 24/3/75, p10
11 George Perkin, *Concrete Quarterly,* January-March 1977, p39
12 *Concrete Quarterly,* October – December 1969, p1
13 John Betjeman, letter, 4/10/73, in Curtis, p152
14 Michael Billington, *Guardian,* 12/3/76, p10
15 Peter Hall, *The Times,* 29/6/74, p9
16 Colin Buchanan, *The Times,* 19/9/66, p9
17 *Financial Times,* 28/9/68, p11
18 *Financial Times,* 8/4/71, p12
19 H. A. N. Brockman, *Financial Times,* 4/12/73, p29

INDEX